Cambridge Studies in Chinese History, Literature, and Institutions
General Editor Denis Twitchett

RELIGIOUS EXPERIENCE AND LAY SOCIETY IN T'ANG CHINA

Other books in the series

William T. Graham, Jr. 'The Lament for the South': Yü Hsin's *Ai Chiang-Nan Fu*
Michael Godley The Mandarin-Capitalists from Nanyang: Overseas Chinese Enterprise in the Modernisation of China, 1893–1911
Charles Backus The Nan-chao Kingdom and T'ang China's Southwestern Frontier
A. R. Davis T'ao Yüan-ming: His Works and Their Meaning
Victor H. Mair Tunhuang Popular Narratives
Ira E. Kasoff The Thought of Chang Tsai
Robert Hymes Statesmen and Gentlemen: The Elite of Fu-chou, Chang-hsi, in Northern and Southern Sung
D. L. McMullen State and Scholars in T'ang China
Tim Wright Coal Mining in China's Economy and Society, 1895–1937
Chih-P'ing Chou Yüan Hung-tao and the Kung-an School
Arthur Waldron The Great Wall of China: From History to Myth
Hugh R. Clark Community, Trade, and Networks: Southern Fujian Province from the Third to the Thirteenth Centuries
Jo-Shui Chen Liu Tsung-yüan and Intellectual Change in T'ang China, 773–819
Brian E. McKnight Law and Order in Sung China
J. D. Schmidt Stone Lake: The Poetry of Fang Chengda
Denis Twitchett The Writing of Official History Under the T'ang
David Pong Shen Pao-chen and China's Modernization in the Nineteenth Century
J. D. Schmidt Within the Human Realm: The Poetry of Huang Zunxian, 1848–1905
Eva Shan Chou Reconsidering Tu Fu: Literary Greatness and Cultural Context

Religious Experience and Lay Society in T'ang China

A Reading of Tai Fu's Kuang-i chi

Glen Dudbridge

University of Oxford

Published by the Press Syndicate of the University of Cambridge
The Pitt Building, Trumpington Street, Cambridge CB2 1RP
40 West 20th Street, New York, NY 10011-4211, USA
10 Stamford Road, Oakleigh, Melbourne 3166, Australia

First published 1995

Printed in the United States of America

Library of Congress Cataloging-in-Publication Data

Dudbridge, Glen.

Religious experience and lay society in T'ang China : a reading of Tai Fu's Kuang-i chi / Glen Dudbridge.

p. cm. – (Cambridge studies in Chinese history, literature, and institutions)

Includes bibliographical references and index.

ISBN 0-521-48223-2

1. Tai, Fu, chin shih 757. Kuang i chi. 2. Occultism – China. I. Title. II. Series.
PL2677. T35K83 1995
895. 1′33 – dc20 94-46149
CIP

A catalog record for this book is available from the British Library.

ISBN 0-521-48223-2 Hardback

Contents

Acknowledgements

The years spent in preparing this book have brought encouragement and support from many colleagues and friends. Among them I particularly thank David McMullen, Robert Chard and Stephen Teiser, who read my drafts and responded with excellent advice; also Daria Berg, who obtained certain material for me and helped prepare the book for publication.

It is a pleasure to record thanks to the Council for Cultural Planning and Development, Executive Yuan, in Taiwan, which supported the research for this project with a generous grant.

I am equally grateful to those bodies which, no less generously, made it possible to develop ideas and material for this book in talks at Sinological centres in three continents. In Taiwan the Hsin Chu Bank sponsored a lecture series at National Tsing Hua University; the Institute of Chinese Literature and Philosophy, Academia Sinica, and the Departments of History and of Chinese Literature at National Taiwan University treated me with similar hospitality. In America the Metropolitan Museum of Art and the University of Pennsylvania and Princeton University welcomed me to their colloquia and seminars. The European Commission's ERASMUS programme supported lecture courses in Germany at the Sinological Seminars of Heidelberg and Munich Universities, and in Denmark at the Universities of Copenhagen and Aarhus. In Britain the School of Oriental and African Studies and the British Association for Chinese Studies hosted lectures which formed the early basis of the whole project. It has been a privilege to share work in progress with so many keen-minded audiences. The book which follows has been shaped by the experience.

Note to the reader

Full reference data for the source abbreviations used in the footnotes and Appendix appear in the List of Works Cited.

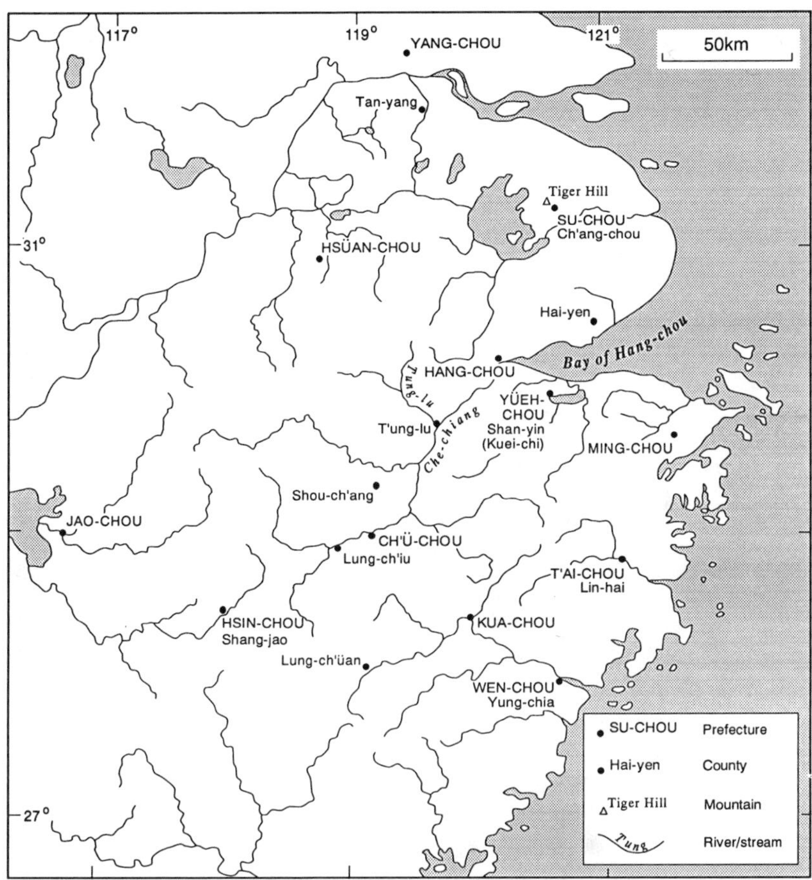

One hundred miles around T'ung-lu in the 760s (*showing places mentioned in Chapters 1, 3, 6 and 7*)

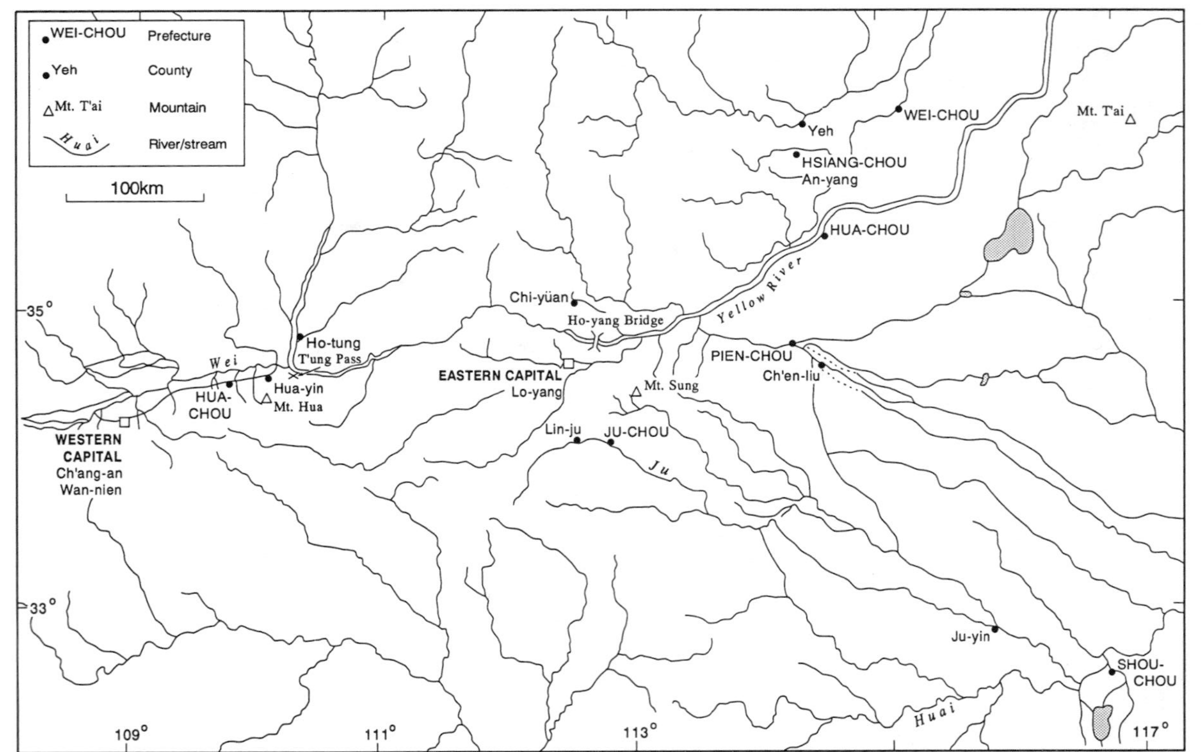

Two hundred fifty miles around Lo-yang in the 760s (*showing places mentioned in Chapters 3, 4, 5 and 7*)

1
A sequence of voices

The voice that will open this book belonged to a young provincial woman of the eighth century:

A girl of T'ung-lu named Wang Fa-chih has served the spirit of a young man since early in life. During the Ta-li period [766–779] the spirit was suddenly heard speaking out in an adult voice.

Fa-chih's father asked: 'Isn't this some sage or worthy speaking?' And the answer came: 'It is. My name is T'eng Ch'uan-yin. I came from the metropolitan county of Wan-nien; my house was in Ch'ung-hsien ward. And I have an affinity with Fa-chih from the past.'

In the exchange of remarks which followed he showed deep understanding of natural principles.

A succession of prefectural and county administrators have paid him high regard. The magistrate of T'ung-lu county, Cheng Feng, an enquiring man, often summons Fa-chih to his residence. He tells her to bring down Master T'eng XII, and after a long interval the spirit comes. His conversation is very much that of an educated man, and Cheng never tires of listening to him. In the company of writers or poets he will happily share in literary conversation and composition all day long.

A travelling Buddhist monk once approached Fa-chih for alms. The spirit spoke with him and dedicated this poem:

> You stand aloof, do not seek fame as a Buddhist.
> Your single purpose, held constantly in mind, lies high up in
>   the blue mists.
> The men of the hour may radiate forceful energy –
> But which of them could stay long enthroned on the precious
>   lotus flower?

Another time he dedicated the following poem to someone:

> All through life my abilities have been less than adequate,
> But in dealing with the world my sincerity is more than enough.

> I can proudly claim that I have given 'no grave cause':
> Let the good gentleman not shun my presence.[1]

In the sixth year, on the night of the twenty-fifth of the second month, Tai Fu forgathered in Cheng Feng's residence with Hsü Huang, from the Troop Service in the Guards of the Left, Ts'ui Hsiang, magistrate of Lung-ch'üan, Li Ts'ung-hsün, assistant magistrate of Tan-yang, and two local residents, Han Wei and Su Hsiu. As it happened Wang Fa-chih made an appearance, and we told her to summon T'eng Ch'uan-yin. After a long pause he came. He joined with Hsü Huang and the others in an exchange of courtesies that went on for hundreds of words. Then he addressed the whole company of gentlemen, inviting each of us to compose a piece of verse. We did this, then we all asked for a poem from him, and he dashed off two:

> In comes the tide at the river-mouth: at first the waters run high.
> In a rocking boat a lotus-gatherer cannot pick the blooms.
> So I go back empty-handed, my springtime mood let down.
> I must wait for the slack water to try picking once more.

('Don't smile at me, gentlemen,' he said.) Then:

> Suddenly a wisp of cloud scuds across the lake.
> In my boat I find that rain has wet my clothes.
> I forget all about the lotus blooms just picked,
> And turn back, simply shielding my head with a lotus leaf.

His own comment was: 'That was done in quite a flurry, too!' And he caused his 'younger brother' Fa-chih to exchange hundreds more words in courtesies with Cheng Feng. Then he departed. (**84**)[2]

This party at the magistrate's residence in T'ung-lu 桐廬 took place on 15 March 771. They were in the wooded hilly country on the edge of the western Chekiang uplands, at a point where the south-flowing T'ung-lu River entered the great tidal stream, then called Che-chiang 浙江, that would flow out to the Bay of Hang-chou some fifty miles to the north–east.[3] The company brought together guests from different walks

1 A Confucian allusion: 'None who have been long in his service does [the gentleman] dismiss without grave cause,' *Lun-yü* 18/10. Cf. Arthur Waley, *The Analects of Confucius*, London 1938, pp. 222–3.

2 *TPKC* 305.2414. Numbers in bold type refer to the contents of *Kuang-i chi* as listed in the Appendix.

3 The county seat stood 140 paces north of the Che-chiang River, and one *li* west of the meeting waters: *Yüan-ho chün-hsien t'u-chih* 25.607–8. (On modern maps the main river at this point is called Fu-ch'un chiang 福春江.) This situation seems to explain the reference in one of the poems to spring tide waters entering a river-mouth: the famous tidal bore on the Ch'ien-t'ang River sometimes pushed many miles upstream. Bishop Moule, on a branch river somewhat further downstream on 29 May 1888, described how 'a smooth wave (perhaps 2 feet above the previous level) came swiftly up and took us up stream at a great pace, I should say full 5 miles an hour': see Osborne Moore, 'The bore of the Tsien-tang kiang (Hang-chau Bay)', *Journal of the China Branch of the Royal Asiatic Society*, 23, 1889, p. 244; cf. pp. 227–8. Compare the high-running waters

of polite society – a military officer, some county administrators, some untitled local residents – and Tai Fu 戴孚, the man whose bare name and lack of description mark him as the author of this account. From the voices of such men, in such situations, will come the chief material for the studies that form this book.

Already, of course, several voices are speaking. The young woman Wang Fa-chih 王法智 holds centre-stage. But she is only the mouthpiece of a ghostly intruder, a man otherwise unknown to history, who speaks up in this cultured male society claiming a past address in the T'ang capital Ch'ang-an.

So Wang Fa-chih is a woman possessed. Although her age in 771 is not given, we know that she was still a child when, no more than five years before (at the opening of the Ta-li 大歷 period), the male soul with a Ch'ang-an address made his first appearance in her life. There are features here well known to students of possession around the world: a change of voice – young girl's into grown man's;[4] new, unexpected skills and knowledge passed from spirit to host.[5] But other aspects of possession behaviour remain to be guessed at. The state of trance which allows a new personality to emerge and communicate is widely, even universally, brought on by stressful physical stimuli – drugs, rhythmic drumming, bell-ringing, handclapping, dancing, inhibition of normal breathing – and while such things have been familiar sights in the public conditions of village shamanism in traditional China, we cannot easily imagine them within the polite setting of a magistrate's residence. 'After a long pause he came,' says the text. What happened in that pause, which also intervened on those other occasions when Cheng Feng 鄭鋒 required her to summon the spirit? It is tempting to imagine the girl overbreathing and causing changes in her body chemistry that would bring on the trance.[6] But the literature on possession suggests that states of trance, once established and repeated, are more and

which rock the lotus-gatherer's boat in the poem. Widespread damage from a summer tidal surge at Hang-chou was reported for the year 767: *CTS* 37.1361–2.

4 Sampled in the standard literature: see T. K. Oesterreich, *Possession, demoniacal and other* (trans. D. Ibberson), London 1930, pp. 19–20, 33–4 and 66–7; I. M. Lewis, *Ecstatic religion*, Harmondsworth 1971, p. 94; William Sargant, *The mind possessed*, London 1973, pp. 47–8.

5 Oesterreich, *Possession*, pp. 137, 144. Cf. Sargant, *The mind possessed*: 'In hypnoidal states people can remember languages which they have consciously long forgotten, or they can construct new languages. They can act or give impersonations or produce art or music with a degree of skill which is not normally available to them . . . the brain absorbs and records far more information than is normally remembered, but which can come to the surface in abnormal states of mind' (pp. 36, 37).

6 Sargant, *The mind possessed*: 'overbreathing produces a state of brain alkalosis when the carbon, an acid, is blown out of the blood stream, and this often brings about hysterical dissociation and states of increased suggestibility' (p. 135; cf. p. 117).

more easy to enter; and heightened suggestibility opens the subjects to powerful influence from their surroundings in fixing the content of their trance experience.[7]

We cannot fit Wang Fa-chih easily into any of those categories of traditional Chinese society for whom possession was a routine experience. She was no village exorcist or professional medium in the service of a temple cult.[8] She came instead from a background of some literary culture and operated strictly within its bounds. Her father, in conversation with the ghostly T'eng Ch'uan-yin 縢傳胤, was able to appreciate his 'deep understanding of natural principles'. Young girls, of course, would not enjoy conventional access to the polite male society which talked about such things. But trance made all the difference. The first possession by T'eng came unexpectedly, perhaps involuntarily, but now it rewards the girl with a place of honour and respect as a centre of attention in the local officials' social circle. In these new circumstances her fits of possession are sought at the magistrate's bidding; they come, however slowly, in response to voluntary efforts. And the possessing spirit acknowledges and dignifies his hostess as a 'younger brother' (弟). Possession is sometimes seen as a strategy of repressed or marginal groups in society: it gains them attention and fulfilments denied in conventional life.[9] Wang Fa-chih, the possessed girl whose male persona has officials and gentry hanging on her every word, might answer well to this view. But she functions (and this is our main point of interest) as an individual, not as a member of a profession.

Her inspired verse is lucid and graceful. The second poem of dedication boasts a modest Confucian allusion. And the last piece, in which the lotus gatherer retires in a shower of rain, reminds the modern critic Ch'ien Chung-shu of the same conceit pursued by other more celebrated poets.[10] Spirit-poets were not rare in Chinese life. In later periods we often read of verses revealed by spirits through automatic writing séances.[11] But spirit-verse produced in a state of possession is as ancient in China as the traditions of inspired poetry revealed to fathers

7 Oesterreich, *Possession*, pp. 95, 99; Sargant, *The mind possessed*, p. 54. I have myself watched a young man in T'ai-pei county rapidly enter trance and possession in a tranquil temple setting, with no strong physical stimuli at work.

8 Examples of these practitioners in Tai Fu's China are discussed below, in Chapter 4.

9 This view is argued in Lewis, *Ecstatic religion*, particularly Chapters 3 and 4, which discuss the more developed context of 'peripheral cults'.

10 Ch'ien Chung-shu, *Kuan-chui pien*, Peking 1979, pp. 772–3.

11 The visible procedures are carefully described in Justus Doolittle, *Social life of the Chinese*, vol. 2, New York 1865, pp. 112–14. Many examples will be found in the eighteenth-century poetic memoirs of Shih Chen-lin 史震林, *Hsi-ch'ing san-chi*: see 1.1–11, 17, 20, 23–4, 27; 2.27, 53, 57, 61, 83; 3.119, etc.

of the Taoist movement,[12] and continues today in the temple-cults of modern Chinese societies. Such, essentially, is the style of Wang Fa-chih, comfortably adapted to an urbane secular setting and happily accommodated by its hosts.

We hear her voice from the depths of the past only with the help of another, the voice of Tai Fu, who was one of the company she entertained that night in 771. He compiled the book from which this account first came – the *Kuang-i chi* 廣異記, or *Great book of marvels*, a collection of more than three hundred such items – and here he makes his first and almost his only bow as witness and informant. The *Kuang-i chi*, or the remains of that lost collection, will provide the themes and material for most of what follows in this book. Its scope and subject-matter, its place in literary tradition, the extent of its survival – all these will need scrutiny in the next chapter, together with the few facts we know about Tai Fu and his life. But he faces us here as a witness. Named without title or introduction, the author addresses us in his own voice.

Time and place, we shall see, square exactly with his life and the contents of his book. The scene, as in a score of other stories from the 760s and 770s, lies in the region of modern Chekiang.[13] And it comes with a precision that tells us important things about the author, the society he kept, his personal interests and, effectively, how he collected much of the material we find in his book. Tai Fu ended his own career in a minor provincial post. Military staff, county officials and local gentry were his natural associates and, we find in many other stories, his main informants. This episode came from his own experience, but he drew a multitude of others from hearsay gathered among men like these. What they told him he now transmits through the loosely assembled pages of his book. And that, in a fashion I have described elsewhere, owes its partial survival to the accidents of anthology, manuscript transmission and belated printing.[14]

12 See K. M. Schipper, *L'empereur Wou des Han dans la légende taoïste*, Paris 1965, pp. 12–14, 55–7.

13 Although the various provincial colleagues gathered in the official residence of T'ung-lu county, their own postings lay quite far afield – one in Tan-yang 丹陽, which is many miles to the north on the main Chiang-nan canal, just before its entry into the Yangtze River; one in Lung-ch'üan 龍泉 at a similar distance away in the south. If we draw a circle on the map to take in these places, T'ung-lu is close to its centre, and the radius reaches 140 miles around. Only just outside the circle is Jao-chou 饒州 in the west, the scene of Tai Fu's own last appointment (see below: Chap. 2, p. 44). We can only guess whether he was really based there in 771, but it remains clear that the séance described here did not have a strictly local audience. Other stories in the collection with a Chekiang setting are: **6, 29, 33, 36, 54** (set in T'ung-lu), **60, 85, 132, 141, 167, 176, 187, 202, 217, 233, 292, 307, 310, 315, 316, 318.** Stories with Chekiang-based informants are: **24, 80, 115, 122, 128.**

14 Tu Te-ch'iao, '*Kuang-i chi* ch'u-t'an', *Hsin Ya hsüeh-pao* 15, 1986, 395–414.

Tai Fu serves as an informant, but not a neutral observer. Faced with Wang Fa-chih he plays a part with the rest of the company in endorsing the view that she is indeed possessed by a dead man's spirit. He joins in the exchange of poems and conversation with which that secular gathering greets and accommodates its supernatural visitor. His motive in recording the occasion grows out of their communal perception of the girl's trance behaviour. For them Wang Fa-chih speaks with a voice from beyond the grave: for us the voice of Tai Fu speaks from within his own society.

In this complex system of voices the last to speak is the modern historian who recovers the story from the old tenth-century source where it lies preserved. A certain kind of relationship to the past is implied here. The French historian Le Roy Ladurie put this well when he considered the career of Arnaud Gélis, canon's servant and assistant sexton in the mediaeval village Montaillou, who served his community as a messenger of souls:

> His chief role was to make the dead speak. Rather comparable, at the end of the day, in spite of immense chronological and cultural differences, to the role of the *historian* in our contemporary societies.[15]

That role goes perfectly with the business of this book, and not simply because so much of Tai Fu's traffic runs between the living, the dead and those caught in between. It is rather that the *Kuang-i chi* and its like preserve, at many points, the oral history of a remote age. Buried within those hundreds of anecdotes are statements by ordinary people about their times, their surroundings and often about their own experience. We study them, not really to build up a knowledge of events and institutions with documentary data, but rather to explore the perceptions of that long dead generation as it confronted the visible and invisible worlds all around. To deal with material like this is to handle an awkward and slippery critical task. The historian must find ways to distinguish between subtly different forms of testimony that face him, often in disguise, and the challenge of this task will remain alive at every point in the studies that follow.

In the sequence of voices chosen to open this book Wang Fa-chih speaks first. A humble individual, a remote period, an obscure provincial situation – yet we observe and in some ways understand this woman through the eyes of a personal witness from her own time and place.

15 'Son rôle capital: faire parler les morts. Rôle assez comparable, en fin de compte, en dépit d'immenses différences chronologiques et culturelles, à celui de l'*historien* dans nos sociétés contemporaines': Emmanuel Le Roy Ladurie, *Montaillou, village occitan de 1294 à 1324,* rev. edn., Paris 1982, p. 601.

Here is the simplest scheme of testimony available to us in the *Kuang-i chi,* though even this, presented through Tai Fu's ways of perception, his cultural assumptions and cast of mind, takes on a quite different character when we analyse it ourselves. To make progress from here to the more complex testimony and interpretation that lie ahead, some ground rules will be needed. We shall approach them through reading about a second provincial individual.

36 Wang Ch'i comes from the T'ai-yüan family, and his home is in Ying-yang. He has abstained since childhood from all meat and strong-flavoured food. Early in the Ta-li period he became revenue manager in Ch'ü-chou. He is deeply devoted to regular reciting of the *Kuan-yin sūtra,* and throughout his life this practice has never failed to cure him of his frequent bouts of serious illness. Always, as he recites, strange creatures and phantasms come to vex and assail him, but Wang is right-minded, so they cannot interfere with him.

When he was nine years old he suffered an illness for five or six days which left him unable to speak. Suddenly he heard someone outside the gate calling his name, with the words: 'We're coming after you!' So he went off with them and walked some fifty *li,* when they came to an official building.

The senior officer inside said, in great alarm: 'Why did you make the mistake of bringing this little boy here? You must send him back at once!'

A man at his side said: 'Whoever has been summoned here ought not to be let go. You must commission him to do an errand – only then can he leave.'

The officer said there was a dog that was due to die and told Wang Ch'i to fetch it. But Wang pleaded that he was too young and could not cope with the journey alone. So the official told him to go in company with a messenger. On the way the messenger gave Wang Ch'i a pill shaped like a little ball and told him to knock at the gate of the house where the dog lived. The dog came out, and he threw the pill to it. It swallowed this down and instantly died. The official said: 'Your errand is done: you may go home!'

Later on he fell sick again. Suddenly he felt through all his limbs the presence of eighty-two people: eyes, eyebrows, nose and mouth – all had their keepers, and those inside his arms and legs were moving to and fro, attacking his flesh and blood. Whenever they came into the wrist-joints there would be collisions and blows. The illness was unendurably depressing.

When Wang Ch'i asked: 'Do you people want to kill me?', they replied: 'Of course we are not killing you. We are curing you of your disease!'

He said: 'If you do cure me I'll provide a rich feast to feed you with!' And the demons cried out within his flesh in great delight. The next day a meal was served for them, and when it was eaten they all departed. He also recovered from the other symptoms.

Wang has a consecrated knife kept in readiness, more than a foot long, which he holds in his hand whenever he is reciting the scripture. And when seasonal epidemics break out he keeps it constantly at the head of his bed for self-protection.

On a later occasion when he was seriously ill he forced himself to rise in the dark and invoke the name of the Bodhisattva Kuan-yin. Suddenly the darkness became as bright as day, and he saw the blade of the knife pointing upwards. A monk came in and sat down with Wang, asking him what knife this was.

Wang said it was a devil-killing knife, and the monk then abruptly vanished. Before long an iron flail descended from mid-air and struck at the knife. It delivered more than 200 blows in succession, until the flail was all smashed in pieces, while the knife was unharmed. Then he saw a huge water cask, banded with iron and large enough to hold more than 250 gallons. It was turned facing downwards, and beside it were two giants wielding staves.

They asked Wang: 'Do you know what this is?'

He said he did not, and they told him: 'It is an iron-banded prison!'

Wang said: 'Just the very thing I need to imprison devils in!'

With these words they both vanished. Then he saw a feast of delicacies being carried out through the gate on stands, about a hundred of them. Again, he saw several hundred people dressed in radiant clothing, drawn up in lines inside his residence; and he saw his late father, sword in hand, furiously saying: 'I have no rooms for you to stay in!' And the people all at once broke up and fled. Not long after this he recovered from the illness.

In the Ch'ien-yüan period [758–759], when he was in Chiang-ling, he once again suffered a serious illness, and returned with devout heart to invoking the name of Kuan-yin. In the distance he could see hundreds of demons coming towards him in boats. They were famished from their long journey and begged Wang for food. So he told his servants to prepare a meal, which was laid out in the courtyard. The crowd of demons sat down in rows, while from Wang's own mouth two demons leaped out and took their seats. When the meal was finished they said at first that this was still not enough.

Wang said: 'You want some clothes, don't you?'

And the demons replied: 'Exactly!'

So he told his servants to make several dozen suits of paper clothing and also tunics in the official colours, such as red and green. These were burned in the courtyard: the demons put them on, then scattered. And consequently he recovered from his illness.

In the Yung-t'ai [765] period he again fell seriously ill. So with pure heart he recited the *Heart sūtra* by lamplight. And suddenly a sound like the fluttering of birds gradually worked its way from his seat right up through his body and made his mouth gape open uncontrollably. He reflected that this must be a demon vexing him, and redoubled his mental clarity and composure. In a few moments he was back to normal. Then again he saw bloated corpses beside his bed, serpents as thick as jars, with a multitude of demons, most of them dead men he had once known, who wildly sought to destroy him. Wang closed his eyes and devoutly recited the *sūtra* through twenty-four times. All vanished clean away. And after thirty-nine readings he relaxed and got some sleep. The next day he was well again.

His wife Li once also fell sick of an epidemic disease. Wang recited the *Heart sūtra* on her behalf, by lamplight. After four or five phrases he suddenly saw three human heads under the lamp, one of them belonging to a maid of Li's who had recently died. Then he heard a cry from the mouth of Li, who pulled herself up into a sitting position. She stared, unable to speak, just pointing to this side and that, or up and down, as though she saw things there. Wang ordered a slave with a long sword to slash through whatever place she pointed at.

At length she awoke and said: 'Is that Master Wang III?' (No doubt she was addressing Wang Ch'i as a younger brother.)

Wang asked her what she had been pointing at.

She said: 'I saw someone at the window, with a nose several feet long. Then I saw two creatures beside the bed that looked like camels. And I also saw red curtains spread out all over the room. All these things were broken up by the slave hacking at them with his sword, and all at once they vanished.'

For his part Wang recited the *sūtra* through forty-nine times, and Li accordingly recovered.

This Wang Ch'i 王琦 belongs to the same company of petty provincial officials in the Chekiang region with whom Tai Fu mixed in the 760s and 770s. The signs are that this piece, with its detailed private chronology, its domestic particularity and the family circle that populates its scenes of hallucination, represents Wang's own testimony as noted down by his friend Tai Fu.

Wang stems from an eminent clan,[16] and from a branch associated with the ancient town of Ying-yang 滎陽 on the south bank of the Yellow River. His current (or most recent) appointment places him, *ca.* 766, on the staff of a prefecture in the post-rebellion province Che-tung 浙東.[17] His medical history, which occupies the whole of this story, is so subjective in symptom definition and so vague in aetiology that clear diagnosis is hardly possible. The hallucinations could come from different organic causes, ranging from pathogenic foodstuffs or drugs to feverish episodes during bouts of malaria or other epidemic disease. But certainly Wang's perception of experienced sickness makes an interesting comparison with the literature of possession in traditional societies. This man is clearly prone to hallucinations. He relies on his

16 A lineage belonging to the group of Seven Great Surnames 七姓 recognized as an aristocratic elite by an edict of 659 (see *T'ang hui-yao* 83.1528–9) and by Shen Kua (1031–95) in his essay on the T'ang and pre-T'ang aristocracy (*Meng-ch'i pi-t'an chiao-cheng* 24.773). Cf. *HTS* 72B.2632–3; Denis Twitchett, 'The composition of the T'ang ruling class: new evidence from Tunhuang', in A. F. Wright and D. C. Twitchett, eds., *Perspectives on the T'ang*, New Haven and London 1973, pp. 47–85, with pp. 56 ff.

17 Ch'ü-chou 衢州 (now Ch'ü-hsien 衢縣 in modern Chekiang) was one of seven prefectures since 756 under the administrative control of the civil governor of Che-tung 浙東觀察使: *Yüan-ho chün-hsien t'u-chih* 26.617; *T'ang fang-chen nien-piao* 5.770.

own ritual therapy to deal with them, and for this purpose favours two well-known Buddhist scriptures, both long used in China for talismanic effects.[18] Certain episodes of his history also imply the belief, widespread in traditional societies, that organic diseases are caused by demonic possession. Oesterreich excluded that loose conception from the analysis set up in his classic book on possession.[19] Nonetheless Wang's case history does invite a closer look, and each bout of illness reveals a character of its own.

The childhood illness at nine *sui* 歲 (eight years by the Western count) takes him into an episode of bureaucratic muddle in a courtroom of the other world. This we recognize at once as a standard narrative format, repeated many times in the *Kuang-i chi* and elsewhere. But its familiarity does not invalidate, and may even explain, the episode's status as a subjective experience in a child on the brink of death. Such is the décor with which the surrounding culture has furnished his mind.[20]

The second illness shares characteristics with possessions in other societies and times. Multiple spirits at large in Wang's body are closely associated with physical discomforts: he seems to suffer the symptom known to modern pathology as 'formication', a crawling or needling sensation all over the skin. It compares with a condition leading up to convulsive fits once reported among the Samoyed women of Arctic Russia:

> Some subjects declare that they have the sensation of a rat running all over the body and inflicting on the limbs innumerable and very painful bites.[21]

More characteristic of possession strictly defined is the possessing spirits' ability to speak up for themselves in dialogue with the subject, and their

18 *Kuan-yin sūtra* 觀音經 was a popular name for the 'P'u-men p'in' 普門品 chapter of the famous *Lotus sūtra* (*Saddharma-puṇḍarīka*), describing the saving grace of the Bodhisattva Kuan-yin. Its most widely used Chinese version was by Kumārajīva (350?–409?): *T* vol. 9, no. 262. For descriptions of its early devotional and talismanic use, see Tsukamoto Zenryū, 'Koitsu Rikuchō *Kanzeon ōkenki* no shutsugen', *Silver Jubilee volume of the Zinbun kagaku kenkyūsyo, Kyōto University*, Kyoto 1954, pp. 234–50. The so-called *Heart sūtra*, a distillation of the great body of Buddhist wisdom literature, was also translated by Kumārajīva (*T* vol. 8, no. 250), but its earliest known version using the title *Hsin-ching* 心經 was apparently by Hsüan-tsang 玄奘 (602?–664) (*T* vol. 8, no. 251); others soon followed (nos. 252–5). Hsüan-tsang's own use of this protective text is described in his early biography *Ta-T'ang Ta-tz'u-en ssu San-tsang fa-shih chuan* (*T* vol. 50, no. 2053) 1.224b: see G. Dudbridge, *The Hsi-yu chi*, Cambridge 1970, pp. 14–15.

19 Oesterreich, *Possession*, pp. 119, 124.

20 Elsewhere this is explicit. Story **259** describes how a boy sees a vision of an ox-headed man, 'truly as seen in pictures of hell'. It turns out to be an ape. The boy is so severely shocked by his experience that he soon dies.

21 Oesterreich, *Possession*, p. 204.

willingness to leave upon fulfilment of a condition – here the serving of a rich meal.[22] And when they go, the other symptoms go too.

Wang's adventures with the ritual knife in his third serious illness suggest a sequence of delirious hallucinations. But in the Ch'ien-yüan 乾元 episode we see him once again meeting external conditions for the possessing spirits, some of whom make their exit through his mouth. He serves them by burning paper clothes for their use – and serves us by providing this uniquely early evidence of a ritual act, practical and enduring, still widely performed in Chinese society.[23] He adds tunics in the colours laid down for official wear by an ordinance of 630: red (緋) for fifth-grade officers, green (綠) for the sixth and seventh grades.[24]

The Yung-t'ai 永泰 episode shows Wang most effective in his disciplined mental resistance. Two perspectives are possible here. For Oesterreich this man might confirm his observation that people of intense religious commitment are traditionally prone to obsessions and phenomena of psychic compulsion, but that, while in people of weak character obsessions easily become full possessions, the lives of saints and mystics often show how strength of character and discipline can keep possession at bay.[25]

The clinical psychiatrist William Sargant rejected Oesterreich's distinction between states of hysteria and possession in favour of distinctions in social context and prevailing belief; and he stressed his finding that normal people are far more susceptible to hypnotic states than the mentally disturbed.[26] On this view, Wang Ch'i's successful battles with

22 Cf. ibid., pp. 106–7, 228 (Japan), 136–7 (Abyssinia), 232 (Mecca).

23 Cf. story **104**. Tsien Tsuen-hsuin, *Paper and printing* (vol. 5, part I, of Joseph Needham, *Science and civilisation in China*, Cambridge 1985, pp. 104 ff.), cites twelfth-century sources for the burning of paper clothes and other objects for the dead in the Sung period. W. Eberhard, *The local cultures of south and east China* (trans. A. Eberhard, Leiden 1968, p. 467), cites *T'ung-yu chi* 通幽記 (in *TPKC* 332.2637) and *Ming-pao chi* B.27 as examples of the use of paper and textile imitations of persons in funeral ceremonies, 'definitely before the T'ang period'. Both, however, are T'ang sources. For the burning of paper clothes for the dead he cites *I-chien san chih, hsin* 辛, 5.1422: a reference no earlier than 1198. The present reference thus has some historical interest. The burning of paper money from this period or before is more richly documented: see the discussion by Hou Ching-lang, *Monnaies d'offrande et la notion de trésorerie dans la religion chinoise*, Mémoires de l'Institut des Hautes Études Chinoises, vol. 1, Paris 1975, pp. 3–17; and cf. below, Chap. 3, p. 54, with n. 11, and Chap. 4, n. 37.

24 *CTS* 45.1952. Cf. *TCTC* 210.6686.

25 Oesterreich, *Possession*, pp. 80–3. The terminology used here reflects the theological definition given by the mediaeval Catholic church to its doctrines of *obsession*, in which the assault of devils was external, and *possession*, in which it came from inside the patient's body. Compare the discussion in Keith Thomas, *Religion and the decline of magic: studies in popular beliefs in sixteenth and seventeenth century England*, London 1971, pp. 477 ff.

26 Sargant, *The mind possessed*, pp. 56–7, 31.

invading spirits may have been the symptom of a long-standing mental pathology.

A final episode shows his sick wife susceptible to suggestion, both from her husband's prior visions and from his trusted ritual therapy.

If we discuss Wang Ch'i's medical history in terms of religion, ritual and possession, it is because he does so himself. His experience of sickness may or may not have stood out as unusually colourful and eventful in his own time, but it has one quality which certainly attracted Tai Fu and must surely interest modern readers too: the patient's private, subjective experience finds precise and articulate expression. We know exactly what sensations Wang was aware of, what visions filled his mind, what actions he took and why he took them. We may also notice what forms of treatment were absent from his sickbed – for no professional specialists, medical or ritual, appeared to attend him there. He seems to have put all his trust in the power of mental discipline, the magic of certain Buddhist scriptures, the use of physical weapons and in fearless dialogue and crude transactions with his tormentors.[27]

This, then, like the story of Wang Fa-chih, also testifies to human perceptions within its parent culture. But it differs in one clear and fundamental way. While the woman Wang Fa-chih comes before us only as an observed performer, the man Wang Ch'i takes us inside his felt experience. Tai Fu reports them both, but from different vantage points. With one he picks up hearsay and joins other spectators in watching the outer surface of events (though even the spectators enjoy indirect communion with an unseen ghost). With the other he lets the consciousness of an articulate patient take charge (though even that active expressionist watches blankly from the outside as his wife wrestles with visions he cannot see himself).

The distinction drawn here will run through all our attempts to read and interpret Tai Fu's testimony. To make it quite clear these two unusually pure specimens have been picked out to stand at the head. They suggest a first rule: *to separate the viewpoint of secular observers from the inner eye of a participating subject.* A second rule will follow from the first: *to recognize both kinds of vision at work within the same account.* And for this we now turn to a third provincial.

85 Li Tso-shih, assistant magistrate of Shan-yin county, fell ill from exhaustion in Ta-li 2 [767]. After several weeks of illness he enjoyed an intermission and

27 With this we can contrast the case of Yen Feng-hsiang in story **152**, whose struggle with a sequence of demon visitors involves the systematic use of professional ritual assistance – spirit mediums, Buddhist monks, Taoist priests of the Liu-ting 六丁 school – all without apparent effect.

made his way from Kuei-chi to Lung-ch'iu where, as it happened, his kinsman Li Shu was magistrate. Tso-shih stayed a few days in the magistrate's chamber, at night sitting by lamplight with his companion Li Chü.

Suddenly he saw twenty men in uniforms of crimson and purple, all bearing arms, come rushing into the lower end of the courtyard. Tso-shih asked who they were, and they said:

'We are demon warriors. The Great King has appointed you as an administrative assistant, sir, and we are under special instructions to serve as your welcoming party. So we are performing our mission.'

Tso-shih said: 'I am in a period of mourning – that would be in breach of due ritual. And how did the king know of my existence?'

They answered: 'It was Tou K'an, the magistrate of Wu-i county, who recommended you.'

Tso-shih said: 'He is no acquaintance of mine. Why should he recommend me?'

They replied: 'Now that the gracious command is issued you cannot refuse it.'

Very soon Tou K'an appeared and greeted him with due courtesy, poised and urbane as any ordinary man. He took a seat and said to Tso-shih: 'The king is looking for a son-in-law, and has further commanded me to choose one from a leading clan. That is why I have recommended you. Your destiny decrees that it must be so, after all!'

Tso-shih's vigorous attempts at refusal were fruitless.

Before long the king's daughter likewise appeared, scented and fragrant, with a vast attendance of carriages and riders. Tso-shih came down from the dais to bow in welcome. He saw her good looks, her robes and coaches, and felt quite delighted with her.

Tou K'an told him: 'We all must die. Not many can be as fortunate as you: you should not provoke the king to anger by refusing too many times.'

And Tso-shih knew that he would have to submit in the end. In due course the king's daughter departed with Tou K'an, leaving more than two hundred generals and attendants to wait respectfully upon the administrator.

The next day, when Li Shu and his brother Li Tsao went together to call on Tso-shih, he told them the whole[28] story. He added: 'If I am really going to lose my life, I must ask for a square meal.' And Li Shu had sumptuous food brought for him.

Suddenly, as Tso-shih was eating the pheasant soup, he said: 'My bowl has disappeared!' He shouted to the servants: 'Why have you cleared the soup away?', and slumped on to the table, dead.

His wife Cheng was in Kuei-chi. On the night that his funeral boat reached her there, a maid suddenly spoke with the voice of Tso-shih's spirit: 'The king's daughter has already married another man. I have just been sent to escort my wife on her journey home.' His speech sounded very mournful.

28 For 且 read 具 (conj.).

Here is another personal anecdote of Chekiang official society in the 760s.[29] The mythology is standard. Mortal officer called to judicial duties in the underworld, tempting hopes of union with a lovely goddess, imposing escort party of spirit warriors – all these we meet in other stories. The interest here lies elsewhere – not only in the story's sad final twist (after all the blandishments and bait the man finds he has died to no purpose), but more solidly in its human setting. We enjoy a double spectacle. On the outside, a man in the terminal stages of what is probably heart disease enters with premonitions upon the last day of his life and collapses with a spectacular attack as he feasts greedily on his last rich meal. But on the inside we share the familiar visions with which his mind clothes those premonitions. It seems implied in the telling that Li described his visions in detail to his friends and kin, so that both sides of the story could find their way as hearsay to Tai Fu. And clearly the substance of those visions entered into the mind of the servant-girl who, under the stress of her master's sudden death and his body's arrival by boat, fell into trance and possession and spoke in his person with the grown man's voice.

Yet the vision narrative is so orthodox, so smoothly presented (unlike the random turbulence of Wang Ch'i's hallucinations above), that we must suspect the work of some practised hand crafting it into shape and plausibility. It certainly stands apart from the low-key, inconsequential social contacts and movements that make up the outer dimension of Li Tso-shih's 李佐時 last days.

Those two self-defining elements within the whole narrative we can call, respectively, *inner story* and *outer story*.[30] Each speaks for a distinct set of perceptions. It scarcely matters if, as just suggested, the inner story has been enhanced by the author or some intermediate informant to fit standard mythological norms, for those norms both prescribe and reflect the mental imagery of their parent culture. The society to which Li Tso-shih and Tai Fu belonged often chose to explain sudden and untimely deaths in terms of judicial summons to the underworld – a mirror image of the mortal world with its bureaucratic order. The appeal

29 Shan-yin 山陰 and Kuei-chi 會稽 are two names for the same place, the modern Shao-hsing. Lung-ch'iu 龍丘 county lay 110 miles to the south-west, in Ch'ü-chou prefecture: all in modern Chekiang.

30 These terms were used by Karl S. Y. Kao to analyse a story in his 'Introduction' to *Classical Chinese tales of the supernatural and the fantastic*, Bloomington 1985, p. 32. I have discussed their further use in other, preliminary publications, the substance of which is reworked in this book: 'Tang tales and Tang cults: some cases from the eighth century', *Proceedings of the Second International Conference on Sinology*, Academia Sinica, Nan-kang, 1990, Section on Literature, 335–52; 'Yü-ch'ih Chiung at An-yang: an eighth-century cult and its myths', *Asia Major*, Third Series, 3, 1990, 27–49; 'Three fables of paradise lost', *Bulletin of the British Association for Chinese Studies*, 1988, 27–36.

to destiny and the theme of divine marriage were likewise always close to hand. Perhaps Li's own mind formed its visions in those very terms. Or perhaps his companions built up the familiar details around whatever confused utterances they heard him make. Perhaps again Tai Fu clothed rough, sketchy reports from friends or kin with the mythological circumstance which he knew should belong there. Whichever case applies, the inner story – a highly coloured adventure with beings from the other world, the centre of attention for the anecdote's earliest readers – will interest the historian precisely as mythological property shared between subject, author and society at large. Its character is defined by that common ownership. Its interest is both general, for belonging to a whole society, and specific, for belonging to a given situation at a given time.

The outer story creates a distance from all this. At first sight its work of observation seems to give us what we ourselves might have seen if we had been there to see it. But of course the detachment is more apparent than real, for those observations are filtered through the minds of informants and shaped by the hand of the compiler Tai Fu. They perceive (as we should perceive) selectively and express their perceptions in forms their culture has laid down for them. The results need interpreting with care. And here too, as we have found with each of the stories above, the historian's own mind will interpose itself as he tries to 'make the dead speak'.

Students of history are driven by two very different instincts, both of which are at work in this enterprise. One is the need for synthesis – to go beyond simply knowing what happened in the past, rather to make sense of it. By its nature the work of synthesis demands distance from the scenes it places under scrutiny. It needs the high ground and wide perspectives of the present time to put all manner of historical documents into an order that seems meaningful now, in the view of modern minds. But another, more primary instinct at work in us wants to know and come close to the men and women of the past. It fuels our hypnotic interest in personal documents like photographs, recordings and film footage (from the recent past), or letters, diaries, travel journals, even business correspondence (from deeper in the past). Of course, such documents serve the synthesis-driven historian too, and the best historical writing feeds both kinds of instinct. But its most powerful effects come from using rare chances to catch people from the past functioning and articulating at certain points in their existence. The deeper we search into the past, the harder it becomes to find and capture such chances, but the relish in doing so grows that much stronger.

This, then, will be the main business of the studies that follow. They will treat a number of Tai Fu's reports analytically, trying to identify the specific personal situations which underlay them, to distinguish their core of individual, often spoken, testimony from other intervening voices. But there will be many other kinds of evidence, from the documentary records of the time to the comparative vantage point of other cultures. When those touch the contents of an outer story, the results can give rich and striking insights into the social life of provincial China. It becomes possible to know something of the ordinary life which flowed on in complicated patterns of relationship with the decrees of state policy and the evolving institutions of organized religion.

Three voices in sequence, individuals from a certain level of provincial society in eighth-century China, have served to reveal the aims of this book, to illustrate its methods and to sample its chief source. But the same *Kuang-i chi* can of course be used to serve other aims and support other methods. In Europe it attracted the attention of the ethnographer de Groot, who wrote: 'It forms one of the most valuable sources for the study of Chinese folklore, and we shall afterwards borrow from it very often.'[31] He went on to translate thirty-five stories from the collection. For him it belonged to a class of *hsiao-shuo* 小說 literature which gave access to China's timeless folklore:

> Though produced in ages so wide apart, the whole class shows a striking uniformity of character. Not the slightest change or progress in the animistic notions have we been able to trace in it, which corroborates our statement that China on the whole has always been as she was.[32]

The texture of de Groot's volumes 4, 5 and 6 often reads as a thematic anthology of that literature, in which the stories speak simply and without further analysis for the customs and beliefs revealed in them. They are used as a literature of record in the most uncomplicated, even indiscriminate sense.

The present book, searching out voices and distinguishing inner story from outer, attempts a more analytical design. It also, by identifying individuals in their setting of time and place, takes an interest in historical particularity (a question to be further explored in Chap. 3). But it shares with de Groot the basic view that the *Kuang-i chi* did indeed belong to a literature of record, not of fantasy or creative fiction. We should declare this assumption at the outset, since it enjoys at best an uncertain status in modern China. There, with the May Fourth Movement, the twentieth century brought redefinitions of literary values and categories. Creative fiction rose to high canonical status, and the

31 J. J. M. de Groot, *The religious system of China*, vol. 4, Leiden 1901, p. 73, n. 1.
32 Ibid., p. IX.

ancient term *hsiao-shuo* was co-opted to cover it. In this new climate mediaeval anecdotal literature took on a historical interest as proto-fiction – an early stage in a perceived evolutionary progression.[33] And in that progression the T'ang represented the dawning age of creative fiction – a view, first formulated in the sixteenth century,[34] which has successfully overlaid more ancient perceptions. Only recently have literary historians turned to the task of recovering the original values and definitions of mediaeval *hsiao-shuo* writing.[35] This task we shall now find to be integral with the introduction of *Kuang-i chi* as a record of its times.

33 The classic statement of fiction's evolutionary progress in China is Lu Hsün's still influential *Chung-kuo hsiao-shuo shih-lüeh* (1923), reprinted in *Lu Hsün ch'üan-chi*, 20 vol. edition, vol. 9.

34 By Hu Ying-lin (1551–1602) in *Shao-shih-shan fang pi-ts'ung* 36.486; endorsed by Lu Hsün in *Chung-kuo hsiao-shuo shih-lüeh*, chap. 8, p. 211. For typical Western endorsements of the same notion, see Kenneth J. Dewoskin, 'The Six Dynasties *chih-kuai* and the birth of fiction', in Andrew H. Plaks, ed., *Chinese narrative: critical and theoretical essays*, Princeton 1977, pp. 21–52; and Kao, 'Introduction' to *Classical Chinese tales of the supernatural and the fantastic*, pp. 1–51.

35 A particularly clear reappraisal is by Ch'eng I-chung, 'Lun T'ang-tai hsiao-shuo ti yen-chin chih chi', *Wen-hsüeh i-ch'an* 1987.5, 44–52.

2
A contemporary view

The true introduction to *Kuang-i chi* already exists in the shape of an original preface, written after Tai Fu's death by an old friend, the poet and painter Ku K'uang 顧況 (d. 806+).[1] This piece is well known to scholarship, and rightly so, for in justifying his friend's enterprise and revealing its setting in an archaic but still living tradition, Ku K'uang created a document of independent interest and importance. It deserves our close study. The author sets before us a defence and a catholic survey of Chinese lore of the supernatural, drawing richly from ancient, mediaeval and (to him) contemporary sources.

But the value of this document needs judging with care. Do not look here for creative insights, experimental style, intellectual power or critical scholarship. For the historian its interest lies precisely in the middle-of-the-road quality of its format, its ideas, its scope of reference. This is how, in the High T'ang, a whole class of writers and readers understood and justified their taste for strange tales. Just as the *Kuang-i chi* itself takes us through the byways of a vanished society, so this preface speaks for ordinary, forgotten men who lived in that society. Its documentary value is of the same kind. This is no systematic, library-based bibliographical research, but a free response to books and names in recent currency, and with Tai Fu and his work it carries the authority of first-hand personal contact – things which no imperial librarian or critical historian could give us.

Ku K'uang's preface offers certain technical difficulties. It is undated.

1 For a critical study of Ku K'uang's life and career, see Fu Hsüan-ts'ung, *T'ang-tai shih-jen ts'ung-k'ao*, Peking 1980, pp. 379–408. Chao Ch'ang-p'ing 趙昌平 has reviewed the biographical evidence again in Fu Hsüan-ts'ung, ed., *T'ang ts'ai-tzu chuan chiao-chien*, vol. 1, Peking 1987, pp. 633–54. Chao gives evidence suggesting that Ku was born in 727 (pp. 635–6). One firmly known date is 757, when he took the *chin-shih* 進士 degree in Soochow, together with Tai Fu (Chao, pp. 636–7, and see below). A later preface mentions the passing of fifty years from that time, implying that he was still alive *ca.* 806 (Fu Hsüan-ts'ung, p. 385).

Its text seems damaged in parts. It is also densely, almost totally, allusive and not easy to read intelligently without the help of a detailed commentary. The pages which now follow will tackle these problems, giving a translation of the preface with a running commentary that studies its allusions and references in their literary, intellectual and historical context. A more general discussion of the preface's opening passages was broached in an earlier book.[2] Here now is the promised background to that discussion.

The preface survives in only one early source, the tenth-century compilation *Wen-yüan ying-hua* 文苑英華, transmitted in a sixteenth-century reprint from Foochow.[3] This text has its share of problems and imperfections, but it does show evidence of attention to graphic variants. A much later text, collected in a family edition of Ku K'uang's surviving work,[4] was also prepared with some care, consulting P'eng Shu-hsia's 彭叔夏 critical *Wen-yüan ying-hua pien-cheng* 文苑英華辨證 (preface 1204). The nineteenth-century *Ch'üan T'ang wen*, though widely used by T'ang specialists, is not a primary source, and with this item (at 528.13b–15a) it offers a text whose numerous variants betray a mixture of careless transcription and silent emendation. My translation is therefore based simply on *Wen-yüan ying-hua.*

The writer follows a well-tried pattern. **I.** He opens with general principles, cosmic processes, scriptural maxims. Then step by step he narrows the focus upon his subject: **II.** Ancient authorities prove the incidence of irregular transformations in nature. **III.** High antiquity begins to document the spirit world. **IV.** Then comes a list of transmitted records – from before the T'ang and from the T'ang itself – in a steady and continuing tradition up to the very moment of writing. **V.** And finally we meet Tai Fu, learn of his ancestry, his career, his literary work and his *Kuang-i chi,* all presented with crisp numerical clarity. These self-defining paragraphs form the framework of our commentary.

I

When we wish to observe the relations between Heaven and Man, [we find that] **in the signs of transformations, in the sources of omens good or ill, there are things which even sages do not know, even gods cannot fathom. It is when the primal matter suffers interference, when the five**

2 G. Dudbridge, *The tale of Li Wa: study and critical edition of a Chinese story from the ninth century*, London 1983, pp. 61 ff.

3 *WYYH* 737.5b–7a.

4 *Ku Hua-yang chi* 顧華陽集, family edition of 1613, reprinted 1855, 3.9a–11a.

elements are disorganized, that the Sage shows us 'prodigies, feats of strength, disorders, spirits' and 'rites, music, punishment, government'. He proclaims the sagely way in order to bring things together. Thus, according to Hsü's explanation, when the pattern of Heaven sends down signs it is no doubt to show them to men. The character 示 ['show'] **in the old script resembles the modern character 不, and some Confucians, failing to grasp the root of his intention, say that 'the Master would not** [不] **speak of such things'. That completely destroys his maxim and impugns the very basis for establishing teaching by observing signs.**

The opening words are drawn from the 'I-chi' chapter of *The book of documents*:

The Emperor [Shun 舜] said: 'You ministers are our legs and arms, our ears and eyes . . . **When we wish to observe** (予欲觀) the emblematic figures of the ancients [worked upon their robes], . . . it is for you to make clear [the distinctions of rank].'[5]

In this phraseology 'observation' forms part of the solemn task of regulatory government. It is directed, in the words that follow, at **the relations between Heaven and Man** 天人之際, a phrase proclaiming the traditional 'phenomenalist' cosmology which the imperial institutions of the High T'ang inherited from the Han. *Chi* 際, 'points of contact', related the human and the natural world within a single system of mutual sensitivity: 'it was as if ethical irregularities were disturbances in the cosmic pattern at one point which were bound to induce other (physical) disturbances elsewhere, not by direct action but by a kind of shock signalled through the vast ramifications of one organic whole.'[6] The sage emperor would wish to monitor these significant disturbances, which offered him an index to the moral health of the universe. And such cosmic vigilance is indeed implied in **the signs of transformations** 變化之兆, a phrase from the 'T'ien-hsia' chapter of *Chuang-tzu*:

One who takes nature as his main principle, virtue as his foundation, the way as his school, who **takes his** [guiding] **signs from** [natural] **transformations** (兆於變化): such a man is called a sage.[7]

To warn of the impenetrable mysteries of this solemn scrutiny of omens (**things which . . . even the gods cannot fathom** 神有不測) the author

5 *Shang-shu chu-shu* 5.4b–5a and commentaries on 5.5b–8b.

6 Joseph Needham, *Science and civilisation in China*, vol. 2, Cambridge 1956, p. 378.

7 For the purpose of this allusion I accept the interpretation of the seventh-century Taoist commentator Ch'eng Hsüan-ying 成玄英: see *Chuang-tzu chi-shih*, ed. Kuo Ch'ing-fan, Peking 1961, 10B.1066.

recalls words from the ancient poetry of Ch'u, in which the Great Diviner admits that his instruments and skills are inadequate to deal with Ch'ü Yüan's bitter questioning:

There are things to which my calculations cannot attain, **over which the divinity has no power** (神有所不通).[8]

The argument then moves on to develop a traditional rationale for irregularities in nature. Its key terms, **primal matter** 元氣 and **five elements** 五行, are another typical legacy from the Han cosmologists. 'Primal matter', long established in literary usage, seems to have begun life in the apocryphal scriptures of the Han. The standard *Wen-hsüan* 文選 commentator Li Shan 李善 (*ca.* 630–689) refers no less than four times to a statement from one of the pseudo-*Ch'un-ch'iu* apocrypha:

It is when **the primal matter** is correctly balanced (正) that the eight trigrams of Heaven and Earth are brought forth.[9]

The formulation fits Ku K'uang's purpose well. For primal matter is not merely the pre-existent, inchoate material from which Heaven and Earth with all their phenomena were first synthesized,[10] it is always with us, volatile and dynamic, as the next paragraph will clearly state. In a healthy universe it is 'regulated' (調)[11]; conversely, Ku K'uang now points out, **interference** with its balance provokes symptoms of disorder and irregularity. So too with the five elements: but here the author draws his words directly from that classic text of the Han phenomenalist cosmology, the 'Hung-fan' chapter of *The book of documents*:

I have heard that long ago, when Kun 鯀 dammed up the flooding waters, **the arrangement of the five elements was disorganized** (汨陳其五行). The Lord was stirred to mighty anger and would not bestow the Great Plan in nine divisions.[12]

The consequences of elemental disturbance are put in familiar scriptural language: **prodigies, feats of strength, disorders, spirits** are notoriously the subjects upon which, in the received text of the *Analects*, Confucius declined to speak.[13] (But the author will soon argue that this familiar passage in fact expressed an exactly opposite position.) The

8 From the poem 'Pu-chü' 卜居 (Divination), as translated by David Hawkes, *Ch'u Tz'u, the Songs of the South*, Oxford 1959, p. 90. Cf. *Wen-hsüan* 33.7a.

9 Citing *Ch'un-ch'iu ming-li hsü* 春秋命歷序: *Wen-hsüan* 1.27a, 11.20b–21a, 34.15a, 45.6b.

10 Such definitions were familiar to T'ang readers in the early literary encyclopaedias *Ch'u-hsüeh chi* 1.1, and *I-wen lei-chü* 1.2.

11 Pan Ku 班固, 'Rhapsody on the Eastern Capital' 東都賦, in *Wen-hsüan* 1.27a.

12 *Shang shu chu-shu* 12.2b. This passage opens a classic early exposition of the 'Five Elements' theory: see discussion in Needham, *Science and civilisation*, vol. 2, pp. 242–4.

13 *Lun-yü* 7/20.

ruler's articulated response to disordered nature – **rites, music, punishment, government** – is a well-known formula from *The book of rites* chapter on music.[14]

Ku K'uang now appeals to an authority. **Hsü's explanation** of Heaven and its signs is loosely quoted from Hsü Shen's 許慎 gloss on the character 示 in *Shuo-wen chieh-tzu* 說文解字. The transmitted text of the original gloss will clarify points both here and in the next line:

Heaven sends down signs, revealing **omens good or ill**, as a means of showing them to men.[15] [The graph] derives from three things extending down from above: they are the sun, moon and stars. We observe **the pattern of Heaven** and thus discern the changes in constant progress . . .[16]

The graph in the **old script** from which Hsü Shen drew his etymology and to which Ku K'uang compares the modern 不 is given at the end of the gloss as 𡕛. In context it visually depicts the sending down of signs, but Ku uses it to controvert and reconstruct the Confucian refusal to speak of 'prodigies, feats of strength, disorders, spirits': quite simply he believes that scholars misread the ancient text by finding the negative 不 where he prefers to read '**show**' 示.[17] The true role of the sage he expresses with a phrase from the 'Judgement' 彖 on the twentieth hexagram, '**Observation**' (*kuan* 觀), in *The book of changes*:

They **observe** Heaven's divine way: the four seasons proceed without variation. The sage uses that divine way to **establish teaching**: the whole world submits to him.[18]

But a revealing parallel to Hsü Shen's phrasing lies elsewhere, in the 'Hsi-tz'u' appendix to *The book of changes*:

Heaven sends down signs, revealing omens good or ill, and the sage treats them as signs.[19]

Such is Ku K'uang's position – totally orthodox as a theory of omens for the Chinese imperial state, and not necessarily very novel as a defence of omen-reading by laymen. But the solid, central and predictable character of his language serves a necessary purpose as he now moves on to polemic. For he acknowledges an opposition within the Confucian

14 'Yüeh chi' 樂記: see *Li chi chu-shu* 37.3ab, 11a.

15 The graph 蓋 in the preface, translated as **no doubt**, reveals itself more intelligibly in the original gloss as 所.

16 *Shuo-wen chieh-tzu* 1A.2a.

17 I am indebted to David McMullen for proposing this reading of an otherwise difficult passage and for producing convincing parallels in middle and late T'ang sources for bold emendations to the canonical *Lun-yü* text.

18 *Chou I chu-shu* 3.9a. This reference too I owe to Professor McMullen.

19 Ibid., 7.29b.

tradition. An ancient counter-movement sought to separate the sphere of human ethical responsibilities from a surrounding universe of unrelated phenomena: in modern times it has been acclaimed as a 'sceptical tradition' and described in its broad sweep by Joseph Needham.[20] The shades and degrees of scepticism about relations between Heaven and Man in the mid-T'ang period have been usefully sketched out for us by H. G. Lamont in a monograph on the sceptical essays of Liu Tsung-yüan and Liu Yü-hsi.[21] But Ku K'uang, writing a generation before those major figures, identifies no specific opponent. He confronts no argument more precise than the alleged silence of Confucius on natural irregularities (the most elusive and non-committal position available to a sceptic), and deals with it bluntly by reconstructing the scriptural text and by appealing to the established precedents of his opening lines: to defy them, he affirms, will destroy the principle of enlightened government.

When, more than a century later, the Taoist divine Tu Kuang-t'ing 杜光庭 defended literature of the supernatural in the preface to his own collection *Lu-i chi* 錄異記,[22] he would begin by admitting the silence of Confucius. But, with his reliance on ancient authority and his flood of illustrations, he would closely match the style of what follows here.

II

When matter is distributed on the great potter's wheel it does not stagnate in one place. T'ao-wu became a yellow turtle, P'eng-sheng a large boar; Ch'ang-hung['s] blood became green jade, Shu's daughter a stream; Niu Ai became a tiger, Huang's mother a giant turtle; the superior men became apes and cranes, the inferior men insects and sand; the woman of Wu-tu turned into a man, the man of Ch'eng-tu into a woman; Chou O was buried alive in a tomb and came back to life after ten years, the Ying spy was exposed in the market-place but revived after six days; the Shu emperor's spirit is known as the cuckoo, the Fiery Emperor's daughter as the *ching-wei* bird. From the dim remoteness of primordial times it has never been possible to say where it stops.

20 Needham, *Science and civilisation*, vol. 2, pp. 365 ff.

21 H. G. Lamont, 'An early ninth century debate on Heaven: Liu Tsung-yüan's *T'ien Shuo* and Liu Yü-hsi's *T'ien Lun*', Part 1, *Asia Major* (New Series), 18, 1973, 181–208, in particular 193 ff. But it is misleading to imply, as Lamont does (p. 194), that Liu Chih-chi 劉知幾 (661–721) contributed to the sceptical tradition by attacking the 'Five elements monograph' in the *Han shu*: the strictures in chapters 10 and 11 of his *Shih t'ung* 史通 (*wai-p'ien* 外篇) concern technicalities of historical presentation and documentation; they do not develop a theoretical critique.

22 Transmitted in *Tao tsang*: HY 591.

To bring his grand apology to bear upon the world of recorded events, Ku K'uang borrows a metaphor from the early Han poet Chia I 賈誼. It appears in his 'Owl rhapsody' when the poet, alarmed by the appearance of this ill-omened bird, asks for its guidance on his uncertain fortunes. Some phrases from the owl's response will show clearly why Ku K'uang wanted to use it here:

> All things undergo change without ceasing . . . form and matter alternate in succession, passing into one another by a process of transformation . . . destiny cannot be explained . . . who knows where it might end? . . . **All things are distributed on the great potter's wheel** (大鈞播物), boundless and unlimited . . . What cause for lingering enjoyment if you suddenly become a man? Or for distress if you change into some alien thing?[23]

The metaphorical potter's wheel is not the instrument of a Supreme Craftsman so much as the working engine of a freely mutating creation.

We are now prepared for the list of irregular transformations which follows. Individually the items lead back to a number of very different sources, but it seems likely that Ku K'uang drew them from the 'transformations' (變化) section of some early literary encyclopaedia, or at least from the more diffuse stock of cultural data in general literary circulation. We find parts of the same list in the poetry of Po Chü-i.[24] The items are presented in a series of carefully balanced pairs – a scheme of parallelism that runs right through the preface and will become important in our examination of breaks and flaws in the text below.

T'ao-wu 檮杌 is a name from archaic mythology – one of the monsters banished by the Yellow Emperor; it was Kun 鯀, the father of Shun, also banished by the Yellow Emperor, who **changed into a yellow turtle**, but some texts identify one with the other.[25] **P'eng-sheng** 彭生 appears in *Tso chuan*: the young nobleman, put to death by the marquis

23 *Han shu* 48.2227–8; *Wen-hsüan* 13.17a–19a.

24 *Po Chü-i chi* 7.146. Cf. Dudbridge, *The tale of Li Wa*, p. 63.

25 References in ancient literature collected by Marcel Granet, *Danses et légendes de la Chine ancienne*, Paris 1926, pp. 240 ff., and Bernhard Karlgren, 'Legends and cults in ancient China', *Bulletin of the Museum of Far Eastern Antiquities* 18, 1946, 247–51. For the identification of the two figures, see Tu Yü's 杜預 comment on *Tso chuan* Wen/18: *Ch'un-ch'iu Tso chuan chu-shu* 20.18b. On the term *t'ao-wu*, see Yang Liu-ch'iao, '"T'ao-wu" cheng-i', *Wen-shih* 21, 1983, p. 100. Although I have adopted the traditional reading of 熊 as *nai*, 'three-legged turtle' (see Sarah Allan, *The shape of the turtle: myth, art, and cosmos in early China*, Albany 1991, p. 70 and p. 194, n. 60, citing *Erh-ya* [*Erh-ya chu-shu* 9.20a]), we should note that Karlgren insisted on taking the creature as a bear ('Legends and cults', p. 250, n. 1). For this reading of the character, cf. *Erh-ya chu-shu* 10.14b and 10.15a; also Allan, *The shape of the turtle*, p. 71, where the same character represents what is clearly a creature of the mountains. See also Ku Chieh-kang, '*Chuang-tzu* ho *Ch'u-tz'u* chung K'un-lun ho P'eng-lai liang-ko shen-hua hsi-t'ung ti jung-ho', *Chung-hua wen-shih lun-ts'ung* 1979.2, p. 50; and T'u Yüan-chi, 'Kun hua huang-lung k'ao-shih', *Min-chien wen-i chi-k'an* 3, 1982, 35–49.

of Ch'i, later confronted him during a hunt in the form of **a large boar**; this apparition caused the marquis an injury.[26] **Ch'ang-hung** 萇弘 appears in early historical texts as a high lord at the Chou court; the story of his **blood turning to jade** (血 . . . 化為碧) three years after his death in exile is mentioned in *Chuang-tzu*, echoed in *Lü-shih ch'un-ch'iu*, elaborated in the *Chuang-tzu* commentary by Ch'eng Hsüan-ying, and abandoned to fantasy in the fourth-century *Shih-i chi* of Wang Chia.[27] The local legend of **Shu's daughter** 舒女 is quoted in various reference works of the T'ang and Sung, which give the source as *Hsüan-ch'eng chi* 宣城記 by Chi I 紀義:

Long ago there was a girl of the Shu family who cut firewood with her father at this stream [the Shu Maiden Stream, near Lin-ch'eng county]. When the girl sat down it proved impossible to pull her away, so he went and told them at home. By the time they returned there was nothing to see but the clear, tranquil stream . . .

The stream responds to the stimulus of music, and so they know it as their daughter.[28] The tragic fate of **Niu Ai** 牛哀, a man of Lu, was first told in *Huai-nan tzu* and widely used in later writings: after a short illness he **turned into a tiger** and mortally attacked his brother – for as a man he had no knowledge of being a tiger, as a tiger no knowledge of being a man.[29] **Huang's mother** 黃母 was found to have **turned into a giant turtle** while taking a bath: her story was noted in the 'Five elements' monograph of the *Hsü Han shu* 續漢書 and taken up in Kan Pao's 干寶 *Sou-shen chi* 搜神記.[30]

At this point the scheme of parallels expands into two pairs of antithetical transformations. According to the fourth-century *Pao-p'u tzu*,

26 *Tso chuan*, Huan/18/4 and Chuang/8/12. Cf. Karlgren, 'Legends and cults', p. 251.

27 *Tso chuan*, Ai/3/6; *Kuo yü*, 'Chou yü', 3.148 (ed. Shanghai 1978); (politically motivated death of Ch'ang-hung at the hands of the Chou). *Chuang-tzu*, 'Wai-wu' 外物 chapter, opening lines (*Chuang-tzu chi-shih* 9A.920); *Lü-shih ch'un-ch'iu chiao-shih* (ed. Ch'en Ch'i-yu) 14.828 ('Pi chi'); Ch'eng Hsüan-ying, in *Chuang-tzu chi-shih* 9A.920–21; *Shih-i chi* 3.74 (ed. Ch'i Chih-p'ing, Peking 1981). By T'ang times the story had an 'encyclopaedia' existence of its own: cf. *Fa-yüan chu-lin* 32.531b.

28 *I-wen lei-chü* 9.165–6; *Ch'u-hsüeh chi* 15.378. For further details see notes by Wang Shao-ying in his edition of T'ao Ch'ien, *Sou-shen hou-chi* (Peking 1981) 1.8 – a work into which this passage was evidently introduced by later compilers. The story appears among the same complex of allusions in Po Chü-i's poem 'Gaining the truth, 2' (see n. 24, above).

29 *Huai-nan tzu*, 'Chu-chen' 俶真 chapter, 2.2b. Cf. Chang Heng's 張衡 rhapsody 'Thinking of mysteries' (思玄賦) in *Wen-hsüan* 15.8b; *Pao-p'u tzu nei-p'ien chiao-shih* 2.14 (rev. ed. Wang Ming, Peking 1985); *Fa-yüan chu-lin* 32.530c; *Po Chü-i chi*, 3.146.; *TPYL* 888.1a.

30 *Hou Han shu*, Monograph section, 17.3348; *Sou-shen chi* (ed. Wang Shao-ying, Peking 1979) 14.175, with details of other references. (But *TPKC* 471.3880 cites *Shen-kuei chuan* 神鬼傳, not the title given by Wang Shao-ying.)

the army of King Mu of Chou on campaign in the south suffered a morally discriminating change – **the superior men into apes or swans, the inferior into insects or sand**.[31] This antithesis is balanced by a matching pair of sex changes – a phenomenon recorded from various parts of China in the Han 'Five elements' monographs.[32] The girl who **was buried alive in a tomb, but came back to life after ten years** was a favourite maid of Kan Pao's father, thrust into his tomb by a jealous wife, found there alive ten years later when the tomb was opened for the newly dead wife: this was one of the family experiences which spurred Kan Pao to compile his classic *Sou-shen chi*.[33] The **'Ying spy'** 嬴諜[34] was captured when, in 601 BC, the state of Chin was attacking his own state, Ch'in: 'they put him to death **in the market-place** of Chiang; **six days later he revived**.'[35]

The long, spectacular list ends with a pair of bird myths. One is attributed, but in various forms, to Yang Hsiung's 揚雄 lost *Annals of the Kings of Shu* 蜀王本紀: in essentials it tells how one of the kings, Tu Yü 杜宇, who resigned his throne for reasons of personal inadequacy, changed into a bird at his death; the bird was named after him – *tu-chüan* 杜鵑, **the cuckoo**.[36] **The Fiery Emperor** of the next and final reference appears in Warring States and Han literature as a divine adversary of the mythical Yellow Emperor,[37] but the myth of his daughter Nü-wa's 女娃 sea change is told in the 'Northern Mountains' section of *Shan-hai ching*: 'she voyaged over the Eastern Ocean, was drowned and never returned; so she became the *ching-wei* 精衛 bird, which constantly carries wood and stones from the western hills to fill up the Eastern Ocean.'[38]

31 As quoted in *TPYL* 74.6a, 85.3ab, 888.1b. (*TPYL* 916.4a has 'cranes' 鶴 for 'swans' 鵠.) Contrast the simpler version in *Pao-p'u tzu nei-p'ien* 8.154.

32 *Han shu* 27CA.1472 (woman to man, man to woman); *Hou Han shu* 82B.2741 (woman to man); Monograph section, 17.3349 (man to woman). None of these cases are linked with the places named by Ku K'uang. But a man–woman change in **Wu-tu** is recorded in *Hua-yang kuo chih* 3.2b.

33 *Chin shu* 82.2150.

34 I read 嬴, with *Wen-yüan ying-hua pien-cheng* 2.10b. It was the traditional surname of Ch'in: *Shih chi* 5.173.

35 *Tso chuan*, Hsüan/8/spring.

36 Compare citations by Liu K'uei 劉逵 (third cent.), commentary on Tso Ssu 左思, 'Shu-tu fu' 蜀都賦, in *Wen-hsüan* 4.26a; by Liu Chih-chi, who holds up the story to ridicule, in *Shih t'ung t'ung-shih* 18.519–20; by Hsü Shen in *Shuo-wen chieh-tzu* 4A.12ab; and in *TPYL* 923.8a.

37 Mark E. Lewis, *Sanctioned violence in early China*, Albany 1990, pp. 174 ff., analyses the myths of the Yellow Emperor and his adversaries. He rejects the ancient identification of the Fiery Emperor with Ch'ih-yu 蚩尤 (p. 305, n. 35); Yüan K'o reviews the textual evidence on this question in *Shan-hai ching chiao-chu*, '*Hai-ching* hsin-shih', 11.415–16.

38 *Shan-hai ching chiao-chu*, '*Shan-ching* chien-shih', 3.92. For other references, see *Pao-p'u tzu nei-p'ien* 8.155, and *TPYL* 925.9b.

So, in a sequence of allusions both balanced and breathless, Ku K'uang displays the mutability of created things. His list already dwells upon the specialized subject-matter of the literature that he will survey below. He ignores the comets and eclipses, climatic disasters, freak animal and vegetable growths which occupied the professional omen-readers of the imperial court, and pursues only abnormalities of category – movement between the categories of human and non-human, of dead and living, of male and female.[39] He has drawn them, perhaps indirectly but no doubt often consciously, from many of the sources in the list to come. He has also, as we shall see, implied a definition of subject-matter which well fits the contents of his friend's book *Kuang-i chi.*

III

In antiquity – when Ch'ing-wu divined [the sites of] **mounds and tombs, when Po-tse investigated spirits and demons, when Shun commissioned K'uei to bring the spirits into harmony** [with men], **when T'ang questioned Chi, who spoke of strange matters – sounds were heard in the Lu wall, shapes were cast on the Hsia tripods; in 'jade slips and stone records', in 'five diagrams and ninefold tube', accounts came in great profusion. Thus, when Emperor Wen of Han summoned Chia I to inquire about ghosts and spirits, at midnight he moved his seat forward.**

In this new sequence of allusions, still in matching pairs but organized in a common syntax, the author explores the ancestry of recorded *arcana.* He moves in chronological steps, beginning from the very dawn of civilization. **Ch'ing-wu** 青烏 and **Po-tse** 白澤 were, in the eyes of mediaeval writers, the ultimate authorities for geomancy and spirit-lore. In the fourth century Ko Hung 葛洪 (283–343) brought them together as two of the many specialists from whom the Yellow Emperor had to seek knowledge of the world and its mysteries:

To **investigate the spirits and demons** he recorded the words of **Po-tse**, to **divine** the earth's patterns he wrote down the sayings of **Ch'ing-wu**.[40]

Texts of spirit-lore and grave-siting that bore these creatures' names circulated in the Middle Ages.[41]

39 Some literary implications of this point in eighth- and ninth-century literature are explored in Dudbridge, *The tale of Li Wa,* pp. 63 ff.

40 *Pao-p'u tzu nei-p'ien chiao-shih* (rev. edn.) 13.241, with nn. 25 and 26 on p. 248. Ko Hung's dates are discussed by Nathan Sivin, 'On the *Pao p'u tzu nei p'ien* and the life of Ko Hung (283–343)', *Isis* 60, 1969, 388–91.

41 *Po-tse t'u* ('The illustrations of Po-tse'), in one chapter, is listed in *Sui shu* 34.1039 and *CTS* 47.2043. *Ch'ing-wu tzu,* in three chapters, appears first in *CTS* 47.2044. Both works

The chronology now advances from primary culture hero to legendary sage emperor. **Shun commissioned K'uei** 夔 as director of music in a passage from the part of *The book of documents* known and accepted in T'ang times as 'Shun-tien' 舜典. Music was to be the medium of education for the young; moreover – and here we glimpse again the workings of the Han organic universe – 'if the eight tones can agree together without one usurping the due place of another, thus will **spirits and men be brought into harmony**'.[42]

T'ang 湯, first ruler of the Shang dynasty, **put questions to Chi** (問革) near the opening of *Chuang-tzu*, where the sense of their dialogue meets with the philosopher's approval, and he goes on to illustrate the relativity of different creatures' horizons with his celebrated fable of the birds.[43] An extended account of this exchange between T'ang and [Hsia] Chi 夏革 later takes up a chapter of the book *Lieh-tzu* (*ca.* AD 300): the questions elicit first a probing of concepts by means of logic and paradox, then an exposition of ancient mythological lore.[44] It is to these **strange matters** (怪) that Ku K'uang apparently refers.

The move now from spoken to written revelation is also a move into the historical era. The *Han shu* tells how, notoriously, 'ancient texts' of the Confucian scriptures and commentaries were found in **the walls** of the master's old house **in Lu** while it was being demolished in the second century BC: work stopped when **sounds were heard** of bells, chimes and zithers.[45]

To learn about the **shapes cast on the Hsia tripods** we must consult

are classified under 'Five elements', though Anna Seidel argues for counting at least the *Po-tse t'u* as a text from the apocryphal literature known as *ch'en-wei* 讖緯: 'Imperial treasures and Taoist sacraments – Taoist roots in the apocrypha –', in Michel Strickmann, ed., *Tantric and Taoist studies in honour of R. A. Stein*, vol. 2 (Mélanges chinois et bouddhiques, vol. 21), Brussels 1983, p. 321.

42 *Shang shu chu-shu* 3.26a. 'Shun tien', not attested as an archaic division of the *Shang shu*, was accepted and maintained by the standard T'ang editor K'ung Ying-ta 孔穎達 (574–648).

43 'Hsiao-yao-yu' chapter: see *Chuang-tzu chi-shih* 1A.14. On 1A.15 the modern editor Kuo Ch'ing-fan establishes the identity of the name Chi written 棘 (*Chuang-tzu*) with 革 (*Lieh-tzu* and Ku K'uang).

44 Yang Po-chün, ed., *Lieh-tzu chi-shih*, 5.147 ff. For discussion of the philosophical part of the dialogue, see Richard Wilhelm, *Liä Dsi: das wahre Buch vom quellenden Urgrund, Tschung Hü Dschen Ging, die Lehren der Philosophen Liä Yü Kou und Yang Dschu*, Jena 1921, pp. 132 ff.; Needham, *Science and civilisation*, vol. 2, pp. 198–9; A. C. Graham, *The book of Lieh-tzu: a classic of Tao*, second edn., New York 1990, 'Preface to the Morningside Edition', pp. xiv–xv. Elsewhere Graham argues that the opening, philosophical part of the dialogue may come from a lost passage of *Chuang-tzu*: see his *Studies in Chinese philosophy and philosophical literature*, Singapore 1986, p. 271. But Ku K'uang's interest no doubt lay rather in the marvels that follow, which were most likely assembled with the transmitted text of *Lieh-tzu* in the early fourth century AD: see Graham, *The book of Lieh-tzu*, pp. 281–2.

45 *Han shu* 53.2414.

a speech recorded in the *Tso chuan*: when the viscount of Ch'u began to ask presumptuous questions about the tripods which were the sacred warrants of the Chou royal sway, an officer of Chou lectured him on the tripods of antiquity and their close bond with the ruler's kingly virtue:

'When the Hsia was at the height of its virtue, pictures of [exotic] creatures [were made and submitted] from distant parts, and metal was sought in tribute from the heads of the nine provinces. Tripods were then cast with these creatures depicted on them. With all the creatures [thus revealed], precautions were taken against them, so that the people might recognize the spirits and demons . . .'[46]

Ku K'uang's next phrase, **jade slips and stone records**, is a purely literary quotation from the sonorous opening lines of Tso Ssu's 'Rhapsody on the Capital of Wu'. There, together with 'bird'-script on bamboo slips and 'seal'-script on silk, it evokes the entire heritage of writings from the past.[47] And in turn the **five diagrams and ninefold tube** evoke the authority of transmitted esoteric texts. This is a literary borrowing from a Taoist poem by Pao Chao 鮑照 (405–466): as, late in his career, the poet aspires to everlasting life and seeks the guidance of immortals in remote mountains –

The **Five Diagrams** display records [concerning alchemical] gold,
The **ninefold tube** encloses scriptures [on the alchemy] of cinnabar.

The *Wen-hsüan* commentator Li Shan, referring to *Pao-p'u tzu*, identifies the ***Five diagrams*** as a Taoist text (*Chart of the true forms of the Five Sacred Peaks* 五岳真形圖) or as a corpus of alchemical writings stored in the fivefold citadel on Mount K'un-lun. He points out that the 'tube' 籥 was an ancient receptacle for written documents: the mysteries of cinnabar nine times refined would require a ninefold tube.[48]

This section ends, as the last one began, with Chia I. Summoned by the Former Han emperor Hsiao-wen Ti 孝文帝 to the Proclamation

46 Hsüan/3/Spring: *Ch'un-ch'iu Tso chuan chu-shu* 21.15b–16a. This passage is analysed by Chiang Shao-yüan in *Chung-kuo ku-tai lü-hsing chih yen-chiu*, vol. 1, Shanghai 1935, repr. 1937, pp. 6–13, 82–4; [trans. by Fan Jen as Kiang Chao-yuan, *Le voyage dans la Chine ancienne, considéré principalement sous son aspect magique et religieux*, Shanghai 1937, pp. 130–47]. See also Needham, *Science and civilisation*, vol. 3, pp. 503–4; and Seidel, 'Imperial treasures and Taoist sacraments', pp. 299 and 320–1.

47 'Wu-tu fu' 吳都賦, *Wen hsüan* 5.1b, copiously annotated by the author's contemporary Liu K'uei and by Li Shan.

48 Pao Chao, 'Sheng t'ien hsing' 升天行, in *Wen hsüan* 28.23b. For a detailed study of the *Chart of the true form of the Five Sacred Peaks* as it evolved in literature and Taoist ritual, see K. M. Schipper, '*Gogaku shinkyō zu* no shinkō', *Dōkyō kenkyū* 2, Tokyo 1967, 114–62. See also comments by Seidel, 'Imperial treasures and Taoist sacraments', pp. 325–7.

Chamber 宣室 in the Wei-yang Palace, he was questioned on the 'fundamentals of ghosts and spirits' and responded in detail. **'When midnight came, Wen Ti moved his seat forward.'** Chia I's compelling performance earned him a position as tutor to the emperor's youngest son. It also set up, for others as well as Ku K'uang, a landmark in recording the dealings of the other world.[49]

IV

The men who recorded strange things: Liu Tzu-cheng's *Illustrious immortals* and Ko Chih-ch'uan's *Gods and immortals*; Wang Tzu-nien's *Neglected things gathered up* and Tung-fang Shuo's *Gods and marvels*; Chang Mao-hsien's *Manifold knowledge* and Kuo Tzu-heng's *Insights into obscurity;* Yen Huang-men's *Scrutiny of the superhuman* and Hou Chün-su's *Signal wonders.* Among them, some spiritual and profound: Master Ku's *Declarations of the perfected* and *Chou's communications with the unseen world.*

And as for the *Assembly of marvels* and the *Spirits searched out*, the *Scriptures of mountains and seas* and the *Transcripts of the other world*, the *Ancients of Hsiang-yang* and the *Former worthies of Ch'u*, the *Universal principles of manners and customs* and the *Recording of seasonal observances, Wu-hsing* and *Yang-hsien, Southern Yüeh* and *Western Capital, Glosses upon things ancient and modern* and writings entitled *The Huai and the ocean*, P'ei Sung-chih and Sheng Hung-chih, Lu Tao-chan . . . – all these produced testimony in a luxuriant, unending abundance.

Under our own dynasty – . . . [and Chang] Yen-[kung]'s *Tale of the four gentlemen of Liang*, T'ang Lin's *Records of retribution from the other world* and Wang Tu's *Memoir concerning an ancient mirror*, K'ung Sheng-yen's *Record of gods and demons* and Chao Tzu-ch'in's *Records of destiny preordained*; and then the likes of Li Yü-ch'eng and Chang Hsiao-chü – they pass the testimony on, one to another.

It is tempting to wave aside this cascade of titles and names as a mere gesture of extravagant citation, and it would scarcely be wise to seek too much significance in its sequence and groupings. But this remains an interesting list. It stands authors and books which are household names in Chinese mediaeval literature beside others which have virtually sunk from view. Many of these ancient books have long been lost

49 *Shih chi* 84.2502–3; *Han shu* 48.2230. The 'Proclamation Chamber' of this incident was used in the title of a ninth-century collection of supernatural tales, the *Hsüan-shih chih* 宣室志 by Chang Tu 張讀.

to transmission as independent texts: what we know of them has to be recovered from indirect survivals in quotation or anthologized form. Some have left only their names behind, others hardly even that. This preface adds usefully to the patchy record. More pertinently, it creates a context for Tai Fu's work. Where bibliographers and historians of literature might wish to pin down generic categories and assign Tai Fu a small pigeon-hole among them, Ku K'uang allows him the freedom of a vast, richly assorted company.

This company answers to one general description – **men who recorded strange things** (志怪之士) – a phrase that found its first known use in *Chuang-tzu*,[50] and was destined to become the label for a whole literature of sub-historical anecdotes and *mirabilia*.[51] Within that grand category the overall organization is chronological: the writer identifies a broad tradition running from Han to Sui, then finds it loyally maintained in his own age, even by men younger than himself and Tai Fu. His exposition is essentially no more than a list which makes vague gestures at holding its contents together in a loose syntax. Like the rest of the preface it is textured in parallels, and two flaws in its careful sequence of doubles betray likely problems of textual integrity.

The list opens with a group of eight titles, for the most part early and famous. *Lieh-hsien chuan* 列仙傳 (Biographies of **illustrious immortals**), circulating in various forms in T'ang China, was then believed to be the work of the great Former Han scholar **Liu** Hsiang 劉向 (styled **Tzu-cheng** 子政, 77–6 BC); traditionally it contained seventy-two brief biographical notices of immortals known in ancient times.[52] **Ko** Hung's (**Chih-ch'uan's** 稚川) successor work, *Shen-hsien chuan* 神仙傳 (Biographies of **gods and immortals**), added notices of many more, of which about half come down to us.[53] Both collections celebrated dedicated men who triumphed over the limitations of their mortal flesh by dint of physical techniques and spiritual discipline. The collection called *Shih-i chi* 拾遺記 (Records of **neglected things gathered up**) was known to T'ang China in two forms, associated in different ways with

50 'The man Ch'i Hsieh was one **who recorded strange things**': *Chuang-tzu chi-shih* 1A.4 ('Hsiao-yao yu').

51 This process is carefully described by Li Chien-kuo in *T'ang ch'ien chih-kuai hsiao-shuo shih*, Tientsin 1984, pp. 9 ff.

52 On these and other questions of authenticity and transmission, see Max Kaltenmark, *Le Lie-sien tchouan*, Peking 1953, pp. 1–8.

53 The Confucian scholar Liang Su 梁肅(753–793) reported 190 in his essay on this work, '*Shen-hsien chuan* lun' (*WYYH* 739.14b); and the tenth-century Taoist master Wang Sung-nien 王松年 reported 117 in his preface to another collection, *Hsien-yüan pien-chu* 仙苑編珠 (*Tao tsang*: HY 596). There are recent reconstructions by Sawada Mizuho, *Shinsenden*, in *Chūgoku koten bungaku taikei*, vol. 8, Tokyo 1969, and by Fukui Kōjun: *Shinsenden*, Tokyo 1983.

the fourth-century hermit magician **Wang** Chia 王嘉 (**Tzu-nien** 子年).[54] In the form known to us it is an assembly of rarities, historical apocrypha and mythological scraps, arranged chronologically through known history and ending with a chapter of sacred mountain lore. The shorter work *Shen-i ching* 神異經 (Scripture of **gods and marvels**) was in T'ang times still accepted as the work of **Tung-fang Shuo** 東方朔 (154–93 BC), the colourful figure presented in his official biography as a jester at the court of Han Wu-ti.[55] One T'ang catalogue classes it under 'Geography', reflecting the regional character of its reported wonders.[56] **Chang** Hua 張華 (**Mao-hsien** 茂先 AD 232–300), a scholar of the Western Chin deeply versed in apocryphal and magical literature, was reputed to have produced a massive compilation of reports from such sources, of which his ten-chapter *Po-wu chih* 博物志 (Records of **manifold knowledge**) was said to be a reduced version. Its richly varied contents cover mountain and river lore, historical figures, rare creatures, magicians, immortals and other mythological subjects.[57] **Kuo** Hsien 郭憲 (**Tzu-heng** 子横) had a place among the magicians of the Later Han whose brief biographies survive in the *Hou Han shu*.[58] He was traditionally accepted as the author of a short work, *Han Wu tung-ming chi* 漢武洞冥記 (The record of Emperor Wu of Han's **insights into obscurity**), dealing with that emperor's quest for immortality and lore of distant parts.[59]

54 A ten-chapter version entitled *Wang Tzu-nien shih-i chi* was credited to Hsiao Ch'i 蕭綺 (probably a sixth-century member of the Liang imperial family); and a two-chapter *Shih-i lu* was ascribed more directly to Wang Tzu-nien: *Sui shu* 33.961; *CTS* 46.1995. The surviving text is edited and discussed with its credentials analysed, by Ch'i Chih-p'ing: *Shih-i chi*, Peking 1981.

55 *Han shu* 65; translated by Burton Watson in *Courtier and commoner in ancient China*, New York and London 1974, pp. 79–106. Although *Shen-i ching* was not credited to his name in Liu Hsiang's catalogue of the Han imperial library, there are signs that it did exist by the Later Han and was associated with Tung-fang Shuo by the sixth century: see Yü Chia-hsi, *Ssu-k'u t'i-yao pien-cheng* 18.1124–6. Questioning of the ascription began with Ch'en Chen-sun, *Chih-chai shu-lu chieh-t'i*, ed. Shanghai 1987, 11.315; cf. *Ssu-k'u ch'üan-shu tsung-mu* 142.4b–6a.

56 *CTS* 46.2016; cf. *Sui shu* 33.983. But the mid-eleventh-century *HTS* 59.1520 lists it under 'Immortals' 神仙.

57 The original title echoes a phrase from *Tso chuan*/Chao/1 (41.25a). What we now have of the book, corrupted and confused in transmission, falls short of what was known and cited in the T'ang. Evidence on the complex questions of survival and authenticity is examined in *Ssu-k'u ch'üan-shu tsung-mu* 142.39b–43a; Yü Chia-hsi, *Ssu-k'u t'i-yao pien-cheng* 18.1154–8; Fan Ning, ed., *Po-wu chih chiao-cheng*, Peking 1980, pp. 157–68; T'ang Chiu-ch'ung, 'Fan Ning *Po-wu chih chiao-cheng* p'ing-lun', in *Chung-kuo ku-tien hsiao-shuo yen-chiu chuan-chi* 6, Taipei 1983, pp. 315–31.

58 *Hou Han shu* 82A.2708–9.

59 This is the title of the one-chapter work listed in *Sui shu* 33.980. There were other forms. Cf. *Shih t'ung t'ung-shih* 10.275; *CTS* 46.2004 ('four chapters'). Later bibliographers have argued that the surviving text was composed by the Liang emperor Yüan-ti 元帝 (r. 552–555) and falsely ascribed to Kuo Hsien, but this is still questioned:

The last two titles in this group fall later in time and command less celebrity. A work called *Chi sheng fu* 稽聖賦 (Rhapsody on s**crutiny of the superhuman**) is credited in certain Sung catalogues to **Yen** Chih-t'ui 顏之推 (531–591+), vice-president of the **Yellow Gate** 黃門侍郎 under the Northern Ch'i.[60] It does not survive. The work receives no mention in Yen Chih-t'ui's official biography,[61] and only a few tiny scraps of quoted text appear in sources from the ninth and eleventh centuries; its mention in Ku K'uang's preface may be the earliest of its kind.[62] The *Ching-i chi* 旌異記 (Book of **signal wonders**) by **Hou** Po 侯白 (**Chün-su** 君素), though all but lost now, was well documented throughout the T'ang,[63] and a few scattered extracts remain in compilations of the period.[64] Hou was a figure at the early Sui court in the 590s, brilliant, witty and popular, employed in compiling the official history.[65] It is said that his *Ching-i chi* was prepared at imperial command; it seems to have specialized in Buddhist stories of retribution, visions and monastic lore.

Ssu-k'u ch'üan-shu tsung-mu 142.8a–10a; Yü Chia-hsi, *Ssu-k'u t'i-yao pien-cheng* 18.1135–7; Li Chien-kuo, *T'ang ch'ien chih-kuai hsiao-shuo shih*, pp. 159–67.

60 *Ch'ung-wen tsung-mu* 12.10b (one chapter, under 'Individual collections'); *HTS* 60.1622 (one chapter, commentary by Li Ch'un-feng 李淳風, under 'General collections'); *Chung-hsing kuan-ko shu-mu* 中興館閣書目 (commentary by Li Ch'un-feng 李淳風), see *Chih-chai shu-lu chieh-t'i* 16.466 (also listing three chapters, commentary by grandson Yen Shih-ku 顏師古). The latter sees the work as an imitation of the 'T'ien-wen' section of *Ch'u-tz'u*.

61 *Pei Ch'i shu* 45.617–26. As an author Yen Chih-t'ui is best known for his *Family instructions*: see Wang Li-ch'i, ed., *Yen-shih chia-hsün chi-chieh*, Shanghai 1980. On his career and cast of mind, see Albert E. Dien, 'Yen Chih-t'ui (531–591+): a Buddho-Confucian', in Arthur F. Wright and Denis Twitchett, eds., *Confucian personalities*, Stanford 1962, pp. 43–64; and *Pei Ch'i shu 45: Biography of Yen Chih-t'ui*, Frankfurt 1976. Although the T'ang bibliographies do list other works by Yen Chih-t'ui which would clearly belong among the titles dealt with here (*Chi-ling chi* 集靈記 in ten or twenty chapters, and *Yüan-hun chih* 冤魂志 in three), Ku K'uang ignores them. See *Sui shu* 33.981; *CTS* 46.2006. On surviving texts of *Yüan-hun chih*, see Wang Chung-min, *Tun-huang ku-chi hsü-lu*, Peking 1979, pp. 226–8.

62 Wang Li-ch'i assembles a small group of phrases quoted in various sources: *Yen-shih chia-hsün chi-chieh*, Appendix 3, pp. 639–41. One may be roughly contemporary with Ku K'uang: Hui-lin's (737–820) *I-ch'ieh ching yin-i* 51.643c. Here and elsewhere the reference is to commentators on the *Chi-sheng fu*.

63 A fifteen-chapter version is reported in *Sui shu* 33.981, and *CTS* 46.2006 (see *Chiu T'ang shu chiao-k'an chi* 28.31a for a variant in the author's name). *Hsü kao-seng chuan* (whose compiler Tao-hsüan 道宣 died in 667) reports a twenty-chapter version (2.436a); so does *Fa-yüan chu-lin* (whose compiler Tao-shih 道世 died in 683) (100.1023a). The book is also listed as a source by Tao-hsüan in *Chi shen-chou san-pao kan-t'ung lu* C.431a, and in *Tao-hsüan lü-shih kan-t'ung lu* 436a.

64 Mostly in Buddhist compilations: *Chi shen-chou san-pao kan-t'ung lu* B.414a, B.420ab, C.427c; *Ku Ch'ing-liang chuan* A.1093a; *Fa-yüan chu-lin* 13.383bc, 14.389c, 18.418bc, 85.909b–910a, 91.956b (cf. *TPKC* 99.660–1); *Hsü kao-seng chuan* 28.686ab, 29.693c.

65 Biography in *Sui shu* 58.1421.

At this point Ku K'uang sets apart two works as **'spiritual and profound'**. Both were fundamental texts in the important school of Taoism associated with Mao-shan 茅山 and crucially promoted by T'ao Hung-ching 陶洪景 (456–536).[66] The movement first sprang from divine revelations set down in written form and spread later among its followers through edited transcriptions of those revealed texts. A fifth-century scholar, **Ku** Huan 顧歡, was said to be the first to attempt a systematic compilation, entitled *Chen chi* 真迹 (Traces of the perfected), which offered facsimile copies of the revealed writings. His work was superseded by the more critical and comprehensive attentions of T'ao Hung-ching, whose *Chen kao* 真誥 **(Declarations of the perfected)** survives to provide our richest source of information on the birth of Mao-shan Taoism. The earlier *Chen chi* does not survive, nor do we have evidence that it did even in T'ang times.[67] So this preface creates a puzzle by linking the superseded editor Ku Huan with the work that took the place of his own, and by making no mention of T'ao Hung-ching.[68] But its other reference gives less trouble. *Chou-shih ming-t'ung chi* 周氏冥通記 (A record of **Chou's communications with the unseen world**) is the title of a known and surviving work, T'ao Hung-ching's annotated edition of visionary transcripts left behind in 516 by his own disciple Chou Tzu-liang 周子良.[69] It is interesting that Ku K'uang should include, and single out, these texts of Taoist revelation in what is otherwise a more predictable list of *chih-kuai* literature. For in or soon after 793 he was himself to go to Mao-shan and there receive induction into the so-called Shang-ch'ing 上清 order of Taoism,[70] and although that circumstance gives no direct insight into the dating of this preface, it does confirm the special interest its author took in the inspired texts of the Mao-shan school.

66 The brief comments which follow derive from the historical accounts given by Michel Strickmann in three important studies: 'The Mao shan revelations: Taoism and the aristocracy', *T'oung Pao* 63, 1977, 1–64 (see esp. pp. 31–4); 'On the alchemy of T'ao Hung-ching', in Holmes Welch and Anna Seidel, eds., *Facets of Taoism*, New Haven and London 1979, pp. 123–92 (esp. pp. 140–1); *Le taoïsme du Mao chan: chronique d'une révélation*, Paris 1981.

67 The *Sui shu* records other scholarly works by Ku Huan (on *Shang shu* and *Mao shih*: 32.914, 917; on *Lao-tzu*: 34.1000–1; on 'Barbarians and Chinese': 34.1002), but not his *Chen chi*. Cf. *CTS* 46.1970; 47.2028, 2030.

68 The nineteenth-century editors of *Ch'üan T'ang wen* substituted T'ao's surname for Ku's at this point in the text (528.14b), with what authority is not clear. They also supplied the particle *chih* 之 in this phrase to balance the same in the next.

69 *Tao tsang*: HY 302. See Strickmann, 'The Mao shan revelations', p. 5; 'On the alchemy of T'ao Hung-ching', pp. 158–61; *Le taoïsme du Mao chan*, pp. 25–6. *Sui shu* 33.981.

70 The contemporary references which make this dating possible are examined by Chao Ch'ang-p'ing in Fu Hsüan-ts'ung, ed., *T'ang ts'ai-tzu chuan chiao-chien* 3.645–9.

The names and titles of the pre-T'ang group that follows next can be dealt with more summarily:

I-yüan 異苑(**Assembly of marvels**), by Liu Ching-shu 劉敬叔 (*fl.* 409–465): listed with ten chapters in *Sui shu* 33.980; compare *Shih t'ung t'ung-shih* 10.274 and 17.480. Extant version gives wide range of rarities, apparitions, abnormalities.[71]

Sou-shen chi 搜神記 (Record of **spirits searched out**), compiled in thirty chapters by Kan Pao 干寶 (*Chin shu* 82.2150): listed (thirty chapters) in *Sui shu* 33.980, *CTS* 46.2005, and cf. *Shih t'ung t'ung-shih* 10.274. Subsequently lost, but partially and unevenly recovered from quotations. Collected stories of divine beings, uncommon men, transformations, in ancient and modern times; the most famous of its kind.

Shan-hai ching 山海經 (**The scriptures of mountains and seas**): composite text dating in parts from Warring States times, assembled by the time of Han Wu-ti (*Shih chi* 123.3179; *Han shu* 30.1774); revised with commentary by Kuo P'u 郭璞 (276–324); listed with twenty-three chapters in *Sui shu* 33.982, with eighteen in *CTS* 46.2014.[72] The classic collection of mythological lore of distant regions, fabulous creatures and growths: territorial subjects associated in ancient times with shamans and magicians. Early classified as 'Geography'.

Yu-ming lu 幽冥錄 (**Transcripts of the other world**), by Liu I-ch'ing 劉義慶 (403–444: see *Sung shu* 51.1475–80, *Nan shih* 13.359–60), a member of the Sung royal house celebrated for his stylish collection of conversations and characterizations *Shih-shuo hsin-yü* 世說新語. Listed with twenty chapters in *Sui shu* 33.980, with thirty in *CTS* 46.2005; cf. *Shih t'ung t'ung-shih* 10.274;[73] lost by Northern Sung times, now known through excerpts. Regional, mythological and supernatural anecdotes.[74]

Hsiang-yang ch'i-chiu chi 襄陽耆舊記 (Records of the **ancients of Hsiang-yang**), by Hsi Tso-ch'ih 習鑿齒 (d. 384), native of Hsiang-yang in modern Hupeh (*Chin shu* 82.2152–8). Listed with five chapters in *Sui shu* 33.975 and *CTS* 46.2001. Now lost and represented only by excerpts. An example of the literature of regional traditions, dealing with persons, lands, settlements, official incumbents.[75] Although seeming different in kind from many other titles in this list, it shares with them a common early classification: 'Assorted traditions' (雜傳).

Ch'u-kuo hsien-hsien [chuan-tsan] 楚國先賢傳贊 (Biographies and eulogies of

71 A detailed account of the transmission and current state of this text, together with notes on the author, is given by Li Chien-kuo, *T'ang ch'ien chih-kuai hsiao-shuo shih*, pp. 372–82.

72 The surviving version is in eighteen chapters: see Yüan K'o, ed., *Shan hai ching chiao-chu*, Shanghai 1980.

73 These T'ang sources give the title in a variant form: 幽明錄.

74 For a careful study of the survivals, see Wang Kuo-liang, '*Yu-ming lu* yen-chiu', *Chung-kuo ku-tien hsiao-shuo yen-chiu chuan-chi* 2, Taipei 1980, 47–60; cf. too Li Chien-kuo, *T'ang ch'ien chih-kuai hsiao-shuo shih*, pp. 356–68.

75 Compare the specimens of this literature cited by Liu Chih-chi, *Shih t'ung t'ung-shih* 10.274.

the former worthies of Ch'u), by Chang Fang 張方. Listed with twelve chapters, under this title and author, in *Sui shu* 33.974. But *CTS* 46.2001 ends the title with *chih* 志 and ascribes it to Yang Fang 楊方, a much more likely author.[76] Lost, and known only in excerpts.

Feng-su t'ung[-i] 風俗通義 (**Universal principles of manners and customs**) by Ying Shao 應劭 (who died before AD 204): designed as a project of social and political reform, giving a survey of society and institutions in the Eastern Han, and including observations on regional and religious matters. Full title listed with thirty-one chapters in *Sui shu* 34.1006, with thirty in *CTS* 47.2033. Apparently current in complete form during T'ang; survives now only in ten-chapter versions.[77]

[Ching-Ch'u] sui-shih chi 歲時記 (**Record of seasonal observances** in Ch'u), by Tsung Lin 宗懍 (*fl.* 520–554): the ancestral work in China's literature of calendars, recording regional festivals and customs by season. Listed with ten chapters in *CTS* 47.2034. Not transmitted in its full early form, only partially available in quotations.[78]

Wu-hsing [chi] 吳興記 (**Records of Wu-hsing**): appears under 'Geography' in *Sui shu* 33.982, with three chapters, and credited to Shan Ch'ien-chih 山謙之 (state historian of the Sung, d. *ca.* 454). The work, recording traditions of the place now known as Hu-chou, in Chekiang, is lost and known only in quotations.

Yang-hsien [feng-t'u chi] 陽羨風土記 (A record of the characteristics of **Yang-hsien**): a title which is inferred from its abbreviated form here. The author Chou Ch'u 周處 (240–299), a native of Yang-hsien in I-hsing 義興 (southern Kiangsu), served with heroism as a general under the Chin.[79] His *Yang-hsien feng-t'u [chi]* is cited as a source of local information in *Shih t'ung t'ung-shih* 3.74 and 5.132. It is listed, with three chapters, in *Sui shu* 33.982, with ten chapters in *CTS* 46.2014. Now known only in quotations.[80]

Nan-yüeh [chih] 南越志 (Account of **Southern Yüeh**), by Shen Huai-yüan 沈懷遠 (*fl.* 424–465):[81] listed in *Sui shu* 33.960, with eight chapters, in *CTS* 46.2016,

76 Chang Fang (d. 306) was a fighting man who served as a general in the Rebellions of the Eight Princes at the end of the Western Chin; his biography contains no suggestion that he wrote books: *Chin shu* 60.1644–6. But Yang Fang (also early fourth century) built a career on his literary skills and nourished an attachment to his native land: *Chin shu* 68.1831.

77 See modern editions by Wu Shu-p'ing, *Feng-su t' ung-i chiao-shih*, Tientsin 1980, and Wang Li-ch'i, *Feng-su t'ung-i chiao-chu*, Peking 1981. The abridged title *Feng-su t'ung* adopted by Ku K'uang was current elsewhere in T'ang writing: cf. *Shih-t'ung t'ung-shih* 10.291.

78 Yü Chia-hsi, *Ssu-k'u t'i-yao pien-cheng* 8.440–7, finding that the transmitted texts do not reflect the organization or carry all the contents of the work reflected in early quotations.

79 *Chin shu* 58.1569–71; *Feng-t'u chi* noted on 58.1571.

80 Recovered in Wang Mo 王謨 et al., *Yang-hsien feng-t'u chi*, in *Su-hsiang shih ts'ung shu* 粟香室叢書.

81 *Sung shu* 82.2105. Shen spent much of his career in exile in Kuang-chou, and his study of Southern Yüeh must owe its origins to that circumstance.

with five chapters. Though it survived into the thirteenth century,[82] this monograph on the remote south has now vanished but for quotations.[83]

Hsi-ching [tsa-chi] 西京雜記 (Miscellaneous notes from the **Western Capital**): a work believed in T'ang times to be compiled by Ko Hung (283–343), using data omitted from a history written by the Han scholar Liu Hsin 劉歆: see *Shih t'ung t'ung-shih* 10.274; listed in *Sui shu* 33.966 with two chapters (but no named author), in *CTS* 46.1998 with one.[84] The book has survived, though exposed to critical doubts.[85] Its mixed anecdotal contents include supernatural material.

Ku-chin chu 古今注 (**Glosses upon things ancient and modern**): two books with this title were known in T'ang China – one by Fu Wu-chi 伏無忌 of the Later Han, assembling various data on state affairs, omens and signs;[86] the other by Ts'ui Pao 崔豹, assistant preceptor in the court of the Chin emperor Hui-ti 惠帝 (*r.* 290–306).[87] This second work, a collection of terminological notes on carriages and clothes, cities and towns, music, birds and beasts, fish and insects, flora and more heterogeneous topics was much quoted in T'ang writings. It survives in largely complete form.[88]

Huai-hai [luan-li chih] 淮海亂離志 (Disorder and distress on **the Huai and the ocean**) is another inferred title. It is listed in *Sui shu* 33.958, with four chapters, credited to Hsiao Shih-i 蕭世怡 and described as 'recounting the rebellion of Hou Ching 侯景 at the end of the Liang'.[89] We know little more of this lost work, beyond its mention by Liu Chih-chi 劉知幾 (661–721) in the section of his *Shih t'ung* which deals with commentary and annotation: it is one of those he cites for appending circumstantial detail in the form of interlinear comments.[90] Perhaps this characteristic is what links it in a pair with *Ku-chin chu*, above.

82 *Chih-chai shu-lu chieh-t'i* 8.259: entry lists seven chapters.

83 For some comments on the literature to which this book belonged, see Edward H. Schafer, *The vermilion bird: T'ang images of the south*, Berkeley and Los Angeles 1967, p. 148.

84 Second entries appear in both bibliographies: *Sui shu* 33.985 ('*Hsi-ching chi*: three chapters'), *CTS* 46.2014.

85 Yü Chia-hsi sums up the debate in *Ssu-k'u t'i-yao pien-cheng* 17.1007–17 and concludes that this was a compilation by Ko Hung drawing upon many different Han sources.

86 Listed in *Sui shu* 33.959 and *CTS* 46.1995: both give eight chapters and class as 'Miscellaneous history'.

87 *Sui shu* 34.1007 (three chapters); *CTS* 47.2033 (five chapters). Both class under 'Miscellaneous schools of thought' (*tsa-chia*).

88 See the critical study by Yü Chia-hsi: *Ssu-k'u t'i-yao pien-cheng* 15.857–68, with p. 859 on quotations in T'ang literature. Modern edition: *Ku-chin chu, Chung-hua ku-chin chu, Su-shih yen-i* 古今注, 中華古今注, 蘇氏演義, Shanghai 1958.

89 Hsiao Shih-i, a nephew of Liang Wu-ti, died in 568: *Chou shu* 42.754. Hou Ching's biographies appear in *Liang shu* 56.833–64 and *Nan shih* 80.1993–2017: a general serving under the Liang, he started a rebellion in the lower Yangtze valley in 548 which lasted until his death in 552; these troubles made the Liang vulnerable to attacks from the Western Wei, and it came to an end in 557.

90 *Shih t'ung t'ung-shih* 5.132. For a discussion of the style of annotation referred to, see Ch'eng Ch'ien-fan, *Shih t'ung chien-chi*, Peking 1980, pp. 92–3. On p. 94 Ch'eng briefly examines the uncertain authorship of *Huai-hai luan-li chih*: three different names appear in the T'ang sources.

P'ei Sung-chih 裴松之 (372–451) is the first of paired authors' names that now begin to appear. He was known in T'ang times, as now, for his massive supplement to Ch'en Shou's 陳壽 (233–297) *San-kuo chih,* interspersed throughout its text.[91] While now we value P'ei's work for its extensive quotations from lost ancient books, Liu Chih-chi disdained him as one of those 'inquiring men who want to proliferate strange lore, but whose talents and powers are too slight to be able to express themselves. So . . . they pick out strange passages from the histories to fill gaps in earlier writings'.[92]

Sheng Hung-chih 盛弘之 is known to us only in T'ang references to his book *Ching-chou chi* 荊州記, a collection of strange lore from the vast and ancient province Ching-chou.[93] *Sui shu* 33.983 describes him as a secretary in the service of the prince of Lin-ch'uan 臨川 under the Sung dynasty, hence a mid-fifth-century figure.[94] Liu Chih-chi grouped him among authors who described their own region's territory and landscape, products and procedures, customs and culture; he classed their books as 'Geography' (*ti-li*).[95] The same authors, according to Tu Yu 杜佑 (735–812), 'describe their own country's spirits and demons, the quality of its men, the abundance of its created things; when checked against other writings, they are mostly in error'.[96]

The last two names, following the texture of the whole preface, form a careful verbal parallel – even seem chosen for that purpose, since little else links them together. But what now follows them is a single name, with no fellow to pair with it, and no identity that we can attach to it. I have not discovered **Lu Tao-chan** 陸道瞻 outside the text of this preface, and am tempted to wonder whether the name that appears here masks the broken remains of what once may have been a matching pair of other names. At any rate, the pre-T'ang list breaks off at this point.

To introduce the tradition inherited by T'ang writers, Ku K'uang has used a term, *chih-kuai*, that would not be adopted as a generic category by bibliographers until modern times.[97] He defines the field for himself

91 The *San-kuo* commentary is listed in *Sui shu* 33.955; see also *CTS* 46.1989 and 1992. Other works from his hand appear to have been a book of commentary on funeral dress (*Sui shu* 32.920), a history of his family (*Sui shu* 33.977, *CTS* 46.2013), and collected literary work in thirty chapters (*CTS* 47.2068).

92 *Shih t'ung t'ung-shih* 5.132. More criticism of P'ei's indiscriminate prolixity appears on the same page. For further comment, see Ch'eng Ch'ien-fan, *Shih t'ung chien-chi,* p. 95.

93 As defined in *Chin shu* 15.453–8, this covered an area greater than the present Hupeh and Hunan. Compare the 1898 preface by Ch'en Yün-jung to his reconstruction of the three-chapter text of *Ching-chou chi* in *Lu-shan ching-she ts'ung-shu,* 1ab; also the postface of the same year by Ch'en I 陳毅 (appended at the end of that text), 3a–5a.

94 Ch'en I in his postface narrows the book's date of composition to between 431 and 440, and identifies the prince of Lin-ch'uan as Liu I-ch'ing (403–444).

95 *Shih t'ung t'ung-shih* 10.275.

96 *T'ung tien* 171.907a.

97 Li Chien-kuo, *T'ang ch'ien chih-kuai hsiao-shuo shih,* p. 11.

and at first sight lets it sprawl bewilderingly across known classifications. I have documented his names and titles from sources that reveal other perceptions from the High T'ang period, and the results are confusing.

The book listings of the *Sui shu* and *Chiu T'ang shu* ultimately reflect catalogues of imperial library holdings compiled in the mid-seventh and mid-eighth centuries.[98] In almost exact unison they classify the titles mentioned here under a number of heads.[99] Most heavily represented are 'Miscellaneous traditions' (*tsa-chuan*) and 'Geography' (*ti-li*); on the margins are 'Miscellaneous histories' (*tsa-shih*) and 'Miscellaneous schools of thought' (*tsa-chia*). Other classes (mostly in the *Chiu T'ang shu*) cover isolated titles: 'Taoism' (*Tao-chia*) for *Chen kao*; 'Standard histories' (*cheng-shih*) for P'ei Sung-chih; 'Histories of usurping dynasties' (*wei-shih*) for *Huai-hai luan-li chih* and P'ei Sung-chih's work on the Kingdom of Wu; 'Commonplaces' (*hsiao-shuo chia*) for *Po-wu chih*. The main categories cast a long shadow: even the modern historian of *chih-kuai* literature Li Chien-kuo borrows them for his own threefold classification into 'Geographical science' (*ti-li po-wu*), 'Miscellaneous histories and traditions' (*tsa-shih tsa-chuan*), 'Miscellaneous records' (*tsa-chi*).[100] But formulated as they were by officials for an institutional purpose, they reflect bureaucratic thinking. The *Sui shu* compilers, for instance, shaped their view of geographical literature and miscellaneous history around the idealized administrative arrangements of ancient regimes.[101]

Liu Chih-chi covers similar ground in his short chapter 34, 'Miscellaneous records' (*tsa-shu*).[102] Marking off this whole sector from the formal records of ancient rulers (which carry prescriptive force for later times), he divides it into ten specialized classes and so isolates, for instance, regional monographs from family histories. He exposes certain representative titles to uncompromising assessments of veracity and reliability, and these austere judgements obviously serve his overall project of establishing standards of critical procedure for historians.

But Ku K'uang adopts a more deeply conservative style. For him no clear line divides historical and geographical writing from records of gods and spirits: the charting of supernatural agencies and the survey of the world's regions blend in a single historical continuum. His integrated system echoes the interesting thesis developed in the 1930s by Chiang Shao-yüan 江紹原, who identified an ancient tradition of

98 *Sui shu* postface, pp. 1903–4; *CTS* 46.1962–6.

99 Apart from five titles which appear in only one of the two bibliographies, and three assigned to different classes in each, both sources assign all titles to the same classes.

100 This scheme is developed from p. 126 on in his *T'ang ch'ien chih-kuai hsiao-shuo shih.*

101 *Sui shu* 33.981–2, 987–8. For a discussion of the official scheme of categories, see David McMullen, *State and scholars in T'ang China*, Cambridge 1988, pp. 159–60.

102 *Shih t'ung t'ung-shih* 10.273 ff.

regional reporting designed to inform, warn and protect those embarked on the dangerous enterprise of travel. In the eyes of that tradition spirits and demons were simply part of the natural fauna at large in the environment, apt to menace the stranger who entered their territory. A literature of regions and creatures – *Shan-hai ching*, *Chiu-ting chi* 九鼎記, *Po-tse t'u* and their like – was there to give voyagers in strange lands practical guidance on what perils to expect and how to deal with them.[103] Although narrative collections like *Kuang-i chi* would claim no place in that literature, the idea of a continuum linking geographical and supernatural lore does provide a relevant and useful tool for reading them. And by now it becomes clear that the archaisms of Ku K'uang's preface yield more than a formal rhetoric: they show the character of the tradition within which Tai Fu was working – old, fundamentally conservative, but tenacious and lasting.

A briefer list of authors and titles from the T'ang period, much used in modern times for data on rare and lost works, winds up this part of the preface. It begins in a way that suggests more damage to the text, for while the underlying pattern of matching parallels persists to the end, the first title of this group appears with no fellow and with a much-mangled author's name. Here again are some summary comments:

Liang ssu-kung chuan 梁四公傳 (**Tale of the four gentlemen of Liang**) survives only in three excerpts in *T'ai-p'ing kuang-chi*, one of which probably gives the opening of the work. Contents are mostly reports of exotic lore.[104] Data on authorship confused: the Sung catalogue *Chih-chai shu-lu chieh-t'i* (7.196) gives Chang Yüeh 張說 (667–731), duke of Yen 燕公, chief minister during Hsüan-tsung's early reign,[105] but adds details of variant ascriptions, to Lu Shen 盧詵 or Liang Tsai-yen 梁載言 (*chin-shih* 675) (cf. *HTS* 58.1484). This preface appears to confirm Chang Yüeh as author, though only the name of his ducal fief Yen appears in the text.[106]

Ming-pao chi 冥報記 (**Records of retribution from the other world**) by T'ang Lin 唐臨 (*ca.* 600–*ca.* 659) has survived in manuscripts preserved in Japan, as well as in early quotations.[107] The author enjoyed a distinguished official career, which included the presidency of three government boards, before ending his life in the relatively modest status of prefect.[108] His *Ming-pao chi* was apparently

103 The subject of Chiang Shao-yüan's study *Chung-kuo ku-tai lü-hsing chih yen-chiu*; trans. Fan Jen, *Le voyage dans la Chine ancienne.*

104 *TPKC* 81.517–22; 418.3403–4; 418.3404–6. All citing *Liang ssu-kung chi* 記.

105 *CTS* 97.3049–57; tomb inscription by Chang Chiu-ling, *WYYH* 936.4a–6a.

106 *WYYH*: 'Yen'; *Ch'üan T'ang wen*: 'Yen-kung'.

107 Ed. in *T* vol. 51, no. 2082; also Uchida Michio, *Kōhon Meihōki*, Sendai 1955. The most recent critical edition is by Fang Shih-ming, published with his edition of *Kuang-i chi*, Peking 1992.

108 Biographies in *CTS* 85.2811–3, *HTS* 113.4183–4. See also the study by Uchiyama Chinari in *Zui Tō shōsetsu kenkyū*, Tokyo 1977, chap. 2, sect. 2, pp. 85 ff.

composed between 650 and 655 (*Fa-yüan chu-lin* 100.1024b). It assembles from personal testimony fifty-odd tales showing the workings of karmic retribution, with particular interest in the Buddhist underworld.

Ku ching chi 古鏡記 (**Memoir concerning an ancient mirror**): text survives in *T'ai-p'ing kuang-chi* 230.1761–7 and (part) in *T'ai-p'ing yü-lan* 912.3b–4a. Narrative sequence of early seventh-century episodes involving a mirror with properties of exorcism, illumination and protection, in the possession of Wang Tu 王度. This preface and other sources treat Wang Tu as the author, but various scholars have argued for later authorship. Historians of fiction have seen this work as a transitional step towards the fictional literature of the later T'ang.[109]

One brief item from a work called *Shen-kuai chih* 神怪志 (**Record of gods and demons**) appears in *T'ai-p'ing yü-lan* 559.7b and *Meng-ch'iu cheng-wen* A.51a, another, from *Shen-kuai lu* 錄, in *Pei-t'ang shu-ch'ao* 136.10a and *T'ai-p'ing yü-lan* 716.1b. Both are anecdotal encounters with the supernatural. The author **K'ung Shen-yen** 孔慎言 is listed as great-grandson of K'ung Ying-ta 孔穎達 (574–648) (*HTS* 75B.3433) and may have been active in the early eighth century.

Chao Tzu-ch'in 趙自勤 served in court and provincial posts during the T'ien-pao period [742–756], with a sudden rise to high office when the court took refuge in Szechuan in 756; he later held posts in Soochow and Hangchow around 760.[110] His *Ting-ming lu* 定命錄 (**Records of destiny preordained**) appears in *HTS* 59.1542 as *Ting-ming lun* 論 ('Discourses . . .'), in ten chapters. *Sung shih* 206.5225 gives *Ting-ming lu* in two chapters. Sixty-two anecdotes remain in *T'ai-p'ing kuang-chi, T'ai-p'ing yü-lan* and *Lei shuo,* dealing mostly with events in the first half of the eighth century.[111] They share a common thematic interest in the predestined nature of human life and the insights to be gained from seers, soothsayers and diviners, with particular reference to official careers in the middle to upper reaches of the T'ang bureaucracy.[112]

Of the two remaining names in this list, I can identify only the second. **Chang Hsiao-chü** 張孝舉 is recognizable as Chang Chien 薦 (744–804), who held a succession of court posts, served as official historian and led two embassies to the Uigurs.[113] Grandson of Chang Cho 張鷟 (658?–730?), the author of a famous anecdotal collection (*Ch'ao-yeh ch'ien-tsai* 朝野僉載), Chang Chien produced his own two-chapter collection of ghost and demon stories: *Ling-kuai chi* 靈怪集 (*CTS* 149.4025, *HTS* 59.1541). *T'ai-p'ing kuang-chi* and *Lei shuo* contain a small handful of items ascribed to it, but there are problems of anachronism and multiple ascription.

109 For an extensive survey of modern scholarship on the subject, see ibid., chap. 2, sect. 3, pp. 110–37.

110 For this reconstruction, see ibid., pp. 289–93.

111 Three items with much later dates may be derived from a continuation to this work by Lü Tao-sheng 呂道生: see ibid., pp. 293–5.

112 Uchiyama Chinari illustrates and analyses this theme in its T'ang context: see ibid., pp. 296–305.

113 Biographies in *CTS* 149.4023–5, *HTS* 161.4979–82; tomb inscription in *Ch'üan Tsai-chih wen-chi* 22.6a–8b. See also Chu Ying-p'ing, '*Ling-kuai chi* pu shih Liu-ch'ao chih-kuai', *Wen-hsüeh i-ch'an* 1987.1, 18.

So ends this dense and stimulating section of the preface, with its detailed contextual statement. The T'ang list, as often pointed out, appears to stretch in rough chronological sequence from the seventh century down to the very time of writing. The last named author was a generation younger than Ku K'uang, and his mention here must be the earliest of its kind. But more interesting is the broad generic sweep of these few selected works. They include a traditional collection of exotic marvels, a more forward-looking narrative treatment of a magic object, two titles devoted to specialized themes of predestination and retribution, as well as two collections of hauntings. To see *Kuang-i chi* in this context helps to make clear the point of its own title. For it will not submit to any such straightforward classification, and as we shall see, both in length and in catholic range of interest what we have loosely translated as *The great book of marvels* makes up a project of 'comprehensive' (*kuang*) coverage.

V

Master Tai Fu of the Ch'iao-chün [line] **was most deeply versed in the occult. He was descended from An-tao and from Jo-ssu; Miao was a vice-president in the Chin, and K'uei was a hermit in Wu. Service to society and civilized refinement have kept his family name in high esteem. It was early in the Chih-te period, as disorder broke out through all the world, that I and he first graduated together in the same metropolitan examination. He began as a collator and ended his life as administrative registrar in Jao-chou, at the age of fifty-seven. There is a collection of his literary work in twenty scrolls and this book, also in twenty scrolls, comprising a thousand strips of paper, with a good hundred thousand characters or more. Although his allotted life-span was not long, his clear and ringing tones can nonetheless render the spirits some service! His two sons Yüeh and Yung have explained to me his original intention and addressed a tearful request to their father's friend. Receiving** [his book], **I have written this preface to it.**

It seems likely, as Uchiyama Chinari suggests in his close look at this part of the preface, that the list of selected ancestors reflects not so much a significant family tradition as the expression of a simple pride taken by Tai Fu and his sons in great names from their family's past. In fact it is by no means clear that 'An-tao' and 'Jo-ssu' came from the same line.[114] **Tai K'uei** 戴逵 (*tzu*: **An-tao** 安道) did belong to the

114 Uchiyama, 'Chū Tō shoki no shōsetsu – *Kōiki* o chūshin to shite', in *Kaga hakase taikan kinen Chūgoku bunshi tetsugaku ronshū*, Tokyo 1979, pp. 527 ff., in particular p. 529.

Ch'iao-kuo 譙國 branch which Tai Fu claimed as his own. A disciple and son-in-law of the austere scholar-hermit Fan Hsüan 范宣,[115] he entered history as one who firmly refused service under Emperor Hsiao-wu of the Eastern Chin. Settled in the Kuei-chi area, devoted to gentlemanly pursuits, he sought refuge in Soochow and stayed briefly in the villa (belonging to Wang Hsün 王珣) that would later become the famous Buddhist monastery on Tiger Hill. Returning to Kuei-chi, he died *ca.* 395, leaving a small body of literary and scholarly work.[116] His son Yung 顒 (378–441), a hermit of similar stamp, settled in Soochow but died without heir.[117] In 755, according to a story from the *Kuang-i chi* (**116**), the ghost of this man would appear to someone staying at his former Soochow villa and beg the visitor to marry his daughter. All this confirms, at least anecdotally, that Tai Fu's own branch of the family had old associations with Soochow.

Tai Yüan 戴淵 (*tzu*: **Jo-ssu** 若思) and his brother **Miao** 邈, on the other hand, were from the Kuang-ling 廣陵 line of their family.[118] The former began his career as a freebooter and ended it as a distinguished general, losing his life in 322 at the hands of the rebel Wang Tun 王敦. The brother reached high civil office after Wang Tun's death in 324.

Wishful ancestral memories tell us less about Tai Fu than the career details which now follow. The disorders of the **early Chih-te** 至德 **period** that determined the circumstances of his *chin-shih* examination arose of course from the mid-century rebellion of An Lu-shan. In itself this was a complex of events in which historians have by common consent seen great turning-points in the political, social and economic life of imperial China, and distant echoes of that national disaster do sound here and there in the pages of *Kuang-i chi*. But the young Tai Fu was most immediately affected by the disruption of the metropolitan examinations. Military rebellion had broken out in the winter of 755, and the emperor Su-tsung took the throne in succession to Hsüan-tsung on 12 August 756: this was the opening of the Chih-te period. Metropolitan examinations had already taken place that year in Ch'ang-an, but in the next year they had to be held in three provincial centres, one of which covered the eastern provinces from Soochow. It seems clear that Ku K'uang (himself a Soochow native) and Tai Fu (perhaps also based

115 *Chin shu* 91.2360.

116 *Chin shu* 94.2457–9 (biography); *Sui shu* 32.938, 33.976, 34.1000, 34.1007; *CTS* 46.2002, 47.2066; *HTS* 58.1482, 60.1589; *Shih t'ung t'ung-shih* 10.274.

117 *Sung shu* 93.2276–8; *Nan shih* 75.1866–7.

118 Biographies in *Chin shu* 69.1846–9. *TCTC* 92.2903 (for Yung-ch'ang 1/3) records that Jo-ssu was the *tzu* of Tai Yüan.

there) took their degree there together in 757.[119] This association, giving them the status of fellow-students under the presiding examiner Li Hsi-yen 李希言, would be basis enough for Tai Fu's sons later to approach Ku K'uang as **their father's friend**, requesting a preface; but it does not really follow that the two men remained in close personal touch through their careers. For this reason the minimal data we have here on Tai Fu's official career – beginning with the junior court appointment of **collator** (*chiao-shu-lang* 校書郎) and ending with a modest prefectural staff post as **administrative registrar** (*lu-shih ts'an-chün* [*shih*] 錄事參軍事) in **Jao-chou** 饒州 – give us tantalizingly little to work with and certainly no firm dates.

We depend instead on the stories of *Kuang-i chi* to provide a sense of chronology. Their internal dates range widely through the eighth century, building up to the year 780, when the sequence abruptly ends. Tai Fu must certainly have died no earlier than this, and possibly not very much later. Given that he **ended his life at the age of fifty-seven** *sui*, we infer his earliest possible date of birth as 724. His age at graduation would then have been thirty-four *sui* – similar to that of Ku K'uang, who was perhaps around thirty. Tai Fu may of course have been younger, but not younger than (say) twenty; in which case he was born not later than 738 and died not later than 794.[120] We have already noticed, in Chapter 1, how many of his stories reflect contact with provincial bureaucrats and gentry in the eastern coastal region during the 760s and 770s: perhaps that is the surest clue to the shape of his career.

But Uchiyama Chinari, tempted by the notion of parallels with Ku K'uang's own career, constructs a radically different picture. This would leave Tai Fu unemployed for thirty years after his graduation, finally achieving the post of collator under Ku K'uang's old associate Liu Hun 柳渾 (715–789), *ca.* 787, and suffering demotion to Jao-chou when Ku K'uang suffered the same fate in 789.[121] The entire hypothesis, it must be said, rests on no visible evidence. And if Tai Fu ever reached senior official status between the beginning and the end of his career, no sign of it remains.

His substantial **collection of literary work** has not survived. Nor indeed has **this book**, the *Kuang-i chi*, in its original form. The last trace of its presence in a library appears in a list of books lost from the imperial collection during the sack of the Northern Sung capital in

119 Evidence reviewed in Fu Hsüan-ts'ung, ed., *T'ang ts'ai-tzu chuan chiao-chien*, vol. 1, pp. 636–7. Cf. *Teng k'o chi k'ao* 10.343–4.

120 I have documented these points in detail in Tu Te-ch'iao, '*Kuang-i chi* ch'u-t'an', pp. 395–6, 401–2.

121 Uchiyama, 'Chū Tō shoki no shōsetsu', pp. 529–32.

1127.[122] But Ku K'uang's remarks give a useful perspective on the remains of its contents found in other Sung sources. Throughout this discussion I have for convenience rendered the bibliographical term *chüan* 卷 as 'chapter', but here it has seemed best to keep the true meaning 'scroll'. Ku K'uang wrote at a time when Chinese books still took the form of manuscript scrolls made up from sheets of paper (*chih* 紙) pasted together laterally (the term used here is **strips** 幅). He seems to describe in broad but literal terms what Tai Fu's collection actually looked like. The **twenty scrolls** appear as physical objects, each with about fifty sheets of paper. The **hundred thousand characters** were spread over a thousand sheets, about a hundred on each, perhaps in ten columns of ten characters. Ku K'uang's estimates must reflect a loose calculation built up in this way. They obviously do not give surgical accuracy. But when we assemble the three-hundred-odd items preserved in *T'ai-p'ing kuang-chi* and the half-dozen others in *Lei-shuo, Sui-shih kuang-chi, San-tung ch'ün-hsien lu* and *T'ai-p'ing yü-lan*, we can estimate the number of surviving words at around 80,000, or eighty per cent of Ku K'uang's estimate.[123] The discrepancy no doubt reflects a combination of looseness in both estimates, textual incompleteness in the survivals, and disappearance of an unknown number of original items. But it is slight enough to reassure us that we have a good proportion of the book that Tai Fu's **two sons** brought to their father's friend in the last years of the eighth century, when its preface was probably composed.

What we cannot know is whether the author left it at his death in a final, settled shape, and if so whether that shape embodied some thematic scheme. It seems just as likely that his sons inherited a pile of notes built up through the years, which they made it their business to edit and copy into book form. Conceivably they even supplied the title. So Ku K'uang's preface, for all its rich statement of context, leaves unanswered questions at the heart of the subject. What did Tai Fu himself see the business of his book to be? What was his own conception of the world that appears there, and what were his assumptions about it? Since we have recognized his voice as our point of access to that world, we must find answers to these questions, and seek them in the one place they can be found – the stories themselves.

122 *Pi-shu sheng hsü-pien tao ssu-k'u ch'üeh shu-mu*, ed. Yeh Te-hui, 1903, 2.66. The title is annotated 'one chapter (*chüan*)', with what authority we cannot know. I have elsewhere examined the doubtful status of two later manuscript versions held in the Peking National Library: Tu Te-ch'iao, '*Kuang-i chi* ch'u-t'an', pp. 408–11. They would appear to be based on *T'ai-p'ing kuang-chi.*

123 The items are listed in the Appendix. My examination of the number and authenticity of individual items appears in Tu Te-ch'iao, '*Kuang-i chi* ch'u-t'an', pp. 396–407.

3
The dynamics of Tai Fu's world

Ever since Mencius divided mankind into the rulers and the ruled, the feeders and the fed, analysts of Chinese society have delighted in the use of paired antithetical categories. North and south, centre and provinces, city and countryside, aristocrats and bureaucrats, elite culture and popular culture – matching concepts like these reach to all parts of the subject and still run through the routine discourse of historians, in China and out of it. Yet students of China's past and present also know that close scrutiny makes those great categories blur and dissolve into complexity as their boundaries lose definition. Contact with specific situations in even a limited area usually brings out a welter of phenomena showing little obvious coherence. There is, in short, a fundamental tension between schematic simplicity and focused intimacy. That tension will shape our study of *Kuang-i chi* at every point.

Flawed oppositions

We have already seen Ku K'uang's preface take a thematic interest in the bridging of alien categories – human and non-human, dead and living, male and female. For him the cases cited in his preface, gleaned from a heritage of older literature, were visible signs of a material cosmos in process of constant mutation. But although that underlying cosmic process might offer to other eyes a scene of total, random complexity, Ku K'uang's way of representing it, equally inherited from past cosmologists, is shaped by the same familiar discourse of matching oppositions. So, as we turn from his preface to the actual pages of *Kuang-i chi*, certain questions arise. First, and simplest of all: did Tai Fu, from whom we have no preface or other theoretical statement, think exactly as Ku K'uang did about the stories he had collected? What was his own programme, conscious or unconscious, as he carried out his long labour? A second, more serious and fundamental question underlies the first: would the style of analysis broached in the preface, with its many pairs of matching categories, find its counterpart in the world that produced the stories themselves? Or was it a system imposed externally upon complex material that would really call for different handling to bring out its implications? Jack Goody has argued that the schematic, essentially graphic device of a table with lines and matching columns easily tempts anthropologists into distorting rich and subtle patterns of concepts in pre-literate societies.[1] A similar danger faces us here: not only the tendency of external analysts to seek convenient, relatively simple patterns for grasping a society that would otherwise overwhelm with its complexity, but the very same tendency practised and bequeathed by the Chinese scholarly tradition itself. Confucian-trained scholars were arguably also external observers of many things reported here. Even when engaged in polemic they had a characteristic, strongly delineated picture of the world to affirm. By putting ourselves in Ku K'uang's hands to gain insight into traditional thinking, we also accept the constraints of a scholastic style of thought. But freedom from those constraints may open new and wider prospects for interpretation. That is why the text of the stories themselves now becomes an important subject for direct study.

Ku K'uang described his friend Tai Fu as 'most deeply versed in the occult' 幽賾最深 and added that 'his clear and ringing tones can . . . render the spirits some service'. These less than precise comments represent the only outside information we have on Tai's approach to his work. But they take on a clearer focus when we examine the broad shape of what remains of it, and for this purpose the subject categories used to organize the material in *T'ai-p'ing kuang-chi* give a crude but useful framework. Stories from *Kuang-i chi* are by no means spread randomly and evenly through that collection: most of them lie densely clumped in groups within certain categories. Needless to say, the distribution reflects decisions taken (perhaps casually and hastily) by the imperial editorial staff, but it does provide a first point of reference in discovering the character of Tai Fu's background work.

The heaviest concentration falls in the section headed 'Ghosts' (*kuei* 鬼), where fifty-six *Kuang-i chi* stories pack closely together within ten chapters (328–39) of a group comprising forty (316–55). These stories deal chiefly with dead people in communication with the living world: possessions, hauntings by spirits bearing some grudge, matings with female dead, activity by men freshly laid in their coffin, underworld

1 Jack Goody, *The domestication of the savage mind*, Cambridge 1977, pp. 54 ff. On p. 59 he comments on one example that 'the categories listed in the table are sometimes those of the actor, sometimes those of the observer'.

office-holders and the like. The next most important group is 'Return to life' (*tsai-sheng* 再生), in which thirty-five *Kuang-i chi* stories turn up between chapters 375 and 386: they deal mostly with premature summons to the underworld, where varied adventures end with permission to return among the living. Another important group, under 'Rewards' (*pao-ying* 報應), has twenty-nine stories dealing almost exclusively with the fruits of *sūtra* piety: devout recitation of certain Buddhist texts, particularly the *Vajracchedikā*, earns merit and brings benefits in this world and the next. Twenty-one stories under 'Gods' (*shen* 神) deal mostly with temple cults dedicated to famous mountains. There are fifteen stories under 'Dreams' (*meng* 夢), with omens, warnings, premonitions, cures, but also communications from the dead and abortive descents to the underworld. Substantial groups of stories also appear under the various animal categories – particularly richly under 'Foxes', 'Tigers' and 'Snakes'. These are stories of afflictions, possessions or transformations, drawing humans into relation with the animal world. For the rest, *Kuang-i chi* stories are scattered more thinly through such categories as 'Divine immortals' (*shen-hsien* 神仙), 'Female immortals', 'Yakṣas', 'Demons' (*yao-kuai* 妖怪 and *ching-kuai* 精怪), 'Mounds and tombs', 'Thunder', 'Treasures', 'Plants', 'Birds', 'Watery tribe' (*shui-tsu* 水族) and so on. Many stories could be moved about among these overlapping categories, and indeed some appear twice in different places (see **141, 179, 202/309, 216/312**).

Equally striking are the large number and wide range of categories in *T'ai-p'ing kuang-chi* which carry nothing at all from the *Kuang-i chi.* Chapters 164 to 217 of that collection explore secular human characteristics and activities – remonstrance, avarice, chivalry, percipience, precocity, as well as institutional matters such as imperial examinations, official positions, military command and the marks of elite culture – essay writing, music, calligraphy, painting, divination. Not a single entry from *Kuang-i chi* shows up there, nor in later sections on food and drink, friendship, extravagance, deceit, flattery, humour and cruelty, women and servants. The broad implication is clear: Tai Fu paid little direct attention in his collection to the affairs of secular society. His interest lay rather in its contact with presences beyond normal secular consciousness – the dead, the gods, the spirits and the demons that invisibly shared his own world or administered the underworld. That surely is what Ku K'uang meant by describing him as 'deeply versed in the occult'.

To say this is to propose an even simpler scheme than those discussed above: a single great divide between a seen and an unseen world, each enfolding its own mass of complexity. But the single division has good claim to stay at the centre of our thoughts as we read the *Kuang-i chi*:

it speaks out repeatedly through the mouths of the players themselves, the only general theoretical principle to find expression there. Time and again they appeal to a saying which in various forms defines and limits their situation: 'Men and spirits go different ways' 人神道殊 (**116, 159, 291**); 'men and ghosts go different ways (different roads)' 人鬼道殊 (路殊) (**96, 97**); 'dark and light are different ways' 冥陽道殊 (**181**); 'shade and brightness are separate in principle' 幽明理殊 (理絕) (**27, 57**); 'the shady path is beyond reach' 幽途不達 (**89**). In their context these linked sayings (which had currency beyond the pages of *Kuang-i chi*)[2] show up a paradoxical dynamic running through all its stories: for while they affirm a solid, stable separation of the dark world from the light, they come up precisely when the two worlds have abnormal traffic together. They are heard at moments of first contact across the great divide, testing the possibility of the traffic to follow (**27**), or at moments of parting, when contact across the divide comes to a necessary end (**57, 96, 97**); they remind the players that physical contact across the divide is restricted (**291**) or prescribe conditions of physical separation once contact is established (**159**); they express regret that contact across the divide is so hard to achieve (**89, 181**) or give reassurance that bonds in this world carry no force in the other (**116**).

Although the sayings have a proverbial, formulaic character, they represent more than a literary mannerism. Many stories analysed in this book will show how practices and institutions set up to regulate contacts with the other world – funeral rites, temple cults, prescribed acts of piety – fail to control irregular outbursts and interventions striking through directly at vulnerable human beings without routine mediation. Human society needs and seeks an ordered relationship with the unseen world: when the relationship runs out of control society's members appeal to that order and strive to restore it. Proverbial sayings on the theme of 'different paths' are a sign of this mechanism at work. But their appearance in *Kuang-i chi* also confirms that, in his study of dealings with the other world, Tai Fu's characteristic interest lies in irregularity and disorder.

The same point goes for the parallel structures of this world and the next. Here, if anywhere, is a well-worn cliché of Chinese religion. Yet the stories of *Kuang-i chi* show that it belongs seriously and integrally in the mental map of Tai Fu's society. To find systematic statements we have

2 Cf. *Sou-shen chi* 4.45 (no. 74), 16.200 (no. 394), and *Lu-i chuan* 錄異傳 (*TPKC* 316.2498); *Shu-i chi* 述異記 (*Pei-t'ang shu-ch'ao* 87.9a and *T'ai-p'ing yü-lan* 532.8b); *T'ung-yu chi* (*TPKC* 332.2636); the famous story of Liu I 柳毅 (*TPKC* 419.3410); also comments by Anthony C. Yu, '"Rest, rest, perturbed spirit!": ghosts in traditional Chinese prose fiction', *Harvard Journal of Asiatic Studies* 47, 1987, pp. 413–14.

to look in other texts, such as the seventh-century *Ming-pao chi*, where a being from the other world explains how Taoist rituals take effect:

> The Monarch of Heaven has general control of the six paths, and he is the divine authority. King Yama is like the Son of Heaven in the human world; the Lord of Mount T'ai is like the Director of the Department of State Affairs; the Gods Recording the Five Paths are like the Board Presidents.[3] A kingdom such as ours is like a large prefecture. Whenever there is business in the human world for which a Taoist priest submits a memorial seeking blessing, that is like asking grace from the gods. The heavenly officers receive it and send it down to King Yama, reporting that on a certain date the plea in question was received from a certain person: it should be attended to in full, without any malfeasance. King Yama respectfully accepts and carries out the request, as men accept an imperial command.[4]

Different hierarchies show up in other texts, and it is clear that no fixed orthodox position imposed itself on the whole society.[5] But certainly the echoes of a similar hierarchy are constantly on the lips of players in Tai Fu's stories.

The ultimate authority of a supreme but remote Monarch of Heaven 天帝 sounds through stories **12, 65, 72, 76, 223, 265**. In **181**, where some wronged sheep talk of appealing to him for justice, we read: 'The Monarch is Monarch of Heaven! How could that sort get access to him? Just like the terrestrial Son of Heaven – if ordinary folk apply to see him it's impossible, isn't it?' In **72**, on the other hand, the Emperor Hsüan-tsung addresses inquiries straight to the monarch in his Jade Capital to learn whether his empress will produce an heir. That reflects an institutional reality, for the monarch enjoyed a supreme position in the state cult of Hsüan-tsung's reign.[6]

3 Through much of mediaeval literature the God (or General) of the Five Paths is represented as a single figure, as studied by Oda Yoshihisa, 'Godō daijin kō', *Tōhō shūkyō* 48, 1976, 14–29. But here the usage is explicitly plural. Multiple gods appear each to be responsible for one of the five *gati*, or paths of rebirth in the Buddhist system. Hence the analogy with the Six Boards of the Chinese government, each with a president (*shang-shu* 尚書). Oda's study makes it clear (p. 26) that the work of this god was concerned with the recording (*lu* 錄) of human affairs: I therefore prefer the punctuation of this section of text given in *T* vol. 51, no. 2082, B.793b, to that given by Fang Shih-ming in his edition of *Ming-pao chi* (Peking 1992) and in *TPKC*, where the character *lu* is placed in the previous phrase.

4 *Ming-pao chi* B.28; cf. *TPKC* 297.2367.

5 Oda Yoshihisa cites passages from Tun-huang manuscripts P 3135 and S 980 with hierarchies more strongly influenced by Buddhist ideas: 'Godō daijin kō', pp. 25–6.

6 *CTS* 21.833–6; *Ta T'ang chiao-ssu lu* (ed. *Shih-yüan ts'ung-shu*) 4.1a–18a. On the subject of the supreme deity, see Fukunaga Mitsuji, 'Kōten jōtei to Tennō taitei to Genshi tenson: Jukyō no saikōshin to Dōkyō no saikōshin', *Chūtetsu bungakkai hō* 2, 1976, 1–34; also Howard J. Wechsler, *Offerings of jade and silk: ritual and symbol in the legitimation of the T'ang dynasty*, New Haven and London 1985, pp. 116–17; David McMullen, *State and*

The Indian god King Yama 閻羅王 appears in some of those stories which bring minor officials before the underworld tribunal (**39, 167, 168, 171, 172, 174, 200**). He represents, it seems, the senior and central figure of authority in the routine affairs of the underworld. His role is shared by other less clearly defined figures known simply as 'the king' (**20, 23, 25, 44, 52, 69, 85, 118, 175, 180, 182, 183, 184, 187, 191**), but there is no sign in this eighth-century text of the named group of Ten Kings of Hell which entered the literature and iconography of Chinese Buddhism around this period.[7] The Lord of Mount T'ai runs a separate establishment with his own register (**184**) and staff of administrative assistants (**166**, cf. **131**); but his authority, with deep roots in Chinese tradition, is still petty and localized (**65**);[8] he defers to the ancient astral deity Grand Prime (*T'ai-i* 太乙) (**68, 76**).[9] And the same goes for the Lord of Mount Hua, to whom we devote a particular study in Chapter 4. All these figures appear most familiarly as judges of the spirit world and the dead. They summon mortals when their due time has come, confront them with aggrieved plaintiffs (often animals), bring them to account for political, moral or ritual offences, and occasionally release them for return to life.

The God (or General) of the Five Paths is a more shadowy figure in the *Kuang-i chi*, where his name appears just twice (**54, 82**). But there

scholars in T'ang China, Cambridge 1988, p. 135. Cf. below, Chap. 4, n. 91. The Jade Capital is mentioned again in **65**, which likewise reports a request for information by Hsüan-tsung.

7 There are brief studies of this subject by Arthur Waley, *A catalogue of paintings recovered from Tun-huang by Sir Aurel Stein, K.C.I.E.*, London 1931, pp. xxvii–xxx; and Sawada Mizuho, *Jigokuhen – Chūgoku no meikai setsu*, Kyoto 1968, pp. 22–30. But it receives a detailed study in Stephen F. Teiser's monograph *The Scripture on the Ten Kings and the making of purgatory in medieval Chinese Buddhism*, Honolulu, 1994. This explores the background and production of the *Shih-wang ching* 十王經, a text represented by many manuscripts in the Tun-huang collection.

8 Since at least the first century AD, Mount T'ai had been seen as an underworld: souls of the dead were summoned there, and registers of human life were kept there; its divine ruler was a master of life and death: see *Jih-chih lu chi-shih* 30.28b–29b; *Kai-yü ts'ung-k'ao* 35.751–2; Chavannes, *Le T'ai chan*, pp. 398–415; Sawada Mizuho, *Jigoku hen*, pp. 43–53. The Lord of Mount T'ai 泰山君 already appears by name on an inscribed talismanic urn from a first- or second-century tomb: *Chen-sung t'ang chi-ku i-wen* 15.33a, discussed in Wu Jung-tseng, 'Chen-mu-wen chung so chien-tao ti Tung-Han Tao-wu kuan-hsi', *Wen wu* 1981.3, 56–63. Sawada distinguishes two stages of historical development: from a position as petty sessions judge over the human dead, responsible to higher authorities in the underworld and in heaven, the Lord of Mount T'ai advances in later times to a high position of general power; his titles change accordingly (Sawada, *Jigoku hen*, pp. 45–8). Story **65** aligns itself clearly with the earlier phase: it uses the ancient title and calls upon the deity to give local advice on the affairs of his own territory.

9 Cf. Chapter 4, p. 113 and nn. 89–92, where the historical context for this precedence is made clear: the Grand Prime stood high in the state cult hierarchy of the eighth century.

is rich evidence elsewhere in mediaeval literature that, against the background of an earlier blood-sacrifice cult in eastern coastal China, he joined the divine hierarchy of the T'ang underworld, though the Buddhist theology of the five *gati* ('paths' of rebirth, or conditions of sentient existence) remained confused. His function, as the passage from *Ming-pao chi* suggests, was to record good and evil deeds. Eventually, though not in the *Kuang-i chi*, he joined the group of ten kings.[10]

This brief sampling of dignitaries in the other world shows two distinct processes at work. Individual figures converge from totally different historical origins to join in a single, loose mediaeval system. But the society which makes ritual use of that system strives to match it to the shape and working patterns of its own secular bureaucracy. To describe the other world simply as a 'mirror image' of Tai Fu's own will not really meet the case. At this level it presents instead a jumble of historically distinctive mythological figures; but men and women deal with them as they would deal with the authorities of their own society. So here is another version of the earlier paradox: Tai Fu presents a society for which the unseen world is by definition alien and apart, yet which systematically binds and assimilates that world to its own institutions.

It happens that story **82**, in which a man receives warning that he is due to become General of the Five Paths, nicely illustrates a dynamic link between the seen and the unseen worlds. Offices in the divine bureaucracy are held in succession by the souls of dead men. In many cases, usually at the bidding of Yama, men are recruited directly from the bureaucracy of the living world into that of the dead. Or a man might be recruited locally by spirit powers close to his tomb (**104:** Yellow River). For Tai Fu, mixing with the middle and lower ranks of the official class, this was a subject of lively interest, explored in many of his stories (cf. **52, 85, 125, 166, 167, 168**). His underworld employs figures from among the great and the good of China's past: Yang Hu 羊祜 (221–278), a famous commander of the Chin dynasty, is an underworld king (**182**); Ṭi Jen-chieh 狄仁傑, known in life for his great purge of southern cults in 688 (**66**; cf. **89**), serves in death as Grand Censor (**178**); Li Chiung-hsiu 李迥秀, a board president in life, serves as a general in death (**105**). But no functionary is too humble to escape attention, since the underworld bureaucracy requires clerks and assistants too. Even an immigrant seller of cakes plies the same trade in the other world (**191**). Marriage as well as office sometimes plays a part in this perceived movement across the divide, both for men (**85, 116**) and

10 Oda Yoshihisa, 'Godō daijin kō', gives a thorough study of this figure. A number of further references can be added to his material: I hope to return to this subject elsewhere.

for women (**68, 69, 71, 76**); but that is best seen as part of the more complex subject discussed in Chapter 7 of this book.

As represented by Tai Fu this movement of personnel is part of the inevitable order of things, but also something which men resist and avoid in every way they can. (For holding an office does not guarantee release from punishment: **183.**) Above all they come back, breaking the rules by means of bribery (**118, 193**) or personal influence (**175, 181, 187, 189, 192**), turning their fate upon other victims by tampering with documents (**92**) and performing hasty acts of Buddhist merit (**167**). Most commonly they establish that the underworld has made bureaucratic errors (**105, 176, 180, 198**), or use legal casuistry to escape blame (**182, 183**). So the paradox persists. And it is heightened at every turn by a multitude of small ways in which the surroundings, customs and institutions of the unseen world are likened to those of T'ang China. We can take a few examples at random to make the point, though almost every story plays in some way or other upon the ambiguous situation of men or women caught between the two worlds, often without realizing which side they are on.

A man taken to court in the underworld (**176**) begins his description of the scene by observing:

> The courtroom was like the court of a modern county magistrate. There were two rows of chambers, all with closets inside that were fronted with slanted lattice-work. Behind the lattices were benches for people to sit on.

The precise physical visualization brings an added interest: by implication this is a glimpse of what a real courtroom in T'ang China looked like, something we could scarcely hope to find in other sources. In another story a dead woman returns by arrangement to tell her female relatives what the other world is like. She speaks on various separate occasions through a possessed maidservant:

> 'I have already met King Yama and my relatives . . . The Lord of Mount T'ai is holding a wedding for his daughter. He knows that I am good at make-up and hairdressing, so I have been called in. I won't be back until tomorrow, when it is all over . . . The Lord of Mount T'ai's wedding for his daughter is really splendid. He has told me to do his daughter's toilet, and I've brought some rouge and powder today to give to the girls.' (She opened her hands, in which were the rouge, very red, and the powder – both no different from things in the human world.) 'The coins used in the lord's house for scattering on the bridal curtains are huge: forty ghosts can't lift up one of them. I've brought one of those, too.' (A coin as large as a dish fell through the air.) 'The lord knows that I am good at dyeing things red, so he has told me to do the dyeing. I explained that though I can do dyeing I don't put my own hands in: it's usually

done by a maid under my direction. The lord has told me to collect a maid, so now there is nothing for it but to take the maid with me. I'll send her back tomorrow!' (**131**)

And so on. The interest here lies in the spontaneous creation of a women's world on the other side by a society of women on this: the maid is not mouthing to her audience some prescribed or ritualized vision of the unseen world, but extending the familiar features of their own world into it. And transit between the two, though unexpected, proves easy: when summoned by her mistress the possessed maid lies inert for two days until the note of a chime brings her back, with hands stained red from the dye.

The same sense of a fraternal bond with the other side comes through in stories of official corruption and personal favour. The accessory clerk in **118**, when summoned by the king, begins by asking his escorts what job they do in the underworld. They tell him: 'Arrests'. And he says: 'Fortunately I smell roughly the same as you gentlemen do – can you save me?' It is an appeal to solidarity among the lowest menials in the public service, extending easily across the absolute divide between living and dead. And the appeal takes effect, particularly when the clerk follows it with an offer of ten thousand paper cash.

With the mention of money we come to the most active system of transaction between the two alien domains. Its use runs widely through the whole collection of stories. And the players themselves tirelessly explain how their system of currency exchange works. 'What we use in the underworld is the human world's paper cash' (**127**); 'our gold cash is simply the human world's yellow paper cash, our silver cash simply the human world's white paper cash' (**180**). Strings of paper cash are transferred to the underworld in these stories by burning, which straightforwardly reflects the ritual practice familiar in China until modern times (**118, 127**). The *Hsin T'ang shu* comments, 'grave coins were used in burials from Han times, but in later generations the vulgar custom progressively used paper cash in dealing with spirits'. And Hou Ching-lang, in the standard modern study of this subject, shows that paper substitutes for sacrificial coinage were established in use by the Sui period.[11] The *Kuang-i chi* characteristically enriches our picture of how mediaeval society perceived its underworld transactions to work. A character in **180** asks how to direct a personal remittance to an individual officer. The officer explains:

11 *HTS* 109.4107. Hou Ching-lang, *Monnaies d'offrande et la notion de trésorerie dans la religion chinoise*, Paris 1975, covers the historical background and evolution on pp. 3–17, with the Sui on p. 5. He lists modern Japanese and Chinese studies of the subject on p. 132, nn. 4 and 5.

'The world makes cash in the city, and most of it is collected by the underworld establishment. You should call a cash-stringer[12] to make some in a private room at home. When that is done, put it in a bag. You must burn it at the waterside, and I'll be sure to get it. If a side wind disturbs the ash as the cash is received, that means I have got it. If the wind lifts up the ash, then it is being received by the underworld establishment and the spirits of the earth.'

Cash transfers move the other way too. In **112** the ghost of a dead girl goes shopping for a lacquered mirror in Yang-chou: a young man sells her one for three thousand gold coins, but later finds the money is merely three strings of yellow paper. Gifts and payments of money from the dead always turn out to be paper once the visionary personal contact is over.[13] On one level we can explain this two-way system of cash transfers as a mythological device echoing the fundamental use of paper and fire in Chinese ritual practice. Its material instability (paper into ash one way, coinage into paper the other) reflects the basis of actual ritual procedures.[14] But its very existence points to another more secular implication: in Tai Fu's world social and bureaucratic (as well as economic) transactions require the use of money, and this characteristic of the seen world is duly extended to the unseen.[15]

The material culture associated with tombs and their contents raises more searching questions. T'ang China, as we know from documentary sources and from archaeological discoveries, was a society which buried its dead with objects for personal entertainment and use. The stories of *Kuang-i chi* proclaim unambiguously that the tomb is a dead person's home, equipped according to family means with a staff of guards, attendants or servants, and a stock of domestic and personal property (**104, 106, 107, 161**). But T'ang China was also a society which opened tombs and robbed them of their contents. Once again the *Kuang-i chi* shows this being done (**94, 162, 202**) and reveals that the secular

12 The threading of individual cash on strings is described in story **272**, where a fox is required to produce 2,000 strings as bride-price: 'Ts'ui gave orders to spread out a mat beneath the eaves of the hall and make strings to thread the cash. The cash came down from the eaves, while all the maids threaded it. It came exactly to 2,000 strings.'

13 See **63**, **97**, **145**. In **282** a gift of clothing from a fox turns out to be paper. In **313** a gift of money from the other world turns out to come from a family of turtles with a sunken hoard of *p'ai-tou ch'ien* 排斗錢, a type of counterfeit coin 'specifically excluded from circulation': D. C. Twitchett, *Financial administration under the T'ang dynasty*, second ed., Cambridge 1970, pp. 300–1, n. 84.

14 It is worth noting here that these stories make no mention of written memorials to effect the transfer of funds, as reported from modern fieldwork by Kristofer Schipper in his article 'The written memorial in Taoist ceremonies', in Arthur P. Wolf, ed., *Religion and ritual in Chinese society*, Stanford 1974, pp. 310–11.

15 For anthropological discussions of this topic, see Gary Seaman, 'Spirit money: an interpretation', *Journal of Chinese Religions*, 10, 1982, 80–91; Stephan Feuchtwang, *The imperial metaphor: popular religion in China*, London and New York 1992, pp. 17–20.

authorities prosecute men found in unauthorized possession of grave goods (**161, 202**).[16] So these material objects, unchanging in themselves, have a double identity – they are possessions of the dead in the other world, but also desirable objects of value in this. That contrast of course corresponds to two essentially different physical situations: the undisturbed coffin enclosed in its tomb[17] and the open milieu of secular society. Grave goods either repose in the one or circulate in the other. Time and again *Kuang-i chi* stories represent these goods as the absolute property of their dead owners: to steal them is an offence, not only against the state's criminal code, but against the dead. It attracts pursuit and revenge (**58, 94, 202**). But while the owners thus exercise a right to reclaim items illicitly removed, they may also choose to bestow their goods as gifts, pledges and tokens (**12, 114, 123, 128**). It follows that objects move in and out of coffins and tombs in response to two conflicting agencies – the intervention of thieves and the wishes of the dead.

But that picture is still too simple. Grave goods which to mortal eyes seem no more than artefacts take on lives of their own in the other world. Servant-figures will perform their duties when their ghost masters hold a banquet (**119**). Or they may hold celebrations themselves (**159**). Guards will fight hard to keep tomb robbers at bay (**202**) but may prove quarrelsome and insubordinate and fight among themselves (**161**). The giant wooden *fang-hsiang* 方相 figure, used in funerals for exorcistic purposes,[18] may attack strangers in the open (**158**). One figure of an old man, out of the tomb, sits throwing stones at the neighbours (**160**). All these are objects so firmly rooted in the material world that

16 The T'ang Code provided for punishment of those who disturbed the coffins and bodies of the dead (article 267) or violated tombs and stole their contents (article 277): *Ku T'ang-lü shu-i* 18.343–5, 19.354–5. See discussion by Herbert Franke, 'Archäologie und Geschichtsbewußtsein in China', in *Archäologie und Geschichtsbewußtsein*, Munich 1982, pp. 69–83, esp. pp. 74–5. Also Tu Cheng-sheng, 'Shen-mo shih hsin she-hui shih?', *Hsin shih-hsüeh* 3.4, 1992, 108–10. Discoveries of ancient artefacts buried underground were covered by article 447 in the code: *Ku T'ang lü shu-i* 27.520–1. This provided that ancient objects of unusual construction were to be handed in to the authorities, on pain of punishment. See discussion by Herbert Franke, 'Der Schatzfund im chinesischen Recht', *Archív Orientální* 59, 1991, 140–51, esp. 142–3. Story **202** duly reports the submission to the throne of thirty-odd objects from a Han tomb by the prefect of Ming-chou.

17 But note that a number of stories in *Kuang-i chi* deal with coffins given temporary burial in huts known as 'funeral palaces' (*pin-kung* 殯宮), from which they are liable to be moved on to permanent tombs (**25, 98, 109, 111**). Further details on these dead-houses are given below, Chapter 7, n. 28. The unstable, liminal situation of dead people before their final entombment is discussed again below, Chapter 6, pp. 143–6.

18 Special carriages for these figures drove in T'ang funeral processions: see *T'ang hui-yao* 38.693 ff. and *Ta T'ang liu-tien* 18.20ab.

things like them can outlive their era by hundreds of years to take on the status of archaeological items and appear in our museums; yet for the society which created them they shift restlessly between the seen and the unseen worlds.

Grave goods in fact offer a clear and strong symbol of the whole system of oppositions explored in these last few pages. Tai Fu's society in its collective wisdom may define the separation of the two worlds as absolute, but his reports show this separation to be fragile and flawed. Its boundaries are ambiguous. Mortals and spirits, living and dead move across them constantly, though irregularly. And the control of that movement represents the chief task facing ritual specialists in T'ang China.

With such a rich, dynamic and productive opposition creating a theme for the whole collection, it is surprising that other forms of binary opposition are almost impossible to find there. However much we might wish to polarize the material into neatly balanced antithetical categories, it refuses to give consistent results. We can test the point by recalling the habit, mentioned at the start of this chapter, of splitting China and its society into north/south regions, or into status categories such as metropolitan/provincial, urban/rural, noble/common, bonded/free. In each case Tai Fu comes back with a catholic, even pluralistic, view of a world whose strongest features are mobility and instability.

He does exercise a sense of geographical space, and indeed his stories range from end to end of the T'ang empire, including the deep south, the far west, the eastern seaboard, and the Shantung Peninsula fronting on the Northern Ocean. The inhabitants of this space, whether in the seen or the unseen world, move about in it far and wide. In certain stories the very centre of interest lies in a dynamic link between remote places bound together by some human or other-worldly relationship: a local deity from the tribal south follows his persecutor Ti Jen-chieh across the whole face of China to Pien-chou, on the Yellow River (**66**); an imperial guardsman travels to and fro on an east–west axis bearing messages for dragons of the Northern Ocean (**70**); a family abandons lands near Lo-yang to escape east to the coast in the An Lu-shan rebellion, but their dead cousin returns home alone as a ghost (**128**).[19] In all this China seems to function as a single land mass, connected throughout by its system of established communications. No one part is intrinsically distinctive nor laden with the emotive values that we find in the poetry of this and earlier periods.

It is true that the *Kuang-i chi* does pay particular attention to certain

19 Cf. story **122**.

areas: the prefectures of Chiang-nan East, covering modern Chekiang and part of Kiangsu, show up repeatedly here as settings for stories; so do other locations, such as Lo-yang.[20] But this most likely reflects the chance circumstance that Tai Fu served there and picked up material during his service. It also appears from many stories that the other world has its own strong sense of territory: certain powers and spirits exercise their authority within defined territorial limits, which they patrol and defend with armed forces.[21] Regionalism of this kind seems to look back to a time when China was controlled by smaller dynastic units: their institutions clinging on in the unseen world while the secular world moves on.[22] Taken all together the book presents a China of many small parts, linked up in a system of loose mobility. It is a scene of free multiplicity rather than of paired contrasts.

It has to be said too that Tai Fu's stories situate themselves indifferently in the twin capitals Ch'ang-an and Lo-yang or in the great expanse of the provinces. They contain a noticeable element of court and metropolitan gossip – something which circulates easily in any elite society without much careful verification. We cannot really monitor how many stories in *Kuang-i chi* come from first-hand witnesses, how many from remote hearsay or from written reports in circulation. Certainly Tai Fu, who often volunteers the names of his informants as an act of authentication, remains equally interested in items that might have come to him through many removes. He shows no signs of favouring or rejecting stories on grounds of source or setting, and the metropolitan cities prove no more or less fertile a ground for the marvels he has to tell than other centres around the land.

At first sight the urban/rural contrast offers better promise as an analytical tool. The narratives of *Kuang-i chi* attend with some care to details of physical environment. They are sensitive to the difference between protective buildings in fortified centres of population and the

20 For Chekiang, see Chapters 1 (with n. 13) and 6. For the Eastern Capital Lo-yang, see **9**, **39**, **55**, **68**, **76**, **92**, **97**, **99**, **101**, **102**, **147**, **151**, **186**, **188**, **275**, **276**, **279**, **313**.

21 The cases of Mount Hua and Mount T'ai are examined in Chapter 4. Compare also the armed escorts provided by the ghostly Yü-ch'ih Chiung (d. 580), discussed in Chapter 5. See also note 22.

22 Story **74** documents this point with its comments on the Lord of Mount Sung, the Central Peak. He maintains a military command structure 'like the Generals of the Four Commands in times of old' – a conscious reference to the military establishments of the Northern and Southern Dynasties: *Wei shu* 113.2977; *Sung shu* 39.1225; *Nan Ch'i shu* 16.313. Mount Sung lay in the territory of Wei. The commander in **74** wears the ceremonial headgear of military officers since the Southern Ch'i: *Nan Ch'i shu* 17.342. For further discussion of this story, see Dudbridge, 'The tale of Liu Yi and its analogues', pp. 75–9.

open wilderness of mountains, waterways, marshes or farmlands, studded with tombs and roamed by spirits at large. Many of the book's most spectacular adventures happen to long-distance travellers or to individuals caught outside their home settlements. Those summoned by the underworld kings routinely find themselves led out of city walls, often through closed gates, to march through open country before arriving at fortified citadels on the other side. In any case, much of the agricultural and landowning population in this society lives on manorial estates, where human dwellings stand outside of fortified settlements and in close relation with the countryside. Manor houses and estates are the scene of frequent contact with the spirit world: a man takes a stroll outside and meets an attractive female neighbour, whose home turns out to be a tomb (**107**); another is watching threshers at work outside his gate when a ghost comes by with a wooden horse in need of repair (**138**); yet another is joined in his studies at a Lo-yang manor house by a young boy who turns out to be a fox (**284**).

It is tempting to see in all this a use of the countryside as a liminal region between the world of mortals and the other world. But a closer look reveals, as usual, a much more blurred distinction between the urban and rural environments. Contact with the other world is certainly not limited to the open air. It makes its presence felt quite readily in centres of administration (**73, 84, 86, 89, 127, 248, 293, 295**), in the streets and wards of capital cities (**9, 19, 68, 92, 99, 102, 122, 147**) and in homes (**27, 58, 103, 124, 153, 154, 168**). Indeed homes in themselves are a site of complex interaction between the seen and unseen worlds. A residence has its own elaborate staff of household spirits to protect the occupants: 'the well, the stove, the gate, the latrine, the twelve hours[23] and dozens of others, some tall, some short, in appearance singular and bizarre' (**261**). Accordingly a man may be advised to use his home as a place of refuge, not to be left without risk of death (**140, 193**). Yet even so, as we have only just seen, unwanted spirits easily find their way inside if the conditions are right. In some cases they recruit the soul of a living man to help them in (**102, 103**). In others they use the eaves of a house as a perch from which to communicate with and approach the residents (**285, 293, 294**). So once again a simple and appealing antithesis collapses: however evocative the link may seem

23 A set of grave-figures representing the twelve hours was found in a tomb dating from 745; it is illustrated in *Wu-sheng ch'u-t'u chung-yao wen-wu chan-lan t'u-lu*, Peking 1958, pl. 97; cf. pl. 103. Such figures were also routinely engraved on the stone covering a tomb inscription: see several examples illustrated in 'Pei-ching chin-nien fa-hsien ti chi-tso T'ang mu', *Wen-wu* 1992.9, 71–81.

between the spirits and the open land, it is not an exclusive link. We cannot really use an urban/rural or settlement/wilderness opposition to illuminate the workings of Tai Fu's world.

In no area does that world reveal its pluralistic, even egalitarian character more strongly than in its treatment of social status. Tai Fu, whose own position in the social order is so clearly marked and whose personal contacts seem so closely linked to that position, strikingly lets his interest play on the whole of society from top to bottom, and beyond it into the animal kingdom. He deals with emperors and empresses (**51, 65, 67, 72, 117, 174, 199**), princes and princesses of the blood (**198, 199**), high officials, his own more humdrum provincial colleagues, women of all stations in life from naturalized princess (**60**) to bondmaid (**6, 59, 85, 96, 111, 131, 134, 139, 155**), farmers (**140, 202**), traders (**4**), immigrants (**7, 135, 168, 191**)[24] and slaves (**82, 149, 191, 200, 241, 242, 245**). All sorts and conditions of men are exposed equally to the attentions of the other world, though they may approach it in different ways according to their station. While the great engage famous divines to communicate with the gods (**68, 72, 147, 198**), more ordinary citizens employ mediums and ritual specialists. The bondmaids and slaves often find themselves serving as direct intermediaries with the other world, as they fall into coma or trance (**82, 85, 131, 139**).

This whole stratified human community is fused into one by the great leveller, death. When the youthful Chu T'ung is led off by two village headmen of his acquaintance, he is furious at their off-hand, insolent treatment. They reply: 'You're dead now, sir: why do you have the same looks as you did when you were alive?' (**192**). It is above all the Buddhist-inspired perspective of reincarnation that undermines the world's structures. All status becomes relative, all positions insecure. The chance to be reborn as a prince of the blood means nothing to a monk whose merit has earned him a place in the Tuṣita heaven (**198**). But to be a slave in a noble household is positively desirable for a man who in earlier lives has been a wild cat and a beggar's son (**200**). This last example shows too how closely animals are integrated with the worlds of the quick and the dead: the scheme of rebirth makes them virtually continuous with the human race. They have souls of their own

24 In general I understand *hu* 胡 to refer to speakers of Iranian languages from Central Asia (cf. Edwin G. Pulleyblank, 'A Sogdian colony in Inner Mongolia', *T'oung Pao* 41, 1952, 318 ff.). Occasionally, as Pulleyblank argues, they are identifiable more precisely as Sogdians. In story **7** Shih Chü 石巨 possesses one of the nine recognized Sogdian surnames (*HTS* 221B.6243, 6246; Pulleyblank, pp. 320–3, 336, 340, 346, 351): it was equivalent to Tashkend. Many references to *hu* do not distinguish clearly between settled residents and international traders, although sometimes a low-status occupation like cake-selling suggests immigrant status (**191**).

(**245**), and in the courts of the underworld they appear as articulate and determined plaintiffs at the trials of men who have treated them cruelly or wantonly taken their lives (**23, 180–4;** cf. **42**).[25]

Reincarnation creates ironies of another kind. Story **185**, one of a very small number dealing with times long before the T'ang, presents a man whose family for generations have followed the Taoist Five-Pecks-of-Rice teachings: he scornfully refuses to believe the alien creed of Buddhism. But the underworld confounds him: he learns there that in earlier lives he was a Buddhist himself, slowly losing his faith until, 'born now into the world, he met evil men in his youth; not grasping the difference between error and truth 邪正, he was beguiled by false teachings 邪道'. The story voices here an opposition deeply ingrained in the texture of organized religion in China. The language of orthodoxy and heterodoxy traces back to the early conflict of Buddhist teachings with Brahminical traditions in India. In China it became and has remained part of the basic discourse of schools of doctrine and ritual, almost a structural element in their scheme of mutual relationships.[26] But only in story **185** does Tai Fu use such language. Significantly, this story appears to be transcribed from an earlier written source.[27] If Tai Fu did in fact adopt it in his own collection, it is characteristic of him that he should choose to reproduce here the language of orthodoxy in order to silence a sceptic and affirm the general truth of Buddhism.

For he is no narrow zealot in religious matters himself. If he has a serious commitment it is to open-mindedness: scepticism is the only position with which his stories regularly take issue.[28] A woman who dismisses warning dreams as 'not worth taking seriously' comes to see that things do in the end fall out as the dreams foretold (**60**). Family

25 When animals adopt human form to seek justice in secular courts, however, they are likely to be exposed and driven off: see **273**.

26 It naturally does not follow that this terminology, as used within schools of religious practice or teaching, assures verifiable historical legitimacy for one or another school. The problems that arise when it is reproduced in historical or empirical research are examined by Michel Strickmann, 'History, anthropology, and Chinese religion', *Harvard Journal of Asiatic Studies* 40, 1980, 201–48, esp. 222–36. Compare the same author's comments on Japanese schools of Esoteric Buddhism in *Mantras et mandarins*, chap. 2, 'Sous le charme de Kouan-yin'.

27 The same text appears in *Fa-yüan chu-lin* 55.709ab, ascribed to the fifth-century *Ming-hsiang chi* 冥祥記. It is possible either that Tai Fu transcribed it from there or another source into his own collection, or (as Fang Shih-ming asserts, p. 240) that the ascription in *TPKC* to *Kuang-i chi* is mistaken. *Ming-hsiang chi* was the work of Wang Yen 王琰, a committed Buddhist whose convictions are clearly reflected in its contents: see Li Chien-kuo, *T'ang ch'ien chih-kuai hsiao-shuo shih*, pp. 414–19.

28 This was of course traditional in *chih-kuai* literature: see Anthony C. Yu, '"Rest, rest, perturbed spirit!"', pp. 404 ff., and Robert F. Campany, 'Ghosts matter: the culture of ghosts in Six Dynasties *zhiguai*', *Chinese Literature: essays, articles, reviews* 13, 1991, pp. 23–4.

members who deliberately flout the ancient taboo on disturbing ground associated with the planet *T'ai-sui* 太歲[29] have to cope with a fleshy object which escapes their control and later visits death upon them all (**149**). A magistrate whose predecessors have died in mysterious circumstances disagrees high-mindedly with friends who suspect a bedevilled tree: 'Fate lies with heaven, reproach does not come from trees'; but the friends are right – a dead man lies under the tree, trying to communicate with them (**127**). Even this small handful of examples shows the range of phenomena accepted in Tai Fu's world. There is room both for a scheme which leads the dead into future rebirths, and for a limbo in which they linger on, communicating through possessed mediums and dreams. Moreover, in spite of the humbling of the Taoist Ch'eng Tao-hui in **185**, there is no lack in this book of Taoist immortals (**1–3, 5, 7, 15**), alchemists (**9, 17, 209**) and drug users (**1, 2, 4, 59**). And we have already sampled the vast range of other beings inhabiting the spirit world, some at large among men as animals or physical objects, others residing in cult temples. Though sparing with open comment, Tai Fu makes it clear in his choice of subjects that all these things must be taken seriously: they are real forces in human lives, not to be lightly set aside. It is a view with a well-known literary precedent – the much quoted preface to *Sou-shen chi*, whose contents, says the author, 'are able to show that the spirit world is not a falsehood'.[30] The same sentiment speaks out once again in the words of Ku K'uang recalled near the start of this chapter: Tai Fu's 'clear and ringing tones can render the spirits some service'. By now that phrase takes on a sharper meaning.

At first sight, as we look out over Tai Fu's eventful religious landscape, any opposition between orthodoxy and heterodoxy seems to fade away. He is no adept, no disciple under the sway of an established priesthood, no spokesman for a given spiritual authority. Rather he is an all-purpose layman, witnessing the visible, exoteric manifestations of spiritual powers in the social world. The Buddhism in his book is that of lay believers for whom the discipline of piety means mechanical generation of merit: systematic repetition of sacred texts, copying of

29 *T'ai-sui* is the planet Jupiter. A system of ritual taboos linking the twelve phases of the Jupiter cycle to tabooed ground can be traced to the early Han period and survives into recent times. See *Kai-yü ts'ung-k'ao* 34.724–5; Tsung Li and Liu Ch'ün, *Chung-kuo min-chien chu-shen*, Shih-chia-chuang 1987, pp. 127–38; also Hou Ching-lang, 'The Chinese belief in baleful stars', in H. Welch and A. Seidel, eds., *Facets of Taoism*, New Haven and London 1979, pp. 200–209.

30 *Chin shu* 82.2151. This section of Kan Pao's biography cites the family experiences which moved him to assemble his collection and express his aims in the preface. For a discussion of this and other early prefaces, see Dewoskin, 'The Six Dynasties *chih-kuai* and the birth of fiction', pp. 29 ff.

sūtras, production of consecrated images, sponsoring of rituals, sparing of animal lives.[31] In the words of story **184** (where a man recites the *Vajracchedikā* three thousand times) 'merit enters the bones', and may redeem a lifetime of sin. But even a lifetime of piety still leaves the layman's hunger for secular profit intact (**297**). The mysteries of Taoism are seen through the same eyes: secret techniques for making precious metal and dietary recipes for permanent youth are coveted as secular assets and may be stolen or abused.[32] Specialists in ritual exorcism by talisman are brought in by ordinary members of the public to cope with crises inflicted by the spirit world. And so on. In all this the *Kuang-i chi* presents a set of perceptions as close to the man in the street as we are ever likely to find in our sources from T'ang China.

For me the book's quintessential interest lies here. Paradoxically it can after all be expressed in terms of an orthodox/heterodox antithesis, even though the *Kuang-i chi* itself is virtually silent on the matter. For in spite of his standard education, *chin-shih* degree and career in the bureaucracy, Tai Fu rarely if at all endorses an official Confucian view of the phenomena described in his book.[33] Nor does he ever show sympathy with the tensions felt by Confucian intellectuals trying to distance themselves from the surrounding religious culture.[34] Here and there the signs of his detachment appear in the open: when local administrators are challenged by popular cults, for instance, it is often the cults that come out on top (**2, 7**).[35] But deeper in the texture of the *Kuang-i chi* there lies a quality, looked at more closely in the next two chapters, which is best described as 'vernacular'. The distinction implied

31 But in the last case certain stories reverse the action. Animals kept at Buddhist monasteries for the sake of meritorious sparing of life are sometimes deliberately killed – either to control a haunting (**245**), or (at the animals' own request) to deliver them from a wretched existence (**247**).

32 See stories **9**, **11**, **17**, **209**. Ko Hung's classical account of precious metal alchemy makes it clear that in principle Taoists did not make gold and silver for profit. His mentor Cheng Yin 鄭隱 explains: 'When Perfected Ones make gold it is because they want to ingest it and make themselves gods and immortals, not to make themselves rich': *Pao-p'u tzu nei-p'ien chiao-shih* 16.286. (For an extended discussion of Ko Hung's precious metal alchemy, see Needham, *Science and civilisation in China*, vol. 5, pt. 2, pp. 62–71.) Ch'en Kuo-fu observes that, although the profit motive was not new to alchemy, by T'ang times Taoist adepts commonly used their synthetic gold more for profit than for ingestion: *Tao tsang yüan-liu k'ao*, Peking 1963, pp. 375, 392 ff.

33 For possible exceptions we might consider stories **66**, **90** and **148**, in which moral calibre or official seniority give certain dignitaries power to quell spirits, or protection to repel them.

34 For fuller discussion of these tensions, see Chapter 4, pp. 94–7, and Chapter 5, pp. 131–2.

35 This orthodox–heterodox clash is the subject of Jean Lévi's article 'Les fonctionnaires et le divin: luttes de pouvoirs entre divinités et administrateurs dans les contes des Six Dynasties et des Tang', *Cahiers d'Extrême-Asie* 2, 1986, 81–106.

here is not between elite and popular levels in a stratified society, but rather between the values prescribed and fostered by a centralized state power and those prevailing in local communities at large through the land. Members of a social elite may participate not only in the high culture shaped by the state examination system and imposed through the state bureaucracy, but also in the rich local cultures surrounding them as individuals. The *Kuang-i chi* grows out of this latter environment. It reports the perceptions of men and women involved with abnormal phenomena in their own surroundings: it does not submit these to review or rejection by a central authority, nor to reinterpretation by a critical orthodoxy. So its stories speak for a far more massive population than do the formal writings of China's articulate elite. They reveal many features of the broader milieu within which that elite's literary and intellectual activity should be seen. And this vernacular culture was, as we have seen, open to participation by the whole community.[36]

Movement in time

All through Tai Fu's book there runs a tension between the large scale and the small, the long term and the short. The stories seem at first to present unique, specific subjects, each with its own little spot in time and space occupied by individual people, who often bear names we can identify. Yet the same stories also offer things that we recognize from other periods of Chinese history and know from other, quite different parts of the world. So how do we analyse that free mixture of general with particular? Even when the 'voices' discussed in Chapter 1 have been identified and accounted for, the task still remains of placing each story in a meaningful setting. No item has a uniqueness that transcends all relation to the surrounding world; but neither does it give a complete, unqualified and permanent statement about Chinese society. It calls instead for an act of historical interpretation, making a context within which it can take its place. And that requires a sense of time which can give meaning to these peculiar records.

For various reasons it would not be enough, nor even particularly useful, to draw here a picture of the political and literary culture of the middle T'ang, as it would be in studying a book from the orthodox

36 The distinction drawn in this paragraph, further explored in Chapters 4 and 5, is designed for a pragmatic purpose, to help interpret material remaining from the T'ang period. It may be compared with the ideas on Chinese religion in a late imperial and modern context reviewed by Catherine Bell in 'Religion and Chinese culture: toward an assessment of "popular religion"', *History of Religions* 29.1, 1989, 35–57.

literary tradition. Tai Fu is not writing formal prose; his book does not belong to the orthodox tradition; it has no significance in public life; it does not address the public issues of its day. Nor does Tai Fu show any interest in advancing a particular doctrine. He puts down his records with an open mind, untroubled by orthodox scepticism and indifferent to ideological pressures. His subjects come in from all parts of society. True, many of his stories do mention personalities and episodes from the great public events of the mid-eighth century, but usually only as incidental details. The main interest nearly always lies in a broader time-scale: that is what we now need to define.

Historians sometimes use geological metaphors ('layers', 'substrata') to describe traditional society, sometimes put signs or markers at single points in time to separate out historical periods. I avoid both practices, because they suggest static, frozen structures and deny the complex, dynamic movement going on in all societies as they pass through time. Instead we shall look at the Chinese world, in particular its religious culture, as evolving simultaneously at many different speeds. The governing metaphor should really be the movement of a mass of water, with slow-moving depths, fast-flowing surface, irregular currents and localized eddies. But this metaphor, however evocative, is hard to put usefully to work. So for a simpler scheme I shall borrow and adapt Fernand Braudel's celebrated three levels of historical change – the first 'a history whose passage is almost imperceptible . . . in which all change is slow'; then 'another history . . . with slow but perceptible rhythms'; and last, 'the history of events . . . of brief, rapid, nervous fluctuations'.[37] Of course Braudel's great structures were designed to cover the whole range of human activity seen in relation to its physical environment; here the programme is more specialized and more modest. Certainly mediaeval China's religious culture – with the size of its parent society, its geographical spread, reach in time, variety of cultural influences at work – is still too vast a subject to deal with in a single book. But using the *Kuang-i chi* as a focus does at least allow us to work on a more human scale – not, of course, with the prospect of studying every feature of its three hundred stories, but by picking out samples among them which attract close attention and hint at wider implications.

We might regard each story as a single image taken from the flux of

37 For these quotations and the argument which forms their context, see Fernand Braudel, *The Mediterranean and the Mediterranean world in the age of Philip II* (trans. Siân Reynolds), London 1972, 'Preface to the first edition', pp. 20–1. Braudel himself at the very end of his career constructed a metaphor from a moving body of water to describe his conception of *la longue durée*: see *L'identité de la France*, Paris 1986, vol. 3, p. 431; *The identity of France*, vol. 2, *People and production* (trans. Siân Reynolds), London 1990, pp. 678–9.

the past – like a photograph or a frame of film. If several distinct histories are moving together at different speeds through time, then each image, photograph or still frame should show signs of them all caught in suspension together. So the work of analysis must begin by finding perspectives for each level of historical time.

For the history of imperceptible change a useful starting-point came up already in Chapter 1, with de Groot's comment on *hsiao-shuo* literature: 'Not the slightest change or progress in the animistic notions have we been able to trace in it . . . China on the whole has always been as she was.'[38] We can agree that these statements are limited and misleading as comments on the Chinese world in general. But the point about them is this: they grow out of the assumptions and methods that de Groot adopted in his own studies. For he chose to investigate those things in Chinese life which have lived on from archaic times into the visible present. They include the characteristic Chinese treatment of the dead, perceptions of the human soul, and the many procedures for ritual and shamanistic control of spirits. These are themes through which we can gain a clear first view of what Braudel called *la longue durée* in China's religious culture.

The sequence of events from the death of a family member through to the conclusion of burial rites, though complex, goes through various recognizable stages. There are procedures of ritual control; there is a carefully graded hierarchy of mourning obligations; there is an establishment of new forms of relationship between dead and living. If we look at all this with the eyes of historians we see how such age-old, stable institutions cope with the effects of passing time. They display a rich variation in their detailed execution, not only through time but also more obviously through space, in the vast diversity that spreads over the face of China in modern times. But there still remains a background relationship with ancient prescriptions for funeral rites in the texts of the Confucian canon. That is what particularly interested de Groot, who took the view that Chinese society had successfully preserved its ancient ritual laws by transmission through the hands of its educated class. Of course there are other ways to explain the living relationship with ancient texts: they could themselves be reflecting underlying and lasting patterns of social behaviour.[39] Whichever view we take, the same general point holds true: deep within the varied scene of China's treatment of its dead there lies a central pattern at the core, blending in with the various local features that surround it in

38 See Chapter 1, n. 32. The discussion in these pages refers to de Groot's main work, *The religious system of China*, 6 vols., Leiden 1892–1910.

39 See below, Chapter 7, p. 165, with n. 33.

specific situations. Sometimes this core of behaviour is seen as a test or index of belonging to the Han race – a way for other ethnic groups to adopt the characteristics of Han society as their peoples become submerged in the spread of Han settlement.[40] But for students of *Kuang-i chi* it holds the further interest of explaining why, as we shall see, a bond can so easily be discovered between the mediaeval funeral scenes in that book and similar death rituals observed by fieldworkers in modern China.[41] This bond stands as an example: other ritual practices connected with the dead can be seen to stretch over similarly vast periods of time.[42]

De Groot also gave detailed attention to what is described above as the 'unseen world' – man's complex relations with the souls of the dead and with other spirits emerging from the environment. He studied the professional activities of those whose work was to regulate or manipulate such relations – priests, exorcists, magicians, spirit-mediums. In all this his range of reference covered texts from antiquity down to recent times, supported of course with his own nineteenth-century fieldwork. The passage of a further hundred years has done little to banish these activities from the Chinese countryside, where modern researchers are now returning to investigate them. And the idea that shamanistic behaviour continues to be present at a deep level in Chinese social experience remains well established in modern thinking.[43] De Groot found the *Kuang-i chi* a rich source of evidence for his study of relations with the spirit world: the book blends easily with the long sweep of literature which explores those relations, and it is not hard to see why. Both Tai Fu, the compiler, and Ku K'uang, the preface-writer, were interested in the same subject-matter and shared some of the same attitudes towards it. For them too the activity of spirits and other mutant creatures was a permanent feature of human experience. They clearly felt a need to record when it happened, how it happened, and how it was to be controlled.

Such an approach to religious activity in China does light up long historical vistas. But it also casts long shadows, one of which lies over

40 These ideas are explored in the papers collected in James L. Watson and Evelyn S. Rawski, eds., *Death ritual in late imperial and modern China*, Berkeley and Los Angeles, 1988; particularly in Watson's introductory essay, 'The structure of Chinese funerary rites: elementary forms, ritual sequence, and the primacy of performance' (pp. 3–19), and Rawski's 'A historian's approach to Chinese death ritual' (pp. 20–34).

41 This will be studied below, in Chap. 6: see in particular pp. 144–6, with notes 19–22.

42 See remarks on spirit marriage in Chap. 7, pp. 165–6.

43 In an influential article Piet van der Loon writes of 'China's shamanistic substratum' (*substrat chamaniste de la Chine*) as a tradition more ancient than organized Taoism and Buddhism: 'Les origines rituelles du théâtre chinois', *Journal Asiatique* 1977, 141–68.

the archaic institution of blood sacrifice. Not that this is ever denied as a fundamental and permanent presence in Chinese ritual life: rather its presence is often left implied in the background by historians interested in studying other institutions. There has been more study of 'higher' systems of religious doctrine and cult, which emerge in the course of time and often define themselves by refining or transcending the sacrificial use of 'bloody food' (*hsüeh-shih* 血食).[44] By this they claim superiority to the lower cults, referred to with contempt as *yin-ssu* 淫祀. But the very use of this language and the strength of this reaction reveal that the use of bloody food keeps up its continuing and powerful presence in Chinese society, still there today for us to observe in religious practice. Reading the *Kuang-i chi* we never see sacrificial matters addressed as a main point of interest, yet that reticence itself hints at how widely the practice of sacrificial cult runs through life – so much taken for granted that only passing references remind us how ordinary and necessary it is (see **80, 86, 104, 105, 111, 139, 219**). Even a small handful of stories like this shows different forms of sacrificial activity at work, with the use of alcohol, dried meat and cooked food alongside the bloody food of standard sacrifice. Once again there comes a sense of complex variations playing around a central, long-term phenomenon in society. The very act of identifying such lasting phenomena seems to bring with it a need to acknowledge their restless surface complexity in relation to time and space.

We need to look beyond the unchanging vision of de Groot's analysis to find the signs of a measured movement in historical time. Tai Fu's book is peculiarly well suited to this. Although it comes to us in such a broken and scattered form, it does deal with a well-defined period. My own survey of internal dates shows a sequence leading up to a late limit of 780, concentrating heavily in the reigns of Hsüan-tsung (712–755), Su-tsung (756–762) and Tai-tsung (762–779), with a smaller number of dates in earlier T'ang reigns, and very few indeed from earlier periods.[45] The period so defined loosely fits the span of Tai Fu's own life, and accordingly his book presents the perspective of one man's lifetime in relation to the movement of secular change in the Chinese world.

44 This subject is explored in a series of studies by R. A. Stein in *Annuaire du Collège de France*, vols. 69, 71–3.

45 My figures are given in Tu Te-ch'iao, '*Kuang-i chi* ch'u-t'an', p. 401. Comparable figures, though slightly different in detail, are given by Uchiyama Chinari in 'Chū Tō shoki no shōsetsu', pp. 535–6. The editor Fang Shih-ming tends to treat items with pre-T'ang dates as spuriously attributed to *Kuang-i chi* – a point of view which we need not automatically accept. See below, opening remarks to Appendix.

By coincidence the middle half of the eighth century has long been recognized by historians as a time of basic change in China's institutions and society: structures of power, administration of political, economic and legal affairs, land tenure, population dynamics, currency, trade, urban development – all these embarked on a transformation process in the eighth century which we now see as one of the chief reference points in Chinese history.[46] Serious change was under way in religious culture too.[47] Some tiny signals of larger movements in progress have already shown up in this chapter: the Lord of Mount T'ai, once a local, subordinate figure in the divine administration, later becomes a national cult figure invested with imperial titles;[48] the *Kuang-i chi*'s anonymous 'kings' who administer local justice in hell develop around this time into a team of ten, with their own names, well known throughout the Chinese culture area.[49] These are mere details in a larger process by which, in the view of some recent studies, certain local or regional cults reached out beyond the strictly limited territory of their ancient following to take on new identities as national institutions, often formally recognized by the imperial state.[50]

In each case, we can identify the *Kuang-i chi* with the earlier, more conservative end of these changing systems. I have even suggested that the map of underworld jurisdictions, the layout of power in the underworld in relation to the territory of China that seems implied in the *Kuang-i chi*, carries echoes from the period of political disunion before the Sui.[51] But a closer look at certain stories in the collection brings out signs of later changes to come. One of these (**73**) is studied in Chapter 5 of this book: it discovers a local administrator deep in the provinces caught in what we can now see as a moment of transition. In many ways an ancient, well-established situation is in place: a dead military hero has reappeared as a ghost, bringing trouble and even death to the

46 It is surveyed by Denis Twitchett in two sections of his 'Introduction' to *The Cambridge history of China*, vol. 3, *Sui and T'ang China, 589–906, Part I*, Cambridge 1979, pp. 8–31.

47 A recent volume of studies is devoted to this subject: Patricia Buckley Ebrey and Peter N. Gregory, eds., *Religion and society in T'ang and Sung China*, Honolulu 1993. These editors survey 'the religious and historical landscape' in their opening chapter.

48 See above, n. 8, referring to Sawada Mizuho, *Jigoku hen*, pp. 45–8.

49 See above, n. 7.

50 The imperial granting of titles to local gods and the rise of regional cults in Sung China are studied by Valerie Hansen in *Changing gods in medieval China, 1127–1276*, Princeton 1990, pp. 79–104, 128–59. Terry Kleeman studies a particular case in 'The expansion of the Wen-ch'ang cult', chapter 2 in Ebrey and Gregory, eds., *Religion and society in T'ang and Sung China*, pp. 45–73.

51 See above, p. 58, n. 22.

officials who come to administer the Hsiang-chou prefecture at An-yang; they build a temple in his honour and make him regular offerings of bloody food; he then protects and supports the administrators who are responsible. As historians we might argue that the administrators are dealing with a community in which ancient fears and beliefs about dead heroes are still strong – something we see reflected by cults in different parts of China through the Northern and Southern Dynasties period. But the solution to the problem at An-yang seems to look forward to a more modern institution – the City God (*ch'eng-huang* 城隍), whose cults began to spread through the fortified towns of China's provinces in the ninth and tenth centuries.[52] The word *ch'eng-huang* is not used in story **73**, although the dead hero's new role of support for the administration in return for worship in a local temple makes him look like a *ch'eng-huang* god. But the word does appear just once elsewhere in the *Kuang-i chi* (**77**) – enough to confirm that the new type of cult is already advancing over Tai Fu's horizon.

In a paper published elsewhere I have discussed certain other cults in the *Kuang-i chi* emerging through tension between provincial administrators and religious leaders of the Taoist persuasion.[53] This too is something with its own significance in time. There is much to be said about the spread of schools of Taoism and Buddhism through China during the centuries before and during the T'ang: learned studies have been written about the traditions of doctrine and scripture transmitted through the churches of those great religious systems. Yet that is not what we see directly reflected in the *Kuang-i chi*. Instead we see a lay society using and responding to what it has absorbed from the 'high' traditions over a period of centuries. The most visible signs are reflections of mythology and the practice, both personal and professional, of ritual.

The Taoist Master P'u P'u in story **2** confronts the prefect of Kuang-chou with a speech which claims for him the status of teacher to some of the classic figures in Taoist legend:

'Such people as Ma-ku 麻姑, Ts'ai Ching 蔡經, Wang Fang-p'ing 王方平, K'ung Shen 孔申, and the Three Mao 茅 brothers have sought my instruction on the Tao, and I have not yet finished my explanations. I remain here for this reason and no other.'

52 David Johnson, 'The City-God cults of T'ang and Sung China', *Harvard Journal of Asiatic Studies* 45, 1985, 363–457. Compare the discussion below in Chapter 5, p. 136, with refs. in nn. 71–6.

53 G. Dudbridge, 'Tang tales and Tang cults: some cases from the eighth century', *Proceedings of the Second International Conference on Sinology: section on literature*, Academia Sinica, Nan-kang 1990, pp. 335–52.

The situation, in what is admittedly an inner story, requires that these names[54] have a resonance in lay ears. It speaks for a China where, in particular, the Shang-ch'ing school of Taoism, with its traditional centre upon the mountain named after the Mao brothers, has established itself in the consciousness of mainstream society.[55] The same seems true of the strange story **12**, which plays upon an actual historical sequence of the Shang-ch'ing patriarchal succession in the seventh century: P'an Shih-cheng 潘師正 (585–682), the eleventh Shang-ch'ing patriarch in retirement on Mount Sung, entrusted to his disciple Ssu-ma Ch'eng-chen 司馬承禎 (647–735) the transmission of teachings inherited from T'ao Hung-ching (456–536).[56] Tai Fu's version of the story has garbled virtually the entire record:[57] but its view of the Shang-ch'ing transmission combines with some close attention to the topography of Mount Sung to suggest the work of local tradition, dimly recalling in its own terms the Taoist celebrities of a century past.[58] Stories like this might even, perversely, reveal more about the lay public's view of Taoist divines than records handed authentically down through the orthodox canon.

We can make similar points for ritual matters, about which large questions remain to be answered. Here too, perhaps, the T'ang was a time of transition, as Kristofer Schipper boldly suggested in 1981. He argued that by the end of this period the celebration of many provincial

54 Ma-ku and Wang Yüan 王遠 (*tzu* Fang-p'ing) appeared in splendour at the home of Ts'ai Ching in the period AD 146–167: *Shen-hsien chuan*, in *TPKC* 7.46–7 and 60.369–70. The Three Mao were Mao Ying 茅盈 and his two younger brothers: on this earth in the second century BC, they later conferred revelations upon the fathers of Shang-ch'ing Taoism, and Mount Mao, the famous centre of that school, was named after them: Chavannes, *Le T'ai chan*, pp. 143–4, n. 1. K'ung Shen is not identified.

55 The growing prominence of this school in Chinese religious history down to the T'ang and beyond is traced by Michel Strickmann in *Le Taoïsme du Mao chan, chronique d'une révélation*, Paris 1981, pp. 28 ff.

56 For critical biographical notes on P'an Shih-cheng and Ssu-ma Ch'eng-chen, see Ch'en Kuo-fu, *Tao tsang yüan-liu k'ao*, pp. 50–9. The traditional account of the patriarchal succession is given in *Mao-shan chih* 10 and 11; see especially 10.13a, 11.1a–3b; and *CTS* 192.5126–7. For their association with Mount Sung, see Bernard Faure, 'Relics and flesh bodies: the creation of Ch'an pilgrimage sites', in Susan Naquin and Chün-fang Yü, eds., *Pilgrims and sacred sites in China*, Berkeley and Los Angeles 1992, p. 155.

57 P'an Shih-cheng's name is corrupted to Fa-cheng 法正. His death is moved in time from 684 to the K'ai-yüan period (713–741). T'ao Hung-ching's appointment in the other world, officially registered as inspector of waterways in P'eng-lai (*Mao-shan chih* 10.13a), here becomes Lord of Mount Sung. His hundred-year tenure of the post bears no relation to the lapse of time, real or displaced, between his own death and P'an Shih-cheng's.

58 Even the imperially sponsored temple of Mount Sung here bears a name – Sung-yang kuan 嵩陽觀 – that ceased to apply already in 677, when Kao-tsung's decree renamed it Feng-t'ien kung 奉天宮: see the 699 inscription on P'an Shih-cheng by Wang Shih 王適, in *Chih-shih ts'ui-pien* 62.29a.

cult festivals began to incorporate Taoist rituals performed by Taoist masters, as a way of affirming the new-found strength of local structures; the process would go on to spread widely, even universally in later periods.[59] The idea certainly deserves further investigation. It cannot be disputed that *tao-shih* 道士, or priests claiming to stand in a line of transmission from the early T'ien-shih fathers of the Taoist church, have in the course of time established themselves as the primary ritual specialists of local religion. How did that come about, and when? The *Kuang-i chi* may not give many useful insights into the evolution of communal rites in lay society. But it does show ritual specialists at work on behalf of lay customers, using paper charms (*fu* 符) and summoning spirits to their assistance.[60] These services, despite the disclaimers of theologians, had for centuries been perceived as Taoist practices.[61] And for the society that populates the *Kuang-i chi* they are familiar and accessible to all.

Through a long period that culminated in the eighth century, China, like Tibet and later Japan, was absorbing from India the esoteric lore and practices of Tantric Buddhism.[62] Much of the richest material for studying this process survives in Chinese-language ritual texts of the T'ang period, and much also in later ritual practice in the Shingon Buddhist monasteries of Japan. The transmission of ritual to China seems to have progressed in phases. The incantations known as mantras, or more strictly *dhāraṇī* (in Chinese *shen-chou* 神咒), were well established in use there before the beginning of the T'ang.[63] But only in the eighth century, when Tantric Buddhism reached its full maturity in China, did signs appear of the specialized ritual and meditation

59 K. M. Schipper, 'Taoist ritual and local cults of the T'ang dynasty', *Proceedings of the International Conference on Sinology, Section on Folklore and Culture*, Taipei 1981, pp. 101–15, especially 113–15.

60 For use of *fu*, see **54**, **68**, **69**, **71**, **76**, **78**, **115**, **265**, **268**, **271**, **274**, **299**. For ritual summons, see **65**, **67**, **261** (the last also using *fu*).

61 Ko Hung referred to rites for summoning spirits: *Pao-p'u tzu nei-p'ien chiao-shih* 2.20. His references to *fu* charms are collected by Hu Fu-ch'en in *Wei Chin shen-hsien Tao-chiao: Pao-p'u tzu nei-p'ien yen-chiu*, Peking 1989, pp. 167–9. The ninth-century Taoist scholar and poet Shih Chien-wu 施肩吾 described the summoning of spirits as 'a Taoist rite' 道中之法事, but dissociated it from the spirituality of true Taoist cultivation: see *Yang-sheng pien-i chüeh* 養生辯疑訣, 2b (*Tao tsang*: HY 852).

62 This paragraph is heavily indebted to the late Michel Strickmann's unpublished book *Mantras et mandarins: le bouddhisme tantrique en Chine*, which he was kind enough to show me in typescript. He also, before his sudden death in 1994, did me the favour of reading and commenting on the present chapter in draft.

63 The specific sense of these different terms is discussed by Strickmann at the opening of the first chapter of *Mantras et mandarins*, 'Incantations et eschatologie'. For a study of *dhāraṇī* as used in Chinese society at a later period, see Sawada Mizuho, 'Sōdai no shinju shinkō – *Ikenshi* no setsuwa o chūshin to shite –', in *Shūtei Chūgoku no juhō*, Tokyo 1992, pp. 457–96.

techniques used to summon up the gods of the Tantric universe and make them obey the orders of the ritual master. To the extent that this was a technical and expensive business to undertake, involving secret texts and highly qualified foreign experts, only emperors and high officials could afford to be its patrons. But Strickmann points out that in the long run the inheritors of that esoteric system of Tantric meditation and ritual would be found in China at the humblest level, as we see to this day in the celebration of rites like *fang yen-k'ou* 放焰口 or *shih shih* 施食 at ordinary Chinese funerals or Avalambana celebrations in the seventh lunar month.[64] Once more, a movement of widening access and diffusion has taken place over more than a millennium of historical time. And again the *Kuang-i chi* coincides with a period of incipient change. So here is a chance to look for evidence of that change in secular China.

New research has begun to show that the mid-T'ang saw a complex intermingling of Taoist with Tantric ritual practices. The use of paper charms, the uttering of verbal spells and the summoning of spirits all served as a focus for this convergence of two ancient traditions, in which the predominant influence is sometimes seen on the Taoist side, sometimes on the Buddhist.[65] These are developments that the window of the *Kuang-i chi* allows us to glimpse at work in secular life. We see laymen protecting and empowering themselves with spells both Tantric (**38, 40, 98, 159**) and non-Tantric (**54, 67, 241**). Most interesting is story **146:**

> In late T'ien-pao there was in Ch'ang-an one Second Mistress Ma 馬二娘, skilled in summoning spirits for questioning (*k'ao-chao* 考召). Su Shen, the prefect of Yen-chou, knew her well. Once, wanting to marry his son Lai to a Lu, he said to Ma: 'I only have one son, and I really want to make him a marriage with an excellent girl. We don't know which of the three Lu daughters is the best, and I hope you can summon them here so that his mother can inspect them herself.' So Ma set up an altar in a Buddhist shrine (*fo-t'ang* 佛堂) and performed the summons. In a moment the souls of all three daughters arrived . . .

In this deceptively simple narrative some important features come together: the use of a female ritual specialist (a professional perhaps, but not a cleric), the performance of the rite in the presence of Buddhist images (in what may well have been a domestic shrine), the calling up of souls belonging to living mortals. The story stays tantalizingly silent

64 G. Dudbridge, *The legend of Miao-shan*, London 1978, pp. 94–6.

65 Two works by Hsiao Teng-fu deal with this subject: *Tao-chiao hsing-tou fu-yin yü Fo-chiao mi-tsung*, Taipei 1993, and *Tao-chiao yü mi-tsung*, Taipei 1993. It is also explored in detail by Michel Strickmann in his book *Mantras et mandarins*. Compare remarks by Hu Fu-ch'en, *Wei Chin shen-hsien Tao-chiao*, pp. 169–70.

on the central feature of the rite itself – the medium through which the souls made their presence felt. If Mistress Ma made use of possession, perhaps with specially chosen children as mediums, like those described in the ritual texts analysed by Strickmann,[66] then this story might claim a place in our attempts to document the arrival of Tantric Buddhist practice in lay Chinese life. But in any case its significance lies in showing how ancient and powerful currents of cultural influence flow together in open society at a given moment in the mid-T'ang. And the story takes on this significance only when we can see it in the perspective of dynamic change over time.

A final example of that perspective comes from another branch of Chinese Buddhism, the Ch'an movement. The succession of Ch'an patriarchs, starting with the arrival in China of Bodhidharma in the 470s, was the subject of complicated legends that established themselves during the eighth century – the very period of Tai Fu's lifetime.[67] But that mythology took shape at first privately among the followers of the school itself and did not become famous until the ninth century and later. So we scan the *Kuang-i chi* with interest to see whether this work compiled during the legendary Golden Age of Ch'an shows any recognition of the fact. It comes as no surprise to find only silence on the great figures of the Ch'an movement, a silence which is particularly striking in the case of Mount Sung near Lo-yang. For that mountain group, the very heartland of the classic legends of Bodhidharma and long associated with later Ch'an masters,[68] receives regular attention in the pages of *Kuang-i chi*. There are references both to the imperially sponsored Temple of the Younger Aunt (**83, 115**),[69] and to the Taoist population, both mortal and divine, attached to the mountain (**12, 74, 115, 270**); but none to the 'conquest' of Mount Sung by seventh- and eighth-century Ch'an Buddhist masters of which we read in stories from their sacred biographies.[70] It would seem that the lay public whose world is reflected in the *Kuang-i chi* had no significant contact with the newly arrived schools of Ch'an patriarchs – they had simply not been there long enough to be fixed in the public awareness. The *Kuang-i chi*

66 Strickmann, *Mantras et mandarins*, chap. 4: 'Exorcisme et spectacle'. Compare in particular the story of Vajrabodhi cited at the beginning of the chapter from *Sung kao-seng chuan* 1.711c. Hsiao Teng-fu gives further evidence in *Tao-chiao yü mi-tsung*, chap. 2, pp. 139 ff.

67 For close studies of Ch'an in the eighth century, see Philip B. Yampolsky, *The Platform Sutra of the Sixth Patriarch*, New York and London 1967, pp. 1–121; and John R. McRae, *The Northern School and the formation of early Ch'an Buddhism*, Honolulu 1986, pp. 1–97.

68 Faure, 'Relics and flesh bodies', pp. 156–7.

69 The temple stood on Mount Shao-shih 少室山, one of the lesser peaks in the group.

70 Faure, 'Relics and flesh bodies', pp. 159 ff., citing *Sung kao-seng chuan* 18.823b and 19.828b–c.

would once again appear to present a conservative, backward-looking vision, revealing the more slowly changing features of religious culture at a time when new developments had not yet made themselves felt.

But the point needs making more carefully, for there is a story in this collection that does mention an unnamed Ch'an master. He is an expert in taming wild beasts and is here seen at work in a mountain monastery, helping a man escape from the influence of tiger spirits (**232**). Stories of masters able to control and pacify wild beasts can indeed be found in Ch'an hagiography:[71] but this one, from an early date in the history of Ch'an in China, is passed on independently of the movement's own scriptures – a matter of particular historical interest. To take account of it we need to frame a more judicious conclusion, and this will actually echo what was said above about *ch'eng-huang* gods: the *Kuang-i chi* was compiled at a time when the signs of certain new features in religious culture were first coming into view; a time before really large-scale evidence appeared of their spread throughout the Chinese world; a time of transition in which the signs look confused and sometimes seem to point in different directions. They are the characteristic signs of a history whose change is slow but still perceptible.

What remains is the 'history of events'. Tai Fu and his generation lived through one of the most spectacular and troubled periods of Chinese history. When they were born memories were still fresh of the Empress Wu's colourful reign (**67, 89, 126, 210, 212, 252, 258**), ending with a dynastic crisis – the restoration of the T'ang royal house in the person of Chung-tsung, her son (**67, 174, 258**). They lived their youth through the prosperous and peaceful early reign of Hsüan-tsung, famous for its cultural splendours. But their maturity was darkened by the weakening of Hsüan-tsung's regime in the 750s and the Great Rebellion of An Lu-shan 安祿山 (755–757), which convulsed the empire with warfare and shook its society to the roots. The rebellion forced Tai Fu himself to take the examination for *chin-shih* far from the capital, and his career developed in the troubled decades of imperial weakness which then followed. He had experience, direct or indirect, of the smaller local revolt of Yüan Ch'ao 袁晁 on the eastern seaboard in the 760s[72] and lived just long enough to see the prospects of a new order, and the menace of a new provincial revolt, under the vigorous young emperor Te-tsung (780s).

This whole period saw dramatic swings in imperial religious patronage and policy. While they reviewed and evolved the institutions of state

71 Ibid., pp. 158–9.
72 See below, Chapter 6.

ritual,[73] the T'ang emperors maintained complex and changing relations of power with two established state religions – Buddhism and Taoism.[74] Some, like Empress Wu, would find their own legitimacy in Buddhist prophecy and patronize it lavishly. Others would fill their courts with Taoist or with Tantric ritual experts, and sometimes, like Hsüan-tsung, with both. Their acts of policy might seek to purge the countryside of loose cults, or subject the clerical population to rigorous control.

There are echoes of these great public, but transient, events in the pages of *Kuang-i chi*. But it is not the business of this book to review them in detail. They come up naturally for study in the context of individual stories, and that is the most fitting way to deal with them here – to let them serve as a setting, a background for other subjects, exactly as Tai Fu himself presented the material. Chapter 4 below will look at certain acts of state policy in relation to particular temples and gods during the reign of Hsüan-tsung, Chapter 6 at the rebellion of Yüan Ch'ao in south-east China, 762–763, and so on. What follows here, in the last section of the present chapter, will explore how in practice the history of public events entwines itself with material of more long-term interest. The two cases discussed are both connected with religious communities in the mountains of Wu-t'ai 五臺 and Yen-men 雁門.

13 In the K'ai-yüan period the governor-general of Tai-chou, noting the large numbers of travelling Buddhist clerics in the Wu-t'ai region, expelled all those who had no established superiors, for he feared that incidents of sorcery and quackery would occur. Many of the visiting monks fled before their dreaded pursuers and took temporary refuge in the mountain gorges.

One Fa-lang went deep into the heart of the Yen-men Mountains, where he found a rock cavern in the midst of a secluded mountain stream. It was large enough for a man to go in and out of it. Fa-lang had plenty of dried food with him and was keen to live on this mountain, so he entered and pursued his way through the cavern. After several hundred paces it gradually opened out wide. He came to level ground, crossed a stream and reached the far bank. Sun and moon shone there in full brilliance. He walked on a couple of *li* and arrived among some thatched huts. There were women there, all dressed in grass and leaves, looking most comely and handsome.

They were alarmed at the sight of the monk and asked him: 'What manner of creature are you?'

He said: 'I am a human being.'

73 See the chapter on this in David McMullen, *State and scholars in T'ang China*, Cambridge 1988, pp. 113–58.

74 The subject of Stanley Weinstein's book *Buddhism under the T'ang*, Cambridge 1987.

The women smiled and said: 'How can a human have an appearance like that?'

He replied: 'I serve the Buddha, and disciples of the Buddha have to discard their beard and hair. That is why I look like this.'

Then they asked him who the Buddha was, and the monk told them all about him. They smiled at one another: 'It makes very good sense!'

They went on to ask what his central principles were, and the monk expounded the *Vajracchedikā* for them, earning many appreciative comments.

He now asked what world this place belonged to, and the women said: 'We are Ch'in folk and came here with Meng T'ien to build the Great Wall. He employed women a great deal, but we could not endure the hardships and fled to this place. At first we ate the roots of herbs and so have kept ourselves alive. We have no idea what year it is by now, for we no longer go back to human society.'

They entertained the monk, feeding him with roots of herbs. The taste was so harsh that they were uneatable. The monk lived there for more than forty days, then took his leave to go out briefly to the human world and seek food. When he reached Tai-chou he stocked up with provisions and set off back. But he lost his way and no longer knew where the place was.

This story of the K'ai-yüan period (719–741) is set in the mountain area in Shansi province known as Wu-t'ai shan 五臺山 – mountains that were famous throughout the Chinese Middle Ages as a sacred site of the Bodhisattva Mañjuśrī 文殊.[75] Also involved is the nearby mountain range known as Yen-men shan 雁門山, which contained a historic pass linking metropolitan China on the southern side to the non-Chinese lands immediately to the north.

Several themes come together here. Clearest of all is the 'lost paradise' – the part of the story that so strongly echoes T'ao Yüan-ming's fable of the 'Peach-blossom spring' 桃花源記.[76] There is of course a serious difference. When the adventurous fisherman in T'ao Yüan-ming's piece finds a concealed and forgotten colony of refugees from the harsh age of Ch'in Shih-huang, they are living in a timeless paradise of agricultural order and prosperity; this contrasts sharply with the more specialized society found by the monk Fa-lang in story **13**. But in both cases the refugees greet their visitor with similar hospitality and curiosity; and when he leaves them to return to the outside world, it is for good – no one can find the way there again.

T'ao Yüan-ming's famous piece and its historical and allegorical interpretations have enjoyed long and close attention. But it represents

75 Raoul Birnbaum, *Studies on the mysteries of Mañjuśrī*, Boulder: Society for the Study of Chinese Religions, Monograph 2, 1983.

76 A. R. Davis, *T'ao Yüan-ming (AD 365–427): his works and their meaning*, Cambridge 1983, vol. 1, pp. 195–201.

only one among a number of early documents which report or reflect on remote pockets of society isolated from the main flux of Chinese life.[77] Story **13** must take its place within that wider scene to bring its traditional character into full view.

There are signs that the Wu-t'ai mountains had early legends of their own that could well lie behind this one. A passage attributed to the sixth-century *Shui-ching chu* quotes a tradition that in 309, during the last years of the Western Chin dynasty, five hundred families from Yen-men Commandery fled from disorder into these mountains, where they were guided by the mountain dwellers. So there they stayed, settling in the mountainous wilderness. Few people could ever find them there, and the popular view was that this was the abode of immortal beings.[78] Here is the same strange mix of social history and religious tradition that seems suggested by story **13**. The year 309 lies early in that sensitive period of history when non-Han tribes poured into north China and set up their own small dynasties there. The north of Shansi province was the very area from which came the Hsiung-nu tribes who would set up a Chao dynasty in 316. Chinese communities settled near the Yen-men Pass might well take to the hills and establish whatever agricultural regime they could there. The issue for them in the mountains would certainly be how well they could replicate there the vision of 'fine fields and beautiful pools, clumps of mulberries and bamboos' that T'ao Yüan-ming idealizes in his famous prose and that represent the Han farmers' most cherished setting for peaceful social life. Or how far they would have to compromise with the tough realities of climate and ecology and learn to exploit wild plants for their survival value. The comely women who greet the exploring monk Fa-lang here dramatize exactly this situation. They claim to be Chinese and explain their uprooting from mainstream society by reference to Ch'in Shin-huang and the Great Wall project. Yet they present the appearance of wild mountain tribespeople, with their thatched huts, primitive clothing and specialized diet of roots and herbs. They seem to have no menfolk around, something we might otherwise associate with a hunting and gathering community whose men leave the settlement for periods of hunting. So point for point these women offer an antithesis to the agricultural idyll discovered at the end of T'ao Yüan-ming's 'Peach-blossom spring'. They

77 For a survey, see Davis, *T'ao Yüan-ming*, vol. 2, pp. 140–3. Also Stephen R. Bokenkamp, 'The Peach Flower Font and the grotto passage', *Journal of the American Oriental Society* 106, 1986, 65–77.

78 *T'ai-p'ing yü-lan* 45.3b–4a. Cf. Raoul Birnbaum, 'Secret halls of the mountain lords: the caves of Wu-t'ai shan', *Cahiers d'Extrême-Asie* 5, 1989–1990, 115–40, with p. 124 and n. 26. My reading of the passage differs slightly from Professor Birnbaum's.

bring out the most fundamental clash of culture between Han and non-Han peoples – the basically different styles of food production and food consumption. The women share the attributes of those pockets of aboriginal society pushed into remote hills by the advance of Han agriculture and communal organization.

But there is more. The women's diet of bitter roots has given them long life and unfading youth. The story explores in a simple way the Buddhist traveller Fa-lang's failure to adapt to this alien style of eating that tempts him with the promise of immortality. Although he survives for some weeks on emergency rations of dried food (*kan-liang* 乾糧), in the end the need for cereals drives him away from this place. So the question of specialized diets in relation to human survival is a second important theme looked at in this story. It was explored in the 1970s by Rolf Stein at the Collège de France.[79] He argued that mountain aborigines were an important source of pharmacological and dietary knowledge for Taoists seeking escape from the cereal-based food of the mortal world and access to the diet of immortality; but the dried food used for emergency support by travellers was also similar to the special diets used by Taoist adepts in their quest for long-life nourishment.[80] The Buddhist traveller Fa-lang seems, from this point of view, to be working out an experiment in diet of the kind discussed by Stein from early Taoist writings. Its failure runs parallel to his departure from the women's settlement: the dried emergency rations could have been a transitional diet preparing him for the food that gave the women immortality; but the need for cereals proves too strong, and he withdraws both from the women's austere diet and from their remote settlement. His retreat echoes the shape of other traditional 'lost paradise' tales, in which travellers lose touch with the other world or ideal society they have found, and never discover a way back to it again.

Story **13** is more than a mountain idyll or Taoist excursion. It is also a reminder that the refugee phenomenon is more or less a constant in Chinese history – only the circumstances change. On this occasion the motive force is a tension between uncertified members of the Buddhist order and government authorities anxious to keep them controlled within registered institutions. The sensitive region of Wu-t'ai shan had special significance for both parties in T'ang times. To Buddhists it was the prime pilgrimage centre of the Chinese world; to the imperial

79 In a series of lecture reports published in *Annuaire du Collège de France*: 'Les fêtes de cuisine du taoïsme religieux' (7le année, 431–40); 'Spéculations mystiques et thèmes relatifs aux «cuisines» du taoïsme' (72e année, 489–99); 'Conceptions relatives à la nourriture (Chine)' (73e année, 457–63).

80 Stein, 'Spéculations mystiques', pp. 497–8.

authorities it was part of a northern frontier region where defence against Turkic invaders required a military government-general (*tu-tu fu* 都督府), not an ordinary civil authority. The story explains clearly how local policy triggers off an attack of administrative rigour on 'travelling Buddhist clerics', and expresses its fear that this shifting and ill-defined class of people might lead to cases of 'sorcery and deception'. It does not make clear what precise political and social dangers are implied. But the date in the story does hint at a more general background of persecution. In the K'ai-yüan period the emperor Hsüan-tsung delivered a series of heavy attacks on the Buddhist community. He began by defrocking tens of thousands of illegally ordained Buddhist clergy in 714 and kept up an official scrutiny of monastery personnel from 729 on.[81] Story **13** gives a glimpse at how broad government policies on these lines could translate into action at the local level. And it dramatizes another great theme in the history of Chinese society: here, on the margins of the main Chinese culture area, is a marginal individual at odds with the central system of governmental control.

The story which articulates these various hints and themes, viewed as a historical document, is hardly straightforward. It cannot claim the same documentary status as more conventional historical records. It has instead a value which we might describe as archaeological: everything in the text is a product in one sense or another of the T'ang age and has information to convey about it. Some of this is easily unearthed. It is not difficult to identify the story's context in the 'history of events', with particular government measures, at a known period, directed against the Buddhist community in north China. But it then goes on to describe an experience which already contains its own historical interpretation. We do not and cannot know whether a monk called Fa-lang really did meet a village settlement of women who presented the history of their community with reference to Meng T'ien 蒙恬 and the Great Wall project. But it is certain that this historical gloss was laid upon the story at some point in its transmission, which perhaps passed through other hands before coming to Tai Fu and ourselves. The historical reference to Ch'in Shih-huang's regime has plainly been taken over from an established background in earlier literature; yet it can also be seen as reflecting a long-term series of repeated events in Chinese history, in which groups of refugees have found themselves driven by pressures of state policy or foreign invasion to retreat into mountainous country.

The interpretation which links the travelling monk's experience to

81 Stanley Weinstein, *Buddhism under the T'ang*, Cambridge 1987, pp. 51 ff.

the question of contacts between Han and non-Han peoples comes, not from the text itself, but from modern hindsight. In using it to discuss story **13**, I am echoing in slightly different terms the thoughts of T'ang Ch'ang-ju on T'ao Yüan-ming's 'Peach-blossom spring': he saw it as reflecting a tradition of southern *man* 蠻 tribes, with their pattern of remote, inaccessible settlements, of detachment from Han authorities, sometimes of violent confrontation.[82] Story **13** is even more striking for its picture of a confrontation between two distinct social systems.[83] This view of it really engages a much more long-term perspective on Chinese history, a perspective which cannot really be denied, for those contrasts and tensions still mean something today.

4 In the T'ien-pao period there was a man called Liu Ch'ing-chen who with his associates, twenty in all, were tea traders in Shou-chou. They were each conveying a load to serve as trading stock, but fell prey to bandits when they came as far as Ch'en-liu. Someone served them as guide and took them to Wei-chün. Then Liu Ch'ing-chen and his men set out again, and in turn met with an old Buddhist monk who guided them towards Wu-t'ai.

Liu and his companions were daunted by the hardships of the journey. So, while the Wu-t'ai Monastery was still far distant, the monk invited them all back to his hermitage to spend the night. Talking it over among themselves, Liu Ch'ing-chen and his friends had a suspicion that the old monk was the Bodhisattva Mañjuśrī. So they went back with him, covering several *li* before they reached the hermitage. The buildings there had an air of dignity and purity which inspired in all of them feelings of awe and reverence. The monk preached to them, using such appropriate and well-judged eloquence that Liu and his men with one accord resolved in their hearts to take religious vows, accepting him as their Superior.

More than twenty years went by. Then, suddenly, the monk said to Liu and company: 'Great demons have risen up, and you are certain to have trouble with them. We must take precautions in advance, for otherwise your religious activities will be ruined.' And he told them all to stay kneeling while he proceeded to fill his mouth with water and spit it out in all directions, reciting esoteric spells. Liu and his men all changed into stones: mentally they were fully aware, though unable to move. Very soon, dozens of official runners from Tai-chou came up the terrace, looking to arrest wanted men. Reaching the spot where Liu Ch'ing-chen lay they could see nothing but rank grass and stones, so they gave up the search and left. When evening came the old monk returned and changed Liu and company back into men by spitting out more water. They

82 T'ang Ch'ang-ju, 'Tu "*T'ao-hua yüan chi* p'ang-cheng" chih-i', in *Wei Chin Nan-pei ch'ao shih lun-ts'ung hsü-pien*, Peking 1959, 163–74, citing the passage in *Sung shu* 97.2396 which characterizes the *man* tribes at large in southern China during the fifth century. Cf. Davis, *T'ao Yüan-ming*, vol. 2, p. 142.

83 There are stories in *Kuang-i chi* which describe more developed contacts and interaction between Han farmers and tribespeople in the far south: **225, 252**.

now understood what divine powers he possessed and knew that they had met with a bodhisattva. All strove to advance in religious perfection.

A month or more after this the monk said: 'Now once again demons are going to rise up and will certainly be out looking for you. What shall we do? I should like to take you far away – but will you go with me?'

Liu and company agreed to obey him, and he told them all to close their eyes, warning them: 'Above all, do not peep! It will ruin your great endeavour. But when once you feel yourselves touch the ground, then open your eyes. If you find yourselves in the mountains and see a great tree there, you should all take shelter under it. And if some medicinal substance grows from the tree you should take it as food.'

He then gave them each a pill, saying: 'Eat these, and you will never feel hungry again. But you must keep your thoughts on the Holy Way, for that is your ferry or bridge to the life beyond this.'

With these words they exchanged salutations, then closed their eyes. Gradually they rose up until their bodies were in mid-air, and after the better part of a day their feet reached the ground. Opening their eyes, they saw a great mountain covered with forests. They happened upon a woodcutter and asked him the name of the place. It was Mount Lu.

They walked on some ten *li* and saw a great vine, in girth as large as five or six men's reach, and with blue-green foliage shading out the sun. Liu and his companions exclaimed in delight: 'This must be the wonderful tree that the Great Teacher spoke about!' And each of them cleared a space in the vegetation to sit upon.

Some days later a white fungus grew out of the tree, radiant and lustrous, floating about in constant motion. They said to one another: 'This is the sacred tonic that our Great Teacher spoke of.' And they plucked it down, for all to share in eating it.

But one of the group deceived the others and ate it all first. Every one of his companions was vexed and angry, and they cursed him: 'You have disobeyed our Great Teacher's instructions. But your karma has already appointed that this must be so – we cannot lay blows on you.'

In due course the man disappeared, and looking up they saw him sitting at rest at the top of their tree. Liu and his friends went on: 'It is because you ate that tonic that you are able to rise up on high!'

But the man stayed on up there, not coming down.

After seven days green feathers had grown all over his body. Then suddenly there were cranes hovering overhead, and he addressed the nineteen men: 'I did play you false. But now I am immortal: I am going to part from you and present myself before the Monarch in heaven above. Strive hard, all of you, to achieve nothing less than perfection.'

Liu and his friends begged him to descend from the tree for them to make their farewells, but the immortal paid no heed and rose aloft on a cloud. It was long before he faded from sight.

Since they had lost their tonic, Liu Ch'ing-chen and companions went their separate ways and returned to human society.

Chang Lun of Chung-shan personally heard Liu and the others tell their story in just this form.

The way into this highly coloured episode, I believe, is by putting to work the distinction between inner and outer stories. There is a special feature to observe: the events of the inner story are shared among twenty people. But the distinction still works, because we can separate out a visible 'outer' dimension of their lives. They are traders in tea; their base in Shou-chou 壽州 is a place in modern Anhwei province (the T'ang province was Huai-nan) which did actually lie in one of the main producing areas of the T'ang tea industry.[84] The traders follow a route that we can follow in detail on the map: they go north-west along one of the river thoroughfares linking north central Anhwei with the Pien River near Kaifeng. They are probably heading for Lo-yang or even Ch'ang-an, but the events of the story take them from Ch'en-liu 陳留 (a county south-east of Pien-chou 汴州, near Kaifeng), over the Yellow River and northward to Wei-chün 魏郡, which is now in the south-east corner of Hopei. Then they go further north to the neighbourhood of Wu-t'ai county, under the government-general of Tai-chou. It is striking that these places bear names which match correctly with the historical periods referred to in the story. The place originally called Wei-chou 魏州 did become Wei-chün for the length of the T'ien-pao period when the story begins (that is 742–756), and it reverted in 758; likewise, Tai-chou became Yen-men chün 雁門郡 for just the same period, then reverted too.[85] Since the story ends more than twenty years after its beginning in T'ien-pao, the episode at Tai-chou implies a date somewhere between 763 and 780 – securely within the *Kuang-i chi* time-scale.

Liu Ch'ing-chen and his men (minus one) come back into public view at the end of the story, when they turn up twenty years late and tell their tale to someone called Chang Lun 張倫 – and he is the personal authority for reporting what they have to tell. This is rather typical of the way stories are presented and authenticated in the *Kuang-i chi.* Of course personal hearsay can be no more than just that. In the end Liu Ch'ing-chen's party are their own sole witnesses, and no one else can confirm what they have to say. It is private to themselves. The whole thing could easily be a pack of lies, designed to explain away the passing of those twenty years and the loss of one of their companions. In fact, from our point of view it makes no real difference whether Liu Ch'ing-chen truly believed in his private experience or not. Either way

84 The local speciality was called 'Yellow teeth', *huang-ya* 黃牙, from Huo-shan: *T'ang kuo-shih pu* C.60.

85 *CTS* 39.1493 and 1483.

that experience grows out of the social and religious culture with which his mind was stocked. And that in turn is interesting to study: at first sight, a wild mixture of wizardry and paradise imagery – magic flight, holy mountain, life-prolonging fungus, feathered immortal, hovering cranes, ascent to heaven. But the really interesting figure at the heart of all this is the old monk who recruits them as disciples in religion for the missing twenty years. Liu Ch'ing-chen and his friends surmise this is the Bodhisattva Mañjuśrī himself, something which makes them seem very like real pilgrims to Wu-t'ai shan. The Japanese traveller Ennin, who wrote his famous diary less than a century later, mentions the same pious habits of that place, where people were prepared to see a manifestation of Mañjuśrī in any passer-by. He remarks: 'When one enters this region of His Holiness, if one sees a very lowly man, one does not dare to feel contemptuous, and if one meets a donkey, one wonders if it might be a manifestation of Monju. Everything before one's eyes raises thoughts of the manifestations of Monju.'[86]

The monk actually appears to us as a charismatic teacher. He practises ritual magic by spitting charmed water from his mouth – an ancient procedure, familiar in T'ang literature as an act of sorcery or enchantment, still known to modern students of Chinese religion as a common ritual act of cleansing and exorcism.[87] It would be a natural response from a priest to a perceived threat from demons. The magic itself, which changes the twenty disciples into rocks and stones, has a venerable pedigree in the Taoist religion. We read about it, or something very like it, in one of the scriptures of the Shang-ch'ing corpus, said to have been revealed by divine informants in the fourth century. It is the *Shang-ch'ing tan-ching tao-ching yin-ti pa-shu ching* 上清丹景道精隱地八術經 (HY 1348), a text which deals with 'eight techniques for hiding in the earth'.[88] They are techniques for invisibility and transformation to escape from danger. One of them shows how the body can protect itself by taking on the guise of an earthen mound, while its clothes are changed into vegetation on the mound: 'to other people it looks like a hill'.[89] This theme is actually an ancient one in Taoism and

86 Entry for K'ai-ch'eng 5/5/16 (19 June 840): Ono Katsutoshi, *Nittō guhō junrei gyōki no kenkyū*, vol. 2, Tokyo 1966, p. 461; cf. Edwin O. Reischauer, *Ennin's diary: the record of a pilgrimage to China in search of the Law*, New York 1955, p. 225. Compare similar references from other sources cited by Ono, p. 479, n. 39.

87 It can be traced back to the texts of the second century BC found in tomb no. 3 at Mawang tui 馬王堆: see Hsiao Teng-fu, *Tao-chiao yü mi-tsung*, pp. 227 ff., which discusses the place of this ritual procedure in Taoist and Buddhist traditions.

88 Isabelle Robinet, *La révélation du Shangqing dans l'histoire du taoïsme*, Paris 1984, vol. 2, pp. 141–4.

89 HY 1348, B.3b and 4a.

may well go back to times before what we now recognize as Taoism existed.[90] What we seem to have here is a basic, humble version of religious practices which had long before this been taken up into the transcendent systems of elite Taoism – a reminder, then, of how slow moving and conservative religious behaviour in Chinese society could be.

Liu Ch'ing-chen needs to hide from people his teacher calls 'demons'. We know who these demons are: they come from the government offices in Tai-chou, looking to arrest wanted men. Once again, it seems, the authorities are out to control the spread of unregistered clerics in the area of Wu-t'ai shan. Coming 'more than twenty years' after the T'ien-pao period, this suggests the sudden repressive policy towards Buddhism adopted by the reforming emperor Te-tsung in 779, who ended twenty years of kinder policies under the pious emperors Su-tsung and Tai-tsung.[91] One of his first acts, on 18 July 779, was to ban all applications to found monasteries or ordain monks.[92] Liu Ch'ing-chen and his friends, who say in the story that they freely gave up their secular occupation to follow an inspiring teacher, would scarcely have had the benefit of regular ordination certificates. They would be obvious targets for a government campaign.

So, through all the lurid images and wonders of this story there seem after all to emerge the shapes of knowable historical circumstances and events. It is no easier than story **13** to read as a historical document: finding any social or historical value in it requires a complicated act of decoding. But here, as in perhaps no other kind of literature in mediaeval China, there is at least a small opportunity to glimpse what went on in the minds of ordinary people in that remote time. There are certain signs of long-term continuity in ritual practice, but none at all of orthodoxy in religious discipline. The recognized state religions of Buddhism and Taoism seem to mean little in the lives of Liu Ch'ing-chen and his friends. Instead, their story suggests the perspective (as phrased by Raoul Birnbaum) 'of a common matrix of Chinese religions that is embedded deep in culture yet is continually reformulated, emerging in many guises'.[93]

90 Robinet, *La révélation*, p. 143. On techniques for invisibility and concealment mentioned in *Pao-p'u tzu*, see Hu Fu-ch'en, *Wei Chin shen-hsien Tao-chiao*, pp. 166–7.

91 Weinstein, *Buddhism under the T'ang*, pp. 57–9, 77–92.

92 *CTS* 12.321.

93 Birnbaum, 'Secret halls of the mountain lords: the caves of Wu-t'ai shan', p. 140.

4
The worshippers of Mount Hua

The mountain known as Hua-shan 華山 is one of the most remarkable objects in China. Modern travellers see it for the first time as they move west through southern Shensi province towards the city of Sian: it towers up to the south of the road and the railway line, with a group of sharp peaks and sheer cliffs standing out above the range of mountains behind them.

Mount Hua has been used through the ages as a place of religious retreat. It has also, from quite early in recorded history, been itself an object of sacrificial cult – indeed long before the imperial state set up its official cult of the Five Sacred Peaks, with this mountain as the so-called Western Peak.[1] In the fourth century BC the states of Ch'in and Chin, according to old inscriptions, 'disputed possession of the shrine' (爭其祠), and fortifications were put up to the east of the site.[2] Ch'in

1 On the early historical references, see Ku Chieh-kang, 'Ssu-yüeh yü wu-yüeh', in *Shih-lin tsa-chih ch'u-pien*, Peking 1963, pp. 42–4. For a more recent discussion of Mount Hua in this context, see Aat Vervoorn, 'Cultural strata of Hua Shan, the Holy Peak of the West', *Monumenta Serica* 39, 1990–1, 1–30, particularly 3–13.

2 'Hua-yüeh ming', cited in the sixth-century *Shui-ching chu* by Li Tao-yüan: see *Shui-ching chu shu* 19.1665. In T'ang times an inscription with this brief title was credited to Fu Hsüan 傅玄 (217–278): quotations in *I-wen lei-chü* 7.132, and (with variant title) *Ch'u-hsüeh chi* 5.101. Another such inscription, by the second-century calligrapher Chang Ch'ang 張昶, bears the title 'Hsi-yüeh Hua-shan t'ang-ch'üeh pei-ming' 西嶽華山堂闕碑銘; it was said to have been engraved in AD 205, the year before his death: see remarks by Chang Huai-kuan 張懷瓘 (*fl.* 713–741) in *Shu tuan* B.17b–18a. This piece gives a fuller account of the 'Ch'in and Chin' episode: 'When all the world was under one regime, the Son of Heaven controlled the rites. When feudal lords imposed their rule by force, powerful states took over the sacrifice. It is long since the town received the name Hua-yin ["northern slopes of Hua"], for thus it was recorded in the "Yü-kung" 禹貢 [chapter of *Shang shu*]. But it had a share in the territory of both Ch'in and Chin: on the western border of Chin it was called Yin-Chin 陰晉, on the eastern frontier of Ch'in it was called Ning-Ch'in 寧秦. As the township changed hands, so too did the rites. Both states used force in the struggle to present the sacrifice. The fortifications were strong, and their foundations still stand . . .' (*Ku-wen yüan* 18.6ab). Shih Che-ts'un points out, in *Shui-ching chu pei lu* 4.176, that the phrases cited in *Shui-ching*

Shih-huang included the mountain in the imperial sacrifices he set up in 221 BC; Han Wu-ti paid it homage in 110 BC; and when in 61 BC Han Hsüan-ti 宣帝 introduced regular sacrifices to the Five Peaks, he based the cult to Mount Hua at Hua-yin 華陰, below the mountain's northern slopes.[3]

The temple and its cult

Already in Former Han times there were temple structures here. Wu-ti 武帝 set up a complex of buildings, giving them titles dedicated to the spirits and immortals he supposed to inhabit the mountain. We have a short description by a man from a slightly later time – Huan T'an 桓譚 (*ca.* 43 BC–AD 28) – who visited the place in his youth and wrote a poetic rhapsody to inscribe on the temple walls. Setting the scene, he writes of the Palace of Assembled Spirits 集靈宮 at Hua-yin:

> The palace was below Mount Hua, erected by Emperor Wu. He wished to gather to him there the immortals Wang Ch'iao 王喬 and Ch'ih-sung 赤松, so he named its hall 'Immortal Lodging' 存仙. The main gate faced south towards the mountain, inscribed with the title 'Immortal Prospect Gate' 望仙門 . . .[4]

So those early temple buildings already stood at the mountain's northern foot. It is not clear what relation they bore to the site of the temple complex that now stands some 7 km north of the mountain and 2 km east of the county town Hua-yin, just south of the River Wei. Hsia Chen-ying, whose survey of the existing temple compound gives details of the late-imperial structures that remain on this site, reviews a number of theories on the date of its inauguration. He finds none of them historically convincing, and seeks surer guidance in the evidence of stratigraphy, which reveals bricks of Han date at 1m below the ground surface, and

chu form an intimate parallel with others ascribed elsewhere to Chang Ch'ang's inscription (cf. *Shui-ching chu shu* 19.1657 and 1662), although none of them appear in Chang's transmitted text. Possibly both quotations stem rather from the now lost inscription by Fu Hsüan. It was apparently in 332 BC that the town Yin-Chin passed from the hands of Wei 魏 into those of Ch'in, to become Ning-Ch'in: *Shih chi* 5.205. The site of this ancient town is still found to the east of the present temple compound: see Hsia Chen-ying, 'Hsi-yüeh Hua-shan ku-miao tiao-ch'a', *K'ao-ku-hsüeh chi-k'an* 5, 1987, 194.

3 *Shih chi* 28.1371–2; *Han shu* 6.190, 25B.1249; *Feng-su t'ung-i chiao-shih* (ed. Wu Shu-p'ing, Tientsin 1980) 10.367.

4 'Shan hsien fu' 山仙賦, quoted in *I-wen lei-chü* 78.1338. Cf. *Han shu* 28A.1543–4; *Feng-su t'ung-i chiao-shih* 10.367; *Shui-ching chu shu* 19.1657, quoting the Chang Ch'ang inscription. For another, only slightly later reference to these structures, see the stele inscription of 165 (introduced below, n. 15): *Han Yen-hsi Hsi-yüeh Hua-shan pei k'ao* 3.1b–2b.

in the discovery of a stone figure which he associates with the Han period.[5]

What does seem well established is that local officials of the Later Han carried out restoration and extensions here in the years following 161 and 178.[6] A century later, in 287, officials 'put spare labour to work building altar and temple, and planted cypress trees along each side of the avenue as far as the northern slopes'.[7] The cypress trees would remain a feature here for centuries to come, and aged specimens are still to be found near the site.[8] They possibly served a ritual function, defining a ceremonial avenue for communication between temple and mountain. In due course the Northern Wei emperors, as rulers of this part of northern China with their capital city at Ta-t'ung, 'set up a new temple' at Mount Hua in 435 and restored it again in 453, both times celebrating their work with stone inscriptions.[9] By the early sixth century Li Tao-yüan 酈道元, in his famous topographical work *Shui-ching chu*, could give these clear directions for visitors to the site:

There are often enquiring men who purposely climb Mount Hua to look at the traces [left by the legendary Chü-ling 巨靈 in shaping the mountain]. From the Lower Temple 下廟 they pass along the lines of cypress,[10] going south for 11 *li*, and turn east for 3 *li*, where they reach the Middle Shrine 中祠. Then out to the south-west for another 5 *li*, where they reach the Southern Shrine 南祠, known as the Shrine of the Northern Lord 北君祠. All who wish to climb the mountain offer prayers when they reach this place. And from here they make south up the valley for 7 *li*.[11]

5 Hsia Chen-ying, 'Hsi-yüeh Hua-shan ku-miao tiao-ch'a', pp. 204–5. It proves difficult to find reliable early authority for either of the dates reviewed (134 BC and AD 454): I cannot trace the former in either of the *T'ang histories* (where a citation is allegedly drawn), nor the latter in any source earlier than the doubtful document discussed below in n. 18.

6 For the reference to Wang Mang and a description of how buildings were restored and old inscriptions replaced from 161 on, see *Han Yen-hsi Hsi-yüeh Hua-shan pei k'ao* 3.1–3a. For the restorations of 178–180, which featured wall-paintings of rare treasures and strange monsters, see the inscriptions of those years transcribed in *Ku-wen yüan* 18.1a–5a.

7 Inscription of AD 304 quoted in *Shui-ching chu shu* 19.1663. Shih Che-ts'un casts doubt on the date T'ai-k'ang 太康 8 [287] and suspects a mistake for Yüan-k'ang 元康 8 [298]: *Shui-ching chu pei lu* 4.172.

8 Hsia Chen-ying, 'Hsi-yüeh ku-miao tiao-ch'a', pp. 200, 205.

9 *Wei shu* 108/1.2738 and 2739. For the inscriptions, dated 439 and 455, see *Pao-k'o ts'ung-pien* 10.33b–34a, citing *Chi-ku lu mu* by Ou-yang Fei 歐陽棐 (1047–1113). The former recorded, in summary: 'During the T'ai-yen period [435–] a new temple was set up and sacrifice was offered through Taoist priests, with supplication in spring and thanksgiving in autumn. When major events took place they were reported.'

10 *Ch'u-hsüeh chi* 5.99: 'At the foot of the mountain, setting out from the lines of cypress at the Mount Hua Temple . . .'

11 *Shui-ching chu shu* 4.313. Almost the same passage is quoted in *Ch'u-hsüeh chi* 5.99, from sources given as *Shu-cheng chi* 述征記 and *Hua-shan chi* 華山記.

The relationship between Northern Temple 北廟 (where nine ancient stelae still stood) and southern ('Shrine of the Northern Lord') would remain the same, complete with cypress trees, even in the topography of the *T'ai-p'ing huan-yü chi* in the 980s.[12]

By this time, too, our historical evidence takes on a new, anecdotal dimension. A passage in the official biography of Ta-hsi Wu 達希武 (504–570), a veteran general of the Northern Chou dynasty, begins:

When Wu was at T'ung-chou [from 564] there was a period of drought, and Kao-tsu [of the Northern Chou] commanded Wu to sacrifice to Mount Hua. The Temple of the Mount 嶽廟 had stood from olden times at the foot of the mountain and was the place where prayer and supplication normally took place. Wu said to his staff: 'I . . . should not remain at the place of normal sacrifice, as everyone else does. I must display my sincerity by climbing the summit, and there seek out the divine mystery.'[13]

This passage was written by a historian looking back from the early years of the T'ang dynasty. He makes it clear that the official Ta-hsi Wu, in deciding actually to climb the mountain to offer his sacrifice, first considered and decided against offering it in the usual place. Long before the T'ang period, then, as all these references show, the Temple of the Mount stood north of the mountain itself. Past it ran the government road which led from the capital Ch'ang-an to Lo-yang and the provinces of the empire beyond.[14] When we come to study the contacts between the god of this mountain and society at large in T'ang times we shall see how important this position was, with its access to the passing traffic of the whole empire.

The story of the temple buildings from the time of Han Wu-ti to the T'ang shows the cult activity itself taking different forms. For Wu-ti the point of interest was the supposed presence of spirits and immortal residents on the mountain. Later this changed. The famous inscription of AD 165 puts it clearly:

In the time of Chung-tsung [*i.e.*, Han Hsüan-ti, *r.* 73–49 BC] envoys were regularly sent bearing insignia of office to offer sacrifice there – each year one

12 *T'ai-p'ing huan-yü chi* 29.10a.

13 *Chou shu* 19.305–6. For the date of the T'ung-chou appointment, see *TCTC* 169.5241, under T'ien-chia 5/4.

14 According to a note in *T'ang hui-yao* 27.520, the government road ran past the north end of the temple until K'ai-yüan 12/11/10 [30 November 724], when Hsüan-tsung required the local prefect to erect, 'upon the thoroughfare to the south of the Temple of Mount Hua', the stone stele bearing his own imperial inscription, cited and discussed below (see n. 19). The note adds: 'The old road had been north of [the Temple of] the Mount, but because of this was moved to the south of [the Temple of] the Mount.' See Yen Keng-wang, *T'ang-tai chiao-t'ung t'u-k'ao*, Taipei 1985, vol. 1, p. 33 and map 2.

prayer and three sacrifices. But this was not kept up in later times. Under the fallen Hsin 新 dynasty the site gradually became a deserted ruin. To this day the traces of walls and signs of a fortified camp are still there. At the start of the Chien-wu period [AD 25] a sacrifice took place here, but the rites were subsequently dropped. Only the local prefect would go and pay sacrifice at the seasons of the year. There was always a response to prayers and requests in times of drought and storm. And for a hundred years from that time, whenever events have taken the emperor on a tour in the west, he has always offered sacrifice in passing.[15]

These changing styles well represent the pattern of worship under the emperors who ruled northern China, from Ch'in and Han through Wei and Chou to Sui and T'ang. The sacrifices to Mount Hua served now as an extension of the imperial state cult, now as a seasonal local observance, now as an institutional plea for help in times of natural disaster.[16]

For the T'ang K'ai-yüan period (713–741) we actually have a liturgical text giving the form of rites used in the annual worship of the Five Peaks – in the case of the Western Peak in the first month of autumn – with cantor (贊唱者), invoker (祝), presenters of the initial, secondary and final offerings (初獻亞獻終獻), and many other participants.[17] It is the picture of an established, impersonal state institution. But the emperor Hsüan-tsung himself, in whose name these 'K'ai-yüan rites' took place, presents a new and interesting case. He claimed a personal affinity with the mountain. The first public sign of this came in 713, when he conferred upon the god of Mount Hua the title Metal Heaven King 金天王.[18] Then, on a progress to the Eastern Capital Lo-yang in

15 The text, gathered from rubbings, is reproduced and studied in *Han Yen-hsi Hsi-yüeh Hua-shan pei*, Institute of Chinese Studies, Chinese University of Hong Kong, 1978. The history of this stele and the fate of its classic rubbings are traced by Shih Che-ts'un in *Shui-ching chu pei lu* 4.173–4; according to Ku Yen-wu, in *Chin-shih wen-tzu chi* 1.14b, the original stele was destroyed by the earthquake which devastated the region on 23 January 1556 (see *Ming shih* 18.243). A fragment of stone bearing some phrases from the inscription's opening passage was recovered in 1957: see Li Tzu-ch'un, '*Hsi-yüeh Hua-shan pei* mi-te ts'an-shih i p'ien', *Wen-wu ts'an-k'ao tzu-liao* 1957.5, 80–1; and Hsia Chen-ying, 'Hsi-Yüeh Hua-shan ku-miao tiao-ch'a', p. 204.

16 The rites created in 61 BC prescribed 'one prayer and three sacrifices' (一禱三祠) as the annual programme for all the sacred peaks but T'ai-shan: *Han shu* 25B.1249. For later references apart from those given above in notes 6, 7, 11, see also *San-kuo chih* 4.150 (for AD 264), *Wei shu* 7B.182 (497), *Chin-shih ts'ui-pien* 37.la ff. (567), *Sui shu* 7.140 (614), *CTS* 1.10 (619), *T'ang hui-yao* 22.427 (619).

17 *Ta T'ang K'ai-yüan li* 35.la–5a. This revision of the state ritual code was completed and approved in 732: see David McMullen, *State and scholars in T'ang China*, p. 134.

18 Hsüan-tsung conferred this title in September 713, soon after taking full power in July of that year: *CTS* 8.171 (wrongly giving '9th month' for '8th month'), 23.904; *T'ang hui-yao* 47.834; *Ts'e-fu yüan-kuei* 33.7a; *T'ang ta chao-ling chi* 74.418 (text of decree). A document described as a 'writ' (冊) conferring the title on the god is found in a twelfth-century source, *Hsi-yüeh Hua-shan chih* 西嶽華山誌 (preface 1184) by Wang

724, he stopped at the temple to unveil an inscription in his own name reflecting upon the mountain cult.[19] Here is part of his text:

From the Hsia to the Sui, through five royal dynasties and three thousand years, the sacrificial rites continued in succession, the old rules remained unchanged. Altar and temple were rebuilt from age to age, the single prayer with threefold sacrifice was offered each year without fail . . . With its care and protection high heaven brought fragrance to my glorious ancestors . . . We have commanded the prefectural general[20] to express our reverence at all seasons of the year. We have raised [Mount Hua] to the level and rank of king, we have given him the title of Metal Heaven. Why should this be? There may be a reason for it. When I was born, Jupiter foreshadowed *hsü* 戌 and the moon was at mid-Autumn.[21] I received the rich virtue of Shao-hao 少昊;[22] I coincided in the hour of my birth with Mount T'ai-hua.[23] So at all times, waking and sleeping, the Divine Peak has extended to me his divine communication. Before votive jade and silk have been set before him, deep insight has already laid open my undeclared

Ch'u-i 王處一, preserved in *Tao tsang*: HY 307. The writ is the last item in that work and ends, perhaps fragmentarily, with the unhistorical date 'T'ang Hsien-t'ien 3'. This is not, however, a T'ang document: 1. it incorporates a further title, Shun-sheng ti 順聖帝, conferred on the mount by a Sung emperor in 1011: see *Hsü tzu-chih t'ung-chien ch'ang-pien* 75.1722; 2. it observes none of the formal and stylistic conventions of imperial writs (冊文) as transmitted in *T'ang ta chao-ling chi* 1, 7, 8, 34, 37, 74.418, etc.; 3. most of its text is lifted from Hsüan-tsung's 724 inscription (and the same is true of the scrappy 'Imperial preface by T'ang Hsüan-tsung' which stands at the head of Wang's compilation). We can explain these features only by supposing that it is a fragment of some later piece patched together for a different purpose: broken off after the 'Hsien-t'ien' date, which we must suppose corrupted in transmission, it took on the superficial appearance of a T'ang document.

19 The original stele, said to be fifty feet high, was vandalized by rebels near the end of the T'ang, leaving only four readable characters: *Chin-shih ts'ui-pien* 75.18ab. What remains of it still stands in the temple compound – 3.1 m. long, 1.6 m. thick, 2.1 m. high: see Hsia Chen-ying, 'Hsi-yüeh Hua-shan ku-miao tiao-ch'a', p. 201. The text survives in literary tradition: see *T'ang wen ts'ui* 50.2a–3a, attributing the actual composition of this piece in the emperor's name to his distinguished scholar-minister Chang Yüeh 張說. There are variant dates: K'ai-yüan 10 [AD 722] in *CTS* 23.904; K'ai-yüan 11 [723] in *T'ang wen ts'ui* 50.3a; K'ai-yüan 12/11/4 [24 November 724] in *CTS* 8.187, *T'ang hui-yao* 27.520 and *Ts'e-fu yüan-kuei* 33.9b. I adopt the last because of its precise position in a chronology and because of independent evidence that the stele was displayed to the court on K'ai-yüan 13/5/16 [30 June 725]: *Ts'e-fu yüan-kuei* 24.13a, cf. *T'ang hui-yao* 27.520. The poems which Hsüan-tsung exchanged with three high ministers on this occasion are collected in *WYYH* 170.11ab.

20 'Prefectural general' 州將. For a note on this term of Han origin, denoting the official in charge of a prefecture, see *Feng-su t'ung-i chiao-shih*, p. 93, n. 2.

21 That is, the year was at *yu* 酉 and the month was the eighth. Both dates, in traditional China, bore an affinity with the West and with the element Metal. Hsüan-tsung had been born in the eighth month of the year *i-yu* [685].

22 The legendary son of the Yellow Emperor whose kingly quality derived from the virtue of metal and who bore the name Chin-t'ien-shih 金天氏. The post-Han mythology appears in *Shih-i chi*, attrib. Wang Chia 王嘉, 1.12–14.

23 Because it was the Western Peak.

intent; though my offerings of peppered rice[24] are but poor fare, great blessings have indeed gathered about me in due time . . .[25]

'In China,' wrote Chavannes, 'mountains are deities.'[26] And with this mountain deity Hsüan-tsung now claimed personal communion, a communion mediated visibly by offerings, invisibly through intuition. By the testimony of this inscription he stood in the temple as two figures, not one, for he belonged both with the long line of emperors who had sacrificed here on behalf of the human race, and also with the many individuals of his own age who came here for insights and assistance in living their own lives.[27]

An ancient tradition once credited a spirit from the vicinity of Mount Hua with knowing and predicting the imminent death of Ch'in Shih-huang in 210 BC.[28] In later centuries it was clear that the god of the mount had foreknowledge of other human destinies. Men came to his temple to learn their future. A pattern was evident already in the sixth century, with this anecdote of P'ei Chi 裴寂 (569–628):

In the Sui K'ai-huang reign [581–600] he became a Privy Guardsman of the Left. But the family was poor, and he had no means to build a career. He always made his way to the capital on foot.[29] Passing by the Mount Hua Temple he sacrificed and offered this prayer: 'Poor and wretched as I am, I make bold to present this heartfelt plea. If you possess divine power, examine my destiny. If I can expect wealth and honour, you must send me a lucky dream.' Then, with repeated bows, he left. And that night he dreamed that a white-haired old man said to him: 'Not until the age of thirty will you gain your ambition. In the end you will hold no less than the highest ministerial rank.'[30]

24 Read 椒糈: ritual offerings designed to attract divine beings, according to *Li sao* 離騷 and Wang I's 王逸 comment in *Wen-hsüan* 32.14a.

25 *T'ang wen ts'ui* 50.2b.

26 Chavannes, *Le T'ai chan*, p. 3.

27 This contrasts with his attitude to the imperial sacrifice at T'ai-shan in 725: 'In performing these acts now I do so entirely to seek blessings for the people and have no other private prayers to make' (*CTS* 23.898; *HTS* 14.352; Chavannes, *Le T'ai chan*, p. 224).

28 *Shih chi* 6.259; *Han shu* 27BA.1399–1400; *Hou Han shu* 30B.1078–9; *Lun heng chiao-shih* 22.921–2 ('Chi yao' 紀妖); *Sou-shen chi* 4.48; *Shui-ching chu shu* 19.1564–5; *Ch'u-hsüeh chi* 5.100.

29 Under the T'ang administration the Privy Guards 親衛, ranking officials staffing various corps of guards in the imperial palace, served tours of duty lasting one month. The number of tours was defined by the distance of their homes from the capital: *Ta T'ang liu-tien* 5.13b–14b; des Rotours, *Traité des fonctionnaires*, p. 105, n. 2, and p. 503, n. 3. P'ei Chi, on this analogy, would move regularly between capital and home.

30 *CTS* 57.2285.

A similar tale was told of the early T'ang hero Li Ching 李靖 (571–649).[31] While their career was yet unformed, the pattern went, such men addressed the god with offerings on their own behalf and with words in their own voice, as they sought to penetrate the mystery of their own future. And the response came to them personally, without other mediation, as a dream or a disembodied voice. T'ang literature is rich in anecdotes like these. But we have more direct and eloquent testimony from a scholar who passed the Temple of the Mount on his way to the capital in 806. Chia Sung 賈竦 takes us close to his experience there in a long poem, carved on stone and preserved at the temple . . .

> Travelling in the evening of the year,
> I enter the hall to worship at the precious throne.
> With libation of wine I penetrate to the divine spirit,
> Opening with words full of eagerness and ardour.
> His senior officers extend in dense array,
> Lances and halberds bristle dauntingly.
> . . . .
> No swallows or sparrows haunt the curved rafters,
> Snakes and lizards are quelled by the jade throne.
> Yet all around I seem to hear sounds,
> And dimly I have the sense of a personal encounter.
> . . . .
> I come now on my way to the Imperial Capital,
> Fortunate to fall in with this tradition from T'ao-t'ang 陶唐.[32]
> Straight and true, I know he will not play me false:
> I desire him to say which path I shall take.[33]

Chia follows the now classic pattern – offers his own libation, voices his own words, addresses a god perceived as 'straight and true', and half persuades himself that from the majestic figure surrounded by staff officers and armed guards there comes a whisper or flicker of direct response. He consciously aligns himself with the 'tradition from T'ao-t'ang' – a line of emperors which, to his eyes, reaches back to the beginning of history. And his poem lies in a single continuum with

31 By the eighth-century Liu Su 劉餗, *Sui T'ang chia-hua*, 1.5; *TPKC* 296.2361. The tale gave rise to a spurious inscription purporting to contain Li Ching's address to the god: see comments collected in *Chin-shih ts'ui-pien* 40.31b–34b; rubbing reproduced in *Pei-ching t'u-shu-kuan ts'ang Chung-kuo li-tai shih-k'o t'a-pen hui-pien*, Cheng-chou 1989–91, vol. 41, p. 101.

32 T'ao-t'ang: the mythical emperor Yao 堯, whose resignation of the throne to Shun 舜 was followed by sacrifices at the sacred mountains, Hua-shan in the eighth month. See *Shang shu*, 'Shun tien' 舜典 [3.9b].

33 *Yung-chou chin-shih chi* 5.6ab; *Chin-shih ts'ui-pien* 105.5b–6a.

Hsüan-tsung's inscription – both products of literary high culture, both reflecting on a divine authority as ancient and central as any known to history. Their deity belonged to a group established for centuries in the hierarchy of state cults, the Five Peaks and Four Streams 五嶽四瀆, who now enjoyed a canonical ritual status equal to the Three Lords 三公, highest ministers in the Confucian state.[34] His new kingly title, the first such conferred on a mountain, expressly linked him to a son of the Yellow Emperor.

In all this the ideas of role and perception are crucial. For scholars like Chia Sung found their orthodox and solemn vision threatened by rival perceptions and jostled by different forms of worship. With his privileged knowledge, it seems, the god of the mount was also felt to wield authority and judicial power. Custodian of men's books of destiny, he was also arbiter of human souls. His presence was felt in darkness and storm: 'At night, when the wind rises, I sense the god's coming', wrote Wang Chien 王建 (b. 766?).[35] And Li Shan-fu 李山甫 (*chin-shih* candidate between 860 and 873) echoed him a century later:

> Over the walls white paper cash flutters like snow,
> Before the hall gloomy cypress trees roar like thunder.
> I know you are darkly judging the affairs of men:
> Do not condemn the living in their dreams![36]

These lines betray a quite different level of cult activity at the temple. Votive paper cash in no way corresponds to the meat and alcohol of orthodox Confucian sacrifice. It belonged to the 'vulgar custom' (里俗) of prayer and communication with spirits of the dead by shamans and mediums. And at this temple it served in the trade of a large attendant population of female professionals.[37] Wang Chien's friend and exact contemporary Chang Chi 張籍 (766–*ca.* 830) describes them curtly:

> Below the Metal Heaven Temple, on the road to the Western Capital,
> Shamanesses (巫女) in hordes roam about like writhing smoke.

34 As laid down in *Li chi*, 'Wang chih' 王制 [12.16b]: the Five Peaks ranked with the Three Lords, the Four Streams with the feudal nobility (諸侯). Cf. *T'ang hui-yao* 22.427, 429; des Rotours, *Traité des fonctionnaires*, pp. 19–20.

35 'Hua-shan miao', *Wang Chien shih chi* 9.86. Although Wang Chien's date of graduation as *chin-shih* is given as 775 in certain Sung and Yüan sources, there is other evidence to suggest that the poet was born *ca.* 766 and that he held the examination competition in contempt. The 775 graduate seems to have been another Wang Chien. See Fu Hsüan-ts'ung, ed., *T'ang ts'ai-tzu chuan chiao-chien* 4.151–2.

36 'Yü hou kuo Hua-yüeh miao', in *Ch'üan T'ang shih* 643.7366.

37 See Chapter 3, p. 54, with n. 11. Hou Ching-lang cites some references to the use of paper cash in the Mount Hua cult: *Monnaies d'offrande et la notion de trésorerie dans la religion chinoise*, p. 9.

With handfuls of paper cash they greet passing travellers,
Urging them to pray for blessing and grace in the presence of
the god.[38]

Chia Sung, who had approached the temple with such fervour and unction, was appalled by these aggressive, business-hungry women. He made no secret of his feelings:

The deity himself is faithful and true,
With right judgement assessing loss and gain.
But alas, intelligence is beguiled,
'False words' let shamans and seers run wild.[39]
One follows another, custom sets in –
A wearisome bane to the local village folk,
A thorn in the flesh to travellers passing through.[40]

Wang Chien had seen them too, and sounds similarly shocked:

The shamanesses make travellers stop to buy spirit trays (神盤),[41]
They struggle to take their lutes into the temple to play.[42]

The tension between these different styles of worship and prayer speaks out most clearly in two short literary works of the period. First the confident voice of the statesman and poet Yüan Chen 元稹 (779–831):

The shamaness of Hua[43]

Here is a man, by the side of the god.
The temple is dim, the god is mute.
With the god so silent, what can I do?
If I wish to meet him, how can I manage it?
A shamaness asks me for what I have:

38 *Chang Chi shih chi*, Peking 1959, 6.79. For Chang Chi's date of birth I follow the conclusions in Fu Hsüan-ts'ung, ed., *T'ang ts'ai-tzu chuan chiao-chien* 5.556–7.

39 'False words': a phrase from Ode 183, 'Mien shui' 沔水: 'The false words of the people / Why does no one stop them?' For 'shamans and seers': see below, n. 50.

40 *Yung-chou chin-shih chi* 5.6ab; *Chin-shih ts'ui-pien* 105.5b.

41 For a description of the divination tray and its use by female mediums in modern Korea, see Laurel Kendall, *Shamans, housewives, and other restless spirits: women in Korean ritual life*, Honolulu 1985, p. 72.

42 *Wang Chien shih chi* 9.86.

43 *Yüan Chen chi* 25.300. The piece is dated *ching-hsü* 景戌 (= *ping-hsü* 丙戌), which corresponds to the year 806, when Yüan was aged 28 *sui*: see Hanabusa Hideki and Maegawa Yukio, *Gen Shin kenkyū*, Kyoto 1977, p. 18 and p. 316, no. 728. It was an eventful year in the poet's life. Spending the spring in preparations for the palace examination, he passed it on 4 May and a fortnight later received appointment as Remembrancer of the Left (左拾遺). But in October he was demoted to a junior post in Lo-yang, and within very few days suffered the loss of his mother, who died in Ch'ang-an. He retired from office to observe the period of ritual mourning. It is not clear at what point he might have sought oracular guidance at the Mount Hua Temple.

'Access to the god lies in my hands.
I can present you before him,
And the god will speak, not in his own person, but through my mouth.
If you wish to meet the god and gain personal safety,
Then buy my spirit-cash, purchase my wine!
I am equipped with a spirit tray:
If you present this tray the god will grant you safety.
If you do not, your way will be hard to go –
Your carriage wrecked on land, your boat tossed by waves!'
I sighed deep when I heard these words.
'How could the deity play false to the upright and just?
With you on the main road, who can travel to north or south?
Wantonly you claim to speak for the god, assume his strength.
Yes, assume his strength – yet the god does not come in meeting.
Travellers on the road cannot get through.
If we wish to meet the god we must get rid of shamanesses like you.
How could it be through you that the god lends his blessings?
You, shamaness! Have you really not heard?
Rather than work your charms in this place of mystery,
Far better work them in the kitchen!
If I must grovel before a shamaness like you,
I would prefer to drive on my way!
Shamaness! Look after yourself, now.
My heart has "prayers of my own".'[44]

With this we can compare the reflections of Ch'en An 陳黯, a provincial official of the mid-ninth century, who faced the same challenge in a short prose essay:[45]

As I came from east of the pass to attend the Rendering of Account to the Throne,[46] I passed by the Temple of Mount Hua, where a shamaness led me to offer up prayer. I removed my carriage roof and put my dress in order, took incense-burner and wine-cup, and moved forward to bow with lowered head. Then I withdrew in perfect silence.

The shamaness said: 'Traveller! Is this journey in pursuit of fame? Or office? Why do you perform the ritual acts of prayer without the words? When the god makes his presence felt, surely his answer will unfold?'

44 'Prayers of my own' 丘之禱. The reference is to *Lun-yü* 7/35. The words are spoken by Confucius ('Ch'iu' 丘) as, according to the traditional interpretation, he affirms the value of his own lifelong conduct in preference to prayers offered on his behalf.
45 Ch'en An, 'Pai yüeh yen' 拜嶽言, *T'ang wen ts'ui* 45.1b.
46 'Rendering of Account to the Throne' 隨計. The annual visit by delegates of prefectural government to report to the throne on their administrative and pastoral duties: see Dudbridge, *The tale of Li Wa*, p. 153.

Earnestly I replied: 'I have come here to worship because this mountain is chief among all others – like sages and worthies among men, like pine and orchid among plants and trees, like the Yellow River and the ocean among streams and rivers, like dragon and phoenix among fish and birds. Lofty and towering, it rams against the sky, props up the void. As an object of state ritual it is right that men should show it honour. When I worship here, my thoughts are engrossed with my own veneration. In framing words, I would be fearful about whether the god could hear me. Moreover, if the god's powers of vision and hearing really are high and deep, he will most certainly reward the good with blessings, the sinners with misfortune. And if my conduct measures up to his standards he will most surely look upon me accordingly. Could I pray to the god if I were deceiving him? What need[47] of shamans? If my words are well judged let them be a rebuke to those who speak folly!'

All three writers quoted here are troubled by the same tension. And although they dramatize it through external confrontations and dialogue with the shaman women, we sense that some kind of internal questioning and uncertainty is being played out. Ch'en An self-consciously gropes for an inner spirituality in which actual communication with the deity is neither sought nor required. In this he seems to differ from Yüan Chen and Chia Sung, whose poems both express a clear desire to have their wishes heard and responded to. Unlike them again, Ch'en puts his view defensively, using the shamaness to give (with incredulity and even shock) a more material view of traffic with the god – the view which by implication was expected of normal visitors here. And for all their defiant and hectoring tone, Chia Sung's and Yüan Chen's rebukes manage to imply that same background expectation. Clearly these women could not have plied their trade at the temple for two centuries or more if many customers had not been ready to engage them.[48]

Yet, interestingly, to have dealings with them could bring a stigma. When the provincial governor and ex-minister Yang Shou 楊收 stopped at the temple in 867, presented clothing and engaged shamanesses to pray for him there, the local magistrate denounced it as a fault.[49] The episode is instructive from both points of view: it shows up how ready a scholar-official could be to approach the god through professional mediums, but it also reveals a censorious orthodoxy that publicly rejected this kind of worship – the same orthodoxy that inspired the poems and prose we have just looked at. It is as though the scholar-elite professed one style of worship, but tended to practise another.

47 'Need'. For 心 read 必.

48 Nakamura Jihee 中村治兵衛 cites some further references to temple shamans in *Chūgoku no shāmanizumu no kenkyū*, Tokyo 1992, pp. 37–9.

49 *TCTC* 250.8118–9, for Hsien-t'ung 8/7/*chia-tzu* 甲子.

Now these professionals were, according to the classic definition in Hsü Shen's dictionary of AD 121, 'invokers (祝), women able to serve formless beings and cause spirits to descend by means of dancing'.[50] Once they had played an institutional role in state religion, but now they were marginal and ambiguous in the eyes of the ruling elite. Already in the second century Wang Fu 王符 had deplored their wide and damaging following among women, the social harm they caused with their exorcistic medicine,[51] while in those same times the calligrapher Chang Ch'ang 張昶 had celebrated their presence as one of the splendours of Mount Hua:

The cliffs and steeps are thick with magicians (方士) of all provinces of the land who have come from afar; the valleys and gorges overflow with the shamans (巫覡) who take charge of invocation in country districts. All are buoyant of purpose, joyful of mien, because certain that the road to the heavens can be surmounted, sure that flourishing good fortune can be brought down here below.[52]

These were the forerunners of the women milling about at the Mount Hua Temple, who now offered travellers professional access to the god of the mount through their techniques of invocation and inspired trance. To learn more about them we must look not to the prose essays and *shih* 詩 poetry which carried the values of the high culture and spoke in its rhetoric, but to the rich anecdotal literature of the eighth and ninth centuries. Two or three stories from that literature will show the scope of the women's work. They will also raise some of the characteristic questions of interpretation that form the main focus of this study.

A good century and a half after Hsüan-tsung's visit to the temple his experience was recalled in a story which now embroidered the god's title and the emperor's inscription with a face-to-face meeting between the two:

As his carriage reached Hua-yin the emperor saw the god of the mount come several *li* to greet him. He questioned his attendants, but none of them could see him. So he summoned shamanesses to ask where the god was. An old shamaness called Ah-ma-p'o 阿馬婆 was the only one to report: 'Third Son (*San-lang* 三郎) is just by the left side of the road, with vermilion hair-band and purple gown, welcoming Your Majesty.' The emperor looked round at him with a smile, then through the shamaness commanded the god to go back ahead of him. Reaching the temple, he saw the god, bearing arms, prostrate at the

50 *Shuo-wen chieh-tzu* 5A.11b. The definition of *hsi* 覡 which follows identifies this word as the male equivalent of *wu* 巫.

51 *Ch'ien-fu lun chien*, ed. Wang Chi-p'ei, Peking 1979, 'Fu-ch'ih' 浮侈, 3.125.

52 'Hsi-yüeh Hua-shan t'ang-ch'üeh pei-ming', in *Ku-wen yüan* 18.6b–7a; cf. *I-wen lei-chü* 7.133. On this inscription, see above, n. 2.

south-east of the courtyard, beneath a tall cypress tree. Once again he called Ah-ma-p'o to question her, and her reply matched what the emperor had seen. Showing greater ceremony and respect, the emperor told Ah-ma-p'o to convey his regards and turned about. He issued a decree ennobling [Mount Hua] as Metal Heaven King before all[53] the other sacred peaks. And in his own hand he composed a stele inscription as a mark of imperial favour and distinction. The stele is more than fifty feet high, more than ten feet wide, and four or five feet thick. No stele in the world compares with it.[54]

Apocryphal the story certainly is: its collapsed chronology of kingly title (713) and imperial stele (724) gives evidence enough of that. Yet it is not completely implausible in character. Little more than a dozen years after composing the Mount Hua inscription, Hsüan-tsung, deeply absorbed in Taoist techniques and commerce with spirits, promoted the ritual specialist Wang Yü 王嶼 to high office. Wang, we read, 'perpetually offered prayers, or burned paper cash, beseeching blessing and protection much like a shaman. On this account he enjoyed disproportionate grace and favour.'[55] An emperor with such religious tastes might well not disdain the visions of a shamaness. And for her part, in serving him as a seer and communicator with spirits, she practised one of the functions most widely attested for the shaman's trade since the Han.[56] Her 'village granny' name, too, finds many echoes in T'ang texts.[57]

Ah-ma-p'o's description of the god is interesting for its iconography. The 'white-haired old man' of P'ei Chi's dream is forgotten. The figure here wears the purple robe of senior ministers, befitting a dignitary of the first grade.[58] In this he resembles the city god of Hua-chou 滑州 in story **77** – 'a man little more than three feet tall and dressed in purple gown and vermilion hat' (compare the 'vermilion hair-band' of Mount Hua).[59] It is as though we are reading descriptions of the gods' own images as their temples presented them to public view – diminutive in scale and carefully decked in robes, like their counterparts in Chinese temples now.

The transcendent descends to the everyday. The numinous presence

53 'All'. For 詣 read 諸.

54 *K'ai T'ien ch'uan-hsin chi*, by Cheng Ch'i (d. 899), 3a; *TPKC* 283.2257–8. On the author, see *CTS* 179.4662–3; *HTS* 183.5384.

55 *CTS* 130.3617; *HTS* 109.4107; *TCTC* 214.6831.

56 Documentation on this subject is provided by J. J. M. de Groot, *The religious system of China*, vol. 6, Leiden 1910, pp. 1212–26.

57 Cf. Ho-p'o 何婆 and Ah-lai-p'o 阿來婆 in *Ch'ao-yeh ch'ien-tsai*, by Chang Cho, 3.63–4.

58 'Subsequently [to 656] purple was made the colour for robes of the Third Grade [and above]': *HTS* 24.529.

59 *TPKC* 302.2396. These colours represented the uniforms of high-ranking officials: cf. *Ch'ao-yeh ch'ien-tsai* 3.64, where 'vermilion and purple filled up the gate' of the shamaness Ah-lai-p'o.

whose intimacy Hsüan-tsung cherished in 724 here becomes a mute and compliant subordinate, grovelling before his imperial master and patronized by him.[60] Such, at the end of the T'ang, is the measure of a new, more public perception of the god which made itself felt over 150 years. He now has a vernacular name and a vernacular mythology. 'Third Son' is a style shared by gods far and wide through the Chinese tradition.[61] In relation to Mount Hua the name appears, as above, on the lips of shamans and in other informal contexts, directly identified with the god of the mount himself.[62] The traditions revealed in anecdote books of that period (and more richly in the *Kuang-i chi* than any other) show him as a rough, violent personality with a poorly disciplined domestic regime. Third Son is a judge of the dead and registrar of the living, though some way down the divine hierarchy.[63] His dangerous power can be ritually controlled only by discipline from the highest authority.[64] He has a predatory appetite for the wives of mortal men.[65] And his own domestic affairs are in disorder. An ill-treated bride causes divine warfare to scorch and blacken his mountain.[66] His other

60 Anecdotes of Hsüan-tsung's mediated contacts with the god of Mount Hua can be found elsewhere, as in the ninth-century *I-shih* 逸史, by Lu Chao 盧肇(?) (preface 847), as quoted in *Lei shuo* 27.8ab: 'When Ming-huang had concluded his personal ceremonies of offering to the Western Peak and was moving off to the east, a shaman spoke as he went out of the temple gate: "The Metal Heaven King [*for* 大 *read* 天], wearing armour and wielding a halberd, is walking along leading your carriage." The emperor ordered fine horses and strong knights to conduct him. The shaman expressed approval: "The Metal Heaven King offers humble thanks." After travelling some *li* the horses were sweating and unable to move on. In all there were ten changes of horses before they stopped at the palace. The shaman said: "The Metal Heaven King begs leave to return."'

61 Cf. *San-kuo chih* 48.1171–2, n. 2, in which P'ei Sung-chih's commentary cites *Chiang-piao chuan* 江表傳, by Yü P'u 虞溥; also *Ch'ing shih kao* 357.11329. In the case of T'ai-shan the style Third Son applies not to the god of the mount himself, but to one of his sons: see *Chiu Wu-tai shih* 44.605; *TPKC* 298.2373–4 (story **68**), 305.2418 (*Chi-i chi*).

62 Cf. *TPKC* 341.2705, citing *Ho-tung chi* 河東記: 'The Third Son mentioned by the shamaness was Metal Heaven [King].' Wei Chuang's 韋莊 famous but long-lost poem 'Ch'in-fu yin' 秦婦吟, finally recovered in manuscript from the Tun-huang cave library, contains a passage on the god of Mount Hua; in one manuscript (P 2700) the words 'Metal Heaven God' 金天神 are glossed 'Third Son, Mount Hua' 華岳三郎: see Lionel Giles, 'The lament of the lady of Ch'in', *T'oung Pao* 24, 1926, p. 333. For uses of this name in *Kuang-i chi*, see stories **70** and **75**.

63 Stories **76, 81**; also *Lu-i chi*, by Tu Kuang-t'ing (850–933), in *Tao tsang*: HY 591, 4.1a–3a, and *TPKC* 311.2464; *Tsuan-i chi* 纂異記, by Li Mei 李玫 (ninth century), in *TPKC* 350.2773–5. On the place of Mount Hua in the hierarchy of the underworld, see Sawada, *Jigokuhen*, pp. 56–8.

64 Stories **75, 76**.

65 Stories **69, 76**; also *Chi wen* 紀聞, by Niu Su 牛肅 (mid-eighth century), in *TPKC* 303.2399; *I shih* 逸史, in *TPKC* 378.3012; 'Yeh Ching-neng shih' 葉靜能詩, in *Tun-huang pien-wen chi hsin-shu*, ed. P'an Chung-kuei, [Taipei] 1983–1984, pp. 1104–6. This theme will be examined below, pp. 112 ff.

66 Story **70**.

womenfolk are wanton and promiscuous. He incurs large gambling debts and meets them by selling other-worldly appointments for paper cash.[67] It was apparently to the hero of this colourful and vulgar mythology, which we study below, that the shamanesses of Mount Hua offered access.

The temple cult did not depend entirely on the traffic of career-minded personnel that streamed past on the road to Ch'ang-an. Occasional references show other kinds of worshipper. An early story with an internal date of 660 mentions a man praying at Mount Hua for a son.[68] Another, period unknown, deals with the case of a graduate, Chang K'o-ch'in 張克勤, who bought a concubine:

> His family had for generations invoked the god of Mount Hua, and their prayers had met with some success. K'o-ch'in's mother now prayed to the god to grant him a son, and sure enough they produced a son . . . Five years later . . . his wife was also childless, his mother prayed again for a son, and the woman gave birth to one. But [the first son] Tsui-lien wasted away day by day. She appealed once more for the god's help. And that night the mother saw a man with gold seal on purple cord who said to her: 'Your son is destined to have few children. The previous son was sent by me. Now that the wife has borne another the first son is bound not to thrive. This is not within my power to help.' He departed, merely thanking her for the offerings he had enjoyed.[69]

It comes as no surprise to find Mount Hua engaged to meet this most universal of social needs. But both stories lack detail. Neither describes the manner of prayer or invocation; only the first mentions prayer at the mountain itself, only the second the dream appearance of the god with his seal of imperial office.

All these deficiencies are met in a rare circumstantial account of a village shamaness at work, and one which extends our knowledge of the Mount Hua cult in several directions.[70] We read of a woman, Hsüeh Erh-niang 薛二娘, who claims to serve the Great Metal Heaven King 金天大王. Significantly she works far away from his temple, five hundred miles to the east in Ch'u-chou 楚州 (modern Huai-an 淮安 in Kiangsu), where she exorcizes evil spirits. Some villagers call her in to treat their daughter for demon-inspired madness:

67 *Tsuan-i chi*, in *TPKC* 350.2774.

68 *Ming-pao shih-i* 冥報拾遺, by Lang Yü-ling 郎餘令 (comp. 661–663), in *Fa-yüan chu-lin* 72.833c–834a, and *TPKC* 388.3096. For authorship, see *Fa-yüan chu-lin* 100.1024b. This story gives an interesting account of a shamaness requiring the assistance of a scribe to take down her dictation of utterances by a dead man's invoked spirit.

69 *TPKC* 388.3094. No source is given.

70 *TPKC* 470.3872–3, citing an unknown source, *T'ung-yu chi* 通幽記. The story is translated in full, but with some inaccuracies, by de Groot, *The religious system of China*, vol. 6, pp. 1227–8.

> She set up an altar in a room and laid the patient within its bounds. Beside it she made a large fire pit, in which she brought an iron pot to red heat. The shamaness then performed music in full costume, inviting the god with her playing and dancing. In a moment the god descended, and all the onlookers bowed repeatedly. With libation of wine the shamaness conjured the god: 'Summon the demon here at once!' And with these words she stepped into the fire pit and sat down in it, quite unchanged in appearance. Some time went by. Then she rose with a flourish of her robes and played and danced, covering her head with the heated pot. At the end of the music she removed it, then sat on a folding chair and shrieked at the patient to tie herself up. The patient put her hands behind her back, just as if tied there, and was then ordered to identify herself. At first she wept and said nothing. The shamaness in a rage laid hold of a sword to behead her: the blade sliced through with a crack, yet the body was unhurt. Then the patient said: 'I give in!'

The girl identifies the possessing otter demon, writes out his stylish poem of farewell (though never before able to write), then falls asleep, released from her frenzy. But later she is found to be pregnant, and finally gives birth to three otters sired by the demon who possessed her. They run off to join their father in the lake.

The story's most obvious importance lies in its contribution to the history of shamanism and the exorcistic treatment of possession. But for us it also offers a single, fascinating hint at the wider reach of the Metal Heaven cult in T'ang China. This crucial example shows that even in remote provinces female shamans could invoke the Metal Heaven King as their control in exorcism and healing: they saw his divine authority as spreading, it seems, throughout the land. The god is available not merely for support of imperial interests and enlightenment of the devout elite, but for a far more catholic service to the rural population in its personal needs and crises. This should not be forgotten as we study the traditions of the relatively metropolitan cult at the Temple of the Mount.

The ethnographer de Groot did not scruple to use such tales of the supernatural to reconstruct the religious behaviour of ancient and mediaeval China. And here once again, approached with a particular focus of interest, they seem to offer something like a documentary value. But they cannot be used casually and without comment. Documentary value requires critical distance and discrimination – things which come only when the stories confront the evidence of other documents, within the Chinese historical tradition or beyond it, and establish a response or a tension with them. The case of Hsüan-tsung's roadside encounter with the god of Mount Hua was clear: flaws in chronology disqualify any claim to record actual events as they happened, yet we can adopt a style of reading which sees the story expressing public perceptions; and these respond to echoes of the same perceptions in other – and other kinds of – sources.

But the stories of Chang K'o-ch'in and Hsüeh Erh-niang call for different handling. No independent historical documents verify or challenge the events they report, and we can respond only by measuring their claims against other standards of plausibility. When Chang's mother prays to Mount Hua for offspring we recognize wider patterns – the fertility cult associated with Mount T'ai 泰山 in more modern times,[71] the many other deities who served this need in traditional China, the same practices followed in traditional societies throughout the world – and expand our view of the cult accordingly. But when the same lady dreams of a dialogue with the god we must respond differently: the event falls in what for us is subjective territory, its narration becomes for us once more the voice of a perception. This, first of all, was one way in which such literature chose to represent communication between spirits and humans. Secondarily, it perhaps also represents the way in which the devout public expected or hoped its answers from the gods to come. Ultimately it might even reflect the felt experience of actual subjects seeking help from the gods. In this way the story reveals norms of cult behaviour; its circumstantial details, without the authority of empirical observation, enrich our sense of those norms to the extent that other documents echo them too.

The shamaness Hsüeh Erh-niang finds echoes in the ethnography of traditional Chinese communities in modern times and, beyond that, in accounts of shamanistic behaviour throughout the world. Her fiery ordeals have their counterpart wherever shamans have been seen at work. And this recognition in turn opens up the story itself. With the words 'the god descended', informed readers will know that the presence of the god possesses the shamaness.[72] When she shrieks instructions at the patient, they will understand that the voice of the controlling deity, Metal Heaven King, is confronting the demon in possession of the patient, which will identify itself and write verses before it leaves. All this can be matched in the annals of possession in human society. But when the story in due course has the pregnant girl patient give birth to three otters sired by the exorcized otter demon, who then join their welcoming father in the lake, modern readers are caught without

71 Chavannes, *Le T'ai chan*, pp. 12–13, 29 ff.

72 Compare the short chapter on female shamans in de Groot, *The religious system of China*, vol. 6, pp. 1323–41; A. J. A. Elliott, *Chinese spirit-medium cults in Singapore*, London 1955, pp. 135–40; Jack M. Potter, 'Cantonese shamanism', in Arthur P. Wolf, ed., *Religion and ritual in Chinese society*, Stanford 1974, pp. 207–31.

preparation from ethnographic literature. Forced to switch to another mode of reading, we recognize once more a statement from the surrounding society of what it perceived to be happening.

Under close study these stories emerge as complex documents. They need analysis and interpretation before they will yield useful social insights.

A vernacular mythology

As readers we sometimes enter both the precincts of the temple and the private world of the worshippers there:

194 Wang Hsün, a metropolitan graduate from Hua-chou, once went into the Mount Hua Temple with Chao Wang-shu and some other companions. He entered the shrine of the Third Daughter and was so taken with her arch beauty that he succumbed to her baleful influence and instantly died. In panic and terror Chao called in a shamaness, brought in food and liquor and had music and dancing performed before the goddess.

At long last Wang came to life, glared angrily at Chao and said: 'I was perfectly comfortable up there! What did you make the shamaness play the lute and call me back for?'

Everyone laughed and asked him what had happened.

He said: 'To begin with the daughter hid me in her carriage. Just when we were getting on really nicely together we had Chao Wang-shu intervene with his lute music and bring the matter to the king's attention. He ordered a eunuch to search all the maids' carriages, and then all the daughters'. There was nothing for it: I was pushed out and fell to earth. And so I am alive again!'

This is perfect material to illustrate the simple analytical units we have called 'inner story and outer story'. The inner story is in this case what we hear about from Wang Hsün. It represents the private and subjective experience of an individual caught up in an adventure on the other side – here a meeting with a known goddess, elsewhere a visit to the underworld, a liaison with a fox, an encounter with a demon. Such were the picturesque other-worldly scenes which must have formed the main point of interest for their original raconteurs, collectors and casual readers.

But the outer story contemplates Wang Hsün through the eyes of his friends. It reveals to us that the god's promiscuous Third Daughter 三女 has her own shrine in the temple complex. The Chinese term is *tso* 座, which I take in the sense of *shen-tso* 神座, the image of a divine being set up for worship, and here evidently enclosed in a way that permits the visitor to 'enter' it.[73] The Third Daughter, like the god's lesser womenfolk, seems also to enjoy the privacy of a 'carriage' 車, which I take to be a litter in which their sacred images might ride in ceremonial procession.

Other anecdotal sources confirm that the Mount Hua Temple housed secondary cults to members of a mythical family dependent on the king. Lu Chao 盧肇, who held an army post at nearby T'ung-kuan 潼關 in the 850s, took responsibility for setting one up: visiting the mountain, he fell asleep there and dreamed of an old lady miserably cooking a supper of acorns. She was mother to the god of the mount, but this status brought her no benefit in the world of the shades: 'where sacrificial offerings are made we cannot partake of them unless we are called by name.' So Lu summoned the invoker at the temple (嶽廟祝) to set up a separate tablet (位) to the mother of the god.[74] We shall see below that the god's Three Consorts had their own cult centre, too.

Faced with Wang Hsün's collapse in the shrine, his concerned friends bring in a temple shamaness. The term *shen-wu* 神巫 (de Groot: 'animated wu') shows the woman subject to possession by a spirit, perhaps some member of the Metal Heaven King's staff who might convey the message. Like the women described above she makes ritual offerings of liquor and food, performs music and dance (鼓舞), and breaks into the spirit world by strumming the *p'i-p'a* 琵琶, a bass lute.[75] Already in the first century AD Wang Ch'ung 王充 (27–97?) had seen shamans playing on strings as they called down souls of the dead.[76] Now, in T'ang times, the *p'i-p'a* was the spirit-raiser's special instrument. Female diviners played

73 A parallel may make this clear. When Hsiao Ch'en 蕭琛 (d. 531) became prefect of Wu-hsing 吳興, he found the people there so committed to the cult of Hsiang Yü 項羽 that 'they had set up couch and curtains in the prefectural audience hall as a shrine to the god (神座), and public and private prayers were made there': see *Nan shih* 18.506 and *Liang shu* 26.397. For further reference to this Hsiang Yü cult, see below, Chapter 5, n. 19. These shrines may be compared with the 'soul shrine' 靈座 mentioned in story **280** and Chapter 6, p. 146.

74 *Yün-ch'i yu-i*, by Fan Shu (*fl.* 860–873), A.18–19 (repr. Peking 1959). For Lu Chao's own account of his career from 843 (*chin-shih* graduation) into the 860s, see the dedicatory memorial with his 'Hai-ch'ao fu' 海潮賦 in *T'ang wen ts'ui* 5.10a–11b.

75 Early specimens of this instrument, imported to Japan in the eighth century, remain at the Shōsōin at Nara: see Eta Harich-Schneider, *A history of Japanese music*, London 1973, pp. 65–6 and pl. 8a. Related instruments were used in Heian Japan by blind Buddhist exorcists, and the 'blind monk's lute' (*mōsō biwa* 盲僧琵琶) has remained marginally in ritual use until modern times. Like lute playing as such, the spirit medium's profession was traditionally reserved for blind people in Japan: the blind girls known as *itako* also use primitive stringed instruments as part of their professional equipment. See Carmen Blacker, *The catalpa bow, a study of shamanistic practices in Japan*, London 1975, pp. 147–8. Cf. de Groot, *Religious system of China*, vol. 6, p. 1333.

76 *Lun heng chiao-shih* 20.876 ('Lun ssu' 論死).

it as they revealed their inspired knowledge.[77] One of them gave the virtuoso performer K'ang K'un-lun 康崑崙 his first lessons in the instrument.[78] The poet Li Ho 李賀 (791–817) in a piece called 'Divine strings' described a spirit-raising séance, with libation of wine, smoking incense, paper cash, and

> Lover's wood, adorned with golden dancing phoenix,
> Brows knit, doubling each word with a plucked note.[79]

Scattered literary references like these sketch out a picture of the professional mediums who served visitors at the Temple of the Mount. But the dynamic of inner and outer stories has more to give: here is our first clear view of how the temple's divine population was perceived to interact with secular human society. The case of the Three Consorts provides a parallel view, and one that will give a background for studying the god's own interventions in human lives.

71 During the K'ai-yüan period one Li Shih of the Chao-chün line made a pious visit to the Mount Hua Temple. As he passed through the Hall of the Three Consorts he suddenly noticed that the goddesses were all living women, inviting him in behind their jewelled curtains. There they indulged in all the pleasures of love, and the Three Consorts took turns to join him in sexual union. When they had done, he emerged, and at the moment of leave-taking they said to Li: 'Every year, from the seventh to the twelfth day of the seventh month, the god of the mount has to render account in Heaven. When that date comes round we shall receive you. Don't be backward! Our meeting with you this time falls on those very dates. That is why we have been able to enjoy ourselves so thoroughly!'

For seven years after this, every time the date came round,[80] he would suddenly expire. His family would watch over him. It would be three days before he became conscious again, and he had this to tell:

> 'Sacred curtains – mats of tortoiseshell –
> Silken bedding – palliasse of muslin –
> Waving a full-moon fan to soothe the summer heat,
> Trailing muslin robes to release their fill of fragrance,
> With cool, pure jades at their waist
> And scented airs weaving a riot of colour,

77 *Ch'ao-yeh ch'ien-tsai* 3.63–4. Elsewhere, a tale of Po Hsing-chien 白行簡 (776–826) describes how a shamaness 'burned incense, played upon her lute and called down [her spirit]': *TPKC* 283.2258, from an unknown *Ling-i chi* 靈異記. The whole piece is translated by de Groot, *The religious system of China*, vol. 6, pp. 1113–14.

78 *Yüeh-fu tsa-lu*, by Tuan An-chieh (*fl.* 894–907), p. 51 (repr. in *Chung-kuo ku-tien hsi-ch'ü lun-chu chi-ch'eng*, vol. 1, Peking 1959).

79 *San-chia p'ing-chu Li Ch'ang-chi ko-shih*, Peking 1960, 4.151. 'Lover's wood', the fine-grained wood of a southern tree, represents the lute.

80 For 悟 read 晤.

They waited for my coming –
Tiny dimples lighting up all their smiles,
A charming bloom on each lovely face.
We talked of our long separation, and tears flowed down;
We spoke of our new delights, and love grew between us.

The Three Consorts were all mine. I am nobly endowed, and they liked me all the better for that: each had her fill of love's pleasure. When it was time to go home they all sobbed disconsolately, drawing out the hours of daylight, so sad were they to see me leave.'

Once returned to consciousness Li Shih's body was bathed in sweat, and he did not recover for more than ten days. A ritual specialist who saw him said: 'You have an evil emanation about you,' and wrote him a charm. From then on, even when he met the ladies, they were not able to come near him. Two of the consorts, one named Wang and one named Tu, told him off: 'This is really ungentlemanly! What are you wearing a charm for?' The youngest, named Hsiao, had a specially deep sense of their old love. She stared at him, shedding tears, and warned him to say nothing of this for three years: 'If you do, it will bring harm not just to you, but to me too.'

Li asked her about his official career. She said: 'You are to gain the *chin-shih* degree and finally become magistrate of a small county.' And all this came true.

The distinction between inner and outer stories imposes itself strongly here. While Li Shih enters through the Mount Hua Temple into a mythological world of erotic adventure, his family watch from the side as he suffers a total collapse for three days at a fixed point every summer. Only a ritual remedy can mediate between these two exclusive worlds.

The imperial cult of Mount Hua, whose presiding god stood in the eighth century among the ranks of the highest in heaven, enfolded a collection of subordinate figures whose history remains obscure and whose influence had a strictly local and individual impact. Whether they ever stood as distinct local deities we do not know, but here they are seen as members of a Chinese family group, all responding to the same seasonal rhythm. That at least is what we learn from the date that appears in this story – the annual visit of the King to render account in heaven on the seventh of the seventh month. Long before T'ang times this was an important date in the calendar of the Taoist church: one of the five *la* 臘 days on which the Five Emperors held an assembly in the celestial capital Hsüan-tu 玄都, and also one of the Three Great Festivals 三會 of the Taoist year.[81] Li Shih's story, though it stands outside the tradition of Taoist priestly literature, reveals that even society

81 Ch'en Kuo-fu, *Tao-tsang yüan-liu k'ao*, second ed., Peking 1963, pp. 317 (three festivals) and 319 (five *la*). Rolf A. Stein, 'Religious Taoism and popular religion from the second to seventh centuries', in H. Welch and A. Seidel, eds., *Facets of Taoism*, New York and London 1979, pp. 69 ff.

at large perceived the god of Mount Hua to play a part in these great celestial assemblies – a part patterned on the prefectural officers in China's provincial administration who took turns to report on their duties before the throne at the annual spring assembly.[82] And the consorts of Mount Hua, with their everyday Chinese surnames, would time their extramarital adventures to fit the King's ritual absence: a fine symbol of how cults at a lower, local level, with their own typical phenomena, could nestle within the very folds of a parent cult that operated on the level of emperors and heavenly courts. Their physical accommodation in the parent temple compound, with their own hall and jewelled curtains, carries the same message.

As he describes it, Li Shih's experience belongs within that ancient tradition of erotic meetings between goddesses and men which, from early origins in ritual and mythology, entered and became sanctioned in the mainstream of Chinese poetry. The writer seems to acknowledge this by making Li Shih render his experience in gorgeous poetic language absorbed from studying the *Wen hsüan*. So the experience is informed by cultural tradition and articulated in a traditional language. But it is none the less interesting for that. Though the inner story by itself might claim little more than a secondary literary status, the outer story locks it quite firmly into a known social situation.

About that social situation there is more to say. The pathological condition of men who fell under the erotic spell of a temple image was not, it seems, uncommon in mediaeval China. It recurs in *chih-kuai* literature early and late. And in an undated Taoist manual on haunting and its ritual remedies we read:

> The Moon Lady sprite 月娘精 has the appearance of a woman. It is lascivious and uncontrolled in sexual appetite. It often takes possession of the body of a clay image, so that when men chance to enter the temple and see a female image there, looking so upright and pure, they will fall in love with it. The creature that then, when evening falls, comes to sleep with the men and seduce them is a changed form of the demon attached to the clay image.[83]

The bewitching of Li Shih in some ways resembles this. Although its aetiology is differently presented, the remedy applied to cure it – charms written by a hired ritual specialist – reflects techniques like those elaborated later in the Taoist work. We could make almost exactly the same point about Wang Hsün's collapse above, though his ritual treatment took a different form.

82 See above, n. 46. The present story has *shang-chi* 上計.

83 *T'ai-ch'ing chin-ch'üeh yü-hua hsien-shu pa-chi shen-chang san-huang nei-pi wen*, in *Tao tsang*: HY 854, A.17b. Dr Judith M. Boltz drew my attention to this interesting text.

Tai Fu's book in general opens to our view a world of quite complex relationships between mortal men and spirit women, a subject explored below in Chapter 7. But here we are ready to ask more particular questions about the wives of Mount Hua. Where did these ladies with such conventional surnames come from? How did the god acquire them? Once again the *Kuang-i chi* leads us into a mythology which suggests historical answers. The story which follows is chosen for its richness and complexity: it will represent a larger literature based on the theme of stolen wives.

76 Ch'iu Chia-fu was from Fu-p'ing in the Metropolitan prefecture: his home was in Pu-t'ai village.

He set out for Lo-yang to be presented for the degree examination. As he left the capital he met a young man who looked like a prince and was lavishly provided with furs and horses, servants and followers. The man seemed very pleased to see Ch'iu and asked him where he was bound.

Ch'iu told him he was off to take an examination in the Eastern Capital.

The man said: 'I am going east too, and would like it if you came along with me!'

Ch'iu asked his name. He said it was Pai 白. But Ch'iu privately recalled that there was no nobleman at court called Pai, and felt some doubts about him.

After a day the man said to Ch'iu: 'Your donkey is not strong enough to keep up with me.' And Ch'iu was then borne along in a carriage at the rear. Several days later they came to the Mount Hua Temple, and the man told Ch'iu: 'I am not an ordinary human. The Monarch of Heaven has sent me to arraign spirits throughout the world. I must go into the temple now to hold an enquiry. It is your destiny to share a friendship with me. Since this is already so, can you go into the temple? When my business is done we shall make our way together to the Eastern Capital.'

Ch'iu had no choice but to follow him in through the gates of the temple. And he saw a blue-green canopy, like lowering clouds. All was laid out in full display, and in front [of the hall] there were benches. The nobleman took his seat at the desk, making Ch'iu sit in a bamboo backed chair.[84] The call then

84 This is one of the earliest references in Chinese literature to the frame chair 倚床. (A similar reference appears in story **267**.) It is clear that by the ninth century the backed chair known as *i-tzu* 掎子 (later 椅) was established in polite use, but for the eighth century literary references are harder to find. A reference appears on the reverse of a stone inscription from 797, 'Chi-tu miao Pei-hai t'an chi-ch'i pei' 濟瀆廟北海壇祭器碑: see *Chin-shih ts'ui-pien* 103.42a. For the ninth century there are several references by the pilgrim Ennin: see Ono, *Nittō guhō junrei gyōki no kenkyū*, vol. 1, pp. 275 (n., pp. 276–8) and 504; vol. 4, p. 104 (and cf. Reischauer, *Ennin's diary*, pp. 52, 111, 353); see also Donald Holzman, 'A propos de l'origine de la chaise en Chine', *T'oung Pao* 53, 1967, 289–90. Holzman also refers to the obscure Wang Fan-chih 王梵志 from an earlier period (Tun-huang MS. P-2718), but here mistakes the use of the character 椅, which in the context does not mean 'chair': see Chang Hsi-hou, ed., *Wang Fan-chih shih chiao-chi*, Peking 1983, 4.114; and Hsiang Ch'u, ed., *Wang Fan-chih shih chiao-chu*,

went up for the god of the mount. The god came, prostrating himself, to be berated several times over by the nobleman, who then ordered attendants to drag him out. All the gods of Kuan-chung province were summoned for roll-call and inspection. At the very end came the turn of the god of K'un-ming Pool, who was called up to the dais for a private word. Ch'iu Chia-fu was asked to move a little distance away and not be present at this discussion.

He went out into the tented enclosure at the rear of the hall and there heard sounds of pain and distress outside the tent. Pulling open the door he saw his own wife strung up by the hair from a tree in the courtyard. He gathered that she must have died, and grew sick at heart and deadly pale.

Quite soon the nobleman called him back, saw that Ch'iu looked bad and asked him why. Ch'iu told him the full truth. The man made him have another careful look, and when Ch'iu returned saying it was quite true the nobleman in great alarm said: 'Your wife is to me like my own wife: of course I must look after her!' And he issued a summons for the god of the mount.

The god came, and was asked why he had taken the wife of Ch'iu Chia-fu of Pu-t'ai village and had her tortured. The god knew nothing at all about it. But a man in a blue robe calling himself a judge spoke up from behind on his behalf: 'This was done on orders from authorities in Heaven. The report is now being written up for delivery.' The nobleman ordered the dossier to be brought to him and commanded his attendants to place seal and stamp upon it and, when they came before the Monarch of Heaven, to hold it out and bring the matter to the monarch's attention themselves. Then, turning to the god of the mount, he told him to let the wife go home.

To Ch'iu Chia-fu he said: 'You were planning to go to the Eastern Capital, but that is no longer possible now. You should go quickly back to Fu-p'ing' – he worked out the length of the journey on his fingers – 'but you would not arrive for four days and might well be too late, so I shall lend you some good horses. If you ever think of me in the future, burn some incense in a purified chamber, and I shall always come.'

After these words Ch'iu took his leave and departed. The divine servants had whipped up horses for him which appeared as he came out of the temple gates. Ch'iu mounted and made his way home.

His family broke suddenly into bitter weeping. Ch'iu Chia-fu went straight in, removed his wife's veil and watched for her breathing. In a short while she came to life. There was general rejoicing in the family, and the village elders congratulated them with jugs of wine. This went on for several days. Four or five days later Ch'iu's body, riding the donkey, returned in company with his slave. His family could not distinguish one Ch'iu from the other until the one inside came out, the one outside went in, they met and fused together. Then everyone knew that the first to return had been his soul.

A year or so later Ch'iu Chia-fu set out once again to be presented for examination in the Eastern Capital. As he came up to the Mount Hua Temple

Shanghai 1991, 4.473–4. C. P. FitzGerald, *Barbarian beds, the origin of the chair in China*, London 1965, offers no literary evidence for the T'ang.

it happened that one Ts'ui, of the Law Bureau in Teng-chou, had suddenly lost his wife. The sound of his mourning was so plaintive that Ch'iu deeply pitied him and went across in person to present his compliments. He told Ts'ui to stop weeping and promised to take care of things for him. Ts'ui was delighted.

Ch'iu Chia-fu burned incense in a purified chamber and turned his mind to the nobleman. Before long the nobleman appeared and, when they had enjoyed their moment of reunion, asked him what the matter was. [Then he said:] 'This was done by the god of the mount. She can indeed be kept among the living. And we shall obtain 200 strings of cash for you. Ask for the cash first, then take action.'

He proceeded to write out nine charms, saying: 'First burn three, and if she fails to recover burn six more. She will then return!' With these words he flew away.

Ch'iu Chia-fu told Ts'ui what the god had said. Ts'ui, not daring to do otherwise, first burned three of the charms. By evening she had still not recovered, so he burned the rest. And very soon she came to life.

Ts'ui asked his wife [about the experience. She said:] 'When we first went into the inn I suddenly saw a carriage of mica at the foot of the steps, with hundreds of tough soldiers, all bearing arms, formed up on either side. Word came that an emissary from the king was on his way to meet me, and suddenly I was going away with him. The king was delighted to see me. He was just about to make love when three men suddenly arrived. They said that the Grand Prime demanded to know why he had abducted a living man's wife. The god, in fear and panic, held out an official paper and said that heaven had matched me with him as his own wife – it was not a forced abduction; he therefore refused to send me back. A little while later five or six great spirits came into the king's courtyard wielding golden staves. All the staff ran off in fright, leaving just the spirits standing there under the tree, asking to have my life spared. Then the king had me led back here.'

It was only after this that Ch'iu Chia-fu knew that his nobleman was the Grand Prime. Thereafter the god would always come whenever Ch'iu turned his thoughts to him. It was very much due to the god's efforts that Ch'iu secured a succession of five or six prefectural appointments.

The reference to degree examinations held in the Eastern Capital Loyang gives this narrative a focus in historical time: they were set up in 764–765 and stopped in 776 or 777,[85] well within the *Kuang-i chi* timescale. Internally, the story falls into a number of distinct episodes, some of which have parallels elsewhere.

Let us begin with the personal drama of the man who finds his wife's soul suffering the torments of the newly dead in the Mount Hua Temple. Point for point this matches story **79**. Speed is essential in both. It is clear that husband and wife are present at the temple in different

85 Robert des Rotours, *Le traité des examens, traduit de la Nouvelle histoire des T'ang (chap. LXIV, LXV)*, Paris 1932, pp. 176–7 (n.), discussing *HTS* 44.1165; *Ts'e-fu yüan-kuei* 640.11ab; *T'ang chih-yen* 1.9; *T'ang hui-yao* 75.1368; *CTS* 11.276 and 190B.5031.

forms: she as a soul newly separated from her corruptible body, he as a man whose soul will now hurry back home in advance of his slower-travelling body. Both will recover their living integrity at home: she as a reviving corpse, he as a delayed fusion of body and soul.

In all this the god of Mount Hua plays an ambiguous role. Here, as often in T'ang literature, he wields official power over the human dead, though subject to higher authority. But in the episode with Ts'ui's wife that follows next he also feels free to take personal possession of a married woman who passes his way. Challenged to account for his act, he claims the pretext of legitimate union with the woman. This, then, would be a likely background to the Three Consorts 三夫人, with their subordinate shrine in the Mount Hua Temple complex: they were perceived to be women from the mortal world who fell by chance under the mountain's power.[86] Perhaps certain real women shared with Ts'ui's wife the experience of hysterical collapse in or near the temple, countered for some by ritual treatment followed by nightmare memories of the ghostly establishment inside. And possibly even the named Three Consorts themselves might be identified with once living women who had succumbed in this fashion when passing the temple.

Variant forms of the last episode – the tale of the stolen wife – recur in the *Kuang-i chi* and elsewhere in T'ang literature.[87] These stories possess many common features – abduction of a minor official's wife, with her simultaneous collapse and death in the mortal world; preparation for her union with a divine figure on a sacred peak; timely intervention of ritual discipline through charms or intercession provided by an obliging specialist; ultimate revival of the wife. In all but one case the god of Mount Hua is the abductor, and in all but two T'ai-i 太一, the Grand Prime, is the source of divine discipline. In four cases the episode takes place at the Mount Hua Temple, and in two the ritual specialist is Hsüan-tsung's Taoist adviser Yeh Ching-neng 葉靜能.[88] Just

86 This is explicit in the Tun-huang MS. S-6836, where the god of the mount claims legitimate union with a woman he needs to become his Third Consort. See P'an Chung-kuei, ed., *Tun-huang pien-wen chi hsin-shu*, p. 1104. Story **75** describes wedding preparations for the god's Third Bride. But we should note that in story **70** his Third Bride is identified as a daughter of the dragons of the Northern Ocean.

87 Cf. stories **68** and **69**; also *TPKC* 303.2399 (*Chi wen*) and 378.3012 (*I shih*); *Tun-huang pien-wen chi hsin-shu*, pp. 1104–6 (S-6836). See Ch'ien Chung-shu, *Kuan-chui pien*, p. 796, who also draws attention to *TPKC* 352.2787–8 (*Chü-t'an lu*), a related version, but different in many details. A comparable 'stolen wife' episode is presented from the heavenly authority's point of view in the twelfth-century Taoist scripture *Tzu-t'ung ti-chün hua-shu* 2.10b–11a, translated and discussed by Terry Kleeman, *A god's own tale: the Book of Transformations of Wenchang, the Divine Lord of Zitong*, Albany 1994, pp. 164–5.

88 *TPKC* 378.3012; *Tun-huang pien-wen chi hsin-shu*, pp. 1104–6. For Yeh Ching-neng see also stories **72** and **198**.

one case involves Buddhist powers. Nearly all forms of the story show talismanic charms at work, and the women's dreamlike memories express clearly for us just how the public perceived them to work: each one, when burned, summons a spirit to perform an assigned task with high heavenly authority.

The standing of T'ai-i as agent of heaven needs some historical comment. Through Chinese history this archaic title had variously stood for primordial cosmic principle, for legendary object of worship by ancient kings, for supreme god of the universe (in the state cult promulgated by Han Wu-ti), for god of the North Star or god of the planet Jupiter. By T'ang times T'ai-i was a star god occupying one of the heavenly Nine Mansions 九宮.[89] The diviners and astrologers who practised this branch of learning offered many, sometimes contradictory, systems of theology. But the T'ang court in the ninth century endorsed a formulation which illuminates the figure we meet here in story **76**, in particular his mysterious surname White (*Pai* 白):

> First mansion: the god is T'ai-i 太一, the star is T'ien-p'eng 天蓬, the trigram is *k'an* 坎, the element is water, the directional colour is white.[90]

In 744–745 Hsüan-tsung had set up altars for seasonal sacrifice to the gods of the Nine Mansions, with T'ai-i at their head. These altars stood half a mile outside the Ch'un-ming Gate 春明門, on the north side of the government road running east from the capital. Their rites were secondary only to those of the Supreme Monarch of Heaven.[91] But in 758, under Su-tsung, T'ai-i gained a special sacrificial altar east of the main Altar of Heaven, which in turn stood south of the city.[92] His high place in the imperially constructed heaven of the mid-eighth century is clear enough. But in this story we see his corresponding place in the functional heaven known to lay society: serving as direct lieutenant to the Monarch of Heaven 天帝, he here sets out on a mission from his base just outside Ch'ang-an.

That now brings us to the opening sequence of this story, which raises the interesting question of territory and jurisdiction. Ch'iu Chia-fu meets his divine companion on the road that will lead them past the Mount Hua Temple towards Lo-yang. The sequence echoes, but antithetically, the same opening in story **81**, where a candidate leaves Lo-yang for an examination in Ch'ang-an: road and mission are the same,

89 All these functions are critically examined in Ch'ien Pao-tsung, 'T'ai-i k'ao', *Yen-ching hsüeh-pao* 12, 1932, 2449–78.

90 *CTS* 24.932.

91 *CTS* 24.929; *Ta-T'ang chiao-ssu lu* 6.1a–4a. Cf. Chapter 3, n. 6.

92 *CTS* 10.252; *TCTC* 220.7056.

but their direction reversed. In story **81** the noble young traveller turns out to be a son of the god of Mount Hua; here he is the arm of divine discipline falling upon that god from above. The scenes which follow in each case are again similar but antithetical – all courtroom sessions with judge presiding and prisoners arraigned, though there the god of the mount sits in judgement, while here he kneels as prisoner. Either way the temple's territorial importance is clear. In this story its other-worldly jurisdiction expressly covers the province 'Within the Pass' (Kuan-nei 關內), including the metropolis itself: hence the presence of the god of K'un-ming Pool 昆明池, an artificial lake to the west of Ch'ang-an.[93] Like Ch'iu Chia-fu's home in Fu-p'ing it was under the Metropolitan prefecture.

From other stories we know that Mount Hua's powers did not extend eastward beyond the strategic barrier defined by the T'ung Pass 潼關, where a form of border-post seems to have been in place in the spirit world.[94] In story **70** the god lies there in ambush with five hundred men, hoping to intercept an imperial guardsman before he can move to safety beyond the pass – a feat which the guardsman achieves by travelling in the emperor's drum-carriage ('spirits most dread the drum').[95] And when in story **68** the wife of Administrator Lu recovers from her collapse in the Eastern Capital Lo-yang, she reports being abducted, not by Mount Hua, but by the Third Son of Mount T'ai: so beyond the T'ung Pass jurisdiction and territorial control clearly lie in other hands. According to this anecdotal mythology the most immediate danger to women lies in the precincts of the parent temple, where four of the Mount Hua stories take place. One of them even ends with the comment: 'From this they knew that spirit temples should not be entered by women.'[96] But in story **69** an abduction by Mount Hua interestingly takes place in Ho-tung 河東 (now Yung-chi 永濟) county, in the extreme south-west corner of modern Shansi province. This place, though not physically distant from the Mount Hua Temple, actually lay on the far side of the Yellow River, which throughout Chinese history has defined a boundary here in human geography. But it seems that

93 First built by the Han emperor Wu-ti in 120 BC, it had been dry since the end of the fourth century and was soon to be restored in 797: *Han shu* 6.177, 24B.1165; *Ch'ang-an chih* (preface 1076), 6.6a; *T'ang liang-ching ch'eng-fang k'ao* 2.1b; *San-fu huang-t'u* 4.3a–4b.

94 Compare story **108**, in which the ghost of a man's wife hoping to pass through is held up for some days by the spirits' border control at T'ung-kuan. She passes this barrier only by joining her husband's living cousin as he travels through to take the examination.

95 Story **70**. (Delete 車, with Sun Ch'ien.)

96 *TPKC* 378.3012 (*I shih*).

the physical barrier of the river was perceived to deter the predatory god of Mount Hua less than the bureaucratic controls defining his territory at T'ung Pass.[97]

This talk of territory, boundaries and jurisdiction leads conveniently to our summing up. The discussion has grown out of an anecdotal literature characterized here as 'a vernacular mythology' of Mount Hua. That term describes, not the language of the various notebook entries, but rather their status vis-à-vis an official mythology ordained by the imperial state and publicly enshrined in works of formal literature. By contrast the informal notebooks collect reports of experiences perceived by a wider society, reflecting different constraints and betraying seriously different ritual practices. We have noted how the reports echo and duplicate one another, showing formulaic characteristics we would elsewhere associate with folklore. There is no point in trying to pin down this literature of hearsay as, in whatever sense, a body of empirical documentation. Any underlying pattern of actual human or social experience – collapses, exorcisms, visions, canonizations – can only remain a matter for inference and hypothesis. More safely attested is the infrastructure of the spirit world implied throughout this group of stories. It enables us to see the T'ang cult of Mount Hua in a perspective of some complexity.

The subject of this cult, an image in a large, ancient temple compound at the foot of a great mountain, exerted his influence on the life of China at several different levels. The temple walls enclosed a shared ritual space in which distinct forms of cult activity went on in parallel, but independently. To some extent we can separate them out. The imperial cult offered alcohol and sacrificial animals at prescribed seasons of the year. But one emperor actually found a personal patron in the mountain that presided at his birth. Individual scholars brought their own sacrifices before the god and sought personal messages from him. Some prayed for sons. Many paid shamanesses to accept the divine presence into their own bodies. Others worshipped and entered into imagined relations with the god's womenfolk. All this activity took place in the temple precincts. But the god's influence was believed, and perhaps felt, to extend throughout the region around the capital Ch'ang-an, arraigning the dead and preying upon the living in the fertile plain of the River Wei, where the empire's main communication artery ran.

Yet even the compact, internally consistent vernacular mythology which reveals the god's menacing presence in those lands 'within the pass'

97 For an example of spirit territory defined by a point on the Yellow River, see story **73**, discussed below in Chapter 5, with n. 58.

fails to give the full picture. An awkward, ragged end is left by the story of Hsüeh Erh-niang, the village exorcist who served him in Ch'u-chou, hundreds of miles outside his home territory. Although that single document offers no more than a hint of further complexities, it does stand clearly outside the tidy systems presented in other sources, formal and informal. Here is one more reminder of the vast, slow-moving and barely visible mass of rural shamanistic practice flowing through Chinese history. It brings a warning that the written record takes us only part of the way in understanding past and present society: outside its narrow bounds runs a different writ.

5
Yü-ch'ih Chiung at An-yang

The suicide of Yü-ch'ih Chiung 尉遲迥 at the citadel of Yeh 鄴 in 580 was a turning point in the history of sixth-century China. For sixty-eight days he had offered the most convincing loyalist challenge to Yang Chien's 楊堅 assumption of power from the ruling house of Northern Chou. Then, within six months of his defeat and death, all further resistance dissolved: Yang took the imperial title and proclaimed a new dynasty.[1] These events ushered in the unified empire of Sui and in a sense created the setting for China's political fortunes in centuries to come. But the early T'ang government, taking power in turn from the Sui, read them differently. The first T'ang emperor saw fit to recognize Yü-ch'ih Chiung's loyal stand against the Yangs whom he had himself replaced: he approved a descendant's request to have the old general reburied, and honoured him with an imperial grant of silk.[2]

All this forms merely the background to the events we shall examine here. For in 737 Yü-ch'ih Chiung's ghost made its presence felt in the prefectural city An-yang 安陽, and the prefect of the day appeased the ghost with temple and sacrificial cult. In itself an unremarkable episode – such things took place, both earlier and later, many times in all parts of China. But the events at An-yang offer a special kind of interest. It happens that we can study them from several early documents – documents that differ radically in character. We have what is for this period probably a unique chance to view an episode of local religious experience from several distinct viewpoints. And we can assess, by comparing them together, the value and authority of different kinds of evidence – historical, epigraphical and anecdotal – for the study of this case, and beyond it of other local religious phenomena in mediaeval China. What

1 See accounts by Peter A. Boodberg, 'Marginalia to the histories of the northern dynasties', *Harvard Journal of Asiatic Studies* 4, 1939, 260 ff.; and Arthur F. Wright in *The Cambridge history of China*, vol. 3, Cambridge 1979, pp. 57–60.

2 *Pei shih* 62.2214; *Chou shu* 21.352.

follows, then, will be the story of a haunting resolved, but also, more basically, an essay in source criticism.

Sixth-century background

The ancient fortified city of Yeh stood on what is now the southern border of Hopei province, between the modern cities of Han-tan and An-yang.[3] Founded, according to tradition, by Lord Huan of Ch'i 齊桓公, it served in Warring States times as a border town in Wei 魏. But for the Han and for several succeeding northern dynasties it was a centre of regional administration.[4] It was one of the 'Five capitals' of Wei in the Three Kingdoms period and served as dynastic capital under the Later Chao (335–351) and the Former Yen (357–370).[5] In 398, under the Northern Wei, it became seat of the newly formed Hsiang-chou 相州 prefecture, in 534 capital of the newly seceded Eastern Wei dynasty.[6] For the Northern Ch'i it was again dynastic capital (550), for the Northern Chou again seat of Hsiang-chou (577).[7] It was to this historic city, with its mixed ethnic population, that the veteran general Yü-ch'ih Chiung was appointed in 579 as regional commander (*tsung-kuan* 總管).[8]

Rapidly changing events at the Chou court forced Yang Chien into a sudden bid for power in the summer of 580. Among other dispositions he summoned Yü-ch'ih Chiung to the capital, hoping to neutralize a man he perceived as a threat, and replaced him as regional commander of Hsiang-chou with Wei Hsiao-k'uan 韋孝寬. This was the moment for Yü-ch'ih Chiung to declare his open defiance. He refused to yield the command and led his troops in a rising designed to save the Chou house from its usurping chancellor. The military campaign lasted until early September. By then Yü-ch'ih Chiung had fallen back to his base at Yeh, there to be defeated by forces loyal to Yang Chien under the command of Wei Hsiao-k'uan.[9] He died in these circumstances:

3 There were two adjacent fortified settlements, 'Northern' and 'Southern'. Their sites lie 18.5 km south-west of the present Lin-chang 臨漳 county town and 15 km north of An-yang, straddling the River Chang 漳. For surveys of the history of Yeh and the present state of its archaeological investigation, see Miyakawa Hisayuki, *Rikuchō shi kenkyū: seiji shakai hen*, Tokyo 1956, pp. 537–46, and Shing Müller, *Yezhongji: eine Quelle zur materiellen Kultur in der Stadt Ye im 4. Jahrhundert*, Münchener Ostasiatische Studien 65, Stuttgart 1993, pp. 23–7. A map showing the relation of the site to modern An-yang appears in *Chung-yüan wen-wu* 中原文物 42, 1987.4, p. 1.

4 The sequence is sketched out, with some inaccuracies, in *Yüan-ho chün-hsien t'u-chih* 16.451–2. See also *T'ai-p'ing huan-yü chi* 55.1a ff. and 6b.

5 *TCTC* 95.3002; 99.3118; 100.3166; 102.3236.

6 *Wei shu* 106A.2456; 12.298.

7 *TCTC* 163.5045; *Chou shu* 6.100.

8 *Chou shu* 21.351; *Pei shih* 62.2211; *TCTC* 173.5392.

9 *Chou shu* 21.351–2; *Pei shih* 62.2211–3; *TCTC* 174.5407–25.

Ts'ui Hung-tu's 崔弘度 younger sister had previously become principal wife to [Yü-ch'ih] Chiung's son. When the fortifications of Yeh were breached and Chiung, hard pressed, climbed the tower, Hung-tu went straight up the ramp in pursuit. Chiung drew his bow to shoot him, but Hung-tu took off his helmet and said to Chiung: 'We are quite well acquainted, are we not? Each of us today is engaged on the nation's behalf: we cannot heed personal interests. But in consideration of our family relationship I have taken care to keep the soldier rabble in check and not let them attack and dishonour you. With things standing as they do, you must take the quick way out yourself. What are you waiting for?' Chiung flung his bow to the ground and cursed the Chancellor of the Left [Yang Chien]. When he had cursed his fill he killed himself. Hung-tu turned to his younger brother Hung-sheng and said: 'You take Chiung's head.' And Hung-sheng beheaded him. [Wei] Hsiao-k'uan massacred all fighting men within the small fortifications.[10]

Yü-ch'ih Chiung's sons were put to death, his youthful grandsons spared. Also spared was Ch'in 勤, the son of his younger brother Kang 綱.[11] The surviving troops suffered execution within the month.[12]

A more far-reaching consequence for local affairs now followed:

Yang Chien . . . then burned down the walled city of Yeh and moved the inhabitants 45 *li* to the south. He made the city of An-yang administrative centre of Hsiang-chou and also of Yeh county. Early in the reign of [Sui] Yang-ti the county administration of Yeh was set up in the Ta-tz'u Monastery 大慈寺 of the old Yeh metropolis. Not until Chen-kuan 貞觀 8 [634] were the small fortifications of the present county town erected.[13]

This marked the end of Yeh as a seat of local power. An-yang, fourteen miles to the south, would remain the prefectural city of Hsiang-chou throughout the T'ang and beyond.[14]

Certain features of this story will stand out in the later discussion. Yü-ch'ih Chiung died by his own hand. His head was removed and taken, according to one source, to the capital at Lo-yang.[15] His close followers were massacred at the site of his defeat; members of his family were

10 *TCTC* 174.5425. Shing Müller, in a personal note on the site of Yü-ch'ih Chiung's death and the 'small fortifications' of Yeh, kindly drew attention to two possibly early references quoted by Ku Yen-wu 顧炎武 in *Li-tai chai-ching chi* 歷代宅京記, Peking 1984, 12.185 and 187. This topic deserves further research.

11 According to *Pei shih* 62.2213–6 the sons of Chiung were I 誼, K'uan 寬, Shun 順, Tun 惇, Yu 祐; those of Kang were Yün 運, An 安, Ch'in 勤, Ching 敬. In *Yüan-ho hsing tsuan* 8.10b the sons of Kang appear as Yün-an 運安 and Yün-an 允安; Ch'i-fu 耆福, who petitioned T'ang Kao-tsu for permission to rebury his great-uncle in the early seventh century, was the son of the latter: cf. *Chou shu* 21.352; *Pei shih* 62.2214.

12 *Chou shu* 21.352.

13 *CTS* 39.1492; cf. *Sui shu* 30.847.

14 *Yüan-ho chün-hsien t'u-chih* 16.452; *CTS* 39.1491–2; *T'ai-p'ing huan-yü chi* 55.1a.

15 *Sui shu* 1.4.

pursued and captured. The entire episode took place at the ancient city Yeh, which was then destroyed and abandoned. An-yang became the seat of prefectural government.

Dynastic history

The career of Chang Chia-yu 張嘉祐 unfolded in the late K'ai-yüan period and ended with his death in 741.[16] His short official biography transmitted in the *Chiu T'ang shu* picks out a single local episode for attention:

> In the twenty-fifth year [737] he became prefect of Hsiang-chou. Since the beginning of K'ai-yüan ten or more Hsiang-chou prefects had died or suffered demotion. Chia-yu learned from his enquiries that Yü-ch'ih Chiung had been regional commander of Hsiang-chou at the end of the Chou and had lost his life in the national emergency. So he set up a memorial temple to the spirit as a way to seek its blessing. After three annual assessments his appointment was changed to General of the Left in the Chin-wu 金吾 guards. Wu Ching 吳兢 became prefect of Yeh-chün 鄴郡 after him[17] and further invested the spirit with ceremonial robes. From then on prefects suffered no more troubles.

To this biographer, it seems, the problem in Hsiang-chou was simply a matter of survival for the incumbent officials. Prefects died; local wisdom placed responsibility with the martyred patriot; Chang Chia-yu and his successor appeased the spirit with a sacrificial cult. We must understand 'memorial temple' (*shen-tz'u* 神祠) as an individually dedicated place of worship used for seasonal sacrifice. There is no sign that relics or remains of the martyr played a part in the cult, and 'shrine' would be too narrow a rendering.

The biographer glosses over a number of questions that closer study soon brings to the surface. He silently accepts the implication that the martyr's spirit wielded power over incumbent prefects. But what, for instance, was the relationship between this public tribute to Yü-ch'ih Chiung and the imperially sanctioned honouring of his remains in the early seventh century? If the loyal martyr had received family burial and imperial silk more than a century before, what now lay behind these new troubles? The biographer mentions the death and demotion of

16 *CTS* 99.3093; *HTS* 127.4449; tomb inscription by Liu Pi – see below, n. 20.

17 According to *CTS* 102.3182, Wu Ching (670–749) began at Hsiang-chou as chief administrator (*ch'ang-shih* 長史) and became prefect of the place, renamed Yeh-chün, *ca.* 742. Earlier in his career he had served in the bureau of historiography and composed a series of histories of the northern dynasties, including the Chou: see Denis Twitchett, *The writing of official history under the T'ang*, Cambridge 1992, p. 65, n. 4. He would inevitably have been familiar with the life and death of Yü-ch'ih Chiung.

certain prefects holding office in Hsiang-chou. But Chang Chia-yu himself certainly lived long enough to serve out his term and move on to a new job in the capital (though he did die there almost at once). To that extent the problem should have been solved. Yet the new prefect Wu Ching had to enhance the cult figure's status even more before the 'troubles' (*huan* 患) would come to an end. If something more than prefect mortality and demotion was involved the biography gives no clue to it. Nor does it deal in any way with the territorial distance between Yeh, where the martyr died, and An-yang, where the prefectural centre now lay.

In the *Hsin T'ang shu* Sung Ch'i 宋祁 (998–1061) echoes this same passage, but with a few key phrases revises its entire scheme of motivation:

> Late in K'ai-yüan he became prefect of Hsiang-chou. Many previous incumbents had died in office there, and the people were stricken with fear and uncertainty. Chia-yu set up a memorial temple to purge and cleanse the minds of the people, on the grounds that Yü-ch'ih Chiung, who had died for his country, was a loyal subject. Three years later he was recalled to court and appointed General of the Left in the Chin-wu guards. Wu Ching became prefect after him and further invested the spirit with ceremonial robes. Then there were no more troubles.

The problem has become merely a loss of public morale. Prefects have died; local memory recalls the bloodshed of 580 and suspects vengeful ghosts; Chang and Wu exorcise the problem in the people's minds by publicly dedicating a cult to Yü-ch'ih Chiung. But the same loose ends remain.

Brevity could explain some of them, but not all. The biographer finds room enough to analyse public morale. He expresses Chang Chia-yu's motives in the deliberately chosen language of a public administrator – 'to purge and cleanse the minds of the people' (解祓眾心) – and in this he gives an early and clear statement of the principle spelled out in a later age: 'gods are not supernatural themselves, but they act supernaturally on the minds of those who believe in them.'[18] It is all a far cry from the dramatic confrontations between incoming prefects and proprietorial gods which we find scattered through the histories of the Northern and Southern Dynasties (and to which we return below).[19]

18 *Hsüeh chih i-shuo* 學治臆說 B.28a (*Ju-mu hsü-chih wu-chung* 入幕須知五種, ed. 1892). This book was by Wang Hui-tsu 汪輝祖, preface dated 1793; cit. E. Balazs, *Political theory and administrative reality in traditional China*, London 1965, p. 63.

19 The best-known example is the cult of Hsiang Yü 項羽 at Wu-hsing 吳興 in the fifth and sixth centuries, discussed by Chao I 趙翼 (1727–1814) in *Kai-yü ts'ung-k'ao* 35.754–6, and (less completely) by Uchida Michio in 'Kō U shin monogatari', repr. in *Chūgoku shōsetsu kenkyū*, Tokyo 1977, pp. 241–59; also Miyakawa Hisayuki, *Rikuchō shi kenkyū: shūkyō hen*, Kyoto 1964, pp. 391–414.

The theological and ritual problems raised by local cults, so powerful in the minds of sixth- and seventh-century historians, win little interest in the eleventh. But those problems will press forward more strongly when we examine evidence on the cult from the time of its foundation.

Inscriptions on stone

For the life of Chang Chia-yu we have one contemporary document: a tomb inscription by Liu Pi 柳賁 written on the occasion of Chang's burial near Lo-yang on 19 March 742, three months after his death in Ch'ang-an on 9 December 741.[20] It deals only briefly with the An-yang episode:

> Before long he was appointed prefect of Hsiang-chou. The men of Yin 殷 had false notions, the warden of Yeh showed a flaring of energy.[21] But [Chang] was rich in loyalty, firm in sincerity. He governed like the very gods. Fussy regulations were removed, harsh policies discontinued. Lapsed rituals were restored to full observance . . . [9b]

The glance at Yü-ch'ih Chiung ('warden of Yeh') discovers on the one hand an ill-founded public panic, on the other a preternatural manifestation of the dead hero. So for Liu Pi the haunting might be apparent or real: and the cult accordingly would serve either to steady the public's nerve or to mollify the threatening spirit. Explicit ambiguity then blurs into formulaic praise of Chang's performance as a model prefect.

By good fortune we have the inscriptions written for the memorial temple itself at the time of its foundation. There are two distinct documents. The first, and by far the more important of the two, was composed for an inaugural stele by Yen Chen-ch'ing 顏真卿 (709–785), with a preface by Yen Po-yü 閻伯璵. The whole was executed by Ts'ai Yu-lin 蔡有鄰 in a *li* 隸-style script and engraved on a stone which would stand in the precincts of the Yü-ch'ih Chiung Temple in An-yang for many centuries to come. For connoisseurs of epigraphy this was a classic piece. Ou-yang Hsiu 歐陽修 (1007–1072) had a rubbing in his famous collection, as we see from his son Fei's 棐 catalogue of 1069.[22] In

20 Liu Pi, 'T'ang ku tso-chin-wu chiang-chün Fan-yang Chang-kung mu-chih-ming ping hsü' 唐故左金吾將軍范陽張公墓誌銘並序, in *Ku-chih shih-hua* 11.8b–10a.

21 'The men of Yin' 殷人: Namely, the people of Hsiang-chou, by association with the traditional site of the Yin capital near An-yang: *Yüan-ho chün-hsien t'u-chih* 16.451. 'Flaring of energy' 氣焰: A phrase more fully translated in another context as 'flarings up of the ether': see McMullen, *State and scholars in T'ang China*, p. 156. It originates in *Tso chuan*, Chuang/14, where it describes ominous manifestations of the supernatural engendered by human irregularity: *Ch'un-ch'iu Tso chuan chu-shu* 9.8b.

22 The lost *Chi-ku lu-mu* 集古錄目, later partly reconstructed from other sources. For this item, see *Pao-k'o ts'ung-pien* 6.31a.

the twelfth century it was studied by Tung Yu 董逌 (*ca.* 1125),[23] in the fourteenth (*in situ*) by Nai Hsien 迺賢 (*ca.* 1345).[24] Both men evidently found a text in good enough condition to read quite coherently. But by the seventeenth century the stone, though still seen in An-yang, had 'lost more than half its surface to erosion'.[25] There are reports that the stele was dug out of the ground during a restoration of the temple in 1690.[26] And there, at a spot near the northern gate of the city wall, it stayed through the eighteenth and nineteenth centuries while a series of distinguished epigraphists studied its badly damaged text.[27]

Their transcriptions give us at best a seriously incomplete document. And it has failed to survive in an organic literary tradition. The transmission of Yen Chen-ch'ing's literary works has been from early times a story of loss and partial reconstitution.[28] When the editors of the *Ssu-k'u ch'üan-shu* project (1773–1782) critically reviewed the existing collection, they noted a number of inscriptions in epigraphical sources which had been lost to literary transmission; the 'Yü-ch'ih Chiung' piece was one of these.[29] It joined the recognized Yen Chen-ch'ing corpus in Huang Pen-chi's 黄本驥 definitive edition of 1845.[30] Surprisingly it appears there quite complete and intact, as it does also in *Ch'üan T'ang wen* (1808–1814), supported by Yen Po-yü's equally complete preface.[31] So, despite the patchily preserved stele and the lack of literary tradition, these nineteenth-century editors had a source-text which for completeness surpassed the best epigraphical work of their time. Such a text in fact lay ready for them in the 1738 gazetteer of An-yang county, where a brief notice on the lately restored temple adds the entire text of the inscription, preface and all.[32] Although we have no information

23 *Kuang-ch'uan shu-pa* 7.10a–11a.

24 *Ho-shuo fang-ku chi* B. 22b–24a.

25 So Ku Yen-wu 顧炎武 (1613–1682) in *Chin-shih wen-tzu chi* 3.29a.

26 Hearsay reported by Liu Ch'ing-li 劉青藜 in *Chin-shih hsü-lu* 2.11ab. For the date of restoration, see *An-yang hsien-chih* (1738) 4.14a.

27 Pi Yüan 畢沅 (1730–1797) in *Chung-chou chin-shih chi* 2.24a–25b; Ch'ien Ta-hsin 錢大昕 (1728–1804) in *Ch'ien-yen t'ang chin-shih-wen pa-wei* 6.14a-b; Wu I 吳億 (1745–1799) and Chao Hsi-huang 趙希璜 in *An-yang hsien chin-shih lu* (1799) 4.1b ff.; Wang Ch'ang 王昶 (1725–1806) in *Chin-shih ts'ui-pien* 82.17b–20a; Chao Shao-tsu 趙紹祖 in *Chin-shih hsü-ch'ao* 2.5a–9b (this item dated 1808), and in *Ku-mo chai chin-shih pa* 4.17a–18a; Hung I-hsüan 洪頤煊 (1765–1837) in *P'ing-chin tu-pei chi* 6.5b–6a; Lu Tseng-hsiang 陸增祥 (1833–1899) in *Pa-ch'iung shih chin-shih pu-cheng* 56.5b–7a.

28 Surveyed by Wan Man in *T'ang chi hsü-lu*, Peking 1980, pp. 64–7.

29 *Ssu-k'u ch'üan-shu tsung-mu* 149.33b. The text accordingly appeared in the supplement (補遺) to the main collection: *Yen Lu-kung chi* 16.12a; see *Ying-yin Wen-yüan ko ssu-k'u ch'üan-shu*, Taipei 1983–6, vol. 1071, p. 692a.

30 *Yen Lu-kung wen-chi* (ed. *San-ch'ang-wu chai ts'ung-shu*, 1845) 6.4a–5a.

31 *Ch'üan T'ang wen* (ed. 1814), 339.8ab and 395.23b–25b.

32 *An-yang hsien-chih* (1738) 4.13b–15b. It also records that sacrifices were still currently offered to Yü-ch'ih Chiung at this temple on the twelfth day of the seventh month. Tex-

on where the local historian found this unblemished text of an inscription long since half worn away, we have little choice but to use it, checking the wording where we can with passages in the early reports.

Headed 'Temple-stele of Master Yü-ch'ih, Grand Preceptor of the Chou and Duke of Shu' 周太師蜀國公尉遲公神廟碑, the stele originally bore a date in the first month of K'ai-yüan 26, and thus in the spring of 738.[33] Its inscription deals with the life, death and burial of Yü-ch'ih Chiung and with the arrival and intervention of Chang Chia-yu. The preface represents Yü-ch'ih's rehabilitation in these terms:

In the T'ang Wu-te 武德 period the court ordained his reburial. They honoured the dead, they mourned the long departed, for state rites had been wanting in former times. They marked the tomb, they remembered the man, for heaven's grace now flowed forth in a later age. In the year *ting-ch'ou* 丁丑 of K'ai-yüan [737] . . . the prefect of Hsiang-chou, Master Chang Chia-yu . . . raised a temple to this loyal and pure-hearted man, established sacrifices with ritual offerings. When he had first alighted from his carriage to inquire about the local customs they had complained in the prefecture of malevolent hauntings. He said: 'If any common man or woman[34] who dies by violence can wreak trouble, how much more, then, can the duke of Shu, whose words and deeds were an example to all! . . . Holders of the prefect's post, though privileged to draw a high stipend, have neglected to perform due rites of celebration: it was right and proper that they should suffer calamities! I, therefore, have laid out my own salary, and a lofty temple has risen in splendour. I have moved in a "stone from another hill",[35] and a magnificent stele completes the words of praise. As long as hills and valleys stand firm they will for evermore record his mighty heroism.'

These are the careful words of a man who expects to be overheard by the presence that threatens him – loudly praising the spirit's past merit, freely endorsing his recent mischief-making, elaborately smoothing his ruffled feathers. The passage expresses a dual motivation: to assuage disturbance to the public by 'malevolent hauntings' (多祟), and to free a scared prefect from the 'calamities' (戾) that his predecessors suffered. Chang's comments recall one of the central positions of Chinese theology: it is so often those who die by violence and by their own hand whose spirits impose their powerful presence on human society and

tual variants suggest that the *Ch'üan T'ang wen* editors used an intermediary source: *An-yang hsien chin-shih lu* (1799) 4.1b–4b, where the surviving remnants of the inscription are collated with the 1738 text, exposing some discrepancies.

33 Compare Ou-yang Fei, Ku Yen-wu, Pi Yüan, Ch'ien Ta-hsin, Wang Ch'ang ('K'ai-yüan **/1/2*'), Chao Shao-tsu, Hung I-hsüan. Only Nai Hsien gives the date K'ai-yüan 26/2/21: *Ho-shuo fang-ku chi* B.24a.

34 匹夫匹婦. The phrase comes from *Lun yü* 14/17.

35 A line from *Shih ching*, Ode 184, 'Ho ming' 鶴鳴.

require service by sacrificial cult. Chang affirms the territorial responsibility of local officials for ritual tasks of this kind: a powerful enough spirit at large within the bounds of Hsiang-chou will aim at the prefect of Hsiang-chou and look for a cult at the official seat of Hsiang-chou, regardless of the particular spot where he met his death. So Chang now accepts, in the dead hero's hearing, that the ceremonies of reburial in the early T'ang have not filled his appetite for public recognition. The new cult will put the matter right. Yen Chen-ch'ing's solemn lines, ringing with echoes from *The book of odes*, sum it up:

In Yeh there is a worthy prefect,
Master Chang is he.
Fragrant in his bright virtue,[36]
Now he builds a closed temple.

Now he builds a closed temple,
And the closed temple is hushed.[37]
Now he sets up a fine stele,
And the fine stele brings rules.

The demon afflictions end forthwith,
Spirits and men look fair,[38]
Blessings and goods in full store,[39]
Offerings and sacrifice never in default.[40]

A month after this a second inscription was carved on the back of the same stone. Composed by Yü-ch'ih Shih-liang 士良, a great-great-grandson of Yü-ch'ih Chiung, and dated K'ai-yüan 26/2/25 [19 March 738], it celebrated the ancestor's loyal career and the incumbent's priest-like mediation. For this piece no full text survives. We have about seventy per cent of the original, copied from rubbing or stone by late epigraphists,[41] but large gaps break up the text so often and so seriously that it yields poor sense. Nai Hsien, who read it in the fourteenth century, offers this brief summary:

The reverse of the stele commemorates miracles wrought by [Yü-ch'ih] Chiung. It says that sunshine and rain always followed in response to prayers. He turned

36 Alluding to *Shang shu*, 'Chün Ch'en' 君陳: 'Perfect government is like potent fragrance, it influences the spirits. It is not millet which has the potent fragrance, it is bright virtue.' See *Shang shu chu-shu* 18.10b–11a.

37 The opening line of Ode 300, 'Pi kung' 閟宮. The Closed Temple was dedicated to Chiang Yüan 姜嫄, mother of the Chou founding patriarch Hou-chi 后稷.

38 'Look fair' 載色. From Ode 299, 'P'an shui' 泮水.

39 'Blessings and goods' 戩穀. From Ode 166, 'T'ien pao' 天保.

40 A further line from Ode 300, 'Pi kung'.

41 *An-yang hsien chin-shih lu* 4.8b–10a; *Chin-shih ts'ui-pien* 82.20b–22a; *Ku-mo chai chin-shih pa* 4.18a; *Pa-ch'iung shih chin-shih pu-cheng* 56.6ab.

back wind, drove off locusts, and thus saved the whole territory from harm. When autumn nights came round two cranes would descend and settle in the temple courtyard. Even now (it says) the local people still talked of it as a wonder.[42]

With this as a framework we can bring some details of the original text into focus. It seems, for instance, more likely that the two cranes made a single appearance on a clear night after Chang's successful prayer for rain, prompting his kinsman Chang Huan 張環 to 'compose a rhapsody on fructifying rain' (賦膏雨). Later, when rainstorms threatened the autumn harvest and Chang prayed again, he used a medium (巫) to communicate with the spirit. And after their successful harvest the people of Hsiang-chou sang a hymn of praise to their model prefect.[43]

These inscriptions share a common character with the biographical accounts we began with. It is not just that they all issue from the hands of the T'ang ruling elite; they all also enjoy in their various ways the status of public documents. Documentary forms of course impose certain distinctive rhetorical demands. But public official status lays down a more basic imperative: inevitably these documents address one, and only one, aspect of the Hsiang-chou cult – its role of support for an imperial officer, his personal security and his duty to preserve order, promote the people's welfare and maintain harmony between human society and the surrounding cosmos.

We first approached the An-yang material from the detached and conspicuously public vantage point of imperial historians, then moved inward towards statements so close in time and space to the temple's foundation that they could claim some part of their own in its earliest ritual function. The whole concentric system, however, shows more consistency than variety. At first sight the authors of the two T'ang histories, though using almost the same form of words, pass quite antithetical verdicts on the whole episode – the old implicitly assenting, the new functionally agnostic. Yet the obituary memoir of Chang Chia-yu shows both judgements standing quite easily together, offering state historians a choice of styles. And we have no real grounds to deny even that the same two judgements might have stood together in the minds of Chang himself, of Yen Chen-ch'ing, Yen Po-yü and Yü-ch'ih Shih-liang. Of course the rhetoric of the temple inscriptions declares a firm and passionate commitment to its presiding spirit. But so would it also if the temple and its inscriptions were merely the product of a calculated and cynical act of administrative policy. There is a sense, then, in

42 *Ho-shuo fang-ku chi* B.23ab.
43 *An-yang hsien chin-shih lu* 4.9b; *Chin-shih ts'ui-pien* 82.21b.

which these documents from the very fountain-head of the An-yang cult present no more than an opaque surface through which we see little of its underlying motivation. Nor (with the doubtful exception of Yü-ch'ih Shih-liang's composition) do they reveal much about its concrete circumstances. They reflect instead what we can only call an official mythology, according to which a troubled episode in local affairs resolves into social and cosmic harmony under a wise and able administrator.

Anecdotal sources

Already in the twelfth century Tung Yu noticed in a book called *Shang-shu ku-shih* 尚書故事 a variant account of Chang Chia-yu's experience in Hsiang-chou. He sharply challenged its version of the facts.[44] This book survives, in a single *chüan.*[45] Its author was Li Ch'o 李綽, its subject the fund of anecdotes shared with Li by a board president (尚書) whose exact identity we are unable to pin down, but who numbered Chang Chia-yu among his forebears. What evidence we have about Li and his elusive President Chang is circumstantial but plausible. It suggests[46] that the book had its genesis in a time of national emergency, probably when Huang Ch'ao's rebellion struck at Lo-yang in the winter of 880. Li Ch'o later lived on long enough to brood nostalgically over a T'ang dynasty already collapsed – hence well into the tenth century. President Chang, it seems, belonged to the same family and generation as the celebrated art critic Chang Yen-yüan 張彥遠. His descent from Chang Chia-yu's generation emerges directly in the piece of family lore about Yü-ch'ih Chiung that we now put under scrutiny:

[President Chang] himself told the story of his great-uncle in the fifth generation,[47] Chia-yu, who in the K'ai-yüan period became governor-general (都督) of Hsiang-chou. There were strange calamities in the official residence, and a succession of prefects had lost their lives. When the general arrived, he sat through the whole night, formally robed, in the principal chamber. Suddenly, at midnight, he heard the sound of a sigh behind the screen, and before long a man emerged from the side chamber to the west. His dress was in tatters, his body limp and worn out. The man mounted the steps one by one and walked straight up to him.

The general now demanded in a stern voice: 'What spirit are you, to present yourself here?'

44 *Kuang-ch'uan shu-pa* 7.11a.

45 I use here the text in *Ssu-k'u ch'üan-shu.* The item in question appears on 7b–8a (*Ying-yin Wen-yüan ko ssu-k'u ch'üan-shu*, vol. 862, p. 472).

46 To summarize the main conclusions of Yü Chia-hsi's powerful documentary study in *Ssu-k'u t'i-yao pien-cheng*, repr. Peking 1980, 15.909–18.

47 *Kao-po-tsu* 高伯祖: the elder brother of his grandfather's grandfather.

The reply came: 'I am Yü-ch'ih Chiung, general of the Later Chou. I died in this place, and my remains are here still. I want to entrust a man of good will to see my burial and funeral sacrifices duly completed. But past incumbents of this prefecture have all been men of weak courage and poor spirit. They were startled and scared to death, not murdered by me.' He then pointed to a ten-year-old girl and said: 'This is my daughter. She too is buried beneath the side chamber.'

Next day the general ordered his staff to dig up the place, and they did indeed find two skeletons. He provided a full set of garments, shrouds and coffin equipment and had them buried with due ceremony.

Two nights later the man reappeared to express his thanks. He then said: 'All I can offer by way of return is to make you disciplined and conspicuous in your government.[48] I am at your service in times of flood or of drought.'

The general now reported the matter to the throne, requesting permission to found a temple and offer blood-sacrifice at the seasons of the year. The emperor specially bestowed a written decree in praise of this wonder. A stele was carved with an account of the matter. And the temple with the stele is there still.

Of course Tung Yu was right: the simplest tests show up this story as full of factual error. We have direct contemporary evidence that Chang Chia-yu knew of Yü-ch'ih Chiung's formal reburial more than a century before his own time. Long before his time, too, imperial histories of the northern dynasties had recorded that Yü-ch'ih died in Yeh, not An-yang (*Chou shu* since 635, *Sui shu* since 636, *Pei shih* since 659). And if Chang did communicate with the throne and obtain in return a special rescript, no hint of this transaction remains in the early sources. All told there is every temptation to discard the whole piece as so much spurious imagining – except, that is, for two features that keep curiosity alive. One is the claimed authority of family tradition – a tradition already a century and a half removed from the event, with all the refractions and distortions that time could bring, but still a tradition that must have found its origin somewhere. The other point concerns an internal feature of the story itself – the ten-year-old girl, supposed to be the dead general's daughter, whose skeleton is unearthed together with his. In any purely made-up story a detail like this would be surplus to requirements: contributing nothing functional to the main action, it hangs there loose and spare. What, we want to ask, lies behind it?

The matter would have to rest there if we did not have another and much fuller version of this story from a date far closer to the events in An-yang. It appears as story **73** in the *Kuang-i chi*. For our study of the

48 The attributes 'disciplined' (*chieh* 節) and 'conspicuous' (*hsüan* 宣) were among those officially used in canonizing meritorious officials: see *T'ang hui-yao* 79.1456–7. I am grateful to David McMullen for pointing this out.

An-yang cult the *Kuang-i chi*, whose internal chronology stops in 780, offers testimony from at most fifty, probably less than forty years after the cult's foundation. Its version of the story both challenges and illuminates the *Shang-shu ku-shih* . . .

In the K'ai-yüan period Chang Chia-yu became prefect of Hsiang-chou. The prefectural residence had long been haunted, and when Chia-yu first arrived ghosts at once began changing around his furniture[49] and creating maximum disturbance. But Chia-yu did not fear them. When the settings for a feast in a small hall in his west court were once again overturned, together with other foodstuffs, Chia-yu went to investigate.[50]

He saw a girl and asked her: 'What spirit are you, young lady?'

She said: 'I am the daughter of my late father Yü-ch'ih, once prefect of Hsiang-chou and grand general of the Chou dynasty. Our family has suffered a great wrong, and he wishes to meet the prefect and set forth his case.'

Chia-yu said: 'I shall hear what he has to say with due respect.'

Before long the man appeared. In look and dress he was stately and grand, in gaze noble and sublime. He began by paying his respects to Chia-yu, who invited him to sit and asked him this: 'You, a man wise and good in life, an honoured spirit in death – why do you now squeak and rustle[51] among the shades, frightening the boys and girls and giving this prefecture the lasting repute of a haunted post?'

He replied: 'In days gone by, when the house of Chou reached the end of its imperial sway,[52] Yang Chien seized power. How could I, who had the honour to serve under the Chou, endure the collapse of its state altars? It was for this that I wished to preserve my integrity as a subject, to take the lead in the great cause. I aspired to restore the cosmos to rights and so maintain Emperor T'ai-tsu's 太祖 heritage.[53] Wei Hsiao-k'uan was once a minister of the Chou house, but he failed to respond to the call of the righteous enterprise. Instead he agreed to be harnessed and used by Yang Chien. I, with the forces of a single prefecture, faced the massed thousands[54] of the entire empire's armies. Even though my good faith reared up to high heaven itself there was no one in the whole world to come to my aid. Upon which my territory fell to the enemy. My whole lineage was put to death, and the bones of my entire family, about sixty of them, lie beneath this hall. The more time goes by the more our sense of grievance rankles. Even if we would,[55] we cannot rot away, but whenever we address ourselves to men we terrify them to death. With no one to hear our

49 'Changing around his furniture'. For 祟迴祐家 read 迴易家具, with Ming MS and Sun Ch'ien.

50 'Investigate'. For 觀 read 視, with Sun Ch'ien.

51 'Squeak and rustle'. For 宵窣 read 屑 (with Sun) 窣.

52 'Imperial sway'. For 作 read 祚, with Sun Ch'ien.

53 'T'ai-tsu'. Yü-wen T'ai 宇文泰 (507–556): see discussion of dates in *Chou shu* 2.43, n. 26. He was the father of the first Chou emperor Hsiao-min ti 孝閔帝.

54 'Thousands'. For 益 read 萬, with Sun Ch'ien.

55 For 別 read 則, with Sun Ch'ien.

complaint we have come to this. I beg you, sir, to cast your eyes[56] upon us. If our forgotten bones can gain your kind attention and our darkened souls[57] be lifted up again, then even death will be to us as life itself.'

Chia-yu gave his consent. Some days later he had the pile of bones dug up and gave them solemn burial at the rear of the hall. He then made the hall into a temple and addressed prayers to the dead at the seasons of the year.

[Chia-]yu had a daughter aged eight or nine. Whenever a member of his family had a question to ask they would make her address it to the spirit, and the spirit would always respond. And when the spirit had something to say to Chia-yu, he too would call the little girl out to meet him. This became a regular practice. And from that time on the spirit would always send ghostly troops with any members of Chia-yu's family who were bound on a journey, to escort them as far as the borders. When the troops returned they would report in full on how far the escort had gone. In the west they never went further than the Ho-yang 河陽 bridge.[58]

This account stands in an interesting relation to the late-ninth-century version from *Shang-shu ku-shih.* Of course they share enough features in common – the prefect's dialogue with the ghost, the ghost's young daughter, his neglected bones in the precincts of the residence, his request for burial and obsequies – to count as variants of the same story. Yet they part company over many important details, none more interesting than those which concern Yü-ch'ih Chiung's slaughtered kin. Once again an earlier stage of evidence brings out a crisper definition. The daughter whose remains so strangely accompany her father's in the later version has a perfectly clear role to play in the earlier: she is chosen from among sixty members of the slain lineage to come out and herald her father's formal appearance before the state official. In this example the *Shang-shu ku-shih* betrays a process of decay, by which an isolated feature of the old story survives beyond the context and function that once gave it meaning. Such loose matching between the two variants guarantees a particular kind of value. For if they had been closely matched we should have to suspect some relatively uninteresting form of routine literary transmission. As it is, we seem rather

56 'Cast your eyes'. For 盼 read 眄, with Sun Ch'ien.

57 'Souls'. For 魅 read 魂, with Sun Ch'ien.

58 Ho-yang was a county on the north bank of the Yellow River, just facing Lo-yang. It was protected by various citadels, one of which, the Chung-tan Citadel 中潬城, stood on an island in midstream. 'A floating bridge spanning the Yellow River was constructed there, with boats as supports and bamboo matting going across them' (*Yüan-ho chün-hsien t'u-chih* 5.144). Compare remarks by Chang Shun-min 張舜民 (*ca.* 1034–*ca.* 1110) quoted by Hung Mai 洪邁 (1123–1202) in *Jung-chai sui-pi* 容齋隨筆 (repr. Shanghai 1978), *hsü-pi* 續筆 12.366. Li Tsu-huan in 'Huang-ho ku-ch'iao shu-lüeh', *Wen-shih* 20, Peking 1983, pp. 67 and 74, dates the Ho-yang bridge to 785. This, I believe, rests on a misreading of the source, which associates the bridge more generally with a strategic garrisoning of the Chung-tan Citadel from 758 on.

to have two independent derivatives of a common background tradition. Of the tradition's source or early currency we may not know anything for sure, but we can at least take its existence as well spoken for.

A more basic question now arises. For reasons already pointed out the variants of this powerful ghost story cannot claim authority as simple factual accounts of events in the An-yang of 737. What, then, is their status? How should they be read? Questions like these lie at the heart of all the studies in this book and very often face us with few options beyond speculation and guesswork. But here, for once, with the story of Yü-ch'ih Chiung's ghost and his provincial cult, we can set certain apocryphal items within a context defined by contemporary documents and study them with the benefit of known historical perspective. At least one level of conjecture can be removed from our attempt at a critical reading.

With the external discipline of other documents we can combine an internal analysis using the inner/outer story categories introduced in earlier chapters. We shall begin to find that both categories need to be drawn with subtlety and care, particularly the outer story, which in practice will often reveal more than one layer of externality.[59] But the analysis can throw some light on the story of Chang Chia-yu and Yü-ch'ih Chiung's ghost.

The initial analysis is simple. Chang enters an inner story at the moment when his personal investigation (*Kuang-i chi*) or deliberate vigil (*Shang-shu ku-shih*) puts him in contact with the ghosts and ends when his staff are called in to deal with their abandoned bones. (In *Shang-shu ku-shih* it resumes briefly for uttering of thanks and offering of service.) All the rest is outer story, and here the richness and interest of the *Kuang-i chi* begin to make themselves felt. There is a prelude, in which a poltergeist haunting strikes typically at domestic and household items: furniture, crockery, foodstuffs. And, with the reburial and the temple cult, there is an aftermath in which Chang's own young daughter serves as a spirit medium for the prefect and his family, allowing them to communicate with the honoured spirit; appended to this is an account of one feature of their cordial communion. But analysis into inner and outer stories offers more than a simple paragraphing device: each of them, once isolated, shows a character of its own and calls for an appropriate style of reading.

The inner story is formal in more senses than one. Not merely does it convey the formality of an official interview: its very composition

59 Some examples are discussed in my paper 'Tang tales and Tang cults: some cases from the eighth century'.

obeys a settled and predictable formula. It belongs to a category we might call 'the tale of the haunted post', in which a sequence of terror and destruction is halted by a local official with the courage to identify the dangerous spirit and bring it within the sphere of public control. The origins of this formula are old, and they are linked (as here) to real historical situations. The example of Hsiang Yü 項羽 has been mentioned above (note 19). There too was an ancient dynastic contender, likewise defeated and beheaded, who for much of the fifth and sixth centuries established a claim to blood-sacrifice in the very audience chamber of the official quarters in Wu-hsing 吳興. Incoming officials were obliged to deal with him, and the sources[60] record different styles of confrontation. Those who brazened it out (with shoes on their feet) in the audience chamber met varying success: one died, one simply survived; one managed to replace bloody victims with Buddhist vegetarian offerings, another with offerings of dried meat. Some officials made friends with him: one, it was said, owed a high promotion to his dutiful service of the god, another won answers to his prayers by sociably carousing with him. All this took place against the background of an established temple dedicated to Hsiang Yü in the territory of Wu-hsing. We might draw several parallels with the case of Yü-ch'ih Chiung, but the most pertinent is this: that a trial of strength between local cult and imperial authority works itself out time after time as a personal transaction between prefect and god in the very seat of official power. The *Kuang-i chi*, which takes cognizance of a Hsiang Yü cult,[61] also reports other such transactions. Each one has an inner story, and each of these takes the form that we have found here: the ghost, boldly sought out, emerges and speaks its mind; the magistrate or prefect responds; and the ghost, its needs met, shows gratitude by rendering him service.[62] This is the sense in which Chang Chia-yu's inner story is formulaic and predictable. When the contact between local official and threatening spirit is articulated in narrative form, it will take the same necessary shape. In much the same way Yü-ch'ih Chiung's ten-year-old

60 The main references, in chronological order and excluding duplications, are: *Nan shih*, ed. Chung-hua shu-chü, Peking 1975, 27.726 (before AD 412); ibid., 18.499 (AD 465); *Nan Ch'i shu*, ed. Chung-hua shu-chü, Peking 1972, 27.508 (AD 486); *Nan shih* 18.501 (AD 499); ibid., 51.1269–70 (early sixth century); ibid., 18.506–7 (AD 510–519); ibid., 9.273 (AD 558). The T'ang dignitary Ti Jen-chieh 狄仁傑 (607–700) uttered an act of formal suppression in 688: see *Ch'ao-yeh ch'ien-tsai*, as cited in *Shuo-fu* (repr. Shanghai 1927), 2.10b–11a, and David McMullen, 'The real Judge Dee: Ti Jen-chieh and the T'ang restoration of 705', *Asia Major*, Third Series, 6, 1993, pp. 11–13.

61 See story **75**. This cult was located as Hsü-chou 徐州, now in the north-west corner of Kiangsu province. The dialogue strongly recalls a speech in *Nan shih* 18.506.

62 Dead requiring reburial: **27**, **86**, **89**, **127**; animals requiring assistance: **247**, **294**.

daughter plays a role which recurs through other ghost stories in the *Kuang-i chi* and elsewhere. The young, subordinate, insignificant figure prepares for the appearance of one more weighty, of greater public moment or social standing – a serving maid heralds the coming of her ghostly mistress;[63] a female shade identifies a receptive mortal while a dead officer waits in the darkened wilderness for his more important turn.[64]

With this inner core of recognized formulas we can now contrast the surrounding outer story. It is familiar ground in a wholly different way, standing squarely in the large, ancient and worldwide literature of poltergeist reports. Psychic research, of course, is no part of our business here, and indeed the documentary status of this piece – an apocryphal anecdote set down decades after the event – would not meet modern criteria of evidence in that field of enquiry. But comparisons can be drawn, and we can still make use of poltergeist literature to illuminate the *Kuang-i chi*. At once it becomes clear that the outer story fits organically with a well-established pattern. Poltergeist stories, routinely filled with moving furniture, broken crockery and spilt foodstuffs, also regularly contain human subjects whose presence appears to stimulate or provoke the disturbances. Modern writers use terms like 'agent' or 'medium' to identify this role, which they treat as a strictly passive and usually unconscious involvement with phenomena that often bring the subjects pain and distress.[65] Poltergeist agents are mostly young and female, often pubescent girls, occasionally true children. In some cases they are possessed by a spirit that links itself with the disturbances. This is the context in which the 'prelude' and 'aftermath' of the outer story come together as an organic whole: Chang Chia-yu's eight-year-old daughter, whose communion with the spirit suggests that she too is possessed, emerges as a likely poltergeist agent by the same token.

The point must be made with care. We are not in a position to treat any of this as empirically verified data, simply to observe its fit with patterns seen in a widely based range of reports. We can even give the fit a quantitative value by using Alan Gauld's register of characteristics drawn from reports of five hundred cases throughout the world.[66] Seven of them are suggested in the outer story:

63 Stories **108**, **109**, **197**.

64 In the ninth-century collection *Ch'uan-ch'i* 傳奇 by P'ei Hsing 裴鉶: see *P'ei Hsing Ch'uan-ch'i*, ed. Chou Leng-ch'ieh, Shanghai 1980, pp. 74–5, 'Chao Ho' 趙合.

65 'Agent' is the term used by Alan Gauld and A. D. Cornell in *Poltergeists*, London 1979, pp. 67–84. I refer to this book in particular for the sake of its chronological list of five hundred cases with source references (pp. 363–98).

66 Ibid., pp. 226–8.

11: Female agent
12: Agent under age twenty
15: House-centred
16: Small objects moved
17: Large objects moved, for example, chairs, tables
41: Possession, obsession
46: 'Deceased person' communicates

(Characteristic 24: 'Phantasms (human)' is excluded, since it belongs only to the inner story.) Of the five hundred cases there are forty-five which share four of these characteristics, and four which share five of them.[67] These rather limited figures conceal some suggestive parallels. A single example will make the point – the story from sixteenth-century Lyons of a defected Benedictine nun who died and was buried in the open without ceremony or memorial. One of the remaining nuns later gathered from the sound of rapping noises that the lost sister wished for reburial in the abbey. When this was organized by the suffragan bishop, the dead nun, through the same personal medium, answered questions about the life after death; she also, in a scene of spirit possession, sought forgiveness and received the church's absolution.[68] Here, in the dress of another culture, is the same tale of the grateful dead, with a system of communication now based entirely on poltergeist knockings and possession. The comparison suggests that our account from the *Kuang-i chi* might stand almost as well without the factitious aid of its inner story.

So the effect of this analysis is to present the story from *Kuang-i chi* as a composite construction, calling for different styles of critical reading. To read one part of it – the inner story – we must recognize a convention for expressing in narrative form the transactions between imperial authorities and local cults. To read the other, outer part we must begin by opening our minds to the variety of social experience reflected in Chinese books of marvels, though ignored in standard literature. The phenomena of spirit possession, we know well, were woven intimately into the fabric of life in traditional China. It should

67 The four are: no. 205, from Stratford, Connecticut, in 1850 – see H. Spicer, *Sights and sounds*, London 1853, pp. 101–10; no. 261, from Amherst, Nova Scotia, in 1878–1879 – see W. Hubbell, *The great Amherst mystery*, London 1888; no. 358, from Lading, Austria, in 1916–1918 – see *Zeitschrift für Parapsychologie*, 1932, 97–101; no. 430, from France (no location) in 1940 – see *Annales de médecine légale et de criminologie* 31, 1951, 67–78.

68 Adrian de Montalembert, *La merveilleuse hystoire de lesperit qui depuis nagueres cest apparu au monastere des religieuses de sainct pierre de lyõ*, Paris 1528; repr. in N. Lenglet Dufresnoy, *Recueil de dissertations anciennes et nouvelles sur les apparitions, les visions et les songes*, etc., vol. 1, Avignon 1751. See Gauld and Cornell, *Poltergeists*, pp. 23–6.

come as no surprise that poltergeist phenomena were probably commonplace too, and naturally stimulated a response from the surrounding community.[69] In this sense the outer story offers a picture of social behaviour that claims a certain documentary status. But however socially plausible we may find its features to be, it still offers no securely historical insights into the events at An-yang in 737–738.

The strongest reminder of this comes not here, but at the end of the story in *Shang-shu ku-shih*, with the words: 'the temple with the stele is there in Hsiang-chou still.' They remove the narrator from his story and place him in a detached, present situation from which he views story and temple on equal terms. This simple concluding device creates an even wider outer story enfolding all the rest. Tai Fu often made use of it, though here he left it implied rather than expressed. Its effect is to give the story the status of a mythological document standing beside the visible institution to which it refers – a myth of resentful spirits and neglected bones crying out for burial, their wishes made known through haunting and possession, their gratitude expressed by protection of secular interests. This, we understand, was the interpretation which society at large (as distinct from government authorities) now linked to the established cult. And as such it more likely reflected the typical than the actual.

Actual or not, it certainly suggests that more complex circumstances may have attended the birth of this cult than the official sources permit us to know. There is no inherent reason why the tradition reflected in *Kuang-i chi* and *Shang-shu ku-shih* should not have been born with the cult itself.[70] It might even offer tempting glosses on certain ill-defined phrases in the official sources: Yen Po-yü's 'malevolent hauntings', Yen Chen-ch'ing's 'demon afflictions', Yü-ch'ih Shih-liang's 'prayers through a spirit-medium'. But that is mere guesswork. In fact our anatomy of the various sources has shown that not many circumstantial facts lie

69 Some examples at random from the twelfth-century *I-chien chih* (ed. Ho Cho, Peking 1981): *Ping-chih* 丙志 9.440, 'Wen-chou lin chai' 溫州賃宅; *Ting-chih* 丁志 3.555, 'Wu Shih-liang' 武師亮; ibid., 4.569–70, 'Tai Shih-jung' 戴世榮; ibid., 7.591, 'Tai-lou men chai' 戴樓門宅. The subject deserves systematic study.

70 I do not find the reference to the Ho-yang bridge (see above, n. 58) a serious obstacle to this point. It occurs in connection with the spirit troops detailed to escort travelling members of the prefect's family, a circumstance made known, it seems, by the usual means of communication through the young daughter. The early-ninth-century *Yüan-ho chün-hsien t'u-chih* makes it clear that a floating bridge spanned the Yellow River during a time of strategic reinforcement after the disasters of the An Lu-shan rebellion (from 758 on), but leaves the situation before the rebellion unclear. Even if anachronism could be proved, it might show no more than the relatively late appearance of this appended detail in the story. The background tradition itself could still have stretched back earlier in time without it.

within our grasp, not even those we should most like to know. (Did a popular cult to Yü-ch'ih Chiung exist in the background? Were actual human remains involved at any level in the community?) Instead we have clearly recognizable products of two different mythologies – one official, affirming imperial control over all phenomena secular and religious within a given territory; the other vernacular, dramatizing and validating a cult in terms of its parent community's own religious values.

Yü-ch'ih Chiung sits awkwardly with the categories proposed in a growing Western literature on mediaeval China's provincial cults.[71] He resembles those 'generals of defeated armies . . . persons who have died a violent death, whose head and body are buried in different places, whose spirits have been dispersed . . . troubling men or causing illness' and who 'look for bloody food', that we associate easily with pre-T'ang society,[72] much less easily with that of the High T'ang.[73] Yet the imperial authorities endorse his cult, rather than undermine it as they might traditionally have done.[74] They establish his temple in an important prefectural centre in the heart of the classic northern plain, where he protects their community in the manner (but without the title) of a city god 城隍. Yet city gods, it is said, were not recruited from the ranks of the dangerous, resentful dead,[75] although the spirits of those who died for their country *could* legitimately receive official sacrifice.[76] So we see the Hsiang-chou prefects struggle to make the best of a paradoxical challenge – their malignant persecutor is officially a loyal martyr – and we must understand their rhetoric in this light. All this will remind us that the great movements of historical change in Chinese religion followed a complex, irregular course, not a simple or neat one. The documents that remain demand careful and critical study, which they generously repay with richer understanding.

71 Miyakawa Hisayuki, 'Local cults around Mount Lu at the time of Sun En's rebellion', in H. Welch and A. Seidel, eds., *Facets of Taoism: essays in Chinese religion*, New Haven and London, 1979, pp. 83–101; Rolf A. Stein, 'Religious Taoism and popular religion from the second to seventh centuries', ibid., pp. 53–81; David Johnson, 'The City-god cults of T'ang and Sung China', *Harvard Journal of Asiatic Studies* 45, 1985, 363–457.

72 Stein, 'Religious Taoism', pp. 66–7.

73 Johnson, 'City-god cults', pp. 425–32.

74 Contrast remarks in ibid., p. 432.

75 Ibid., pp. 424 ff.

76 Ibid., p. 444.

6
Victims of the Yüan Ch'ao rebellion

Yüan Ch'ao 袁晁 made his appearance in recorded history on 17 September 762, rising in revolt in the eastern coastal prefecture of T'ai-chou 台州, which included his native Lin-hai 臨海 county. There, in the post-rebellion province of Che-tung, he won a big following from a peasantry disaffected by heavy taxation, and proceeded to capture other prefectures along the coast. Hsin-chou 信州 fell on 19 October, followed by Wen-chou 溫州 and Ming-chou 明州 on 31 October, as the rising moved west, north and south.[1] He adopted a new reign-title and changed the calendar.[2] A major engagement with government forces followed on 18 January 763, when the senior general Li Kuang-pi 李光弼 sent troops to confront and defeat the rebel at Ch'ü-chou 衢州.[3] On 21 April government troops again defeated the rebels, now said to number 200,000. News of Yüan Ch'ao's capture and the pacification of Che-tung by Chang Po-i 張伯儀 finally reached the throne on 24 May 763. He was executed on 17 December 764.[4]

This rising was a peripheral and minor episode in a China still struggling with serious disturbances after the Great Rebellion. It claims little more attention from the historical and literary record than scattered notes on how the emergency drove many into flight. Two anecdotes of the time describe, for instance, the reactions of famous Buddhist monks: one who followed the advice of a warning dream to move out of the area as the rebels approached, another who disdained to flee with his colleagues, but cowed the rebels with a display of supernatural strength.[5] The Yüan Ch'ao emergency does, however, figure three times in the

1 *CTS* 11.270; *HTS* 6.167–8; *TCTC* 222.7130, 7132 (Pao-ying 1/8, 1/10). Hsin-chou was a prefecture formed in 758 out of counties transferred from Jao-chou, Ch'ü-chou, Chien-chou and Fu-chou: *TCTC* 222.7132.

2 *HTS* 136.4589; *TCTC* 222.7130.

3 *HTS* 6.168, 136.4589.

4 *CTS* 11.272; *HTS* 6.168; *TCTC* 222.7143 (Kuang-te 1/4); *HTS* 6.171.

5 *Sung kao-seng chuan* 15.800b and 26.877a.

Kuang-i chi, twice through the testimony of personal informants, which suggests that Tai Fu was in some way close to these events. He recorded them not long after they occurred, for the whole time-span of *Kuang-i chi* seems to end in 780, only sixteen years after the end of the emergency, and these particular records may well have been set down earlier rather than later in that interval. The reported incidents hint at social and economic conditions in ways which enrich the bare chronology of official records. Read carefully, they also seem to speak with the voice of women caught up as victims in the events. Here if anywhere is a chance to test the statement in Chapter 1 that this book 'preserves the oral history of a remote age'.

Certainly 'oral history' will seem a debatable term to use of material like this. It is a modern term and increasingly associated with modern techniques of systematic interview and recording. It relates above all to the recent past, accessible through living memory and richly covered by more conventional written documents.[6] Applied to tales of a little-known regional emergency more than a thousand years ago, the term can scarcely carry the same force or wield the same authority. To use written hearsay for access to such remote events is vulnerable in obvious ways, some of which were discussed in Chapter 1. The chain of hearsay reporting is exposed at every point to distortion, and the move from oral to written testimony adds its own level of cultural processing. It follows that matters of transmission and authority need examining with care. But so do they also with any other kind of historical record, and we can respond to this series of negative points by arguing that, subject to essential critical disciplines, oral testimony should stand beside the many other kinds of flawed and vulnerable evidence from the past from which our history is constructed. It was indeed a standard source of data and insight for historians through the ages until, relatively recently, the modern profession of history-writing chose to disdain it in favour of written documents alone.[7] Records gained from word of mouth, though locked up inside their own special codes, still represent an important body of knowledge handed down from the past. Their value is there to discover; it is bound up with their special character as subjective, spoken testimony, and to find it out we need particular methods

6 For an account of oral history as a branch of modern historical enquiry, see Paul Thompson, *The voice of the past: oral history*, second ed., Oxford 1988. The classic discussion of oral history in relation to non-literate societies is Jan Vansina's *Oral tradition: a study in historical methodology*, trans. H. M. Wright, London 1965, followed by his *Oral tradition as history*, London 1985.

7 Thompson's chapter 'Historians and oral history', in *The voice of the past*, pp. 22–71, documents and discusses this point.

of reading and analysis.[8] The three stories discussed here give a chance to explore and experiment with the Chinese record.

60 At the beginning of Shang-yüan [760] Tou-lu Jung died in office as assistant prefect of Wen-chou. His wife was a daughter of the Chin-ho Princess. This princess had once been married out to [the *qaghan* of] Tokmak,[9] which became a client state. The princess had come home to China when her royal husband died, and she went with Tou-lu Jung when he received his provincial post as assistant in Wen-chou, spending some years there in the prefecture.

At the beginning of Pao-ying [762] Yüan Ch'ao, the mountain bandit from Lin-hai, attacked and captured T'ai-chou. One night the princess's daughter dreamed of a man, dishevelled and streaming with blood, who said to her: 'Disorder will break out in Wen-chou – you ought to leave the place at once. Otherwise you will be in for certain trouble!'

On waking she spoke of this, but the princess said: 'Dream thoughts are topsy turvy. They're not worth taking seriously!'

Soon they went to bed, and the daughter had another dream, this time of her husband Jung, who said: 'The dishevelled man just now was my father-in-law. He is now a general in the underworld. Che-tung province is about to fall, and he just wants to get his wife to leave. She ought to comply, and not go on vainly clinging to wealth and possessions!'

The daughter again reported this to the princess in an attempt to persuade her.

At the time rice was dear in East China, with the exception of Wen-chou, where it was cheap. The princess had given orders to buy thousands of bolts of Wu patterned silk, and she hung on doggedly to these, refusing to leave.

Another day the daughter dreamed of her father saying: 'Eight prefectures in Che-tung have fallen to Yüan Ch'ao. If your mother does not leave soon she will certainly run into serious difficulties.' And he wept as he spoke.

The princess now moved to live in Kua-chou, and when Kua-chou fell she fled, alone and unattended. It did in the end fall out as the dreams had foretold.

The Chin-ho Princess 金河公主 has her own small page in public history. She was actually a Turk, daughter of A-shih-na Huai-tao 阿史那懷道, a *qaghan* of the Western Turks. The Chinese ennobled her for diplomatic reasons in 723 to marry her to Su-lu 蘇祿, the aggressive and successful *qaghan* of the Turgesh tribe (突騎施). His growing power in Central Asia, based on the lands to the west of the Issyk-kul between Talas and Tokmak (Sui-yeh 碎葉), would preoccupy the Chinese government throughout Hsüan-tsung's middle reign until Su-lu's death in

8 Such methods for studying history in societies without writing form the substance of Vansina's books *Oral tradition* and *Oral tradition as history*. Compare also remarks in Thompson, *The voice of the past*, pp. 101 ff.

9 For 辟葉 read 碎葉: cf. *CTS* 194B.5190.

tribal fighting in 738: the marriage was their barely successful attempt to keep him at bay. Not long after Su-lu died the Chinese intervened and brought back the Chin-ho Princess with her son, who had briefly stood as *qaghan* in his father's place.[10]

The *Kuang-i chi* presents an anecdote of this lady's later life, passed on by implication through hearsay, though without named informants. Only analysis will suggest how authentic a glimpse it gives. But Tai Fu's text certainly confirms, through independent transmission from contemporary evidence, that her title was Chin-ho (not Chiao-ho 交河) Princess: a point on which the standard documentary sources are divided.[11] Whatever authority this piece carries can only trace back to the lady herself. It shows her, unsupported by any son of her own (for Su-lu's son vanishes from the record after the events of 738), following her daughter's husband Tou-lu Jung 豆盧榮, himself bearing a tribal surname and clearly of non-Han descent.[12] His death in a minor provincial post has not threatened her standard of living: she is wealthy enough to speculate with investments. But the ladies of this ethnic minority family find themselves caught in the Che-tung of the 760s at the moment when Yüan Ch'ao's local rebellion breaks out. Its sequence and chronology unfold just as we have traced them in standard historical sources, now bodied out with some details of economic conditions. So the outer story here is solidly anchored in conventional historical evidence.

What is more unique about the present story is its access to the private relations of two women left in a vulnerable situation without the authority or protection of male kin. Timely and prudent advice ascribed to the family's departed menfolk gives the princess's daughter the only authority she can exploit in this emergency to persuade her obstinate mother into flight. That she seeks authority through dreams certainly confirms what other sources have to say about the use of

10 *CTS* 194B.5191–2; *HTS* 215B.6067–8. *TCTC* 212.6754 dates the marriage to K'ai-yüan 10/12/*keng-tzu* (14 January 723). Édouard Chavannes translates and discusses these sources in *Documents sur les Tou-kiue (Turcs) occidentaux*, St. Petersburg 1903, pp. 43–7, 81–3, 284–5. Twitchett reviews the episode in *The Cambridge history of China*, vol. 3, pp. 433–5.

11 Variants are listed in *CTS* 194B.5194, n. 5. Chiao-ho was in fact the title conferred in 740 on another lady, surnamed Li, who was the wife of Ah-shih-na Hsin 阿史那昕: see *T'ang ta chao-ling chi* 42.206–7, and *TCTC* 214.6841 (K'ai-yüan 28/4/*hsin-wei*).

12 The surname Tou-lu was adopted by members of the Mu-jung 慕容 surname, who were descended from the northern tribe Hsien-pi 鮮卑. Since the present Tou-lu Jung died in 760 he cannot be the man of that name, described as a graduate of the Chen-yüan period, whose one surviving poem is given in *Ch'üan T'ang shih* 347.3885. The problem is examined by Ts'ao Hsün, in 'Tou-lu Jung yü Tou-lu Ts'e', *Wen shih* 35, Peking 1992, p. 212.

dreams in her society as a medium of communication between living and dead. But her mother's brisk dismissal of 'topsy-turvy' dream thoughts adds an interesting scepticism to that too simple picture.[13] Belief systems, even in mediaeval society, must stand the test of secular pressures, and they do not always succeed. To the end it remains unclear whether the old lady allows herself to be persuaded by the voices of the dead, or makes her own pragmatic decision to abandon her assets and flee.

To us it makes no difference whether the younger woman has really experienced the dreams she describes, or merely pretends that she has. The authenticity of her warning dreams and their predictive power matter less than the purpose which they serve; and their secular function in these difficult circumstances seems only too transparent. The real point of what she has to say lies in its appeal to authority from beyond the grave. Her dreams imply that the male dead, with privileged knowledge of future events, and sometimes also executive authority in the other world, are seen to play a continuing part in the decisions of family life. But it remains a marginal and uncertain part, invoked in times of extreme emergency.

To speak here of inner story (the dreams) and outer (the women's situation) is easy enough, but brings little analytical gain. A more useful contrast lies between two different readings of the episode: one that Tai Fu offers in his final comment, stimulated by the dreams' accurate predictions, and the other reading suggested here, which values the story both for its actual dealings among the living and for its perceived communication between living and dead. By saying one thing Tai Fu tells us another: his offered 'marvel' becomes for us a secular document of social relations. The irony of this reading creates a level of critical detachment: we can read what the author reports without being manipulated by his assumptions about it, and in that way the story gains some status as a historical document. A similar irony will run through Tai Fu's other adventures from the Yüan Ch'ao rebellion.

13 By using the word 'topsy-turvy' to render the Chinese 顛倒 ('upside down') I have chosen to interpret the old lady's response as sceptical: the word implies that reversal brings meaningless confusion. But we should acknowledge a style of dream interpretation which used reversal 反 as a key to meaning – dreams speak the truth in reverse: see the '*Meng-lieh*' 夢列 chapter in Wang Fu's *Ch'ien-fu lun*, 7.315, 317, 318. (I am grateful to Robert Chard for showing me his unpublished paper 'Divination and dream interpretation in the *Ch'ien-fu Lun*', which discusses the point, pp. 34 ff.) On this view the old lady should interpret her daughter's dream as an affirmation of lasting security in Wen-chou. But the events of the story would then prove the dream (or this method of understanding it) wrong. In any case the lady dismisses it as 'not worth taking seriously': she is rejecting a message which events will later prove to be true, not asserting a rival interpretation.

132 Hsüeh Wan-shih was from a Ho-tung family.

At the beginning of Kuang-te [763] the civil governor of Che-tung, Hsüeh Chien-hsün, appointed him magistrate of Yung-chia. Some months went by, and suddenly he said to his wife:

'In ten days from now the food at home will be used up. When that happens I too shall expire. With grain so scarce and prices so high, what shall we do?'

His wife said: 'You are fit and strong – why say such unlucky things about yourself?'

And Hsüeh replied: 'It is most hateful to die, but someone has given me the word, and I have no way out.'

The time came, and he did suddenly drop dead. They had already enclosed him in the coffin[14] when, from inside it, he commanded his clerical assistants and other staff to be called in. They came, and he said to them:

'I have had the misfortune to die, which gives me much grief to speak about. So far I have not given you trouble. But now my wife is without food or money, and she has no way to travel the long road home. I have called you here because I want to entrust you with the care of my nearest and dearest.'

At the time rice was dear in Yung-chia – as much as 10,000 cash per *tou*. Hsüeh Wan-shih demanded rice from all his staff, clerical assistants and below, according to their grade. In terror the officers obeyed him to a man. Even the assistant magistrates and personnel officers presented some rice.

Some days later he said to his family: 'I am going to Yüeh-chou for a while to pay a call on Mr Hsüeh. Now that you have provisions I need not worry any more.' And from that point on he was silent for more than ten days.

His wife, exhausted from her weeping and mourning, was dozing one day when she suddenly heard him speak. She rose with a start and asked: 'Where have you come from?'

He replied: 'I have come back from Yüeh[-chou]. The vice-president now knows that I am dead and has ordered Chang Ch'ing to come and fetch us. He has also chosen husbands for our present two daughters. He certainly has a strong sense of brotherly duty! You must quickly get dressed and ready, so that you can set out as soon as Chang Ch'ing arrives. Otherwise you will be attacked and robbed by the mountain bandits. Getting away quickly comes before anything else.'

So the family got dressed and packed. Chang Ch'ing arrived just at this point, and they set out the same day. By the time they were 200 *li* from Yung-chia, Wen-chou had fallen to the bandits. In every dangerous emergency along the way the family would burn incense and consult [Hsüeh]. He always had advice for them – whether it was positive or negative.[15]

I personally saw members of the family address him.

The story's reference to 'brotherly duty' makes it more or less clear that the civil governor Hsüeh Chien-hsün 薛兼訓 and the county magistrate

14 殮, 'dressing the body', also implies coffining the body: see de Groot, *The religious system of China*, vol. 1, pp. 95–6.

15 不問即否. There is an alternative translation: 'but not unless they asked him'.

Hsüeh Wan-shih 薛萬石 are kinsmen: the dead man and his family are under the governor's personal protection. We know that Hsüeh Chien-hsün did actually serve as civil governor of Che-tung province 浙東觀察使 and prefect of Yüeh-chou 越州 from 762 to 770, when he moved to a post in T'ai-yüan.[16] And near the start of that period of duty he did rise from vice-president of the Censorate (御史中丞) to president of that body (御史大夫).[17] So this story's references to his civil governorship, his residence in Yüeh-chou, his vice-presidency, fit exactly and verifiably with its internal date of 763. So, or almost so, does the fall of Wen-chou (with its seat of government in Yung-chia 永嘉, where the Hsüeh Wan-shih of this story was magistrate) to the 'mountain bandit' Yüan Ch'ao. The official historical record actually places that event in the autumn of 762, when the reign-period was Pao-ying, some nine months before the new period Kuang-te came in.[18] But in these written reports of oral material a technical discrepancy in the dates paradoxically brings a sense of reassurance. Perfectly coordinated dates are naturally impressive, and for that reason always welcome; but we know from our own experience that memories can slip or play false with such details, and we would expect the same problems with Tai Fu's friends. A minor clash in dates might be expected between two stories drawn from different informants, and actually gives some guarantee that Tai Fu has not intervened to edit them into smooth consistency. A similar question might arise with movements in the local rice market. In story **60**, set in the same place at almost the same time, the prefecture of Wen-chou was an oasis of cheap rice; here the price in its chief town Yung-chia has already risen high. But this could well reflect a genuine surge in prices caused by the emergency.

In either case, with the rebels bearing down, it is time to take flight, and both stories use the voice of a dead husband to urge that advice on stressed and vulnerable womenfolk. Only the medium of the voice is changed: it moves from the private world of a daughter's dreams to an open meeting summoned from within the dead man's coffin. But even in this case it returns to infiltrate the drowsy consciousness of an exhausted wife. Eventually the dead magistrate settles down to the discipline of responding only to the family's ritual invocations as they travel, apparently with his coffin, through the rebellious countryside. We are not told whether his responses to their questions are gathered

16 *CTS* 11.297. For an examination of the date of his Che-tung appointment see *T'ang fang-chen nien-piao* 5.771 (with *k'ao-cheng* B.1405); for his prefectural appointment see Yü Hsien-hao, *T'ang tz'u-shih k'ao*, Hong Kong and Nanking 1987, pp. 1763–4.

17 *Chia-t'ai Kuei-chi chih* 2.32a.

18 *TCTC* 222.7132; 222.7138 and 223.7145.

through divination, spoken through possessions, or received in some other way.

The play of inner and outer story is less obvious here. Clearly the effect of the dead man's voice, however perceived to speak, is to protect and provide for his wife in her vulnerable situation, far from home, with a dead body on her hands, and with no independent claim to money or food. His demands are specific and highly convenient. This woman's interests would scarcely be better served if she dictated the terms herself. Her husband's voice is as timely and effective as the dreams that visited Tou-lu Jung's daughter. How it was first made to speak we cannot know for sure. It is not openly stated, but nor is it quite excluded, that the voice spoke through a medium, and if so perhaps through a female relative, as we presume the ghost of Yü-ch'ih Chiung spoke in story **73** (see Chapter 5). In any case, Tai Fu's own eyes have witnessed the ritual formalities that surround the family's later contacts with the dead man, and his testimony is the outer story's firmest framework.

In all this the story plays a counterpoint to story **101**, in which, as here, a dead magistrate speaks out from his coffin, issuing instructions and offering advice. Li Pa 李霸, we are told,

> was a harsh, fierce official, showing favour to no one who crossed his path . . . all his staff, from assistant magistrate and chief of administration down, suffered his venom . . . After one review period he suddenly died, and his body was coffined. But no visitors appeared in the court to offer condolences. His wife wept bitterly as she stroked the coffin, crying: 'When you were alive, Li Pa, why did you cause your wife to suffer this desertion!' Some days later spoken words came out of the coffin, saying: 'Wife! Don't be afflicted! I shall make my own arrangements to return home.'

He takes on reanimated form, summons his frightened staff and threatens them with death. He demands contributions of silk and proceeds to supervise the journey back home to Lo-yang, feeding on offerings at sacrificial sites and reassuring his family each nightfall. Only when the family party have reached home does the dead man finally announce his departure, first causing his coffin to be opened for the display of his terrifying corpse to curious relatives. Then, requesting due burial, he falls silent.

The comparison shows up Hsüeh Wan-shih as clearly the more reasonable, considerate and gentle of the two ghosts, and this very circumstance heightens the story's most obvious ethnographic point: that even so kindly and responsible a spirit is still an object of terror to the surrounding mortals until they can establish a relationship properly mediated through ritual procedures. In this the two stories reflect exactly the preoccupations of Chinese death ritual as it has been observed in modern times, particularly by fieldworkers in southern provinces. Funeral rites, as distinct from grave rites, are 'characterized by fear of the unsettled spirit'.[19] According to a widely held perception, the sensitive period between the moment of death and the aftermath of burial is a time when a corpse is particularly dangerous. James L. Watson distinguishes between two kinds of danger: one a controllable and essentially passive pollution caused by contact with decaying flesh; the other a 'terrible retribution – described as *sat hei* [煞氣] – from the disembodied, and hence, unpredictable spirit'. People would risk this retribution by looking on the corpse during certain moments of physical transition during the ritual. The most critical transitions are complete at the point when the corpse has been moved to the coffin, settled firmly inside and securely nailed in. A further transition follows when the coffin is raised and carried hastily out of the village towards the place of burial. The threat of danger finally subsides only after burial and mourning rituals are completed.[20] Seen from this point of view, both the 'coffin' stories looked at here share an unsettling, and therefore potentially dangerous, circumstance: the deaths have occurred without warning or preparation far away from home, and a long journey lies ahead before the security of burial can put the dead to final rest. It is in the midst of this emergency, and during the liminal period between death and burial, that the dead men breach the restraints laid on them by funeral rites and play an active, typically unpredictable and terrifying role in the events which follow.[21] Li Pa in particular appears to take shape as a zombie and demonstrates his arbitrary killing power on the horses of his official subordinates. He also feeds regularly on sacrificial offerings set out along the way, betraying the physical needs catered for during conventional funerals with bowls of rice and cooked dishes.[22] In one sense, then, stories **132** and **101** act out the worst fears

19 Rubie S. Watson, 'Remembering the dead: graves and politics in southeastern China', in James L. Watson and Evelyn S. Rawski, eds., *Death ritual in late imperial and modern China*, Berkeley and Los Angeles 1988, p. 205. Her comment sums up a wealth of observation and analysis contained elsewhere in that volume.

20 James L. Watson, 'Of flesh and bones: the management of death pollution in Cantonese society', in Maurice Bloch and Jonathan Parry, eds., *Death and the regeneration of life*, Cambridge 1982, pp. 158–9, 161–2, 163, 165–6. A list of seven 'aversion points', at which the corpse is particularly dangerous, is given on p. 184, n. 9.

21 In story **85**, discussed above in Chapter 1, a similar emergency stimulated the newly dead soul of Li Tso-shih, also concerned to support his widow, to speak up through the mouth of his servant-maid.

22 Stuart E. Thompson, 'Death, food, and fertility', in Watson and Rawski, *Death ritual in late imperial and modern China*, p. 84.

implied, and guarded against, in funeral ritual as modern observers have recorded it.

Two other stories in the collection (**276** and **280**) show newly bereaved families deeply attentive to 'soul-speech' 靈語 heard from the soul-shrines 靈座 of their departed. In each case, as it happens, a fox is masquerading as the soul of the deceased and has to be exorcized by ritual means. But these stories demonstrate a contextual point: speech uttered by the unburied dead is a recognized phenomenon, to be taken seriously even when there is a risk of deceptive trickery by alien spirits.

There is a more analytical point to make. When the unburied dead do speak out, it is not at random: they have a specific personal need to address at a time of emergency, when routine social arrangements are not going to serve the purpose. Women caught in vulnerable situations stand to draw particular benefit from that short-circuiting process. But these individual experiences are not stray local incidents: they respond to a much more general human pattern in traditional societies. Keith Thomas, writing about seventeenth-century England, observed:

> In earlier periods . . . it was commoner for men to be carried off at the prime of their life, leaving behind them a certain amount of social disturbance, which ghost-beliefs helped to dispel. The period when the soul wandered loose was that when the survivors were adapting themselves to their new pattern of social relationships.[23]

In English society too ghosts only appeared with good reason, to play some necessary role or communicate some relevant message. And here too was a society, like that of China, in which links with the dead were deliberately preserved and where the wishes of the dead to some extent shaped the behaviour of the living.[24]

The comparison recalls a point made earlier, in Chapter 3 of this study. In reading the *Kuang-i chi* it is often easy, with the help of so-called outer stories, to define particular historical situations with great precision. But the peculiar value of its stories lies more in their insight into people's lives, and in that sense, for all the particularity of time and place, they are documents of wider significance, testifying to more long-term situations. The family experiences of the Chin-ho Princess, of Hsüeh Wan-shih and of Li Pa express a view of relations among the living and with the dead that echoes on into modern times and far beyond the bounds of the Chinese world.

23 Thomas, *Religion and the decline of magic*, pp. 605–6.
24 Ibid., pp. 596, 602.

6 In Kuang-te 2 [764], when Yüan Ch'ao, the pirate from Lin-hai county, was marauding in Yung-chia, one of his ships was caught by the wind and sailed off thousands of *li* to the east. In the distance there came into view a mountain densely covered with brilliant green. There were walls upon it shining with all the colours of the rainbow. They shifted the helm and put in to shore.

There they saw a hermitage with tiles of glass and walls of tortoiseshell. Going into its chambers and corridors they found everything still, with no sign of anyone there, nor anything in the rooms but twenty or so Central Asian whelps. The fittings and appointments were all of gold – none of any lesser type – and there were quilts and coverlets, equally vivid and bright, many made of the finest Shu brocade.[25] There was also a golden citadel, with whole piles of left-over scraps of gold, too many to count. Seeing no one about, the pirates struggled to grab what they could.

Suddenly a woman was seen to come out of the golden citadel. She was about six feet tall, wearing an upper garment of rich brocade and a purple skirt of raw silk. She spoke to the bandits:

'You are Yüan Ch'ao's gang, aren't you? How did you find your way here? What have these objects to do with you, that you should make bold to take them?[26] The whelps you saw just now – did you think they were dogs? You were wrong! They are no less than dragons.[27] Now I really do not grudge the things you have taken, I simply fear that the dragons will grow angry and drag your ship along behind them. Death could then come at any moment. You had best put it all back quickly!'

The pirates lined up to bow to her, and each one took his plunder back to its proper place. Then they asked what place this was.

The woman replied: 'This is where the compassionate hermit of the Mirror Lake Hills pursues his religious discipline. And you, for no good cause, have become pirates under Yüan Ch'ao. Within ten days you will suffer a major disaster. You should take great care!'

The pirates then prayed for a favourable wind to bring them back to the coast. The woman turned her head, gave instructions, and presently a wind arose. The pirates bowed in farewell, then raised their sails.

Within a few days they reached Lin-hai, but their ship was stranded on a sandy mudflat and they were put to death on the rack[28] by government troops. Only half a dozen women managed to survive.

Hsieh Ch'üan-chih, commander of the headquarters garrison in Che-tung

25 The fine silk brocade of Szechuan, famous throughout T'ang China, gave its name to the Cho-chin chiang 濯錦江 (otherwise Min chiang 岷江), the river flowing past Ch'eng-tu into the Yangtze.

26 For 須爾何與, read 預爾何事, as in *San-tung ch'ün-hsien lu* 18.7a.

27 The motif of dragons posing as more everyday creatures recurs in T'ang fiction: see the well-known tale of Liu I, *TPKC* 419.3410–11. But dragons and dogs in particular exchange their forms and names repeatedly in T'ang and pre-T'ang tradition; see Ch'ien Chung-shu, *Kuan-chui pien*, pp. 661–2.

28 Prisoners were placed on a wooden framework, but did not, as with the mediaeval European rack, suffer stretching of the limbs.

province,[29] has taken one to him as a bondmaid. Her name is Curled Leaf 曲葉, and she tells this story herself.

The simple sentences at the close of this adventure give a precise and quite believable chain of testimony. As usual Tai Fu is in touch with the local military staff and hears, at first or second hand, a tale told at the end of the emergency by the garrison commander's captive woman. We know nothing of her origins before the Yüan Ch'ao episode. But she was lucky to survive capture, and can plainly only expect to serve as a bondmaid. What she has to tell, which is of course an inner story, is full of interest in its own right, but the chance to hear the voice of a female slave from that remote time is more interesting still.

To an extent we can take her story to pieces. It has some familiar features. Certainly the island with its palaces of gold is ancient: it goes back to the 'isles of the gods' in the mainstream of Chinese fable:

> Some have been there in the past, no doubt: all the immortals and death-defying elixirs are there, all living creatures, birds and beasts, are perfectly white, and palace buildings are made of gold and silver. As you approach, they look from the distance like clouds; when you reach them, the three divine mountains are actually under water. But as you look down at them the wind takes you away, so that in the end no one has been able to reach them.

Such is Ssu-ma Ch'ien's report of the islands, which he located in the Gulf of Po-hai.[30] According to tradition they were sought out in due course by Ch'in Shih-huang-ti. Myths of Hsü Fu 徐福, the man he charged with a legendary embassy to the island Tsu-chou 祖洲 in the Eastern Ocean, early became associated with Kuei-chi, the place where Curled Leaf would later tell her story.[31] And the immortal Hsü Fu certainly lived on in Tai Fu's world of discourse. Story **1** tells of a man who sets out in quest of him and his island to find a cure for a hopeless illness;

29 'The principal concentration of troops was at the prefectural seat of the province where the garrison was called the *ya-chün* ('headquarters garrison') . . . Its nucleus was an elite corps of guardsmen responsible for the governor's safety and no doubt used as a general security force at the provincial capital': C. A. Peterson, in Twitchett, ed., *The Cambridge history of China*, vol. 3, part 1, p. 515. Hsieh Ch'üan-chih was no doubt involved in stamping out the Yüan Ch'ao insurgency.

30 *Shih chi* 28.1370.

31 The tale of Hsü Fu's expedition traces back to *Shih chi* 118.3086 (cf. 6.247). In *Hou Han shu* 85.2822, Hsü Fu's island is located in the ocean off Kuei-chi, and the descendants of his expedition are said to frequent the markets of Kuei-chi; cf. *San-kuo chih* 47.1136, and *Kua-ti chih*, cited in *Shih chi cheng-i* (*Shih chi* 118.3087, n. 2). Hsü Fu's story was copied through several generations of mediaeval legendaries: see Li Feng-mao, *Liu-ch'ao Sui T'ang hsien-tao lei hsiao-shuo yen-chiu*, Taipei 1986, pp. 149, 153, 203–4. It also came to serve as a myth of the settlement of Japan: see the study by Gotō Shukudō, 'Jofuku tōrai no densetsu ni toite', *Tōyō bunka* (1926) 25, 60–70; 26, 49–61; 27, 63–72; 28, 55–63; 29, 44–51.

in this he succeeds and returns to the northern coastal prefecture Teng-chou 登州.[32] The twelfth-century *I-chien chih*, also rich in Chekiang stories, shows that fabulous islands lingered on in the folklore of that region.[33]

But story **6** also introduces an unnamed compassionate hermit as the occupant of its wonderful island. Linked with the hills of Mirror Lake (*Ching-hu* 鏡湖), he seems to be a figure of local significance, for this lake (long since dried up) was a known spot in Che-tung just south of the provincial capital Yüeh-chou, where this story ends. No record of such a man's title or of a corresponding cult appears in other T'ang sources, and we are left to guess at his identity. It so happens that Mirror Lake was chosen as a retreat at the end of his long life by a local celebrity, the aged and ebullient statesman Ho Chih-chang 賀知章 (659–744). In 744, with the tender good wishes of the emperor Hsüan-tsung, he retired from public office to enter the Taoist priesthood, and near his retreat on Mirror Lake he established a life-sparing pool (放生池).[34] Although we have no firm evidence that this man became the object of any cult after his recorded death that same year, there was certainly a local Taoist tradition that he lived on in a transcendent form of existence. Here is a passage from a Kuei-chi tomb inscription, dated 879, for the Taoist master Tsu Kuan 祖貫:

Now Director Ho Chih-chang[35] had learned the secret of sustaining life: he lived for nigh on hundreds of years without dying. With satchel on his back he

32 Story **1** in fact consists of two items and is drawn from two sources – *Hsien-chuan shih-i* 仙傳拾遺 and *Kuang-i chi*. The former, a lost work now partly reconstructed by Yen I-p'ing (*Tao-chiao yen-chiu tzu-liao*, vol. 1, Pan-ch'iao 1974), was a collection of short Taoist biographies by Tu Kuang-t'ing 杜光庭 (850–933). The first item in story **1** gives the legends connected with Ch'in Shih-huang-ti's quest for immortality; it appears again, with slight changes of detail, in *TPKC* 4.25, there simply derived from *Hsien-chuan shih-i*. So *Kuang-i chi*, here named second, seems to be the source of the second item, the story of the sick man's quest for Hsü Fu. But both items may well have appeared together in *Hsien-chuan shih-i*, since Tu Kuang-t'ing freely assembled material from many sources. This might explain why the second item here is expressly derived from *Hsien-chuan shih-i* in the fourteenth-century *Li-shih chen-hsien t'i-tao t'ung-chien* 6.7b, where the same two items appear in sequence.

33 *I-chien chih*, *i-chih*, 13.295–6, with an island of retributive punishment; *chih-ting*, 3.986–7, with an island of magic bamboos, inhabited by an old hermit clad in white.

34 *CTS* 190B.5034; *HTS* 196.5607; *T'ang shih chi-shih* 17.246–7. Compare also the Taoist sources *San-tung ch'ün-hsien lu* 14.6ab, and *Hsüan p'in lu* 4.27b–29b (ed. Yen I-p'ing, *Tao-chiao yen-chiu tzu-liao*, vol. 1, 4.113–14). The poems presented to him on this occasion by the emperor and almost forty other court figures are preserved in *Kuei-chi to-ying tsung-chi* 2.6a–15b. On this important compilation, made in 1072 by K'ung Yen-chih 孔延之, see *Ssu-k'u ch'üan-shu tsung-mu* 186.41a–42b; Ch'en Ch'iao-i, *Shao-hsing ti-fang wen-hsien k'ao-lu*, Hangchow 1983, pp. 354–5.

35 He rose to be director of the palace library (*pi-shu chien* 祕書監) under Hsüan-tsung.

sold herbal drugs like Han K'ang-po 韓康伯.[36] Recently he ascended aloft in T'ai-chou, and this was heard of far and wide.

The inscription goes on to state that Tsu encountered Ho Chih-chang in 819, when Ho gave him drugs that would prolong his life. Ho also promised to meet him in heaven after a cycle of sixty years, thus fixing the date at which Tsu would end his own life at the age of ninety-five *sui*.[37] The implication is that many in the northern Chekiang region believed Ho Chih-chang to be surviving there as a Taoist saint until late in the ninth century – a time when he would theoretically be more than two hundred years old.

These little known myths of Ho Chih-chang from the late T'ang have, if not a direct, at least a circumstantial relevance to the pirates' island adventure. He had all the characteristics needed to share the identity of the compassionate hermit of Mirror Lake Hills – an other-worldly Taoist saint, famously settled at Mirror Lake at the end of his mortal life, compassionate in creating a life-sparing pool there, freely at large in the region of coastal Chekiang through the latter eighth and ninth centuries. It would not be absurd if this were the man who came to the minds of folk in Yüeh-chou or T'ai-chou when they contemplated, or imagined, an island oratory in the ocean off their eastern coast.

A more comprehensive insight into the island adventure as a whole comes from a remote and unlikely seeming source – the autobiographical *Peregrinaçam* of the sixteenth-century Portuguese adventurer Fernão Mendes Pinto. This work is one of the monuments of Portuguese prose literature. Pinto poured into it a rich knowledge of Asia gathered both from hearsay and from his own experience with buccaneers in the Far East. Later in his career he underwent a religious conversion, became involved with the early stages of the Jesuit movement and looked back on his past with complex feelings of shame and remorse. Using great narrative and descriptive art his book builds up a dynamic vision of many Asian cultures, strongly coloured with value judgements at the

36 Han K'ang, whose *tzu* was Po-hsiu 伯休, is commemorated with a short biography in *Hou Han shu* 83.2770–1 as a celebrated hermit who for many years sold mountain herbs in the market of Ch'ang-an.

37 'T'ang T'ung-ho hsien-sheng Tsu-chün mu-chih-ming' 唐通和先生祖君墓誌銘, by Hsü Ting 許鼎, in *Kuei-chi to-ying tsung-chi* 17.11b–13b. This tomb inscription marks the burial of Tsu Kuan on 27 December 879. It was transmitted in remarkable circumstances: the engraved stone was found underfoot in a local doorway by P'eng Jui 彭汭, a follower of the early Sung scholar and statesman Hsü Hsüan 徐鉉 (917–992), who wrote a preface in celebration: see ibid., 17.13b–15a. All this came to the notice of Fan Chung-yen 范仲淹 (989–1052), who in 1040 had the texts engraved in the main hall of the Taoist monastery which once had been Ho Chih-chang's retreat at Mirror Lake: ibid., 17.15ab.

expense of his own countrymen and with sympathy for the peoples of Asia they were preying upon.

What he says about China meets with suspicion and reserve from modern critics, who tend to conclude that he was working more from invention than experience.[38] Yet in his chapters 75 to 79 he describes what is essentially the same adventure as we find in story **6**.[39] Portuguese freebooters have sailed up the coast from Ningpo in the year 1542 and, after many weeks at sea, make their way to an island off the 'Gulf of Nanking' called Calempluy. They have in mind to plunder the imperial tombs, which they have been told are there. The island presents a remarkable sight – girt all round by a wall of wrought jasper stones, this topped by a balustrade of brass, the whole studded with metal statuary, rich arches, orchards of fruit trees, chapels and a group of larger buildings 'all covered in gold from top to bottom for as far as the eye could see'.[40] The raiders are greeted by an aged hermit who at once sees through their designs of plunder. Then, as they ransack the coffins for silver, he advises them to put back what they have taken and do penance as a means to gain pardon for the offence. Other hermits later warn them in turn of dire retribution from all the forces of nature. And indeed the Portuguese later go on to be driven aground after a typhoon in the Gulf of Nanking. Pinto himself suffers capture and imprisonment.

For the Pinto scholar Georg Schurhammer this Calempluy episode was simply invented (*erdichtet*), and it is not difficult to see why he should think so.[41] But a comparison with the bondmaid Curled Leaf's story of the Yüan Ch'ao pirates throws a sharper light on both. Though separated by eight hundred years, the two adventures are strikingly similar. They have the same vision of an island walled around with shining stone and adorned with buildings of gold; they both produce a resident hermit – an all-seeing and all-knowing figure who warns the pirates to return their plunder; both give a threat of natural vengeance, and both stage a final beaching on the East China coast.

How could a traditional yarn of the sea-coast be handed down through so many centuries in East China? And how might that transmission be traced? These are inviting questions, but they belong to a type of

38 The most thorough examinations are by Georg Schurhammer, 'Fernão Mendez Pinto und seine "Peregrinaçam" ', *Asia Major* 3, 1926, 71–103 and 194–267; Maurice Collis, *The grand peregrination*, London 1949; Rebecca D. Catz, *The travels of Mendes Pinto*, Chicago 1989, pp. xv–xlvi, and extensive bibliography on pp. 655–63.

39 As numbered in the Portuguese original (ed. Lisbon 1614, etc.). See the modern critical translation by Catz, *The travels of Mendes Pinto*, pp. 144–53.

40 Ibid., p. 145.

41 Schurhammer, 'Fernão Mendez Pinto', p. 217. Maurice Collis gives a more subtle analysis in *The grand peregrination*, pp. 116–21.

historical enquiry we are not pursuing here. Two specimens have surfaced randomly from a background culture now virtually lost to view, in which no doubt innumerable variant forms of the story passed around. One such variant shows up, for instance, in story **311**, where the crew of a passing ship find a castaway on their island: he leads them to rich hoards of precious stones, but warns them to load up and leave quickly in case the god of the mountain attempts to recover his treasures; the god does so, giving chase in the form of a snake. This simpler version of the story, with its jealously possessive territorial god, suggests a general mythological background for the tale of the stolen treasure. But such traditional features of the story are less interesting here than the function it serves in two quite different human contexts. They illuminate one another. In Pinto's case we see a man working out in a narrative his sense of guilt at a career of violence and looting at the expense of gentle and civilized peoples in the East. The episode at Calempluy does that work for him perfectly. It contrasts plundering buccaneers with a population of wise and mild-mannered hermits; it shows violent looters outraging the sanctity of tombs. So typhoon and shipwreck on the mainland coast come as just, natural penalties. Pinto must have found the traditional story he heard a perfect setting in which to cast himself and his fellow adventurers, and to clothe their experience with some of the rhetoric of Catholic piety.

Curled Leaf, who tells the same story for her new masters and owners to hear, seems haunted by a similar sense of natural justice overtaking her. Like Pinto she has cast herself in the setting of a background traditional tale. Unlike him, she deals with the question of the looted treasure by giving the story in a way that lets the pirates return their loot to its place. But into the text of her story she has also insinuated all kinds of disapproving comments on Yüan Ch'ao and his rebels, spoken through the mouth of the lady hermit. So the beaching and capture of the pirate ship later bring a clear sense of retributive justice. How carefully this woman has presented herself to her masters! What she has to tell may not have the documentary status of a seafarer's logbook, but for a woman working in the home of her captors it does effectively dissociate her from the Yüan Ch'ao pirates who led her into such serious trouble. Under analysis, then, this island extravaganza responds to a secular social situation in which an individual's voice appears to be speaking. It is a voice that Tai Fu enables us to identify precisely. But to do so we have once again stepped ironically outside the framework he has offered us.

In all the stories discussed here we receive something that seems, sometimes demonstrably, to come from a truly oral original, even when its communication to us is mediated through writing. What we receive in this way is access to experience and to people beyond the scope of formal written culture. Here is a chance to meet women and servants at large in society, none of them in a position to articulate their personal view of the world in writing. We see them characteristically at the receiving end of public historical events, but also in dynamic situations, reacting and relating to one another, as well as to the dead. And they speak from within a distinctive culture: social relations, religious values, mythological perceptions not determined by received orthodoxy.

7
Mating with spirits

Divine women

Consider first the experience of Chi Kuang-ch'en 季廣琛 (**80**):

In Ho-hsi there are goddesses called the Young Ladies.

Chi Kuang-ch'en once travelled in Ho-hsi when he was young. He rested at an inn and, as he took his siesta, dreamed that a cloud-chariot descended from the air with dozens of attendants. The Young Ladies were announced: both sisters had come to visit him. At first Chi Kuang-ch'en was delighted. But when he awoke and opened his eyes he took a stealthy look and saw that they were apparently still there. Suspecting them of being demons he drew the sword at his side and slashed at them.

The goddesses rebuked him: 'We came to you with long-standing affection. How could you bring yourself to think these wicked thoughts?' And they left.

Chi Kuang-ch'en told this to the innkeeper, who said: 'They were the Young Ladies.' Chi then went off himself to buy some liquor and dried meat to offer in sacrifice, intending to offer apologies for the offences he had committed the previous day. But the goddesses were still displeased.[1] So Chi wrote verses on the temple wall, but the ink would not form the words.

The next night he once again dreamed that the goddesses came to him, even more furious, to say: 'We shall see to it that to the end of your days you never receive title or estate.'

Men had dallied with goddesses in Chinese literature since the days of Sung Yü's 宋玉 'Rhapsody on Kao-t'ang' and 'Rhapsody on the Goddess', and the theme ran on luxuriantly through T'ang verse and prose.[2] But here, as so often elsewhere, the *Kuang-i chi* offers the peculiar savour of a known man's personal experience. We read story **80**, not to enjoy an elegant and allusive literary construct, but to see the teller

1 Omitting 也, with Sun Ch'ien.

2 This is the subject of Edward H. Schafer, *The divine woman: dragon ladies and rain maidens in T'ang literature*, Berkeley and Los Angeles 1973. For the poems of Sung Yü, see *Wen-hsüan* 19.1b–9b. They are discussed by Schafer, pp. 35–8.

struggling to make sense of a perceived encounter. The first task, then, is to identify the teller's voice.

Of Chi Kuang-ch'en we know this much.[3] He passed the decree examination called 'Commanding general with wise strategies' 智謀將率 in 735.[4] Early in 757 he served as general under Li Lin 李璘, prince of Yung 永, on the expedition down the lower Yangtze which developed into an attempted rebellion (made famous by the presence of the poet Li Po); but he successfully deserted the prince before the movement was crushed in March of that year.[5] During the summer and autumn of 758 he moved rapidly from one military governorship to another, until in 759 he was demoted to the prefecture of Wen-chou 溫州. Later, in 761, he moved from Wen-chou to Hsüan-chou 宣州 and took on the duties of military governor in Che-chiang West.[6] This seems to have been his latest appointment before a final promotion, in 774, to Grand Counsellor of the Right 右散騎常侍.[7] As far as our sources permit us to know, the Young Ladies 女郎神 of this story were quite possibly successful in denying him the victorious general's usual reward of feudal title and estate.

An anecdote of his early career takes us closer to the adventure in Ho-hsi 河西, a strategic military command on the Tibetan borders in the north-west. According to this a magic sword, which could attack the enemy ranks as though a dragon of metal were among them, passed from Sung Ch'ing-ch'un 宋青春, a successful campaigner of the K'ai-yüan period, into the possession of Chi Kuang-ch'en, then prefect of the far-western outpost Kua-chou 瓜州. Even the great Turkish general Ko-shu Han 哥舒翰, who led armies against the Tibetans in neighbouring Lung-yu 隴右 from 748 to 755 and in Ho-hsi itself from 753 to 755, cast envious eyes on that sword, but Chi would not part with it.[8] This anecdote seems to place Chi Kuang-ch'en in Ho-hsi during the years before his adventure with the prince of Yung. It also provides him with a special sword, and it is tempting to see in this the weapon that he brandishes so effectively against the Young Ladies in story **80**.

The story itself, with its reference to Chi's young years and its sense

3 The extant sources are critically reviewed in Ts'en Chung-mien, *Yüan-ho hsing-tsuan ssu-chiao chi*, Shanghai 1948, 8.763. Other ancient sources, now lost, are critically discussed in *Tzu-chih t'ung-chien k'ao-i: TCTC* 220.7059–60.

4 *T'ang hui-yao* 76.1388; *Ts'e-fu yüan-kuei* 645.16a; *TPYL* 629.10b.

5 *CTS* 107.3265; *Tzu-chih t'ung-chien* 219.7009 and 7019–20.

6 *CTS* 10.252–3, 256, 260. I accept Ts'en's emendation of the 759 appointment.

7 *CTS* 11.306. There is evidence that he held a position as imperial counsellor as early as 758: *Tzu-chih t'ung-chien k'ao-i* 220.7060.

8 *Yu-yang tsa-tsu* 6.62–3; *TPKC* 231.1770; *Nan-pu hsin shu* 2(乙).13. On Ko-shu Han's military governorships, see *T'ang fang-chen nien-piao* 8.1204–5 and 1223.

of hindsight in explaining his lifelong lack of feudal title, has a plainly retrospective character. Another temptation, then, is to see it as part of the Chekiang gossip of the 760s and 770s so richly retailed in the *Kuang-i chi* – this, after all, was the scene of Chi's official career between 759 and 774. His own voice may lie behind the personal reminiscence we read here.

In one sense the story plays upon a theme already mentioned in Chapter 4 of this book. Wang Hsün disported himself with the Third Daughter of Mount Hua (**194**); Li Shih made love every summer with the Three Consorts of the Mount (**71**). Both were responding to images of goddesses in temple shrines, and the same is quite strongly implied in the story of Chi Kuang-ch'en, beginning as it does with his location in the very region where the Young Ladies enjoyed their cult.

But there is an interesting difference in the way he treats the experience. Wang Hsün and Li Shih, happily engrossed in their erotic adventures, were withdrawn from them through actions by family and friends, who used professional ritual means to protect their men from danger.[9] Chi Kuang-ch'en has a more ambiguous perspective. Are his visitors goddesses or demons? Although he has no doubt seen and admired them in their temple before he enjoyed their visit to his couch, it seems that he cannot make this judgement without local assistance. Their behaviour in his first dream would evidently fit either case, with only their lingering presence to his half-awake eyes prompting a panic reaction. Yet the ritual implications are dramatic: a choice between hasty and violent exorcism, if demons, or suppliant temple offering, if not. His second dream of the goddesses, with their implacable sense of grievance, gives expression to feelings of horror and guilt at his mistake.

So the story dramatizes two starkly different kinds of experience awaiting a man who visits a goddess's temple. One is the subject of a warning already quoted from the Taoist exorcist's manual HY 854: the lascivious Moon Lady sprite can take possession of a clay image, then seduce the men who fall in love with it, visiting them in their sleep at night.[10] Chi Kuang-ch'en suspects something of the sort when he wields his sword at the images flitting before his eyes. But he comes to see this as a mistake: he has been through a different experience, the goddesses were genuinely with him, and he should not have dealt with them in that way. Clearly some other course of action would have been more fitting – the goddesses expected positive, affectionate treatment and

9 The parallel case of women overcome by a male god whose temple they visit is discussed above, in Chap. 4, pp. 112–13.

10 Above, Chapter 4, p. 108, with n. 83.

had power to make their displeasure felt when their lover failed to give it.

Compare now the experience of Chu Ao 朱敖 (**115a**):

In days gone by Chu Ao, now vice-prefect of Hangchow, lived in retreat on Shao-shih Mountain.

Early in T'ien-pao Li Shu, an administrator from Yang-ti county who was at the Monastery of the Mount [Sung], sent over a rider to summon him. Chu Ao mounted and rode off, with the attendant behind him.

A little way along they came up below the Temple of the Younger Aunt.[11] At the time it was high summer. He caught sight of a girl in a green robe, aged fifteen or sixteen and very pretty. Chu Ao presumed that she was someone's bondmaid and felt surprised that she should be wearing warm clothing in summertime.

He urged on his horse and questioned her. She smiled, said nothing, and walked into the temple. Chu Ao accordingly dismounted, but found no sign of anyone there. Then he looked at the paintings on the walls and saw in them a girl in a green robe – the girl he had seen on the road. Lingering on with sighs of regret, he eventually moved on to the monastery, where he told the whole story, winning admiring comments from Li Shu and company.

That night while he slept he dreamed that the girl came to him. And as he seized the blankets in an access of pleasure his semen poured out. This happened several nights in a row.

Wu Yün, a Taoist priest of Mount Sung, wrote out for him a talisman to drive her away, but this proved impossible. Wu then used Taoist ritual to control her, but that too failed.

Another time he lodged in the cell of a Taoist priest called Ch'eng, whose performance of ritual was clean and pure. The goddess now stopped her visits.

Once more Tai Fu reports the personal reminiscences of an acquaintance and fellow office-holder in the Chekiang region. Chu Ao appears again as an informant in story **122**.[12] His account here is circumstantial enough to speak convincingly for a personal experience. Above all, his sexual contact with the disembodied serving girl seen on a temple wall-painting is presented as a physical episode exactly as we should perceive

11 This temple was identified as the 'Temple of [Mount] Shao-shih on Mount Sung' mentioned in the geographical monograph of *Han shu* (28A.1560). Its presiding deity was said to be younger sister to Yü the Great's wife, and therefore younger aunt to his son Ch'i 啟. Empress Wu seems to have patronized the cult as part of her claim to legitimacy as a female ruler with capital based at nearby Lo-yang, and the temple was accordingly celebrated in a long formal essay by Yang Chiung 楊炯 (650–after 693): 'Shao-shih shan Shao-i miao pei' 少室山少姨廟碑, in *Yang Ying-ch'uan chi* 5.1a–6b. (The most up-to-date account of Yang Chiung's career is by Fu Hsüan-ts'ung in *T'ang ts'ai-tzu chuan chiao-chien*, vol. 1, pp. 34–43.)

12 A man with this name also appears in *CTS* 11.313 and 129.3600, as an officer of the censorate sent in 777 to investigate flood damage in Wei-nan 渭南 county.

it ourselves: a dream stimulated by a daytime event is associated with a nocturnal discharge of semen. The compounding of this experience over several nights must raise the usual anxieties about semen loss,[13] and that is surely what moves Chu Ao to seek ritual help in controlling what happens in his dreams. Like Wang Hsün and Li Shih he tastes physical pleasure with his divine visitor; unlike them he takes steps of his own to bring it to an end. But his attitude also contrasts with that of Chi Kuang-ch'en: there is no awed attempt here to win back the approval of a feared and powerful goddess, and we have to conclude that a mere bondmaid in the other world presents no terrors beyond tempting him to physical excess.

What emerges from comparing these two personal episodes is on one hand a basic view of sexual behaviour attributed to women from the world of gods: physically attracted to certain living men, they freely seduce them. The men, for their part, passively receive their attentions in an unconscious state, either comatose or asleep; they feel threatened, either by demonry or by loss of semen, and sometimes seek ritual help in struggling free from their visitors. But certain divine women wield knowledge and power which in themselves can threaten, or maybe privilege, their lovers. This creates scope for a wider, more complex pattern of relationships between them, to which we now turn.

The Third Daughter of Mount Hua, revealed in story **194** as a libidinous and unconstrained sexual partner, shows another face in story **78**. She meets her man away from the temple complex, visiting an inn on her travels. Catching sight of him, she calls him before her and effectively recruits him to live with her as husband and wife. For seven years they live royally in a Ch'ang-an mansion, while the man's family draws wealth and prestige from the connection. During this time she bears him two sons and a daughter.

Then suddenly the princess said that she wanted to find him a wife. The man was taken aback and bewildered that she should speak like this, but the princess went on: 'I am really not human at all – it is not right for me to be your wife for good. And you are destined to be married: I shall know that it is not a change in your affections.'

In due course he did marry another woman, but kept up unbroken contact [with the princess]. His wife's family, finding that he would go off and fail to return for several days at a time, sent someone to watch him. They observed him regularly going into a derelict mansion, and feared he might be bewitched by demons.

One day they got him drunk, then ordered a ritual specialist to write charms

13 The physiological theories underlying this familiar concern are surveyed in Needham, *Science and civilisation in China*, vol. 5, pt. 5, Cambridge 1983, pp. 184 ff.

which were placed within his clothing and all over his body. When the man later went to the princess's home she sent out a family servant to stop him from going in. The man was quite unable to understand why and hung disconsolately around the gate.

Presently the princess came out to the gate and heaped reproaches on him: 'Once you were a poor man, and I advanced you. Now you are a noble lord, and that shows I have not treated you ungenerously. So why did you have your wife's family write charms to come between us, so that I would not be able to kill you?'

It was only when he looked at his own body that the man knew there were charms on it. He earnestly begged pardon, and the princess said: 'I do understand the position you are in. But now that the charm has made its authority felt its force cannot be held back.' And she called all her children, telling them to take leave of their father, while the man wept and sobbed.

The princess ordered attendants to make haste and pack, for they would leave the city that same day. The man asked where she lived and what her name was. She said: 'I am the Third Daughter of Mount Hua.' And with these words she took her leave and left. Once outside the gate she vanished.

The outer story here is little changed from that of Li Shih (**71**): the secular perception of this relationship still finds nothing but menace in it, and ritual protection remains the automatic response. But the inner story is subtly different. While the Three Consorts chided Li Shih merely for ending their shared experience of sexual pleasure, now the Third Daughter, with mortification and a sense of betrayal, appeals to a relationship of greater moral weight. She is the man's patron, his partner, the mother of his children. She has generously made way for the mortal marriage he was destined to make. After serving him so well it is with a sense of sad but unbiddable necessity that she and her children depart from his life.

With an anonymous hero and a formulaic outer story, this piece has less the character of an individual experience than of a mythological item. And indeed its theme echoes again quite clearly in another story, attributed to the ninth-century *I-wen chi* 異聞集. There an examination candidate, entranced by the Third Daughter's statue in her shrine, promises to return and marry her if he gains the degree. The marriage takes place, but at the goddess's request soon makes way for a second, earthly marriage. The tale ends in disaster when a Taoist exorcist exposes and punishes the man's divine liaison, an act which in turn brings divine retribution upon his wife and himself.[14]

These eighth- and ninth-century stories already show signs of a mythological system developing around the Third Daughter which would later

14 The tale survives, probably in abridged form, in *Lei shuo* 28.13a–14b.

emerge as an important theme in popular literature – the legend of Prince Ch'en-hsiang 沉香太子, born of the Third Daughter's union with a mortal man.[15] But a more general theme, of the goddess who becomes a loyal, supportive and enriching wife, seems to have run quite widely through the vernacular and literary culture of T'ang China. The *Kuang-i chi* provides another particularly colourful version of this in story **74**, 'A man of Ju-yin'.[16] Once again, initiative comes from the divine woman's side: the daughter of a general under the god of Mount Sung chooses a young man for his good looks and dashing lifestyle; an orphan himself, he can do little to resist the eager pressure to marry her. What follows is not a loose consensual union, as in other tales, but a formal wedded bond. The married couple embarks on a lifetime of orthodox fulfilment, with cordial relations between the families, abundance of wealth, rejuvenating sexual hygiene and many sons. They part only with the mortal husband's death, when mother and children return to the other world. It is a story which, like the more famous tale of Liu I, affirms a totally positive vision of relations between mortal men and divine women. No hint of exorcism or other ritual antagonism intrudes into this mixed marriage, and the partners thus achieve the difficult feat of conventional marital status.

The picture which so far emerges from these various stories shows divine women relating to mortal men along a continuum of experience: it runs from the horrors of demonic visitation, through increasing degrees of personal intimacy and commitment, to the full condition of wedded union. The further they move along this line the closer they approximate to the ideal state of secular relations between the sexes. A similar continuum is found in T'ang literature covering relations with animal spirits, a subject I have discussed in another book.[17] But that is less fully deployed in the *Kuang-i chi*, where men and women who have relations with animal spirits nearly always seek escape.[18]

15 For a study of this legend, see G. Dudbridge, 'The goddess Hua-yüeh San-niang and the Cantonese ballad *Ch'en-hsiang T'ai-tzu*', *Chinese Studies* (*Han-hsüeh yen-chiu*) 8.1, 1990, 627–46.

16 For an annotated translation of this tale, and a close discussion in relation to the famous story of Liu I 柳毅, see G. Dudbridge, 'The tale of Liu Yi and its analogues', in Eva Hung, ed., *Paradoxes of traditional Chinese literature*, Hong Kong 1994, pp. 61–88.

17 *The tale of Li Wa*, London, 1983, pp. 61 ff.

18 Tigers: **222, 227, 234**; rat: **251b** (though here the girl is exceptionally attached to her mate); wolf: **254**; wild cat: **257**; foxes: **261, 263, 265, 266, 267, 268, 269, 271, 272, 274, 278, 279, 281, 282, 283, 288**; (only **290** and **291** show more positive fox unions). A union with a crane takes place in **305**.

Mortal women

What the *Kuang-i chi* does provide in rich detail is a parallel continuum for sexual and marital relations between living and dead mortals. To begin with there are some insights into the ethnography and folklore of weddings: the custom of *sa-chang* 撒帳 (scattering the curtains of the bridal bed with coins) and the use of red-dyed fabrics are both attested in the transferred image of a wedding in story **131**;[19] the belief that bride and groom are tied together by their feet in the spirit world appears in **88**. Unsurprisingly a belief in predestined marriages pervades the whole system: story **146** stages an interrogation of spirits to decide a choice of fiancée, and this reveals that one of them is destined to be the wife of a prefect; story **141** shows a man bearing the mark laid on him by his lover in a former existence – she will join him later as his wife in this. But far more complex and interesting is the dynamic of relations between sexual partners across the barrier of death.

In the *Kuang-i chi* a profound ritual difference separates the treatment of divine and of mortal lovers. People of the living world do not hesitate to use written charms or other exorcistic rites to control and banish unwanted demon lovers. But dead women, no less prone to visit and seduce attractive men, never receive such treatment.[20] It is as though the forces of discipline and control exercised through the hierarchy of the gods have no sway over mortal souls – a distinction which echoes the analysis of modern anthropologists, distinguishing carefully between the ritual treatment of gods, ghosts and ancestors.[21] The dead women's situations find their own way to a resolution which often depends on the needs and the plight of the women themselves. This is best studied by looking at particular cases.

110 Yang Chun, a man of Sung-ch'eng, belonged to a well-known scholarly family. Once, when out in the countryside, he met a woman of outstanding beauty. Chun dallied with her, and they had sex together.

For more than a month she would keep on coming into his study, and would also beg to take Chun away. Chun refused to go with her. But suddenly he felt unbearable pains in his heart, and said: 'If it is absolutely unavoidable, I will go away with you. Why do you torment me so harshly?' He then became well again.

19 See the discussion and quotation above, Chapter 3, p. 53. This is among the earliest textual mentions of the *sa-chang* custom in China, although later texts refer back to earlier periods: see Ch'en P'eng, *Chung-kuo hun-yin shih-kao*, Peking 1990, pp. 266–9, with p. 281, n. 7, on story **131**.

20 The one apparent exception to this is story **107**, in which an evil-protecting sword spontaneously dispels the buildings conjured up out of a dead woman's tomb.

21 See Arthur P. Wolf, 'Gods, ghosts, and ancestors', in Wolf, ed., *Religion and ritual in Chinese society*, Stanford 1974, pp. 131–82; esp. pp. 169 ff.

> He walked a dozen *li* with the woman, and they reached a house, with courtyards and buildings all quite distinct, though the entrance was small and insignificant. The woman provided Chun with a meal. But each mouthful would leave the bowl empty. He thought this strange, but still did not realize she was a ghost – he knew that only later.
>
> Each time Chun left her he would lie on his bed like a corpse behind closed doors and only come to life after six or seven days. This went on for two or three years.
>
> Chun's elder brother said to him: 'As a son you should be siring an heir. Why have you suddenly taken a ghost as your partner?'
>
> In shame and fear Chun took the robe as a Buddhist monk. The ghost then stopped coming. Later he returned to secular life and was selected to be a district defender. He married a woman from another family.[22]
>
> After one year, while attending to official cases in his courtroom, he suddenly saw the woman come in through the door with a furious look on her face. Chun came down from the dais in terror to beg for his life.
>
> The woman said: 'There is no sparing you this time!', and she cursed and beat him as hard as she could. Chun fell sick and died.

The woman's dwelling with its unimpressive entrance is a tomb (cf. **107**). However slowly he grasps the true situation, Yang Chun does eventually come to see that he has been conducting a love affair with a ghost. It is a relationship he maintains with reluctance, and only because his lover threatens his life. Their liaison has all the characteristics of a demonic affliction, yet Yang seems powerless to keep the woman at bay by ritual means. Only Buddhist monastic vows can hold her off. Living in her tomb as an unattached female, she has enough destructive power to compel a lover to stay with her. Her final act of murderous revenge shows her more powerful than all those goddesses so easily neutralized by the use of paper charms. But it also testifies to the strength of her unsatisfied lust and sense of betrayal – she shows no sign of any other motivation. This story expresses the most fiercely negative view in the whole collection of sexual relations with the dead.[23]

Other dead women behave more positively. Yen Chih's dream lover leaves him a parting gift when the time comes for her to move on from temporary to final burial (**63**); so do the lovers of Wang Hsüan-chih (**114**) and the magistrate of Hsin-fan county (**123**); Li T'ao's lover tends him in sickness away from home, then leaves when his appointment comes through and their affinity is at an end (**108**). There are women who have particular aims of their own to fulfil. The girl in **141** unites

22 Read 別婚人家子 (conj.).

23 But compare the more perfunctory story **133**, with its vengeful ghost-lover.

briefly with her former lover before embarking on the new incarnation in which she will be his wife. And this is the story of Miss Lu (**109**):

Assistant Magistrate Lu of Ch'ang-chou county[24] was from a family that was habitually poor.

[Once], when the whole family made a visit to the Tiger Hill Monastery[25] on the third of the third month,[26] a daughter aged fifteen or sixteen was unable to go for want of clothes and stayed at home alone with a maid.[27] Once her parents had set off she threw herself with much display of emotion into a well, where she died. The parents were upset by this and wept bitterly for days. They gave her temporary burial in Ch'ang-chou county.

About one year later someone called Lu had been visiting his aunt, whose home was close by the daughter's grave, and walked past the dead-house.[28] A

24 Ch'ang-chou 長洲 county was under Soochow prefecture in Chiang-nan East: see *Yüan-ho chün-hsien t'u-chih* 25.601; *CTS* 40.1586. It was one of two counties with administrative centres in the prefectural seat.

25 This famous Soochow monastery was said to have been founded in 368: *Fo-tsu li-tai t'ung-tsai* 6.524c. It stood near Sword Pool 劍池 at the foot of Tiger Hill 虎丘, a historic site linked with Ho-lü, King of Wu from 514 to 496 BC, eight *li* north-west of the county hall: *Yüan-ho chün-hsien t'u-chih* 25.601. In T'ang times the monastery was known as Pao-en ssu 報恩寺. After the suppression of Buddhism in 845 it was removed to the top of the hill, and late in the tenth century renamed Yün-yen ssu 雲巖寺, the name it still bears. The present pagoda on the site dates from the Northern Sung, the other monastic buildings from a fifteenth-century restoration: see Wu Yü-ts'ang, 'Su-chou Hu-ch'iu shan Yün-yen ssu t'a', *Wen-wu ts'an-k'ao tzu-liao* 1954.3, 69–74; Liu Tun-chen, 'Su-chou Yün-yen ssu t'a', ibid., 1954.7, 27–38.

26 The ancient seasonal observances early in the third month had been a Festival of Purgation and Lustration (Derk Bodde, *Festivals in classical China*, Princeton 1975, pp. 273 ff.) By the end of the Han period their defined date had shifted from the first *ssu* 巳 day to the third day of that month, and the festival began to lose its old religious combination of revelry, sexual encounters between the young and care of the ancestral dead, to become 'simply an occasion for springtime picnicking and merrymaking either beside or on the water' (ibid., p. 281). In T'ang times it was the occasion for court entertainment on the Serpentine 曲江 in Ch'ang-an (*Chü-t' an lu* B.27b), a court archery event (*T'ang hui-yao* 26.499–501), an official holiday (*Ta-T'ang liu tien* 2.29a). See the long note in Ono Katsutoshi, *Nittō guhō junrei kōki no kenkyū*, vol. 1, pp. 448–50, dealing with the Japanese pilgrim Ennin's remark that 'This prefecture [Ch'u-chou 楚州, north of the River in Huai-nan province] does not observe the festival of the third day of the third month'. Ono argues that these celebrations were now the preserve of the educated elite, not part of general social experience.

27 Sun Ch'ien notes the variant 'two maids'.

28 The term *pin-kung* 殯宮 has a canonical background: it occurs in the chapter of *I-li* which deals with the 'obsequies of an ordinary officer' ('Chi-hsi li 3' [40.4b]), meaning 'the house where the death took place' (see John Steele, *The I-li or Book of etiquette and ceremonial*, London 1917, vol. 2, p. 92). But in the *Kuang-i chi*, where it occurs four times (cf. **25, 98, 111**), it clearly refers to small building structures used to house coffins given temporary burial above ground. From the nineteenth century there is a careful description in Justus Doolittle, *Social life of the Chinese*, vol. 2, p. 369: 'Sometimes . . . proper burial-places have not been secured. In such cases the coffin is placed temporarily in a certain kind of house, erected for the express purpose of holding such coffins. These houses are some eight or nine feet high, and from eight

young maid came up behind him and said: 'My mistress wishes to meet you.'

He had no choice but to go with her to their home, which was very small. The young lady was smartly dressed, and her looks had a soft beauty. She asked: 'You are a commoner from Ch'ang-chou, aren't you? I am Assistant Magistrate Lu's daughter. But I'm actually a ghost, not a living human being, and I want to ask you to take a message to the assistant magistrate. Mr Li XVIII of Lin-tun has now proposed marriage to me. But it's not right for me, an unwed maiden, to arrange my own marriage. You report to my father for me,[29] and if he permits us to be wed he must send word back here.'

The man stayed on inside the dead-house. Presently a ward headman from the prefectural city [Soochow] came past the dead-house and saw clothing sticking out of it. Taking a closer look he saw a woman inside. He reported it to the assistant magistrate, who went there in person. He had the walls opened and the man brought out and taken into court.

When he recovered the power of speech some days later he was asked how he had been able to get in there. He responded with what the girl had told him. The assistant magistrate sighed deeply, then sent to make enquiries about Li XVIII of Lin-tun. This person really did exist, but in perfectly normal health. To begin with they placed no trust [in the story], but a few days later he fell ill and, after some days of illness, died. The whole family expressed its regret, but in the end the girl was united to young Li in spirit marriage.

Tai Fu had connections of his own with Soochow[30] and may have learned of this story locally. It has the unusual feature of implying a love relationship in the background while the story's primary contact merely identifies an intermediary. If Li XVIII when still alive proposed marriage to the dead Miss Lu, he must somehow have been in contact with her: the inner story invites us to imagine dream or trance meetings of a kind which other stories might treat as their main subject. It was not unknown for dead girls to identify their future husbands as story **109** describes: we find examples in mythological literature and in modern ethnography.[31] But the most interesting feature for us here is the spirit

to twelve or fifteen feet long, and wide enough to hold a coffin lengthwise. Their general appearance is very much like a diminutive dwelling-house without windows. Several coffins are usually, if there be need, placed in one such house, or tomb above ground, where they remain till a suitable burying-place has been obtained, and till it is convenient to inter them. . . . These temporary tombs above ground oftentimes become very much dilapidated, and the coffins are sometimes never taken out for burial in the ground, either because the family to which they belong has become very poor or has become extinct.' Cf. also de Groot, *The religious system of China*, vol. 1, pp. 127–8.

29 For 與 read 為, with Sun Ch'ien.

30 See above, Chapter 2, pp. 43–4, with nn. 116 and 117.

31 In a mythological context: *Tzu-t'ung ti-chün hua-shu* (HY 170), 1.4b–5b, translated and annotated by Kleeman, *A god's own tale*, pp. 99–101. In ethnographic reports: Juan Ch'ang-jui, 'T'ai-wan ti ming-hun yü kuo-fang chih yüan-shih i-i chi ch'i she-hui kung-neng', *Chung-yang yen-chiu-yüan min-tsu-hsüeh yen-chiu-so chi-k'an* 33, 1972, 15–38, with

marriage itself, for it enacts a social practice which has lived on in China from ancient times until the present.

Spirit marriage, often known as *ming-hun* 冥婚, made its first appearance in the Chinese record when the canonical ritual text *Chou li* laid down: 'It is forbidden to transfer the buried and to give deceased minors in marriage' 禁遷葬者與嫁殤者. The Han commentator Cheng Hsüan 鄭玄 (AD127–200) explains: 'transferring the buried' means that those who were not man and wife when alive are transferred after death and burial to be together; 'deceased minors' means unmarried women aged nineteen or younger. Cheng Chung 鄭眾 (d. AD 83) identifies the giving of dead women in marriage with a custom of his own day known as *ch'ü-hui* 娶會.[32] To ban a practice is of course to proclaim its established existence, and not necessarily to bring that existence to an end. What is remarkable about this particular practice is its robust survival into modern times against the grain of Confucian ritual prescription. Here at least is proof that truly long-term social institutions in China have not needed canonical authority to secure their transmission through time.[33] The evidence of standard histories and of notebook literature is there to show the steady practice of spirit marriage through the ages.[34] But the closest observation and most valuable insights come from ethnographic fieldwork done in the twentieth century.

For north China the outstanding monograph, sadly underused by students of the subject, is by Uchida Tomoo; it was based on extensive fieldwork in Hopei and Shantung in the 1940s.[35] More recent reports have covered practice in Taiwan, Hong Kong and Singapore, and anecdotal evidence is forthcoming from contemporary China.[36] But a

p. 25; David K. Jordan, *Gods, ghosts, and ancestors: the folk religion of a Taiwanese village*, Berkeley and Los Angeles 1972, pp. 143–4; and Emily M. Ahern, *The cult of the dead in a Chinese village*, Stanford 1973, p. 236.

32 *Chou li*, 'Ti-kuan: Mei-shih', 14.17a.

33 A question looked at above, in Chapter 3, p. 66.

34 The classic study is by Chao I, *Kai-yü ts'ung-k'ao* 31.649–50, which focuses on the standard histories. References to other literature appear in Ch'en P'eng, *Chung-kuo hun-yin shih-kao*, pp. 155–62, with pp. 157–8 introducing the present story; also Okamoto Saburō, 'Meikon setsuwa kō', *Tōyōshikai kiyō* 4, 1945, 135–63.

35 Uchida Tomoo, 'Meikon kō', *Shinagaku* 11, 1944, 311–73. For earlier ethnographic reporting in mainland China see *Chung-kuo min-shih hsi-kuan ta-ch'üan* (comp. Facheng hsüeh-she, Shanghai 1923; repr. Taipei 1962), 4.31a; *Min shang shih hsi-kuan tiao-ch'a pao-kao lu* [Nanking] 1930, repr. Taipei 1969, pp. 1379, 1392, 1409, 1423, 1557, 1702.

36 Marjorie Topley, 'Ghost marriages among the Singapore Chinese', *Man* 55, 1955, 29–30; and 'Ghost marriages among the Singapore Chinese: a further note', *Man* 56, 1956, 71–2; Li Yih-yuan, 'Ghost marriage, shamanism and kinship behaviour in rural Taiwan', in N. Matsumoto and T. Mabuchi, eds., *Folk religion and the worldview in the southwestern Pacific*, Tokyo 1968, pp. 97–9; David K. Jordan, 'Two forms of spirit marriage in rural Taiwan', *Bijdragen tot de Taal-, Land- en Volkenkunde* 127, 1971, 181–9;

growing body of studies in Japan shows that Chinese practice can be seen in a wider context which includes both Japan itself and, more particularly, Korea.[37] The Chinese reports reveal the same kind of complex variety in detail that, in the discussion of *la longue durée* in Chapter 3 above, was found in more general death ritual. Every aspect of this practice seems variable – its name, the qualifying ages for betrothal, marriage and majority,[38] the link to family succession, the features of the wedding ceremony (or even its absence), the institution's perceived function and so on.

Perhaps the most fundamental point of variation is between those marriages which join a living man to a dead woman, and those which bring together only the dead. At first sight the *Kuang-i chi*'s position on this seems quite clear: to marry a dead woman a man must first die himself.[39] The term *ming-hun* is used just three times in the surviving text and each time refers strictly to marriage between the dead. Miss Lu's chosen husband Li XVIII died before he married her (**109**). When Wei Ching fell sick and died, his family 'dressed him provisionally for the coffin, but did not proceed with the burial because they meant to unite him in spirit marriage with a daughter of his maternal uncle'; later he came back to life (**173**). Here, thirdly, is story **111**:

In Lin-ju commandery[40] there is a government waterway hostel. About half a *li* to the north of it is the Li family estate.

and *Gods, ghosts, and ancestors: the folk religion of a Taiwanese village*, pp. 140–55; Juan Ch'ang-jui, 'T'ai-wan ti ming-hun yü kuo-fang'; Ahern, *The cult of the dead in a Chinese village*, pp. 128, 236; Wolf, 'Gods, ghosts and ancestors', pp. 150–2. For a specimen recent incident in mainland China, see Reuter report in the *Guardian*, 19 February 1992 (Szechuan/Shansi).

37 Work on this subject by the ethnologist Takeda Akira is now reprinted in his book *Sōryō saishi to shiryō kekkon*, Kyoto 1990. A more recent collection of reprinted articles by various scholars is Matsuzaki Kenzō, ed., *Tō Ajia no shiryō kekkon*, Tokyo 1993. This includes a bibliography of studies on China, Japan and Korea. I am indebted to Mr Maruyama Hiroshi for kindly sending me these two books.

38 Uchida analyses the variations in detail ('Meikon kō', pp. 357–65), finally noting that the span from the earliest known age for betrothal (7 or 8 *sui*) to the latest known age for majority (20 *sui*) corresponds to the scriptural prescription for mourning the prematurely dead in *I-li*, commentary on 'Sang-fu', 31.14a: 'The time from nineteen to sixteen is "mature youth"; from fifteen to twelve "middle youth"; and from eleven to eight "early youth". Children who have not reached the age of eight full years are spoken of as dying "a mourningless death."' (John Steele, *The I-li*, vol. 2, p. 27.) But note that the Taiwan evidence includes marriages for females dead in early infancy, some even without names: Juan Ch'ang-jui, 'T'ai-wan ti ming-hun yü kuo-fang', pp. 22, 24; Jordan, *Gods, ghosts, and ancestors*, pp. 143 and 152, n. 19.

39 In stories **85** (translated and discussed in Chap. 1) and **116** marriages are proposed with daughters of dead men, and each time require the son-in-law to die.

40 The prefecture Ju-chou 汝州 was renamed Lin-ju chün 臨汝郡 in 742 and reverted to the name Ju-chou in 758: *CTS* 38.1430. The prefectural seat was at the present county town Lin-ju in Honan.

A man called Wang I passed by the manor gate on his way to a fair. Some way off he saw a girl of fifteen or sixteen giving him the glad eye, and she sent her maid to bring word to him. Wang loitered in the shade of the *huai* trees until evening came, when he went to ask for lodging in the manor house. His host gave him a friendly welcome and entertained him generously.

After the second watch [9–11pm] the maid appeared, saying: 'It's not very late yet: keep a candle burning and wait for her.'

Before long the girl arrived, and they were intimate together. But afterwards the girl, looking wretched, suddenly fell sick.

Wang said: 'We were strangers before, but I've been lucky enough to be called by you,[41] and now we have enjoyed supreme happiness together. Since we have such a strong bond, why feel so unhappy?'

She replied: 'I do love you totally! But when I left just now the gate was shut, and I came over[42] the wall. There was an iron rake at the foot of the wall, and its prongs went into my foot. The pain runs right through me to the heart – I can't bear it.' And she brought out her foot to show him.

With those words she took her leave and went back, adding: 'It is already time that I must die. If you love me, then pay me a visit when you come back here, just to bring comfort to my spirit in the shades!'

Later Wang received an official appointment and came back east. On the way he came past the Li family estate and learned that the girl had died. So in secret he went with her maid to take wine and food and offer it in sacrifice outside the dead-house.[43] Wang then slumped to the ground, dead, and the maid saw his soul go with the girl into the dead-house.

The two families united them in spirit marriage.

This story has the characteristics, not of a known informant's personal testimony, but of a local tradition associated with the Lin-ju government hostel, which is perhaps where Tai Fu came to hear of it. Formally speaking most of the text counts as inner story, with the maid's evidence and the concluding line forming its outer shell. But it makes more sense to treat the whole text as inner story – the perception of a local event as the staff at Lin-ju hostel might have presented it. Once again, *ming-hun* is by implication used to fulfil a bond between the unmarried dead.

The true agents in each case are the families who negotiate and perform the weddings. But their motives are not directly addressed in any of the three *ming-hun* cases in *Kuang-i chi.* These stories might perhaps imply the kind of interpretation voiced in the 1940s by informants in Hopei: 'being indulgent parents to their children'; 'done by

41 Read 見相招, with Sun Ch'ien.

42 For 垣而牆角下 read 踰垣而來牆下, with Sun Ch'ien.

43 See above, n. 28. Sun Ch'ien records variants here and below in which the character *kung* 宮 is lacking.

parents full of tender thoughts about dying while still unmarried'.[44] But the tenderness of parents and the comfort of deceased children are not the only motives alleged in the modern practice of spirit marriage. A Shantung villager outlined a more pragmatic strategy: since the unmarried dead can have no offspring, they need to marry so as to be 'parents' to an adopted son, who would then have living grandparents; and for the latter he would be the living son of their own dead son.[45] Such a strategy, used by parents bereaved of a son and anxious for their own ultimate succession, is only one step away from the more familiar motive driving parents bereaved of a daughter:

> If she dies before being transferred to her husband's lineage, it is felt that she has been caught in the wrong place. She has no right at all to care or worship from the members of her natal lineage . . . No one is obligated to worship her as a parent and no lineage members are obligated to provide for her as an actual or potential contributor to the lineage. Whatever they offer her is intended to propitiate her and prevent her from causing harm to lineage members.[46]

In these circumstances the soul of the dead girl, threatening trouble, may find solace in marriage, for then her tablet will hang on the altar of a posthumous marriage partner. Sons may be co-opted or adopted in her name, and she may partake of offerings from the partner's lineage.[47]

If these benefits flow from marriage to a dead partner, they will flow more strongly from marriage to a live one, a form of the institution richly attested in Taiwan.[48] It raises the interesting problem of inducing a living man to unite himself with the dead. For some men poverty may be spur enough; but there are certain devices used by families to compel the agreement of reluctant partners. Remarkably enough we find one of these fully deployed in the *Kuang-i chi*, in a story (**74**) already cited above in the discussion of union with divine women. It begins like this:

> There was a man of Ju-yin called Hsü, orphaned since childhood. He was fair-skinned and handsome, loved smart clothes and fine horses, and roamed wild and free. Often he would lead out yellow hunting hounds to chase game through wilderness and mountain streams.

44 The words of a functionary from Ts'ang county 滄縣 and a villager from I-tu 益都: Uchida, 'Meikon kō', pp. 366–7.

45 Ibid., p. 330. (He points out at once, however, that other villagers denied any connection between spirit marriage and adopted sons.) Compare the Cantonese informants cited by Topley.

46 Ahern, *The cult of the dead in a Chinese village*, p. 128.

47 Juan, 'T'ai-wan ti ming-hun yü kuo-fang', pp. 15 ff.

48 Juan in ibid. finds it focused more precisely in the Min-nan speaking population of southern and north-eastern Taiwan, less in evidence among the Hakka (p. 15).

He [once] rested beneath a great tree more than a hundred feet tall and several dozen spans in girth. High branches stretched out to either side, casting shade over several *mu*. He glanced up into the branches, and hanging there was a purse made of many-coloured silks. Thinking someone had left it by mistake he retrieved it and took it home. But the knot could not be undone. He prized the purse highly and put it in his personal case.

As evening approached it changed into a girl, who came straight up to him with a name-card in her hand and said: 'The king's daughter has instructed me to pay you her respects.' Thus announcing her name, she departed.

Shortly afterwards a strange fragrance filled the room and the sound of horses and carriages gradually became audible. Hsü went outside and saw in the distance a line of torches. In front there was a youth on a white horse attended by a dozen riders, who came straight up to Hsü and said: 'My younger sister, though of mean family, humbly admires your fine character and wishes to join herself in marriage to a true gentleman. What do you think?'

Hsü dared not refuse too hard, for these people were gods.

This, as I have pointed out elsewhere, exactly replicates a situation which often leads on to spirit marriage in Taiwan: a young man drawn to bait (a purse or red envelope) left deliberately in his way; eager pressure from a dead girl's brothers lying in wait nearby; a presumption that his taking the bait is a sign of predestined union with their sister; the use of money as a further inducement; reluctant acquiescence on the young man's part.[49] With the hindsight of this discussion on spirit marriage, story **74** now takes on an even more interesting character than before. Among the tales of marriage with divine women it stood out, after all, as a rare model of fulfilled and permanent union, with the husband's family gaining security and prosperity and the woman herself having loyal sons at her side to the very end. It is as though the procedures of successful spirit marriage, acted out stage by stage, provide a symbolism for this bold and perhaps unusual statement about relations with divine women.

If Tai Fu's society knew of these ways to recruit living men for marriage to spirit women, we ought to ask whether it also practised that form of marriage for real, even though it might have reserved the term *ming-hun* strictly for dead partners. The story which follows (**128**), the last to be studied in this book, comes close to giving the circumstances of such a marriage without giving it the name:

49 Jordan, 'Two forms of spirit marriage', pp. 181–2; *Gods, ghosts, and ancestors*, p. 140. Story **74** matches Jordan's Type 1. Cf. Juan, 'T'ai-wan ti ming-hun yü kuo-fang', pp. 18, 22; Wolf, 'Gods, ghosts, and ancestors', p. 150; and Dudbridge, 'The tale of Liu Yi and its analogues'.

Li Ying of the Chao-chün clan, magistrate of Shou-ch'ang, had an unmarried cousin, thirteenth in her generation, who travelled south with her brothers at the beginning of Chih-te [756–]. She died and was buried at Hai-yen in the land of Wu.

Her elder brother Min's estate lay in Chi-yüan, with a widowed sister living only a few miles away who had not been able to escape south during[50] the rebellion of An Lu-shan.

In the Shang-yüan period [760–761] this lady suddenly saw her sister come home. When asked how this came about the sister said she had been taken by bandits. She responded quite sensibly, and the family did not question her further. But the elder sister was afraid that, what with the troubles, she would not be able to keep the girl safe. So she hastily married her off to a Mr Chang on a nearby estate. Four or five years went by, and she had a son, extremely bright and able to take everything in. She regularly [came back to] shut herself alone in a room at Li Min's house, and in all her movements to and fro led a quiet domestic life.

Much of Li Min's land had been occupied by squatters, but it was all recovered through legal proceedings. In the Yung-t'ai period [765], when our national affairs were clear again, Li Min and his brothers returned from the east to the capital, where they sat the examination for official appointment. This done, they went home to the estate. A couple of hundred miles before they reached it their sister, there at the estate, suddenly said to the maid:

'My brothers will arrive here in a few days. I must go and live with the Changs for a while.' And she went to take leave of her sister,[51] who asked her the reason.

She said: 'The message has come to me several times in dreams.'

Her maid escorted her halfway there, but then she sent the girl home. Walking a dozen steps, the maid looked back and saw no more sign of her. She thought this a strange business.

Two days later Chang sent news that she had died. Aunt and nephew had only just finished their grieving when the brothers arrived and prepared to hold her funeral.

Li Min pointed out that she had died in the Shang-yüan period and been duly buried in Hai-yen – how could she have come here? He feared this was some ghostly haunting and went over to the Changs' home to view her body. Raising the covering, they saw no sign of her corpse. But when they checked her clothing and mirrors, these were all objects from the time when she was laid in her coffin.

Before long the boy died too.

Li Ying 李瑩 is apparently the author's informant for this tale. Magistrate of Shou-ch'ang 壽昌 (south-west of Hangchow) after 765, he belongs among the same group of Chekiang-based colleague-informants

50 Accepting the addition of 値 by Sun Ch'ien.
51 For 娣 I read 姊.

who lie behind so many of Tai Fu's reports. The dead girl is certainly a cousin of his, perhaps a remote one: his description *t'ung-t'ang mei* 同堂妹 gives her merely the same ancestry as himself: he would use it only if she came from outside his immediate circle of kin.[52] Li Ying is simply passing on a piece of recent lore from his broader lineage; he has no personal role in it himself.

The essential situation remains the same. A generation of the aristocratic Chao-chün Li 趙郡李 lineage[53] evacuates its estate in Chi-yüan 濟源 (on the north bank of the Yellow River, opposite Lo-yang) at the moment when An Lu-shan's rebel campaign engulfs the region. From this point on the Lis provide in miniature a social history of the rebellion years.[54]

An Lu-shan's advance struck south through Ho-pei in late 755. During the first half of January 756 he crossed the Yellow River and moved west, taking the canal ports Ch'en-liu and Pien-chou, then Ying-yang and Lo-yang.[55] It was now that the Lis fled east as far as the canal system would take them. With them went a large section of the northern elite. Mu Yüan 穆員, writing at the end of the eighth century, observes:

> In these times central China was suffering many troubles. The scholar elite made their homes among the three rivers and five lakes [of the eastern coastal region], and settlers in Kuei-chi came in droves . . .[56]

Among them, of course, was the compiler Tai Fu himself, in this same region at this same period to take the government examination which would begin his official career.

While the Lis lay low on the east coast for ten years, burying their dead sister at Hai-yen 海鹽 on the northern shore of Hangchow Bay, their Ho-nan estate was at the mercy of intruders. Another sister trapped there in the rebel-held countryside relied for security on a neighbouring estate owner, while the land fell into other hands.[57] When the brothers, led by Li Min 李岷, resume the life they left behind in 756 –

52 Chinese kin in a single generation are 'brothers' and 'sisters' even when their parents are different: a distinction between sister and cousin does not announce itself. There is a suggestion that the use of *t'ung* 同 in this expression was already obsolete in T'ang times (cf. *Ch'eng-wei lu* 4.14a). The present story nonetheless preserves it. For relationships *within* Li Ying's story I have written 'brothers' and 'sisters' without attempting to guess at further distinctions.

53 On this, see David Johnson, 'The last years of a great clan: the Li family of Chao-chün in late T'ang and early Sung', *Harvard Journal of Asiatic Studies* 37, 1977, 5–102.

54 Compare the parallel situation in story **122**.

55 *CTS* 9.230; *TCTC* 217.6937–9.

56 Mu Yüan 穆員, 'Kung-pu shang-shu Pao Fang pei' 工部尚書鮑防碑 (*ca.* 793), in *WYYH* 896.8b.

57 I tentatively render *ying-chan* 影占, 'shadow occupation', as 'squatting'.

attending the renewed metropolitan examinations in Ch'ang-an[58] and restoring their title to the family estate – they mask some of the deep changes wrought upon Chinese society by the great rebellion: large movements of population to the south-east and, eventually, fundamental changes in the pattern of landholding.[59] They represent, at least in the short term, a pocket of recovered stability and remind us that the grand processes of history are never simple.

The ghostly Thirteenth Sister has a point of her own to make. Spirits of the dead in the traditional Chinese world are often perceived to stay close to the site of their remains, preoccupied with problems of rightful burial. But this need not always be so. Thirteenth Sister, who apparently received due and fitting burial from her rich brothers, is drawn over a vast distance back to her home, where she attempts a ghostly imitation of the life she would have hoped to lead if death had not taken her. In this inner story as elsewhere, grave goods, the property of the dead, associate themselves with the spirit's movements. Their displacement reflects the power of the girl's unfulfilled demands from life. Hers is a situation which in other circumstances might find its expression in a malignant haunting and its resolution in spirit marriage. As it is, without conscious decision on her family's part, she does almost achieve that resolution in effect. She is given in marriage to a living man and bears him a son and heir. The death of this young boy at the end leaves her situation once again unresolved: will the Changs adopt or assign another young man to serve as her ritual offspring? Quite possibly Tai Fu came to hear of this story so soon after the events of 765 that those decisions had not yet been taken; but in any case the matter was one for the Changs and not one of close concern for Li Ying.

I have chosen to end this book with the story of Thirteenth Sister for reasons which reach beyond the particular question of spirit marriage. More than any other report in the *Kuang-i chi* it brings seriously into play all the three levels of historical time we have adopted as a measure of dynamic change. Almost triumphantly it transcends the discourse of ghost story rhetoric to claim the status of historical document. As 'history of events' it lets the accurately reported progress of the An Lu-shan rebellion play a structural part in the family drama which occupies centre-stage. Like the anti-clerical emergency of 779 and the local

58 The examinations were restored in both western and eastern capitals in 764 and evidently first held in the spring of 765: *HTS* 44.1165, and des Rotours, *Le traité des examens*, pp. 176–7. I take *ching* 京 in the text to mean Ch'ang-an.

59 Denis Twitchett, *Land tenure and the social order in T'ang and Sung China*, London 1962, pp. 25–6.

rebellion of Yüan Ch'ao in 762–763, discussed in earlier chapters, this great national crisis of 756 is communicated as the population felt it, not as career historians presented it. But over the later sequence of events, which takes the Li brothers back to their careers and their inherited land, there broods also, for us with the vantage point of long-term hindsight, the sense of big changes about to come in the Chinese world. True, the Lis were able to evict their squatters and re-establish claim to their land. But other owners were perhaps less successful – many estates were no doubt dispossessed, broken up or otherwise compromised by the disordered conditions after the rebellion. A new order of land tenure was to emerge from this troubled scene, and it belongs to that level of historical time associated with 'slow but perceptible change'.

It is, finally, the link with spirit marriage which brings us to the 'imperceptible change' of *la longue durée.* Change takes place even on the slowest scale of historical time, though it remains difficult to chart. Certainly it is possible that spirit marriage was not a truly archaic institution in China.[60] But this example does show how even the lapse of two thousand years has not broken the continuity of a practice which has displeased and embarrassed the cultural legislators of China from Han times until now.

Tai Fu's catholic openness of mind and his relish for the far extremes of human experience filled his notebooks with material from which these questions can be studied. Many others were like him. It can only be a gain if we learn to use their surviving work with the critical care that is taken for granted in more conventional historical study.

60 Uchida Tomoo concludes his study with a historical speculation: spirit marriage can perhaps be seen as contingent upon a more fundamental matrix – the custom of burying husband and wife together; but there is evidence in Chou texts to suggest that this custom was not regarded as an ancient one; it would therefore follow that spirit marriage also, like husband/wife burials, was not archaic. See Uchida, 'Meikon kō', pp. 369–71.

APPENDIX

The stories of *Kuang-i chi*

For convenient use this listing follows the order of stories as they appear, first in *T'ai-p'ing kuang-chi,* then in other sources, although there is no reason to believe that this reflects the order in the original collection. The textual data given here build upon the edition by Fang Shih-ming, published together with *Ming-pao chi* by Chung-hua shu-chü, Peking 1992. Some details are corrected, some new sources added. The present list aims to be inclusive: even when the attribution of a given story to *Kuang-i chi* is open to doubt, it still appears below. I have not followed Fang in assuming that all stories containing early dates or found in earlier collections are by that token wrongly attributed to *Kuang-i chi*: it seems at least possible that Tai Fu transcribed items from other collections into his own. A synopsis of content is given for all stories except those which for reasons of chronology cannot have appeared in the original *Kuang-i chi.* Minimal annotation covers matters of biographical or historical context, but concentrates on less routinely accessible sources. Thus, although place-names are recorded here, no effort is made to document them individually; no systematic references are given to standard early biographies, nor to Ch'ien Chung-shu's observations on many items in his *Kuan-chui pien,* vol. 2, Peking 1979. These are easily found. But details are given of items translated into Western languages, which are scattered inconspicuously in various sources.

1 Hsü Fu 徐福

Text: *TPKC* 4.26–7; *San-tung ch'ün-hsien lu* 16.19a–b, 2.12a; Fang, p. 1.

Note: Double attribution includes *Hsien-chuan shih-i* 仙傳拾遺: see discussion in Chapter 6, n. 32.

Stories: (*a*) Early legends on Ch'in Shih-huang-ti's quest for immortality: he sends Hsü Fu to the island Tsu-chou with three thousand youths and three thousand maidens. They never return.

(*b*) A man sets out in the K'ai-yüan period to find Hsü Fu in the Eastern Ocean, hoping to find a cure for his hopeless illness. In this he succeeds.

2 Master P'u-p'u 僕僕先生

Text: *TPKC* 22.150–1; *San-tung ch'ün-hsien lu* 4.1b–2a; Fang, pp. 2–4.

Note: Double attribution includes *I-wen chi* 異聞集, which may have used *Kuang-i chi* as its source for the first group of anecdotes given here.

Story: A string of anecdotes about the named Taoist immortal, a specialist in the Apricot Elixir. He appears in early K'ai-yüan and victoriously confronts the prefect of Kuang-chou 光州, in Huai-nan. The cult receives imperial blessing. A ninth-century postscript describes its later spread to another site.
Translation: Dudbridge, 'Tang tales and Tang cults', pp. 345–9, with discussion.

3 Two gentlemen called Chang and Li 張李二公
Text: *TPKC* 23.158; Fang, pp. 4–5.
Story: Chang and Li, both Taoist students on Mount T'ai, part company when Li takes up an official career. They meet later in life: Chang entertains Li, who recognizes his own wife among the musicians. Tokens exchanged eventually prove that she has dreamed the same experience. This shows Chang's immortal status.

4 Liu Ch'ing-chen 劉清真
Text: *TPKC* 24.160–1; Fang, pp. 5–6.
Story: Twenty tea-traders lose their way and follow a charismatic monk to the Wu-t'ai Mountains. He conceals them from government officers and flies them off to Mount Lu. One of them there eats a magic fungus, turns into a divine crane and ascends aloft. The men return home after an absence of twenty years. Informant named. Implied internal dates: 755–779.
Translation: Chap. 3, pp. 81–5, with discussion.

5 A man of Ma-yang village 麻陽村人
Text: *TPKC* 39.248–9; *Lei shuo* 8.16a; *San-tung ch'ün-hsien lu* 11.13a; *Kan-chu chi* 7.21a; *Shuo fu* 4.11a; Fang, pp. 6–7, 245, 251–2, 256.
Story: A villager follows a wounded pig and finds immortals at play and at study. An old man with snowy whiskers entertains him and identifies two juniors present as Ho-shang kung 河上公 and Wang Pi 王弼, famous early commentators on Taoist scriptures.

6 The Compassionate Immortal 慈心僊人
Text: *TPKC* 39.249; *San-tung ch'ün-hsien lu* 18.6b–7a; Fang, pp. 7–8.
Story: In 764 one of the rebel Yüan Ch'ao's ships is blown out to sea. The crew discover and plunder a fabulous island. But a woman appears and warns them not to risk the wrath of the dragons that live there. The rebels return the plunder, but still suffer shipwreck and execution on the China coast. A woman survives to serve an officer as a bondmaid. She is the informant.
Translation: Chap. 6, pp. 147–52, with discussion.

7 Shih Chü 石巨
Text: *TPKC* 40.251–2; *San-tung ch'ün-hsien lu* 1.19b–20a; Fang, p. 8.
Story: A Sogdian practises Taoist immortality techniques. During a prolonged illness he consults a female diviner, then turns into a crane and departs with a group of white cranes. His son is required by the administrator Li Huai-hsien 李懷仙 to give proof of his father's divine powers, which he does by successfully praying for rain. A temple cult is then set up. Implied internal dates: 766–768.
Translation: Dudbridge, 'Tang tales and Tang cults', pp. 349–52, with discussion.

8 Old Wang 王老

Text: *TPKC* 41.258–9; Fang, p. 9.

Story: A Ch'ang-an drug seller takes Li, a regular patron, to a remote mountain Taoist establishment. Li observes the community there, witnesses a concert of divine cranes and is then sent back into the world. He never finds the way up again.

Translation: Dudbridge, 'Three fables of paradise lost', *Bulletin of the British Association for Chinese Studies* 1988, pp. 26–8.

9 Immortal Li 李仙人

Text: *TPKC* 42.264; Fang, p. 10.

Story: A comely widow in Lo-yang marries Li, a banished god. He teaches her the craft of gold and silver alchemy, by which they live until his return to heaven. She continues this trade, but is forced to share her secret with the vice-governor, who reports the matter to court. Within a year both are dead, no doubt in punishment. Internal date: K'ai-yüan.

10 Ting Yüeh 丁約

Text: *TPKC* 45.279–81; *San-tung ch'ün-hsien lu* 9.16a–b; *Ch'üeh shih* A.1b–4a; Fang, pp. 235–7.

Note: Seems to be wrongly attributed to *Kuang-i chi*. The implied internal dating runs from 768 to 818. A better version of the text appears in Kao Yen-hsiu's *Ch'üeh shih*, completed in 884. See Ch'eng I-chung, 'T'ang-tai hsiao-shuo so chi', *Wen-hsüeh i-ch'an*, 1980.2, p. 52.

11 The hermit of Mount Heng 衡山隱者

Text: *TPKC* 45.283; *Nan-yüeh tsung-sheng chi* C.1083c–1084a; Fang, pp. 10–11.

Story: A hermit who needs no food visits the mountain monastery, selling medicines. He produces a large amount of gold to acquire a musician's beautiful daughter in marriage. When her parents later visit the couple at home they are given food which takes away their hunger, and a gift of gold. But they never find the place again.

Note: Important early reference to the cash value of gold: 3.5 strings an ounce.

12 Venerable Master P'an 潘尊師

Text: *TPKC* 49.303; Fang, p. 11.

Story: During K'ai-yüan P'an Fa-cheng 潘法正, a Taoist adept of Mount Sung 嵩山, receives the call to succeed T'ao Hung-ching as Lord of Mount Sung 嵩山伯 and dies by 'corpse release' (屍解), informing his disciple Ssu-ma. Later a man offends the lord by washing his private parts in a pool, is brought before P'an and told to return to Ssu-ma with a white fan, originally laid by him in P'an's coffin.

Note: Discussed in Chap. 3, p. 71.

13 The women of Ch'in times 秦時婦人

Text: *TPKC* 62.389–90; *San-tung ch'ün-hsien lu* 19.13a–b; Fang, p. 12.

Story: A monk expelled during K'ai-yüan from the Wu-t'ai Mountains finds a community of women in the Yen-men Mountains. They were brought north in Ch'in times to build the Great Wall, then fled to the mountains, living on roots and herbs. The monk cannot stomach this diet, goes out to find grain, but then fails to find his way back to them.

Translation: Chap. 3, pp. 76–81, with discussion.

14 Ho Erh-niang 何二娘

Text: *TPKC* 62.390; *San-tung ch'ün-hsien lu* 18.14a–b; Fang, pp. 12–13.

Story: The girl weaves shoes for a living in Kuang-chou 廣州, but at twenty flies off to Mount Lo-fu 羅浮山 and begs to serve the monks, showing powers of miraculous travel in collecting fruit for them. In K'ai-yüan a court official is sent to bring her in to the capital, but on the way thinks of seducing her, and she flies away forever.

Note: Other early references gathered by Edward H. Schafer, *The vermilion bird*, Berkeley and Los Angeles 1967, p. 107.

15 Pien Tung-hsüan 邊洞玄

Text: *TPKC* 63.392; *Lei-shuo* 8.16b–17a; *Kan-chu chi* 7.21b; Fang, pp. 13–14, 246, 253.

Story: In late K'ai-yüan, at age eighty-four, this female Taoist meets an old man who gives her boiled noodles. When she eats them she takes on immortal characteristics. With final farewells to her disciples she ascends through the air, watched by a vast crowd.

16 Chang Lien-ch'iao 張連翹

Text: *TPKC* 64.399; *San-tung ch'ün-hsien lu* 12.19b–20a; Fang, p. 14.

Story: After a childhood of visions, pathological laughter and eating disorders, she becomes a Taoist nun. She picks up coins dropped from heaven and eats potent yellow pills which strengthen her. Late in T'ien-pao, as she thinks of her parents, a jewelled carriage appears in the heavens, but she fails to depart in it. Now still alive, she is shrivelled and abstains from food.

17 Fu Shen-t'ung 輔神通

Text: *TPKC* 72.449–50; Fang, pp. 14–15.

Story: A Taoist in Shu-chou 蜀州 is dismissed by his Taoist master when, aged over twenty, he conceals some elixir. After living in rugged caves on herbs, he returns to society, but fails to reestablish contact with his master. His skill in gold and silver alchemy is reported and demonstrated to Hsüan-tsung. All this ends with the An Lu-shan rebellion.

18 The *vajra* figures of Wu-chou 婺州金剛

Text: *TPKC* 100.670; Fang, pp. 15–16.

Story: Two *vajra* figures at the gate of K'ai-yüan Monastery in Wu-chou are famed for spiritual powers. No birds go near them. During K'ai-yüan a local official holds a profane feast on the upper floor of the gate at which a guest scorns their powers. Thunder and lightning break up the feast and strike him dead.

19 A prisoner in Ch'ang-an county 長安縣繫囚

Text: *TPKC* 104.702; Fang, p. 16.

Story: A capital offender in Ch'ang-an recites the *Vajracchedikā* for over forty days. When his cangue is removed for execution it illuminates the county office with brilliant rays. The matter is reported to Hsüan-tsung, who has him pardoned.

20 Lu 盧氏

Text: *TPKC* 104.704–5; Fang, pp. 16–17.

Story: Lu, abroad in Hua-chou 滑州, is summoned by two men in yellow tunics with an official warrant. Leaving his body in its seat he sets off on horseback and comes to the king's citadel, where he meets his cousin Li. Li explains that he has gained merit by reciting the *Vajracchedikā* and asks him to deliver some men caught in the toils of a net by reciting it now. He does this, then returns home to rejoin his body.

21 Ch'en Li-pin 陳利賓

Text: *TPKC* 104.705–6; Fang, p. 17.

Story: Ch'en is a successful metropolitan graduate. Since childhood he was helped by reciting the *Vajracchedikā*. During K'ai-yüan he is sailing across Chekiang when a vortex engulfs the other boats in his convoy. He recites the *sūtra*, and a red dragon rushes out to save his boat.

22 Wang Hung 王宏

Text: *TPKC* 104.706; Fang, p. 18.

Story: Wang is much given to hunting and fishing. During T'ien-pao the chase leads him into a cave where he finds the *Vajracchedikā*. He gives up hunting.

23 T'ien 田氏

Text: *TPKC* 104.706; Fang, p. 18.

Story: T'ien, an administrator at I-chou 易州, recites the *Vajracchedikā*, which he once found in a thicket, but persists in hunting. When called to account in the underworld by the beasts he has killed, he explains about his *sūtra* habit to the king, who checks it and makes him recite it again. The beasts disappear; he earns fifteen more years of life.

24 Li Wei-yen 李惟燕

Text: *TPKC* 105.707; Fang, p. 19.

Story: Three anecdotes are reported from the family of Li, magistrate of a Chekiang county. Reciting the *Vajracchedikā* brings deliverance from the threat of bandits when a boat is marooned on a river, from difficulties in navigating river gorges, and from an advancing enemy during the An Lu-shan rebellion.

25 Sun Ming 孫明

Text: *TPKC* 105.708; Fang, pp. 19–20.

Story: Sun, a manorial tenant in Cheng-chou, has recited the *Vajracchedikā* and abstained from strong food for twenty years. When brought before the king in the underworld, he is questioned, commended for his habit, then sent home. His family have already held a funeral. But a hunter hears his shouts inside the burial hut and saves him. By 755 he has lived six or seven more years in good shape.

26 The Master of Three Cuts 三刀師

Text: *TPKC* 105.708–9; Fang, p. 20.

Story: A man of Shou-chou 壽州 is arrested for stealing a horse and sentenced to be cut in two. But the sword fails to cut him. He explains that he used to recite the *Vajracchedikā* and abstain from strong food. After giving the practice up when fighting in the An Lu-shan rebellion he has resumed it under sentence of death. Now spared, he enters the Buddhist priesthood and is said to be a bodhisattva. Internal date: 758–759.

Note: Identity of Shou-chou prefect further documented by Yü Hsien-hao, *T'ang tz'u-shih k'ao,* Hong Kong and Nanking 1987, vol. 3, pp. 1552–3.

27 Administrator Sung 宋參軍

Text: *TPKC* 105.709; Fang, pp. 20–1.

Story: Sung recites the *Vajracchedikā*. When serving in Fang-chou 坊州 he is visited by the ghost of a woman who died resisting the advances of his predecessor's brother. Her body was cast into the latrine. She entrusts her plea to Sung because of his *sūtra* piety. Her bones are recovered, washed and laid to rest. Her ghost gratefully foretells Sung's and his sons' careers. She also accurately foretells the local prefect's more dismal future.

28 Liu Hung-chien 劉鴻漸

Text: *TPKC* 105.709–10; Fang, pp. 22–3.

Story: Liu was taught by a monk to recite the *Vajracchedikā* in 758, while a refugee in the south. In 760, now in Shou-ch'un 壽春, he is taken over the Huai River by two officers to appear before a censor. His monk-teacher is there and pleads for his *sūtra* piety to extend his life. Liu is made to recite it, forgets the text, but picks it up from an inscribed banner. All vanish. He is finally escorted home by demons and rejoins his dead body.

29 Chang Chia-yu 張嘉猷

Text: *TPKC* 105.710–11; Fang, p. 23.

Story: Chang, who died at Ming-chou 明州 in 762, was buried at Yang-chou. In 765 he appears to his friend Lao (the informant here), reporting that his habit of reciting the *Vajracchedikā* has been to his credit in the underworld. He urges this habit on Lao and his own brother. Chang departs, leaving Lao in a dazed condition.

30 Wei Hsün 魏恂

Text: *TPKC* 105.711; Fang, p. 23.

Story: Wei recites the *Vajracchedikā*. In 697 he becomes general in the Palace Gate Guards. One Ts'ai Ts'e falls suddenly dead, then recovers some days later. He reports that the underworld authorities were trying to bring in Wei Hsün, but failed because his *sūtra* piety secured him the protection of benevolent spirits.

31 Tu Ssu-ne 杜思訥

Text: *TPKC* 105.711; Fang, p. 24.

Story: Tu, a man of Lu-chou 潞州, recovers from sickness by reciting the *Vajracchedikā*. On the days of recitation there is divine radiance.

32 The abbot of Lung-hsing Monastery 龍興寺主

Text: *TPKC* 105.711–12; Fang, p. 24.

Story: At the Lung-hsing Monastery in Yüan-chou 原州 a junior monk offends the abbot, who attempts to strike him, but finds his sleeve held back by a pillar. The abbot leads the community in honouring the great merit which caused this miracle: it was in fact twenty years of reciting the *Vajracchedikā*. Pious respects are paid to the pillar, which releases the sleeve.

33 Ch'en Che 陳哲

Text: *TPKC* 105.712; Fang, pp. 24–5.

Story: Ch'en lives in Yü-hang 餘杭; he devoutly recites the *Vajracchedikā*. In 763, threatened by the local rebel Chu T'an 朱潭, he tries to move his property to safety but falls into the rebels' hands. Provoked by a careless question, they try to run him through with their swords, but find that his body is protected from attack by a coloured aureole.

34 Seng Tao-hsien 僧道憲

Text: *TPKC* 111.768; Fang, p. 25.

Story: Tao-hsien is abbot of a Chiang-chou 江州 monastery during K'ai-yüan. The prefect, sharing his surname, commissions seven Kuan-yin images. Tao-hsien has the paintings punctiliously done, but on the way to have them mounted he falls in a river. Seven bodhisattvas bear him up, bidding him call upon Kuan-yin. He later dies in early T'ien-pao. The images are still there in the monastery. So is a painting of the river miracle.

35 Ch'eng Kuei 成珪

Text: *TPKC* 111.768–9; Fang, pp. 26–7.

Note: Only the Shen Yü-wen MS cites *Kuang-i chi*. Other texts cite *Cho-i chi* 卓異記.

Story: Ch'eng, an officer in Ch'ang-sha county in early T'ien-pao, is accused of stealing timber for which he was responsible. Confined in chains, he is taken by boat to Yang-chou. He invokes Kuan-yin, his chains fall away and he escapes into the river. A log bears him to safety, and villagers help him to reach Ch'u-chou 滁州, where he is able to report the matter. His escorting officer goes into hiding and later into the priesthood.

36 Wang Ch'i 王琦

Text: *TPKC* 111.769–70; Fang, pp. 27–8.

Story: Wang is revenue manager in Ch'ü-chou 衢州 in early Ta-li. All his life he has abstained from meat and strong-flavoured food, and has recited the *Kuan-yin sūtra*. This cures him of frequent bouts of illness and helps him combat the strange visions and delusions that assail him. A sequence of dated episodes illustrates his case history.

Translation: Chap. 1, pp. 7–12, with discussion.

37 Censor Chang 張御史

Text: *TPKC* 112.776–7; Fang, pp. 29–30.

Story: During T'ien-pao Chang is travelling on Censorate business to Huai-nan when a man in yellow joins him. Chang accepts him on the official boat. The man's business is to escort Chang to the underworld after drowning in the river, but he suggests that reciting the *Vajracchedikā* a thousand times will extend his life. A team recitation achieves this, and in the underworld Chang is granted ten more years. His wife has a dream to match.

38 Li Hsin 李昕

Text: *TPKC* 112.777; Fang, p. 30.

Story: He recites a *mantra* of Kuan-yin of the Thousand Arms and Eyes. This gives him power to exorcize a malaria demon. While he is away travelling his sister sickens, dies, then revives. She explains that beings tormenting her in the graveyard recognized whose sister she was and feared his vengeance. So she is restored just before Li returns home.

39 Li Ch'ia 李洽

Text: *TPKC* 115.800–1; Fang, pp. 30–1.

Story: On the way from Lo-yang to Ch'ang-an Li meets an officer who gives him an unintelligible message from King Yama. He entertains the officer, who gratefully advises him to write out the *Chin kuang-ming sūtra* 金光明經 in self-protection. A large troop of soldiers passes by: it appears that Yama has moved off to a Ch'ang-an monastery and has extended Li's life because of his *sūtra* copying.

40 Wang I 王乙

Text: *TPKC* 115.801–2; Fang, pp. 31–2.

Story: Wang is a lifelong reciter of the *Ju-i lun mantra* 如意輪咒. In early K'ai-yüan he accepts a risky offer of a boat ride, reciting the *mantra* for protection. The boatman attacks his party murderously with an axe, but Wang survives to reach the bank and find help. Later the criminal is taken to Pien-chou 汴州 and gives his version of the event: the escape and survival were due to the *mantra.*

41 Ch'ien-erh Han-kuang 鉗耳含光

Text: *TPKC* 115.802–3; Fang, pp. 32–3.

Story: This retired magistrate meets his dead wife. In the large citadel where she now lives they enjoy conjugal relations, and she asks to see her sons. On a later visit there he sees her punished for failing a vow to copy the *Chin kuang-ming sūtra.* Her son sets out for the Wu-t'ai Mountains with money to have the *sūtra* copied. Mañjuśrī, in monk's guise, advises copying the *Vajracchedikā,* which achieves a human reincarnation for the mother.

42 Hsi Yü 席豫

Text: *TPKC* 115.803; Fang, p. 34.

Story: Hsi Yü [680–748], travelling in early K'ai-yüan as investigating censor to Ho-hsi, demands a dish of sheep's liver. But it moves about on the plate, he cannot eat it, and instead pays for a Buddha-image to be cast on the sheep's behalf. Collapsing dead, he is brought to account in the underworld. His plea is supported by the Buddha in question, and he is returned to life.

43 Su T'ing 蘇頲

Text: *TPKC* 121.853–4; Fang, p. 34.

Story: Su T'ing [670–727] achieves the third-grade office of board president 尚書 as predicted in his youth by a percipient man, who added that he was destined for the second grade. But on his deathbed he has still not achieved this, because (a spirit-medium tells him) two years of life were forfeited for the lives of two men taken in an earlier appointment. Su regrets the incident, then dies.

44 Chang Tsung 張縱

Text: *TPKC* 132.942–3; Fang, p. 35.

Story: Chang, a minor county official in Ch'üan-chou 泉州, likes minced fish. He sickens, dies, revives after seven days and reports his experience. The king has punished him by making him a fish for seven days. He is then caught. On the way to the sub-magistrate's kitchen he sees the man's wife in deshabille. He revives as a man when the knife cuts off the fish's head. The mince is served to Li O, a guest at table that day.

45 Tu Hsien 杜暹

Text: *TPKC* 148.1067–8; Fang, pp. 35–6.

Story: As a young man, Tu Hsien [d. 740] is preparing to cross the Yellow River in a crowded boat when an old man calls him back. The boat puts out, then founders, with his attendants and companions on board. The old man has saved him because of his distinguished future career.

46 Huang-fu 皇甫氏

Text: *TPKC* 162.1169; Fang, p. 36.

Story: She is the mother of P'ei Tsun-ch'ing 裴遵慶 [691–775] and a pious reciter of *sūtras* in her youth. Her *sūtra* case contains a little coral tree, beside which there appears a small dragon skeleton – a sign of good fortune for the P'ei family. Sure enough her son wins high office in 760–761.

47 The assistant clerk in Chü-jung 句容佐史

Text: *TPKC* 220.1688–9; Fang, p. 36.

Story: A clerk in Chü-jung county has a vast capacity for minced fish. One day he vomits up something like the sole of a shoe which transforms minced fish into fluid. It is taken for sale in Yang-chou at high price. An Iranian buys it for three hundred strings of cash because, he explains, it can dissolve abdominal growths. The crown prince in his country suffers from that complaint, and the king has offered rich rewards for a cure.

48 Wu Sheng-chih 武勝之

Text: *TPKC* 231.1770–1; *Lei shuo* 8.16b; *Kan-chu chi* 7.21a; Fang, pp. 37, 245–6, 252.

Story: Late in K'ai-yüan, when Wu is an administrator in Hsüan-chou 宣州, he sees a thunder god 雷公 chasing a yellow snake through the clouds. A man hits the snake with a stone, and the thunder god flies away. A bronze sword left at the scene is inscribed with the name of Hsü Ching-yang 許旌陽, destroyer of *chiao* 蛟 dragons.

49 The mountain-splitting sword 破山劍

Text: *TPKC* 232.1775–6; *Kan-chu chi* 7.23a; Fang, pp. 37, 254.

Story: A man unearths a sword which an Iranian agrees to buy for a high price. The man and his wife use the sword to cut through a stone, but then the Iranian finds its lustre gone: it was a mountain-splitting sword which he hoped would open a mountain full of precious ores. Used once, it loses its power. He now pays a much lower price.

50 Ku Ts'ung 顧琮

Text: *TPKC* 277.2195; Fang, p. 38.

Story: Ku Ts'ung [d. 702], serving as a remonstrance official, is imprisoned and awaits execution. In a dream he sees his mother's lower limbs. This scares him, but someone assures him that the omen is good: he has seen his own 'path to life'. His sentence miscarries, and he lives to achieve high office.

51 Hsüan-tsung 玄宗

Text: *TPKC* 277.2196; Fang, p. 38.

Story: The emperor Hsüan-tsung dreams of falling and being helped up by a son in mourning. Kao Li-shih 高力士 interprets the vision of mourning dress as code for Wei Chien-su 韋見素 [687–762], whom Hsüan-tsung soon promotes to ministerial rank.

Note: This promotion took place on 14 September 754: *CTS* 108.3276; *TCTC* 217.6927–8.

52 Lü Yin 呂諲

Text: *TPKC* 277.2200–1; Fang, pp. 38–9.

Story: Lü Yin [712–762] is brought in a daydream to the underworld, where he pleads for longer life. The king accepts a named substitute, K'uai Shih 蒯適, who is deemed distinguished enough to serve. Lü is released, returns to life, and tells his story to his host and brother-in-law Ku K'uang. Before long K'uai is appointed to Wu-hsien 吳縣, then retires there, and one day receives the summons to the underworld. He sickens and dies.

Note: Biographical authenticity debated by Fu Hsüan-ts'ung, *T'ang-tai shih-jen ts'ung-k'ao*, pp. 407–8, and by myself [Tu Te-ch'iao], '*Kuang-i chi* ch'u-t'an', pp. 405–6.

53 Ch'u Shih 楚寔

Text: *TPKC* 278.2203; Fang, p. 39.

Story: Ch'u, an assistant editorial director, falls seriously ill during Ta-li. After many days' delirium he sees a female Taoist in yellow, who tells him he is not to die and calls in a little boy with medicine. This cures him. The next day a real boy with the same name comes with medicine. Ch'u recovers.

54 Hsüeh I 薛義

Text: *TPKC* 278.2210; Fang, pp. 39–40.

Story: Hsüeh, a collator in the Palace Library, stays with his brother-in-law in T'ung-lu 桐廬, where he falls dangerously ill with malaria. His aunt dreams of a spirit in white who gives her charms and the text of a spell to exorcize spirits. The aunt, still dreaming, kills the demon afflicting her own daughter with malaria, then awakes to give the spell to Hsüeh. Both he and the daughter then recover.

Translation: Text of the spell translated by de Groot, vol. 6, p. 1053.

55 Chao Chiao 召皎

Text: *TPKC* 279.2218; Fang, pp. 40–1.

Story: Returning to Lo-yang after a politically dangerous mission in the capital, Chao rests at a posting station. There he dreams of being raised aloft and threatened with death, then released 'because he is not Chiang Ch'ing 蔣清'. Arriving in Lo-yang he is captured by rebels under T'ien Ch'ien-chen 田乾貞, who threatens him as in the dream. Again he escapes because Chiang Ch'ing is really the man due to die.

Note: An Lu-shan had Chiang Ch'ing killed in 755: *CTS* 187B.4895; *TCTC* 217.6939.

56 Li Shao-yün 李捎雲

Text: *TPKC* 279.2218–19; Fang, p. 41.

Story: Li is a wild, dissolute character. His wife, the daughter of Lu Jo-hsü 盧若虛, dreams of seeing him led captive with other male and female revellers. Li has the same dream, and in fear takes up a life of discipline, recites the *Vajracchedikā* and feeds monks. But after three uneventful years he relaxes the discipline and returns to a life of pleasure. He drowns during a boat party with friends and girls on the Serpentine Lake in Ch'ang-an.

Note: This accident happened in 717 at a party to celebrate Li Meng's 李蒙 success in the decree examination, according to *Ting-ming lu* (*TPKC* 216.1655) and *Tu-i chih* (*TPKC* 163.1184). More than ten scholars lost their lives. Cf. *Teng-k'o chi k'ao* 5.188.

57 Li Shu-chi 李叔霽

Text: *TPKC* 279.2219; Fang, pp. 41–2.

Story: Li, an investigating censor, dies early in Ta-li [766–]. A year later he appears in his brother-in-law's dream, talking about meeting after a hundred years. He leaves a poem of separation to transmit to his elder brother, who dies a few years later.

58 Lu Yen-hsü 盧彥緒

Text: *TPKC* 279.2221; Fang, p. 42.

Story: Lu, a director of granaries in Hsü-chou 許州, discovers in his latrine an earthenware coffin containing a woman in her twenties. An inscription dates her to the Ch'in period, destined to be opened up by Lu Yen-hsü after a thousand years. Lu takes out her gold hairpins and jewelled mirror, then closes the coffin. But the girl appears in his dreams to show anger at the removal of her valuables. Lu dies a year later.

Note: A lapse of a thousand years after the Ch'in gives dates ranging from 754 to 794.

59 Chou Yen-han 周延翰

Text: *TPKC* 279.2227; Fang, p. 237. Shen Yü-wen MS gives *Chi-shen lu, q.v.* (1.16b).

Story: Chou, a collator, is a keen user of Taoist drugs. In a dream he receives from a divine visitor a text like a Taoist scripture in verse. One line suggests success with the cinnabar. When he dies he is buried next to the tomb of Sun

Ch'üan 孫權 [182–252], leaving no wife or offspring, only a maid named Cinnabar.

60 Tou-lu Jung 豆盧榮

Text: *TPKC* 280.2229–30; Fang, pp. 42–3.

Story: He dies as sub-prefect of Wen-chou 溫州, leaving his wife and her mother, the Chin-ho Princess, once married to a Turgesh *qaghan*. When Yüan Ch'ao's rebellion breaks out in 762 the wife has dreams in which first her father then her husband warn them to flee to safety. The old lady stubbornly refuses to take heed until it is almost too late.

Translation: Chap. 6, pp. 139–41, with discussion.

61 The magistrate of Fu-kou 扶溝令

Text: *TPKC* 280.2231; Fang, p. 43.

Story: The magistrate dies in 767. Half a year later he appears in his wife's dreams and tells of the punishment inflicted for his habit of satirical writing: snakes and centipedes infest his body for 360 days. He requests a new pair of drawers (and knows what silk is available to make them) and wants a Buddha image cast and *Lotus sūtra* copied. He departs only when all this is agreed.

62 Wang Fang-p'ing 王方平

Text: *TPKC* 280.2233; Fang, pp. 43–4.

Story: A dutiful son, Wang attends his father in sickness. One day in a dream he hears two demons planning to enter his father's stomach with his next meal. Waking, Wang traps the food in a bottle, which he boils until it appears full of flesh. His father recovers.

63 Yen Chih 閻陟

Text: *TPKC* 280.2235; Fang, p. 44.

Story: In Yen's youth, when his father is chief administrator in Mi-chou 密州, he dreams of love visits from a beautiful girl of fifteen or sixteen. One day she sadly takes leave, revealing herself as a previous incumbent's daughter, interred near the city wall. Her brother is now coming to take her for burial. She leaves 100,000 cash for Yen, who awakes to find that amount in paper money beneath his bed.

64 Metropolitan graduate Li 李進士

Text: *TPKC* 281.2237–8; Fang, pp. 44–5.

Story: Li dreams he is arraigned in the underworld court for cheating his brother-in-law over the sale of a horse, and is granted fifteen days to make good the money owed. But waking he dismisses the dream. A travelling mirror-polisher comes telling fortunes and warns him that time is running out: the brother-in-law, though dead, can be repaid through dedicated charity to beggars and monasteries. Li complies.

65 Li Po 李播

Text: *TPKC* 298.2371; Fang, pp. 45–6.

Story: The emperor Kao-tsung, preparing for the Feng/Shan rites on Mount T'ai, sends Liu Jen-kuei 劉仁軌 [601–685] to consult Li Po, a Taoist in retreat on Mount Hua. Li summons the Lord of Mount T'ai, who confirms that the rites should go ahead now, and again in sixty years. Indulgence is sought and granted for Liu Jen-kuei, who has neglected to bow to the Lord of Mount T'ai.

Note: Feng/Shan rites were held in 666 and 725: Chavannes, *Le T'ai chan*, pp. 180, 222 ff.

66 Ti Jen-chieh 狄仁傑

Text: *TPKC* 298.2371; Fang, p. 46.

Story: Ti Jen-chieh [607–700], as investigating censor under Kao-tsung, systematically purges spirit-cults in southern China. In Tuan-chou 端州 he has a tribal god restrained by imperial warrant and his temple burned down. Bent on revenge, the god follows Ti back north to Pien-chou 汴州. But high office gives Ti the protection of numerous spirits.

Note: Ti's purge of southern cults took place in 688, but his Chiang-nan jurisdiction did not extend to Tuan-chou: *CTS* 89.2887; *HTS* 115.4208; *TCTC* 204.6448–9. See David McMullen, 'The real Judge Dee', pp. 11–13.

Translation: Lévi, 'Les fonctionnaires et le divin', p. 88, with discussion.

67 Wang Wan-ch'e 王萬徹

Text: *TPKC* 298.2372; Fang, p. 47.

Story: Empress Wu calls in the exorcist Wang Wan-ch'e to investigate why members of her entourage have died. Wang finds the late emperor [Kao-tsung] responsible and summons his ghost with spells. The spirit explains that his Empress Wang has been demanding vengeance, and Empress Wu herself will suffer. The following year Chung-tsung is set on the throne and the empress dowager dismissed to die in obscurity.

Note: Kao-tsung died in 683, Empress Wu in 705.

68 The wife of an administrator in Chao-chou 趙州參軍妻

Text: *TPKC* 298.2373–4; *Sui-shih kuang-chi* 23.6b–7b; Fang, pp. 47–9.

Story: Administrator Lu's wife goes to market in Lo-yang, collapses with chest pains and dies. Lu consults the imperial counsellor Ming Ch'ung-yen 明崇儼, who identifies the Third Son of Mount T'ai as responsible. On his advice three charms are burned, and the woman revives. She tells how she was taken and prepared for marriage to the third son, until the Grand Prime (*T'ai-i*) intervened destructively to liberate her.

Note: Ming Ch'ung-yen died in 679: *CTS* 191.5097. Legendary user of Grand Prime charms: *TPKC* 74.467; 285.2270; 299.2377; and cf. 328.2605. See Chap. 4, p. 113.

69 The wife of the Ho-tung county chief of staff 河東縣尉妻

Text: *TPKC* 300.2382–3; Fang, pp. 49–50.

Story: In 710–711 the wife of Li, chief of staff in Ho-tung county, collapses lifeless. A man restores her to life with the use of charms. She had been carried off to Mount Hua and brought before the king, who made amorous approaches during a party. Then messengers from the Grand Prime arrived to demand her release. The king complied.

Note: See Chap. 4, p. 112.

70 The imperial guardsman 三衛

Text: *TPKC* 300.2383–4; Fang, pp. 50–1.

Story: In early K'ai-yüan an imperial guardsman, passing the Temple of Mount Hua, agrees to help the bride of the mount by reporting her sufferings to her family in the Northern Ocean. Her father rewards him with rare silk. Warfare then ensues between the dragons of the ocean and the god of the mount, leaving the mountain scorched. The guardsman sells his silk and (helped by the grateful bride) escapes the god's revenge.

Translation: Dudbridge, 'The tale of Liu Yi and its analogues', pp. 64–8, with discussion.

Note: Contains one of the earliest references to safe-deposit banking in China.

71 Li Shih 李湜

Text: *TPKC* 300.2384–5; *Sui-shih kuang-chi* 28.5a–6a; *Kan-chu chi* 7.21b; Fang, pp. 51–3, 253.

Story: In K'ai-yüan Li visits the Hall of the Three Consorts at the Mount Hua Temple. The consorts, whose husband is on an annual visit to heaven, invite Li to join them in love-making. For seven years he returns on the same date to do this. His family watch him expire, then recover after three days. A ritual specialist provides him with a charm that keeps the consorts at bay, to their displeasure. One of them foretells his official career.

Translation: Chap. 4, pp. 106–8, with discussion.

72 Yeh Ching-neng 葉淨能

Text: *TPKC* 300.2385; Fang, p. 53.

Story: The Taoist divine Yeh Ching-neng is called in by the emperor Hsüan-tsung to submit a memorial to the Monarch of Heaven 玉京天帝 asking whether the empress will bear a son. It comes back with a negative endorsement.

Note: Cf. story **198**; also P'an Chung-kuei, *Tun-huang pien-wen chi hsin-shu,* p. 1112. Hsüan-tsung's consort *née* Wang became empress in 712, remained childless, and fell to commoner status in 724: see *T'ang hui-yao* 3.26; *CTS* 51.2177; *HTS* 76.3490.

73 Chang Chia-yu 張嘉祐

Text: *TPKC* 300.2386; Fang, pp. 53–4.

Story: Chang Chia-yu [d. 741] is prefect of Hsiang-chou 相州. The residence is haunted by a poltergeist, but Chang has the courage to meet the ghost, who is Yü-ch'ih Chiung, a loyal martyr of the Northern Chou left unburied in that place. Chang gives him due burial and sets up a temple cult. The grateful ghost maintains communication with him.

Translation: Chap. 5, pp. 129–36, with discussion.

74 A man of Ju-yin 汝陰人

Text: *TPKC* 301.2387–8; Fang, pp. 54–6.

Story: The man is Hsü 許, a lover of horses and action. Out hunting, he picks up a coloured bag, an act which leads to his marriage with a maiden from the divine society of Mount Sung 嵩山. His grateful in-laws make him rich, and his wife rejuvenates him with sexual arts. They have five sons, who go off with their mother when Hsü finally dies.

Translation: Dudbridge, 'The tale of Liu Yi and its analogues', pp. 75–8; cf. Chap. 7, pp. 168–9.

75 Ts'ui Min-ch'iao 崔敏殻

Text: *TPKC* 301.2389; Fang, p. 57.

Story: Ts'ui died at age ten and revived after eighteen years, explaining that he had been wrongly taken. He now retaliates on the spirits, for whom he has no fear. As prefect of Hsü-chou 徐州 he scornfully cows the spirit of Hsiang Yü 項羽. In Hua-chou 華州 his presence subdues the preparations for a spirit wedding in the Mount Hua Temple.

Note: Ts'ui's speech to Hsiang Yü echoes one made in Wu-hsing by Hsiao Ch'en 蕭琛 [478–529]: *Nan shih* 18.506.

76 Ch'iu Chia-fu 仇嘉福

Text: *TPKC* 301.2390–2; Fang, pp. 57–9.

Story: Travelling to take the examination in Lo-yang, Ch'iu joins a young nobleman called Pai who has business in the Mount Hua Temple. While Pai reviews the gods of Kuan-nei province, Ch'iu discovers his own wife being tortured in the temple. Ch'iu has her case reviewed and her life restored. Later, with the help of Pai (really T'ai-i, the Grand Prime) Ch'iu uses charms to revive another man's wife, stolen by the god of Mount Hua.

Translation: Chap. 4, pp. 109–14, with discussion.

77 Wei Hsiu-chuang 韋秀莊

Text: *TPKC* 302.2396–7; Fang, pp. 59–60.

Story: As prefect of Hua-chou 滑州 during K'ai-yüan Wei meets the city god, who asks for help in fighting back the god of the Yellow River. Wei commits some troops, who attack steam rising from the river on the appointed date. The river retreats to its current distance of 5–6 *li* from the city walls.

Translation: Wieger, *Folk-lore chinois moderne,* pp. 49–50; Lévi, 'Les fonctionnaires et le divin', pp. 85–6.

Note: Wei's name should probably read Chi-chuang 季莊: cf. *HTS* 74A.3109; *Yüan-ho hsing-tsuan* 2.28a.

78 The god of Mount Hua's daughter 華嶽神女

Text: *TPKC* 302.2397–8; Fang, pp. 60–1.

Story: An examination candidate on his way to the capital shares a lodging with a princess. He sees her bathing, takes her fancy and becomes her lover. He lives with her as royalty, and in the course of seven years they have three children. Then, because she is a spirit, she tells him to marry a human. His wife's family uses charms to keep them apart, and the princess departs, taking their children. She is the Third Daughter of Mount Hua.

Translation: Dudbridge, 'The goddess Hua-yüeh San-niang and the Cantonese ballad *Ch'en-hsiang T'ai-tzu*', pp. 628–9; also Chap. 7, pp. 158–60; both with discussion.

79 Wang Hsien 王僩

Text: *TPKC* 302.2398; Fang, pp. 61–2.

Story: Wang, a court usher, is borne off by spirits to the Temple of Mount Hua. He sees his wife being tortured, and the divine staff arrange for him to ride home on a spirit fox. His wife revives, and he rejoins his own body, waiting there inertly.

80 Chi Kuang-ch'en 季廣琛

Text: *TPKC* 303.2402; Fang, p. 62.

Story: Travelling in Ho-hsi 河西 as a young man, Chi [*fl.* 735–774] is visited by goddesses called the Young Ladies. Then he suspects his visitors were demons and attacks them with his sword. The goddesses are offended, and he is unable to make amends. They vow that he will never receive title or estate.

Translation: Chap. 7, pp. 154–7, with discussion.

81 Liu K'o-ta 劉可大

Text: *TPKC* 303.2402–3; Fang, pp. 62–3.

Story: Liu, on his way to the examination, joins a young nobleman who takes him into the Temple of Mount Hua. He is the god's son. Liu sees prisoners being flogged, then asks to see the register of his own future. By begging to pass the examination in the current year, he causes his whole career to take a more modest course.

82 Wang Chi 王籍

Text: *TPKC* 304.2408; Fang, pp. 63–4.

Story: In 758–9 Wang, abroad in Kuei-chi 會稽, sees one of his slaves die, then revive. The man was told by an officer in the underworld that his master would become General of the Five Paths 五道將軍. He also saw the banners and guards made ready for this. Wang Chi soon dies, and the guards welcoming him are much in evidence.

83 A village headman in Ying-yang 潁陽里正

Text: *TPKC* 304.2413; Fang, p. 64.

Story: A villager lying drunk outside the Younger Aunt Temple 少姨祠 at Mount Sung is recruited to assist in making rain. He is set upon a creature like a camel and given a bottle, with instructions to hold it firmly upright. He flies up, and raindrops emerge from the bottle. But looking down at his own drought-ridden area he tips the bottle. This causes a flood which sweeps away his house and family.

Note: I read 'Aunt' 姨 for 'Woman' 婦: see story **115** and Chap. 7, p. 157. Ch'ien Chung-shu gives other examples of flooding from a tipped bottle: *Kuan-chui pien*, p. 796.

84 Wang Fa-chih 王法智

Text: *TPKC* 305.2414; *Lei-shuo* 8.17b; *Kan-chu chi* 7.22ab; *Shuo-fu* 4.11a; Fang, pp. 64–5, 246, 253–4, 256.

Story: A young woman in T'ung-lu 桐廬 county is regularly possessed in the late 760s by the spirit of a man from Ch'ang-an. The local magistrate makes her call down the spirit, who exchanges verses and conversation with the local gentry. Tai Fu himself is present at such a party on 15 March 771.

Translation: Chap. 1, pp. 1 ff., with discussion.

85 Li Tso-shih 李佐時

Text: *TPKC* 305.2415; Fang, pp. 65–6.

Story: Li, assistant magistrate of Shan-yin 山陰, falls ill in 767. While visiting a kinsman he is summoned by warriors from the underworld, where the king wants him as an administrative assistant and as a son-in-law. He tells his kinsman that he will soon die and demands a big meal, during which he falls dead. When his coffin reaches his wife in Kuei-chi her maid speaks with Li's voice, reporting that no marriage has taken place.

Translation: Chap. 1, pp. 12–15, with discussion.

86 Chang Ts'ung 張琮

Text: *TPKC* 328.2603; Fang, pp. 66–7.

Story: In 650 Chang, as magistrate in Nan-yang 南陽 county, confronts a spirit haunting the residence. It is a soldier killed in the Chu Ts'an 朱粲 rebellion, whose remains are unburied and pierced by a root. Chang has him duly buried. Later the grateful ghost warns him about a plan to take his life. Chang pays sacrifice and has the tomb inscribed.

87 Liu Men-nu 劉門奴

Text: *TPKC* 328.2603–4; and cf. *Sui-shih kuang-chi* 19.12b; Fang, pp. 67–8.

Story: While the Ta-ming Palace is being built under Kao-tsung, horsemen are heard at night. The medium Liu Men-nu is told to investigate. An answer comes from the son of [Liu] Wu 戊, prince of Ch'u in the Former Han, who was buried with a pair of jade fish. He begs reburial, still with the fish, away from the building site. This done, the trouble ends.

Note: For the original episode in 154 BC, see *Shih chi* 11.440; *Han shu* 5.142–3. The jade fish are mentioned by Tu Fu: *Ch'ien chu Tu shih*, Peking 1958, 15.513–4.

88 Yen Keng 閻庚

Text: *TPKC* 328.2604–5; Fang, pp. 68–9.

Story: Chang Jen-tan 張仁亶 [d. 714] is supported by Yen Keng, from a trading background, who follows him to study in the mountains. At an inn in Ch'en-liu 陳留 county they meet an underworld officer whose work is tying the feet of brides and grooms at weddings. He predicts Chang's long and distinguished future and advises Yen Keng to find and marry the right woman to secure his own career. Both men succeed.

Note: For Chang's career, see *CTS* 93.2981–3; *HTS* 111.4151–3.

89 Ti Jen-chieh 狄仁傑

Text: *TPKC* 329.2614: only the Ch'en Chan collation cites *Kuang-i chi*; Fang, pp. 69–70.

Story: Under Empress Wu Ti Jen-chieh is prefect of Ning-chou 寧州. Although earlier incumbents have died in the haunted residence, Ti insists on moving in and rebuking the ghost. A dead officer emerges to explain that his remains lie under a tree in the courtyard, pierced by a root. Ti has him reburied, and the trouble stops.

Translation: de Groot, vol. 6, pp. 1156–7. See also David McMullen, 'The real Judge Dee', p. 13.

90 Li Kao 李暠

Text: *TPKC* 329.2615; Fang, p. 70.

Story: Li, president of the Board of War, is approached in early K'ai-yüan by an attractive woman. He does not accept her, but gives her to his visitor Chiang Chiao 姜皎. At a party the woman tells the guests' fortunes. When Chiang Chiao takes her aside for dalliance the guests line up to peep at them, ending with Li Kao. She cries out and vanishes, leaving only bones. She is judged to be a ghost intimidated by Li's integrity.

Note: In *CTS* 112.3335–6 and *HTS* 78.3531 Li Kao is president of the Boards of Public Works and Civil Office in late K'ai-yüan.

91 Chang Shou-kuei 張守珪

Text: *TPKC* 329.2615–6; Fang, pp. 70–1.

Story: While Chang [d. 739] is a military commander in Ho-hsi his men seize a consignment of *kaṣāyas* being taken home from China by an Iranian Buddhist and kill his disciples. Chang makes amends by maintaining the monk for some years. On a later mission, when surrounded by thousands of Iranian troops, he is saved by cavalry led by Li Kuang 李廣 of the Han. He rises to military commissioner and censor-in-chief.

92 Yang Ch'ang 楊瑒

Text: *TPKC* 329.2616–17; Fang, pp. 71–2.

Story: When Yang [d. 735] is prefect of Lo-yang, he learns from a soothsayer that he has only two days to live. The man guides him in earning a reprieve: first with personal austerities, then with hospitality to those sent to fetch him to the underworld. These agree to alter his name to that of his neighbour. Finally the sound of wailing next door tells him he is saved.

93 Chang Kuo's daughter 張國女

Text: *TPKC* 330.2618–19 (source given in Ch'en Chan collation and Shen Yü-wen MS); Fang, p. 73.

Story: Chang Kuo's daughter dies at fifteen and is given temporary burial at his post in I-chou 易州, then left there when her father moves on. The son of his successor Liu I becomes her lover. She prompts him to find and open the coffin and restore her body to life. Liu I finally arranges an orthodox marriage, after consulting Chang Kuo.

94 Consort Hua 華妃

Text: *TPKC* 330.2619; Fang, p. 74.

Story: Consort Hua, a favourite of Hsüan-tsung in K'ai-yüan, dies. But in 740 grave-robbers attack her tomb and violate and mutilate her perfectly preserved body. They remove the grave goods by staging a false funeral. But in a dream her son hears his mother explain her plight and vow revenge. He reports to Hsüan-tsung, who has the robbers (all unprincipled aristocrats) arrested. After savage retribution the lady is reburied.

Translation: de Groot, vol. 4, pp. 447–9.

95 Kuo Chih-yün 郭知運

Text: *TPKC* 330.2619–20; Fang, pp. 74–5.

Story: Kuo, a military commissioner in Ho-hsi, dies suddenly in a posting station. His soul returns to his prefecture and puts his affairs in order. It then witnesses his own funeral and takes leave of his family before disappearing into the coffin.

Translation: de Groot, vol. 5, p. 723; Wieger, p. 61.

96 Wang Kuang-pen 王光本

Text: *TPKC* 330.2620; Fang, p. 75.

Story: Wang is assistant prefect in Lo-chou 洛州 in K'ai-yüan. When his wife dies suddenly the family mourn passionately, but she appears to inform them that excessive grief is not well received in the underworld. She arranges for her daughter to become a nun and has her maids set free. Then she vanishes, having been visible only to her husband.

97 Yang Yüan-ying 楊元英

Text: *TPKC* 330.2625–6; Fang, pp. 75–6.

Story: Yang held a court position under Empress Wu, but has been dead for twenty years when his son notices a sword from his father's tomb being repaired at a forge. It is collected by his father's soul, who stays to sort out family affairs and hear family news. Giving them money, he leaves and vanishes into the ancient necropolis outside Lo-yang. The money turns out to be paper.

98 Hsüeh Chin 薛矜

Text: *TPKC* 331.2627; Fang, pp. 76–7.

Story: Hsüeh supervises the East and West Markets in Ch'ang-an during K'ai-yüan. He sees a beautiful woman to whom he offers a silver box. She invites him to visit her, but when he does so the eerie atmosphere troubles him, and he recites the Kuan-yin *mantra*. The woman is veiled. She turns out to have a grotesque face and a voice like a dog. He collapses, and his attendants find him inert inside a burial hut. But he later revives.

99 Chu Ch'i-niang 朱七娘

Text: *TPKC* 331.2628; Fang, p. 77.

Story: She is a Lo-yang courtesan, patronized by a General Wang. In K'ai-yüan Wang dies, without her knowledge, but later appears and asks her to join him in a city residence. Against her daughter's advice she goes, spends the night with him, and is found next day on the general's coffin-stand. Wang's sons are called, and she is taken home.

100 Li Kuang-yüan 李光遠

Text: *TPKC* 331.2628; Fang, pp. 77–8.

Story: Li is magistrate of Kuan-t'ao 館陶 county during K'ai-yüan. He writes a report on local drought conditions, but suddenly dies before it takes effect.

To the despair of the people an assistant prefect rejects the report. But Li then appears on a white horse, promising to see it through, and threatens the assistant into cooperation. Drought relief is approved.

101 Li Pa 李霸

Text: *TPKC* 331.2628–30; Fang, pp. 78–9.

Story: Li, a magistrate of Ch'i-yang 岐陽, is harsh on his subordinates, and when he suddenly dies his wife receives no visits of condolence. From inside his coffin he speaks to her, then appears and demands contributions from his frightened staff. He directs the transport of his hearse back to Lo-yang, on the way helping to recover a stolen horse. He takes leave after a final appearance to curious relatives, and requests due burial.

Translation: Chap. 6, pp. 144–6, in part, with discussion.

102 A student in An-i ward 安宜坊書生

Text: *TPKC* 331.2631; Fang, p. 80.

Story: A student in Lo-yang is visited one night in late K'ai-yüan by a demon who spirits him out of the city. They go to a mound with a skylight, in which they see a family with a sick child. The demon removes the child in a cloth bag. As they return he explains that the company of a living man was needed to collect the child for the underworld. Next day the student checks the crosses that marked the previous night's movements.

103 P'ei Sheng 裴盛

Text: *TPKC* 331.2631; Fang, pp. 80–1.

Story: P'ei, on the staff of I-hsing 義興 county, is led off by a demon during sleep. They come to a child sleeping between his parents, protected by Buddhist sacra. P'ei, as a living man, is told to lift out the child, whose cry wakes the parents. The demon leads P'ei away and returns his soul to his body. Named informant.

Note: There are significant gaps in the text: see Yen I-p'ing, *Chiao-k'an chi*, p. 124a.

104 A traveller in Li-yang 黎陽客

Text: *TPKC* 333.2642–3; Fang, pp. 81–2.

Story: A poor scholar seeking patronage north of the Yellow River receives hospitality near Li-yang from a man named Hsün Chi-ho 荀季和. He learns that Hsün serves as registrar for the god of the river and sees him punish the magistrate of Li-yang for breaching the walls of his compound. This turns out to be a tomb, which the magistrate destroys when he hears the scholar's tale. The scholar later offers food and burns clothes for the bereft soul.

Translation: Laurie Scheffler, in Karl S. Y. Kao, ed., *Classical Chinese tales of the supernatural and the fantastic*, Bloomington 1985, pp. 241–3.

105 Li Chiung-hsiu 李迥秀

Text: *TPKC* 333.2643; Fang, pp. 82–3.

Story: Li [*fl.* 701–709], a board president, was friends with a Buddhist monk before he died. After some years the monk is summoned by two runners and expires. The summons was mistaken. He is taken back past a citadel where he meets Li, now an underworld general. Li weeps at the impending end of his family sacrifices and requests acts of Buddhist merit from his sons. Only one refuses, and he is soon convicted of sedition.

Note: *CTS* 62.2391 records the sedition of Li's son Ch'i-sun 齊損 in 722 and consequent end of the family line. Cf. *TCTC* 212.6752 (K'ai-yüan 22/8/*chi-mao*).

106 A man of Lang-yeh 瑯琊人

Text: *TPKC* 333.2644; Fang, p. 83.

Story: A traveller finds lodging outside the walls of Jen-ch'eng 任城 county town. But his host vanishes at the sight of a small knife with rhinoceros-horn handle. Guarding himself with the knife, the traveller finds himself inside a mound with a rotting coffin. He crawls out through an opening, but gains no further information on the tomb.

107 P'ei Hui 裴徽

Text: *TPKC* 333.2646; Fang, pp. 83–4.

Story: Walking near his manor-house during T'ien-pao, P'ei meets and flirts with an attractive woman. She invites him into her fine home nearby, where the staff entertain him in style. He notices the appearance of bridal preparations. Returning from using the lavatory he sees his evil-protecting sword flashing light. The buildings vanish: he is on an old tomb. Found by his servants, he is left sightless and speechless for some time.

108 Li T'ao 李陶

Text: *TPKC* 333.2647; Fang, pp. 84–5.

Story: During T'ien-pao Li T'ao, travelling in Hsin-cheng 新鄭, is shaken awake to meet a Miss Cheng. At first reluctant to deal with a ghost, he then spends several months with the girl, to his mother's distress, before leaving to take the examination in Lo-yang. The girl goes to tend him there when he falls ill, negotiating the border control at T'ung Pass. But when he receives an appointment she takes leave: their affinity is at an end.

109 A daughter of the Lu family in Ch'ang-chou 長洲陸氏女

Text: *TPKC* 333.2647–8; Fang, pp. 85–6.

Story: Lu, a deputy in Ch'ang-chou county, takes his family to visit Tiger Hill Monastery in Soochow. But his teenaged daughter, left at home, kills herself. They give her temporary burial. Later she sends out word from her burial hut through a passer-by, also named Lu, that she wants her father to deal with a marriage proposal from Li XVIII. This young man, though alive, soon dies. The two families hold a spirit marriage.

Translation: Chap. 7, pp. 163–6, with discussion.

Note: Discussed by Shigehara Hiroshi in 'Chūgoku meikon setsuwa no futatsu no kata', pp. 475–6.

110 Yang Chun 楊準

Text: *TPKC* 334.2650; Fang, p. 86.

Story: Yang meets and unites with a beautiful girl in the countryside. She forces him to follow her into a dwelling with a small entrance, where they eat

together. This and later encounters always leave him prostrate at home. His brother rebukes him for mating with a ghost. He becomes a Buddhist monk, and she leaves him alone. But when he returns to lay life, takes office and marries, she comes to express her anger. He sickens and dies.
Translation: Chap. 7, pp. 161–2, with discussion.

111 Wang I 王乙
Text: *TPKC* 334.2650–1; Fang, pp. 86–7.
Story: Wang I meets a teenaged girl in Lin-ju 臨汝 and joins her in a manor house, where they become lovers. But she is injured and expects to die. When she leaves, she begs him to visit her later. Wang gains office, returns to the girl's manor house and finds she is dead. He sacrifices and mourns outside her burial hut. The girl emerges, Wang dies, and the maid sees his soul go back inside with her. They are joined in spirit marriage.
Translation: Chap. 7, pp. 166–7, with discussion.
Note: Discussed by Shigehara, 'Chūgoku meikon setsuwa no futatsu no kata', p. 476.

112 Wei Li 韋栗
Text: *TPKC* 334.2651–2; Fang, pp. 87–8.
Story: Wei is deputy magistrate of Hsin-kan 新淦 county during T'ien-pao. As they travel there through Yang-chou his daughter asks to buy a lacquered mirror, which he puts off. The girl dies, but when they return with the hearse through Yang-chou she goes shopping for the mirror herself, using gold coins which turn out to be sacrificial paper money. The mirror thus bought from a young man is found in the coffin.

113 Administrative Aide Liu of Ho-chien 河間劉別駕
Text: *TPKC* 334.2652; Fang, pp. 88–9.
Story: In the streets of Ch'ang-an Liu sees and follows an attractive woman to her home, where they enjoy some nights of pleasure. But he feels cold at night, even when covered with quilts. He awakes one day to find himself alone in a deserted garden, covered with leaves. He falls chronically ill.

114 Wang Hsüan-chih 王玄之
Text: *TPKC* 334.2652–3; Fang, pp. 89–90.
Story: Returning to Kao-mi 高密 county, Wang meets and becomes the lover of a young woman. She will not receive him at home, where she lives with her late brother's daughter. One night she takes leave, explaining that she is the dead daughter of a former magistrate, who will now complete her formal burial. They exchange gifts. Meeting the family, Wang verifies that the grave goods have been changed. The woman's dead niece was indeed buried with her.
Note: Discussed by Shigehara, 'Chūgoku meikon setsuwa no futatsu no kata', pp. 478–80.

115 Chu Ao 朱敖
Text: *TPKC* 334.2655; Fang, pp. 90–1.
Story: (*a*) Chu, now vice-prefect of Hang-chou, once lived in retreat on Shao-shih Mountain 少室山. Riding past the Temple of the Younger Aunt 少姨廟,

he met a girl in green whom he then recognized in the wall-paintings there. She appeared in his sexual dreams until a Taoist priest devised a ritual remedy.
(*b*) Later, after a thunderstorm in the same mountains, Chu witnessed a performance of dancing by divine women in the heavens.
Note: See Chap. 7, pp. 157–8, with translation of (*a*). Chu Ao appears again as informant in **122**.

116 P'ei Ch'iu 裴虬
Text: *TPKC* 334.2656; Fang, p. 91.
Story: In late T'ien-pao P'ei stays at the former residence of Tai Yung 戴顒 [378–441] in Soochow, where he suddenly dies, then returns to life. He was summoned by Tai Yung, who wanted him to marry his daughter. P'ei successfully resisted the proposal and was released back to life. Likely informant: Soochow hermit Lu Ch'ü-she 陸去奢.
Note: The Sung official and hermit Tai Yung belonged to Tai Fu's ancestral line: cf. Chap. 2, pp. 42–3.

117 Chao Tso 趙佐
Text: *TPKC* 334.2656; Fang, pp. 91–2.
Story: In late T'ien-pao this state academy student is lying sick when two runners in yellow bring him before a royal figure. It is Emperor Ch'in Shihhuang. He comments on Hsüan-tsung's imperial entertainments at the hot spring beside his own tomb; also warns about forthcoming troubles, and urges the man to leave Ch'ang-an. Then returns him home.

118 The accessory clerk of Ch'i-chou 岐州佐史
Text: *TPKC* 334.2656–7; Fang, p. 92.
Story: While on business in Ch'ang-an this official is summoned before the king by two men accompanied by a headless man. He offers them paper money to let him go; they accept and agree on a deadline for release. When this passes he burns the money. Later they visit him again, confirming that he is secure from sickness until the end of his life.

119 The Wangs of Chün-i 浚儀王氏
Text: *TPKC* 335.2658; Fang, pp. 92–3.
Story: When mother in the family is buried her son-in-law P'ei in a drunken accident is also buried in the tomb. Days later he is dug out and revived. He reports having seen a great company of Wang dead. His mother-in-law pleaded for his life to be spared on her daughter's account. He then watched the ghosts enjoying a lavish party with entertainments. He was fed from food in a bottle. The servants were all grave goods.

120 Chang-ch'iu Chien-ch'iung 章仇兼瓊
Text: *TPKC* 335.2658–9; Fang, pp. 93–4.
Story: Chang-ch'iu serves as military governor in Chien-nan 劍南 [740–746]. Preparing for a visit to court, he is warned by a seer called Yakṣa Chang 張夜叉 not to leave Szechuan. Chang-ch'iu does go, but collapses at Han-chou 漢州. Then a junior official from Chien-nan turns up and also falls dead.

Chang-ch'iu revives and explains that this man has taken his place. He compensates the man's family generously.

121 Yang Kuo-chung 楊國忠

Text: *TPKC* 335.2660–1; *Hsiao-hsiang lu* 瀟湘錄 4b–5b, in the late-Ming revision of *Shuo-fu*, ch. 32.

Note: Only Sun Ch'ien cites *Kuang-i chi*. Ming MS cites *Hsüan-shih chih* 宣室志.

Story: A woman insists on speaking to Yang Kuo-chung [d. 756] at the height of his power. She denounces his policies and abuse of power. She closes with a mocking speech which makes punning use of the character *hu* 胡. Only after the great rebellion does its reference to An Lu-shan become clear.

122 Li Shu-chi 李叔霽

Text: *TPKC* 335.2661–2; Fang, pp. 94–5.

Story: During the An Lu-shan rebellion Li flees south. His wife and sons die on the road, and he travels on. But his wife appears to her aunt, caught in rebel-held Lo-yang, claiming that she has married a rebel after her husband was killed. Providing good food and a gift of silk, the wife then moves off. After the restoration in 758 the aunt compares stories with Li Shu-chi in Yang-chou. She still has a skirt made from the silk. Informant Chu Ao [cf. **115**] claims to have met the rebel in question.

123 The magistrate of Hsin-fan county 新繁縣令

Text: *TPKC* 335.2662; Fang, pp. 95–6.

Story: After his wife's death the magistrate enjoys a love affair with a woman making the mourning clothes. Then she takes leave, since her husband is coming to take her far away. She gives him a silver goblet, he gives her silk. But another county officer, come to collect his own dead wife's body, recognizes the goblet as coming from her coffin and finds the magistrate's silk in her arms inside the coffin. In fury he burns her.

Translations: de Groot, vol. 4, pp. 424–5; Wieger, pp. 244–5.

124 Yao Hsiao-p'in 姚蕭品

Text: *TPKC* 335.2663; Fang, pp. 96–7.

Story: Yao, a man of Hang-chou, dies during a party at home, then revives. He describes being called out, then seized and made to drag along a boat full of officers by the city wall. He did this with difficulty for some distance, then slipped away and escaped.

125 Ch'ang I 常夷

Text: *TPKC* 336.2665–7; Fang, pp. 97–9.

Story: Ch'ang I of Chien-k'ang 建康 hears from a stranger, Chu Chün, dead and buried nearby, who hopes to meet him. Chu is a graduate who died in this place in 559. His talk is full of historical anecdotes otherwise unrecorded. The men become friends. Later, when Ch'ang sickens, Chu announces he is required for office in the underworld and advises him to accept the situation. Ch'ang then dies willingly.

Note: Ch'ien Chung-shu, *Kuan-chui pien*, pp. 786–7, comments on the references to Liang Yüan-ti's partial blindness.

126 Chang Shou-i 張守一

Text: *TPKC* 336.2667–8; *Lei-shuo* 8.13b–14a; *Shuo-fu* 4.10b; Fang, pp. 99–100, 243–4, 255.

Story: Chang, in the Court of Judicial Review, frees some prisoners on death row. One grateful father, a ghost, offers to help with any request. Chang sees a girl at the Imperial Revels and asks the ghost to procure her for him. The ghost does this: while she believes she is in heaven, an inert substitute takes her place. After seven days' lovemaking she goes home. Chang receives a magic pill which later helps in the difficulties of exile.

Note: The 'Ch'ien-yüan' [758–759] date given in both early texts cannot be reconciled with a later reference to Empress Wu (武太后). Perhaps Ch'ien-feng [666–667] was intended.

127 Yü-wen Tu 宇文覿

Text: *TPKC* 336.2668–70; *Fen-men ku-chin lei-shih* 5.3b–5b; Fang, pp. 100–3, 249–50.

Story: In 758–759 the magistrate of Wu-shan 巫山 faces the threat of fatal haunting. A coffin with human remains is found under a tree in the courtyard. The spirit, a Chin general speaking through a medium, shows gratitude for his reburial by warning about the future of the magistrate's friend Yü-wen Tu, whom he later protects from various dangers, including imprisonment for sedition. Yü-wen dies in the act of accepting office.

128 Li Ying 李瑩

Text: *TPKC* 336.2670–1; Fang, pp. 103–4.

Story: Li's unmarried cousin travels south with her brothers in 756 to escape the rebellion, dies and is buried in Hai-yen 海鹽. A sister-in-law, left behind on the family property near Lo-yang, sees her come home in 760. She quickly finds her a husband, and they have a son. When the brothers return in 765 to recover their land the cousin leaves. Her death is reported, but no corpse is seen – just clothes and objects from her original coffin.

Translation: Chap. 7, pp. 170–3, with discussion.

129 P'ei Sheng 裴晠

Text: *TPKC* 336.2671; Fang, p. 104.

Story: P'ei plays the *cheng* 箏 zither and takes lessons from a master on his sister's behalf. He dies while travelling in the south. But later, turning up at home alone, he plays and guides his sister's performance. Then he vanishes, and the funeral cortège arrives.

130 The woman Li 李氏

Text: *TPKC* 336.2671; Fang, pp. 104–5.

Story: The woman Li is visited by her husband's late sister, dressed in white, who chases her around the house and out of the gate. Only a cavalryman dares intervene, striking the ghost with his whip. It evaporates, leaving only a white turban and a skull.

131 Wei Huang 韋璜

Text: *TPKC* 337.2672–3; Fang, pp. 105–6.

Story: She is the wife of Chou Hun 周混, magistrate of Lu-ch'eng 潞城. She agrees with her sisters that whoever dies first will send back news of the other side. She dies in 758–759. Later her voice is heard explaining that she must dress the Lord of Mount T'ai's daughter at her wedding. For the red dye work she needs a maid, who now expires. Later revived by notes from a stone chime, hands all red, the maid repeats poems dedicated by the dead woman. From personal testimony.

Translation: Chap. 3, pp. 53–4 (in part).

132 Hsüeh Wan-shih 薛萬石

Text: *TPKC* 337.2673–4; Fang, pp. 106–7.

Story: In 763 he becomes magistrate of Yung-chia 永嘉, but dies during the local rebellion. From inside his coffin he commands his staff to provide rice for his wife. Then, summoning help from his patron, the civil governor of Che-tung, he orders his wife to set out and escape the rebels. During the dangerous journey the family consults his advice. The author has witnessed this in person.

Translation: Chap. 6, pp. 142–6, with discussion.

133 Fan Ch'u 范俶

Text: *TPKC* 337.2674; Fang, p. 107.

Story: He runs a wine-shop in Soochow in 763. One night an unusual woman comes and spends the night with him, concealing her face. Next morning she has lost her comb. She bites his arm before leaving. Fan later finds a paper comb; but his body swells up, and he dies within a week.

134 Li Huan 李澣

Text: *TPKC* 337.2674–5; Fang, pp. 107–8.

Story: Li, vice-governor of Ho-chung 河中, dies in 764. During mourning he comes riding in, calls out his beloved second wife and explains that she will join him within two years. So why not now? He also details four maids to join them in death and orders his sons to bury him with the second wife, not the first (their mother). Later an escorted carriage comes to collect the women, who make their preparations, then drop dead.

135 Hsiao Shen 蕭審

Text: *TPKC* 337.2679; Fang, pp. 108–9.

Story: Hsiao is magistrate of Ch'ang-chou 長洲 in 765. After some years riders in purple enter his court, cover him with a white tunic and disappear with him. He is found dead. Later his voice speaks from the tomb, chiding his brother and denouncing an Iranian running a racket with their rice and silk. The prefect receives the report and arrests the racketeer. The ghost wants the silk, unlawfully obtained, given away as alms.

Note: The prefect of Soochow, here named Ch'ang Yüan-fu 常元甫, is named in other texts as Wei Yüan-fu 韋元甫, prefect from 765–768: Yü Hsien-hao, *T'ang tz'u-shih k'ao*, p. 1676.

136 Shang Shun 商順

Text: *TPKC* 338.2683–4; Fang, pp. 109–10.

Story: Shang's father-in-law, Chang Ch'ang 張昶, was vice-governor of Ching-chao 京兆 until he died. In Ch'ang-an for the examination, Shang is summoned to the Chang estate, but finds himself lost and locked out of the city at night. Unable to find the Chang manor in the storm, he is led by a mysterious lantern to the slave in charge of his father-in-law's tomb, where the ghost's voice has already announced his arrival.

137 Li Tsai 李載

Text: *TPKC* 338.2684–5; Fang, pp. 110–11.

Story: In 772, when Liu Yen 劉宴 [715–780] is president of the Board of Civil Office, Li Tsai becomes investigating censor and is appointed to Chien-chou 建州, where he dies. But he revives briefly to finish attending to official and family business. He explains to his surviving wife that his late wife is planning to harm her, so she must go back north at once. He punishes the attendant officer who delays departure. Then he finally dies.

Note: For Liu Yen's appointment, see *CTS* 11.302, *HTS* 149.4795.

138 Kao Li 高勵

Text: *TPKC* 338.2685; Fang, p. 111.

Story: While Kao is watching threshers at work, a horseman comes and asks Kao to repair his horse's hoof with glue. The man is a ghost, and the horse is of wood, as Kao soon sees when he does the repair. Taking leave, rider and horse then speed off. Kao's son-in-law Ts'ui Shih-kuang 崔士光 is the probable informant.

139 Chu Tzu-ch'üan 朱自勸

Text: *TPKC* 338.2686–7; Fang, pp. 111–12.

Story: Chu, of Wu-hsien 吳縣, dies in 762. His daughter is a Buddhist nun. In 768 her maid, out shopping, several times meets Chu's ghost attended by horsemen. He sends his daughter gifts of food and silk. Finally he requires her to entertain him and his guests to a meal. The maid collapses, then speaks in his voice. The daughter dedicates lavish offerings, which the guests enjoy before departing. The maid then regains consciousness.

140 Lo Yüan-tse 羅元則

Text: *TPKC* 339.2688–9; Fang, pp. 112–13.

Story: Lo, a farmer travelling to Kuang-ling 廣陵, accepts a passenger on his boat. He finds the man has a register with a list of lives to be taken, including his own. Learning that someone he has wronged is claiming his life, he begs to be spared. The passenger agrees, imposing a condition. But Lo breaks it, and the travelling companion reappears, punished for his indulgence, to explain that Lo must now die, which he does.

141 Li Yüan-p'ing 李元平

Text: *TPKC* 339.2689; and 112.779, where the same item is drawn from *I-wu chih* 異物誌; Fang, pp. 113–14.

Story: Li is the son of the prefect of Mu-chou 睦州. One night in 770, staying in a monastery, he meets a pretty girl with a maid. She is a ghost, once daughter of the prefect of Chiang-chou 江州, and Li was her lover in a former existence. When he died she marked his leg in red. He still has the mark. After a night spent together, she leaves to be reborn. They will be married when she reaches the age of sixteen.

Note: Li Po-ch'eng 李伯成, the Mu-chou prefect, was in post there in 756: Yü Hsien-hao, *T'ang tz'u-shih k'ao,* p. 1849.

142 Chou Chi-ch'uan 州濟川

Text: *TPKC* 342.2715–16; Fang, pp. 237–8. Credited to *Hsiang-i chi* 祥異記; Ming MS gives *Kuang-i chi.*

Note: The story ends with the date 801: it is chronologically and stylistically inconsistent with *Kuang-i chi.*

143 Tu Wan 杜萬

Text: *TPKC* 356.2820. Fang, p. 114.

Story: Tu's brother, on the way to a post in Ling-nan, loses his wife to an attack of malaria. He gives her temporary burial in a mat. Returning later, he finds she has left the mat and borne children to a *yakṣa.* She communicates first in writing, only later in speech. Husband and wife escape with the younger son, while the elder is destroyed by the angry *yakṣa.* Wife and son are still alive during Ta-li.

144 Cheng Ch'i-ying 鄭齊嬰

Text: *TPKC* 358.2832–3; Fang, p. 115.

Story: Cheng, a personnel evaluation commissioner, returns to the capital through Hua-chou 華州. Five men in the five cardinal colours come before him: they are the spirits of his five viscera, signalling his imminent death. Entertaining them to food and drink, Cheng quickly composes a last memorial, bathes, changes clothes, then lies down to die.

Note: Cheng probably died in 765, the date of an inscription listed in *Chin-shih lu* 7.139.

Translations: de Groot, vol. 4, pp. 72–3; Wieger, pp. 72–3.

145 Liu Shao-yu 柳少游

Text: *TPKC* 358.2833; Fang, p. 115.

Story: Liu is a well-known diviner in Ch'ang-an. One day in T'ien-pao a customer asks for an age-forecast. Liu finds he is due to die the same day. But a servant in attendance observes that the customer and Liu are indistinguishable. When the customer vanishes Liu realizes that this is his own soul, leaving him. The silk paid for the consultation turns out to be paper. Liu dies that night.

Translations: de Groot, vol. 4, pp. 97–8; Wieger, pp. 67–8.

146 Su Lai 蘇萊

Text: *TPKC* 358.2833; Fang, p. 116.

Story: In late T'ien-pao Su Shen 蘇詵, prefect of Yen-chou 兗州, consults a specialist in summoning spirits (*k'ao-chao* 考召) to help select one of three sisters as a bride for his son Lai. She performs the ritual procedure, bringing the three spirits before his mother, and recommends one as the future wife of a prefect. They take her. Lai dies in the rebellion, a mere magistrate. But later he is awarded a posthumous prefect's rank.

Note: Yü Hsien-hao revises the date of Su Shen's appointment to early K'ai-yüan, citing an inscription of 719 listed in *Chin-shih lu* 5.93: see his *T'ang tz'u-shih k'ao*, p. 880.

Translations: de Groot, vol. 4, p. 100; Wieger, pp. 68–9; above, Chap. 3, p. 73 (part).

147 A woman of Lo-yang 洛陽婦人

Text: *TPKC* 361.2868; Fang, p. 116.

Story: In Hsüan-tsung's time a woman of Lo-yang is possessed by a demon. She consults the Taoist divine Yeh Fa-shan, who identifies a demon banished from heaven, now due to return. He helps the process by pronouncing a ban beside a pool deep in the mountains. A giant head slowly emerges, then vanishes in a blanket of cloud.

148 Ch'ao Liang-chen 晁良貞

Text: *TPKC* 362.2877; *Lei shuo* 8.13ab; *Shuo-fu* 4.10a; Fang, pp. 117, 243, 255.

Story: Ch'ao, who has no fear of ghosts, breaks the taboo on digging ground associated with *T'ai-sui* 太歲. Finding a fleshy object, he flogs it and leaves it at a crossroad. That night riders and carriages come to ask the object why it accepted such treatment without retaliation. It answers that Ch'ao's fortunes have left it helpless. Then it vanishes.

Note: On the *T'ai-sui* [planet Jupiter] beliefs, see Chap. 3, n. 29. Ch'ao Liang-chen passed decree examinations in 706 and 712: *Teng k'o chi k'ao* 4.140, 5.158.

149 The Li family 李氏

Text: *TPKC* 362.2878; Fang, p. 117.

Story: In 761 the Lis, disbelievers in the *T'ai-sui* taboo, dig up tabooed ground and find a lump of flesh. Giving it the flogging which traditionally brings immunity from harm, they see the object vanish aloft before reaching the required number of blows. The entire family community perishes. A single young son, rescued by slaves posing as demons, survives to continue the line. He is later ennobled as duke of K'uai 蒯.

150 Idem 又

Text: *TPKC* 362.2878; Fang, p. 117.

Story: A man in Ning-chou 寧州 digs up an object like a large fungus with thousands of eyes. A Central Asian monk recognizes it as *T'ai-sui* and urges him to rebury it at once. The man returns it to its place, but he and his are dead within a year.

151 Chang Yin 張寅

Text: *TPKC* 362.2879–80; Fang, p. 118.

Story: While riding south of Lo-yang's old fortifications, Chang finds his horse halt in fright. He sees on a stone column in a graveyard an object like a muslin bag. It grows larger, finally reaches the ground, then roars off at high speed, eventually dropping into a home. The occupants all die. A neighbour explains the background tension between a daughter-in-law and her late mother-in-law.

152 Yen Feng-hsiang 燕鳳祥
Text: *TPKC* 362.2880; Fang, pp. 118–19.
Story: Yen, a teacher of gentlemanly arts, is visited by a series of horrifying creatures. He tries vainly to defend himself by throwing domestic objects, by engaging spirit mediums, by retreating to a monastery and by employing Buddhist monks and Taoist priests to perform rituals. He becomes seriously ill. At last a judicial figure in a dream announces the return of his souls – some coiffured like women, others in red clothing. He recovers.

153 Wei Hsün 韋訓
Text: *TPKC* 368.2930; Fang, pp. 119–20.
Story: Wei is studying the *Vajracchedikā* in the family school when a female monster in red climbs in and attacks the master. Wei protects his body with the *sūtra* text. Dragging the master away, the monster disappears into a dungheap. This is dug up to reveal the body of a bride, which is burned at a meeting of five roads. The haunting ends.
Translation: de Groot, vol. 5, pp. 671–2.

154 Lu Tsan-shan 盧贊善
Text: *TPKC* 368.2930; Fang, p. 120.
Story: He has a porcelain figure of a bride at home, which his wife jokingly proposes as his concubine. But she haunts him, so the figure is sent to a Buddhist monastery. There a boy has visions of a woman describing herself as Lu's concubine, driven out by a jealous wife. His story fits the porcelain figure. They have it smashed and then find blood in the heart.
Translation: de Groot, vol. 5, pp. 669–70.

155 Su P'i's daughter 蘇丕女
Text: *TPKC* 369.2933; Fang, pp. 120–1.
Story: Su is magistrate of Ch'u-ch'iu 楚丘 during T'ien-pao. His daughter, the wife of a man who favours a maid-servant, becomes the object of the maid's sorcery. Husband and maid both die, but years later female figures used in the sorcery come to afflict Su's daughter with sickness. One is caught, chopped up and burned, and the others mourn her. Eventually those are caught too, and the buried secret of the sorcery is unearthed.
Translations: de Groot, vol. 5, pp. 911–12; Wieger, pp. 282–3.

156 Chiang Wei-yüeh 蔣惟岳
Text: *TPKC* 369.2934; Fang, p. 121.
Story: Chiang has no fear of demons or spirits. Sleeping by an open window, he hears human voices and challenges the ghosts fearlessly. When seven men burst in he disperses them with a pillow, and later digs up seven wheel-spokes. Another time, tending his sick brother, he sees three female demons enter and drives them off. His brother recovers.
Translation: de Groot, vol. 5, p. 665 (in part).

157 Wei Liang 韋諒

Text: TPKC 369.2934; Fang, pp. 121–2.

Story: In 758–759, when Wei is magistrate of Chiang-ning 江寧, he sees a small demon in his hall, with face concealed by his lower lip. This is chased off under the dais, where later an old door is dug up, carved at the top like a curled lotus leaf.

158 Huan Yen-fan 桓顏範

Text: TPKC 372.2954; Fang, p. 122.

Story: Huan Yen-fan [653–706], an unconstrained character in his youth, awakes after a drunken party in the wilderness to find a huge creature armed with a lance bearing down on his group. He chases it off, beating it with a willow branch. It sounds hollow, eventually crawls into an old grave-pit. Next day they find a broken *fang-hsiang* 方相 figure there.

Note: Biographies in *CTS* 91.2927–32 and *HTS* 120.4309–13.

Translation: de Groot, vol. 5, pp. 672–3.

159 Ts'ai Ssu 蔡四

Text: TPKC 372.2954–5; Fang, pp. 122–3.

Story: During T'ien-pao Ts'ai Ssu, a poet living in Ch'en-liu 陳留, finds himself attended by a friendly ghost. He has a hut made for it to stay in. But the ghost insists on borrowing Ts'ai's house for a wedding, then wants to borrow equipment for a ceremony. Ts'ai's family go to watch, protected by a Kuan-yin *mantra* and ritual purification. The ghosts scatter and retreat to a graveyard. They are identified as grave-figurines and burned.

160 Li Hua 李華

Text: TPKC 372.2955–6; Fang, pp. 123–4.

Story: Li Hua [*ca.* 710–*ca.* 767] studies in his youth with friends in Chi-yüan 濟源. An old man comes to sit on the wall and throw stones at them every night. They bring in an archer to shoot him down. He turns out to be a wooden grave-figurine.

Note: For Li's position, given here as vice-director in the Board of Civil Office, see *HTS* 203.5776, with a date *ca.* 760.

161 A man of Shang-hsiang 商鄉人

Text: TPKC 372.2956; Fang, p. 124.

Story: A traveller in Shang-hsiang meets a ghost who asks him to help control the rebellious grave-figurines in his tomb. The man must stand before the tomb and pronounce an order of execution. He does this, sounds of execution follow, and the grateful ghost comes out with some headless figurines in gold and silver as reward. Although the authorities suspect him of robbing a tomb, inspection proves his story true.

Translations: de Groot, vol. 2, pp. 809–10; Wieger, pp. 294–6.

162 A daughter of Tung-lai people 東萊人女

Text: TPKC 375.2988; Fang, pp. 124–5.

Story: A girl of Tung-lai dies, then is released and escorted back to life. But she is confined in the tomb and can get out only if it is broken into. Her favourite uncle is chosen for this task, but his virtuous nature must first be corrupted. He joins a gang which opens and robs her tomb, then feels shame when they find her alive. He pleads successfully for her life to be spared and takes her home.

163 Cheng Hui 鄭會

Text: *TPKC* 376.2989; Fang, pp. 125–6.

Story: Cheng, known for strength, lives in Wei-nan 渭南. During the An Lu-shan rebellion most people leave the land to live in administrative centres, but he confidently stays on his estate, patrolling the countryside. Rebels kill him, but his soul speaks out from a tree to his old wet-nurse, guiding the family to his body and its severed head, and asking to be carefully stitched together again. They do this, and he recovers.

164 Wang Mu 王穆

Text: *TPKC* 376.2990; Fang, p. 126.

Story: Wang serves under Lu Kuei 魯炅 [d. 759] in the battle of Nan-yang 南陽 [6 June 756]. Retreating in defeat, he has his head cut off from behind, leaving only the throat attached. He ties it back in place using his hair. His loyal horse helps him to mount, and he is found by his men. In some two hundred days he recovers, with a line of proud flesh round his neck and the head slightly tilted. He goes on to serve as magistrate in several counties.

Note: On the battle of Nan-yang, see *TCTC* 217.6961–218.6962 [Chih-te 1/5/*ting-ssu*]; also *Cambridge history of China*, vol. 3, p. 456. Lu Kuei's name has been corrected accordingly.

165 A son of the T'ang family 湯氏子

Text: *TPKC* 376.2992–3; Fang, p. 127.

Story: A young man is condemned to death after killing the magistrate of Lo-p'ing 樂平, under whom his father has suffered insult. But a physiognomist observes that he is destined for an official career. And indeed he survives repeated execution by garrotting and hanging. Finally returned to his family for dead, he is secretly revived, while an empty coffin is buried. He ends his life in 758–759 as magistrate of Ch'üan-chiao 全椒.

166 Li Ch'iang-yu 李彊友

Text: *TPKC* 377.3001–2; Fang, pp. 127–8.

Story: Li, son of the investigating censor Li Ju-pi 李如璧, becomes assistant magistrate in Shan county 剡縣 *ca.* 755. He is greeted by an acquaintance returned to life from the underworld, who claims that he saw Li there serving as assistant to the Lord of Mount T'ai. He describes the underworld bureaucracy. A relative of Li's also returns from such a visit with a report. Li is later seen regularly setting out with a retinue. Before long he dies.

167 Wei Kuang-chi 韋廣濟

Text: *TPKC* 377.3002; Fang, pp. 128–9.

Story: He dies in 760–761, summoned by Yama to be an assistant. But he finds a cousin, Wei Huang-shang 韋黃裳, prefect of Ch'ü-chou 衢州, already doing the job and is sent back. The mortal Wei Huang-shang is still alive. But Lü Yen-chih 呂延之, military governor of Che-tung [759–760], was warned by a seer that *he* was required by Yama. He saves himself through pious works: Wei Huang-shang is now chosen instead and soon dies.

168 The accessory clerk of Hsi-chou 隰州佐史

Text: *TPKC* 378.3007; Fang, pp. 129–30.

Story: The clerk dies in Hsi-chou, then revives to tell his tale. He was summoned by King Yama to handle documents, but recommended a colleague instead. First punished for killing a snake, he was then allowed to return. The escort demanded a large bribe, to be taken from a pile of money belonging to an Iranian at the clerk's home. The clerk managed this by using violence on the Iranian's son, who guarded the money. Now alive again, the clerk finds the deficit in the money is real.

169 An unassigned official of the K'ai-yüan period 開元選人

Text: *TPKC* 379.3016; Fang, p. 130.

Story: The father of Lu Ts'ung-yüan 盧從願 [668–737], vice-minister in the Board of Civil Office, suffers in the underworld for failing to practise Buddhist piety. He approaches an unassigned official, who after premature death is allowed to return to life, asking him to take word to his son. To save his father Lu Ts'ung-yüan must have *sūtras* copied and images made. He does this, thanks the messenger and learns that his father is reborn.

Note: The father was Lu Ching-i 盧敬一, granted a posthumous provincial post at his son's request: see *CTS* 100.3124; *HTS* 129.4478.

170 Ts'ui Ming-ta 崔明達

Text: *TPKC* 379.3016–18; Fang, pp. 130–2.

Story: Ts'ui is a Buddhist monk in Ch'ang-an, expert in the *Nirvāṇasūtra.* In early K'ai-yüan he is taken to the underworld and comes before a noble youth, who asks him to expound the *sūtra.* Then, after contact with his grandfather, he is returned to life. His escorts demand large cash rewards and collect them at a mourning service marking Ts'ui's death. He revives, then seeks out an old woman sent back to life with him.

Note: Ts'ui's grandfather Yüan-chiang 元獎 was prefect of Hang-chou in 694, his father T'ing-yü 庭玉 prefect of Chi-chou 冀州 during K'ai-yüan: Yü Hsien-hao, *T'ang tz'u-shih k'ao,* pp. 1315, 1729; cf. *HTS* 72B.2752; *Hsien-ch'un Lin-an chih* 45.16a. His Buddhist master Li-she 利涉 was active in Ch'ang-an during K'ai-yüan: *Sung kao-seng chuan* 17.815ab.

171 Fei Tzu-yü 費子玉

Text: *TPKC* 379.3019–20; Fang, pp. 132–3.

Story: Fei, an officer in Chien-wei 犍為, is summoned during T'ien-pao by King Yama. But his *Vajracchedikā* piety has earned him merit with Kṣitigarbha, who floats down to plead his case. He is allowed to live, but warned not to eat meat. Meanwhile he is led to worship a bronze Buddha with many moving parts. After three years of life he eats some meat and dies again. His three former wives appear, bearing grudges against him.

172 Mei Hsien 梅先

Text: *TPKC* 379.3020; Fang, pp. 133–4.

Story: Known in Hang-chou for his *sūtra* piety and good works, Mei dies suddenly during T'ien-pao, but then revives. He describes coming before King Yama, who praises his piety and approves his return to life. Then Mei witnesses the trial of a village headman from Ch'ien-t'ang 錢塘, whose son is required for evidence. When Mei returns to life he finds that this son duly dies within a few days.

173 Wei Ching 魏靖

Text: *TPKC* 380.3023; Fang, pp. 134–5.

Story: As a criminal investigator Wei detects a Buddhist monk harbouring stolen goods. He pardons the monk, but his superior insists on execution. When Wei dies suddenly in 690 he lies unburied while a spirit marriage is arranged, then comes to life again, though partly decomposed. In the underworld the criminal monk testified on his behalf. He was given medicaments to restore decomposed flesh, then successfully revived.

Note: Wei Ching served as investigating censor under Empress Wu: *CTS* 50.2148–9.

174 Yang Tsai-ssu 楊再思

Text: *TPKC* 380.3023–4; Fang, pp. 135–6.

Story: Secretariat Director Yang dies in 705. So does a meat server in the same department. A long list of culpable acts of policy by Yang is read out before King Yama. Yang pleads guilty and is then seized aloft by a huge hairy hand. The meat server, who has witnessed all this, is sent back to life. Chung-tsung orders his report to be inscribed in the hall of the secretariat.

Note: According to *CTS* 90.2919 Yang Tsai-ssu died in 709.

175 Assistant Magistrate Wang of Chin-t'an 金壇王丞

Text: *TPKC* 380.3024–5; Fang, pp. 136–7.

Story: In the capital to deliver tax revenue in late K'ai-yüan, Wang is summoned by the king of the underworld. There he meets an old friend, Ts'ui Hsi-i 崔希逸, who puts in a word for him with Yama. Wang's false accuser is exposed, Wang himself exonerated. Preparing to return to life, he receives a message from Ts'ui to pass to his son Ts'ui Han 崔翰 containing advice on official ethics and Buddhist piety. He then revives.

Note: On Ts'ui Hsi-i, see *CTS* 196A.5233, *HTS* 216A.6085, and *T'ang fang-chen nien piao* 8.1220. On Ts'ui Han, see *HTS* 72B.2773, and *T'ang shang-shu sheng lang-kuan shih-chu t'i-ming k'ao* 3.42a.

176 Wei Yen-chih 韋延之

Text: *TPKC* 380.3025–6; Fang, pp. 137–8.

Story: Wei leaves his post in Mu-chou to live in Chia-hsing 嘉興. He falls sick in 773 and is summoned before a senior official in the underworld. He goes through bureaucratic formalities and appears in a court like that of a modern county magistrate. The proceedings show that he has been summoned by mistake. Curious about his future career, he finds it a blank. Returning home, he meets a nephew just summoned below. This man duly proves to be dead.

177 Cheng Chieh 鄭潔

Text: *TPKC* 380.3028–9. Credited to *Po-i chi* 博異記; Ming MS gives *Kuang-i chi.*

Note: The story contains the date 840 and differs stylistically from *Kuang-i chi.*

178 Huo Yu-lin 霍有鄰

Text: *TPKC* 381.3032; Fang, pp. 138–9.

Story: In late K'ai-yüan Huo serves in Chi 汲 county. Wrongly called to account in the underworld for an offence of the local prefect, he there meets his maternal uncle Grand Censor Ti Jen-chieh, who is just confirming the appointment of Li Shih-chih 李適之 as grand councillor in Hsüan-tsung's government for five years. Ti gives him medicine to combat decomposition when he returns to his body. Li is duly appointed.

Note: Li Shih-chih [d. 747] served as chief minister from 8 September 742 to 3 May 746: see *CTS* 9.215 and 220; E.G. Pulleyblank, *The background of the Rebellion of An Lu-shan,* London 1955, pp. 86 ff. and 193.

179 Huang-fu Hsün 皇甫恂

Text: *TPKC* 381.3033. Extended version in *TPKC* 302.2393–5, from *T'ung-yu chi* 通幽記; Fang, pp. 139–40.

Story: Huang-fu, an administrator in Hsiang-chou 相州 during K'ai-yüan, dies suddenly, then revives. The local prefect hears his story. He met the monk in charge of the K'ai-yüan Monastery, in trouble for killing cattle for beef. The monk begged him for a dedicated *dhāraṇī* pillar when he was later appointed to T'ung-chou 同州: the monk would then be reincarnated as a pig. This comes to pass. A grateful pig bows in thanks.

Note: Several names and places are different in the *T'ung-yu chi* version. For Huang-fu Hsün in K'ai-yüan, see *CTS* 88.2881, 95.3018; *HTS* 75B.3394, 81.3602, 125.4402.

180 P'ei Ling 裴齡

Text: *TPKC* 381.3033–5; Fang, pp. 140–2.

Story: P'ei is on the staff of Ch'ang-an county in K'ai-yüan. During a bout of illness he is summoned by the king. This turns out to be a mistake, and P'ei then sees a market official tried for offences alleged by various animals. He is also shown around Hell. An officer begs for *sūtras* to be copied and rituals performed to secure his rebirth; he also asks for money, to be burned in paper form. P'ei returns to life and meets the requests.

181 The assistant magistrate of Liu-ho county 六合縣丞

Text: *TPKC* 381.3035–6; Fang, pp. 142–3.

Story: He dies suddenly during K'ai-yüan, but soon revives. In the underworld he was brought before an administrator with whom he had personal connections. The administrator dismissed the charge against him. Allowed to return, the man agreed to help a woman from Yang-chou return too: she offered money and service as a concubine. Restored to life, he finds her, but she must marry another and pays him double instead. He is still alive *ca.* 755.

182 Hsüeh T'ao 薛濤

Text: *TPKC* 381.3036; Fang, pp. 143–4.

Story: Hsüeh, an officer in Chiang-ling 江陵, dies briefly in 758–759. During that time he comes before the king to face charges of killing animals. Since this is done on imperial business in a post responsible for falconry, he is pardoned in court, but the victims attack him. He promises acts of merit to help their rebirth. The king identifies himself as Yang Hu 羊祜 [221–278], who died in post in Ching-chou 荊州 and feels nostalgic.

Note: For Yang Hu's biography see *Chin shu* 34.1013–25; appointments in Ching-chou: 34.1014. The circumstances of his death (34.1020–1) differ from those given here.

183 Teng Ch'eng 鄧成

Text: *TPKC* 381.3038–9; Fang, pp. 144–5.

Story: Dying suddenly, Teng comes before an administrator, Prefect Huang Lin 黃麟, who is his maternal uncle. He arranges Teng's release, but Teng still faces the king's rebuke and the threat of attack from animals accusing him. He sees how Huang, though holding office, must daily be burned up and restored. Huang begs for an estate to be sold to pay for acts of merit, and gives a jade pin as proof of genuine contact. Teng revives, and the Huang family accepts the mission.

184 Chang Yao 張瑤

Text: *TPKC* 381.3039; Fang, pp. 145–6.

Story: Chang dies for a few days, then revives. During that time he comes before a king who confronts him with the animals he has killed. His *sūtra* piety has earned significant merit, but his name has been erased from all but one of the registers checked. On balance he is allowed to return, warned not to take life and stamped with a mark on his leg. The mark is still there.

185 Ch'eng Tao-hui 程道惠

Text: *TPKC* 382.3041–2; *Fa-yüan chu-lin* 55.709a–b, citing *Ming-hsiang chi* 冥祥記; Fang, p. 240, rejects attribution to *Kuang-i chi.* See Chap. 3, n. 27.

Story: Ch'eng comes from a line of Taoist believers and does not accept Buddhism. He dies in 390, then revives. While in the underworld he realizes he was a Buddhist in earlier incarnations, and that merit now spares him suffering and redeems his sins. Acquitted, he tours round hell, then returns to life, equipped with a bronze bell and the promise of long life. He gains high office and dies in 429, aged 89.

Note: In 428 he was made prefect of Kuang-chou, as claimed here: *Sung shu* 5.77.

186 The scribe of Ho-nan fu 河南府史

Text: *TPKC* 382.3047; Fang, p. 146.

Story: The man dies in early T'ien-pao, then revives. While in the underworld he is pardoned for heavy drinking and released. But first he tours round hell, seeing his wife (once a wine-seller in Lo-yang) steeped in a lake of excrement, and the Ch'in general Po Ch'i 白起, condemned to regular execution for a whole *kalpa.* His own drinking habit is punished with ulcerated feet, which afflict him for the remaining years of his life.

Note: Mentions Po Ch'i's massacre at Ch'ang-p'ing 長平 in 260 BC: *Shih chi* 73.2335.

187 Chou Sung 周頌

Text: *TPKC* 382.3047–8. Ming MS credits to *I-wen lu* 異聞錄; Fang, pp. 146–7.

Story: A T'ien-pao graduate, he becomes magistrate of Tz'u-ch'i 慈谿 in 765. He dies suddenly and in the underworld meets Liang Ch'eng 梁乘, prefect of Chi-chou 吉州, who agrees to negotiate his release. This is approved by a king with two horns on his head. His escort on the way back demands five thousand strings of cash. Chou revives by being pushed down a well.

Note: Liang Ch'eng was prefect of Chi-chou in 766: Yü Hsien-hao, *T'ang tz'u-shih k'ao*, p. 2066.

188 Lu Pien 盧弁

Text: *TPKC* 382.3048–9; Fang, p. 148.

Story: Setting out from Lo-yang to visit his uncle, the magistrate of Hu-ch'eng 胡城, Lu is taken off to the underworld. While waiting to come before the administrator he watches women being ground and minced. Among them is his uncle's wife, there for jealousy. He stops the millstones by reciting the *Vajracchedikā*, and they both escape to return to life. A happy reunion follows in Hu-ch'eng.

189 Hu Le 胡勒

Text: *TPKC* 383.3051; Fang, p. 240.

Story: Hu dies for three days in 399. The arresting officers block his nose and mark him with a seal. But Hu recognizes his neighbour, dead for a year, who is now a managing clerk. This man agrees to negotiate his release. Hu also notices the neighbour's uncle attending to business in the underworld. Later the uncle indeed dies. Hu, now a county runner, is the informant.

Note: The discrepant date for a contemporary informant is not easily explained. Fang rejects attribution to *Kuang-i chi*.

190 Li Chi 李及

Text: *TPKC* 384.3059–60; Fang, pp. 148–9.

Story: Li, a heavy drinker, lives in Ch'ang-an. He dies suddenly, but sounds come from his body, and the family watch for signs of life. He revives to tell how he was summoned by mistake and was released by the officer in charge. On the way back he saw oxcarts ready to transport the dead of An Lu-shan's imminent rebellion. With difficulty he forced his way into his home and came to life.

191 Number Six 阿六

Text: *TPKC* 384.3060; Fang, pp. 149–50.

Story: Number Six is a slave in a Jao-chou 饒州 monastery. He dies in 762 and comes before the king, but has more time to live and is released. He meets a Central Asian friend who sold cakes when alive and now does so dead. The friend sends him back to life with a letter begging his family for acts of Buddhist merit to secure his rebirth. When this is achieved the friend thanks Number Six in a dream.

192 Chu T'ung 朱同

Text: *TPKC* 384.3062–3. T'an K'ai assigns to *Shih chuan* 史傳. Sun Ch'ien supplies missing column of text at the end, with ascription to *Kuang-i chi.*

Story: When aged fifteen Chu, the son of the magistrate of Ying-t'ao 癭陶, is led by two insolent village headmen before an underworld official. But a recorder who once worked with his father negotiates his release and stamps Chu's arm with his name and seal for protection. This saves him from attack in hell. His grandfather's slave provides a horse, and he goes home, on the way observing a hanged man in the Temple of Confucius.

193 Kao Ch'eng 郜澄

Text: *TPKC* 384.3063–4; Fang, pp. 150–1.

Story: Riding towards Lo-yang for an examination, he lets an old woman read his palm. She warns of impending death unless he stays indoors at home for ten days. But at home he breaks this rule and is tricked into the underworld. He bribes a censor to help him lodge a protest, and thus escapes. His brother-in-law, out hunting, helps him get home.

194 Wang Hsün 王勳

Text: *TPKC* 384.3065; Fang, pp. 151–2.

Story: Wang, a graduate from Hua-chou 華州, falls dead in the shrine of the Third Daughter of Mount Hua. His friends engage a shamaness to bring him back, but on revival he rebukes them for cutting short his pleasure in company with the lovely goddess.

Translations: Chap. 4, pp. 104–6, with comment; de Groot, vol. 6, pp. 1230–1.

195 Ts'ui Shao 崔紹

Text: *TPKC* 385.3068–73. Variously attributed to *Hsüan-kuai lu* 玄怪錄 or *Ho-tung chi* 河東記. Only Sun Ch'ien gives *Kuang-i chi* as a variant source. With an internal date of 806 this story is too late, and also too long, to belong plausibly to Tai Fu's collection.

196 The wife of Chou Che-chih 周哲滯妻

Text: *TPKC* 386.3080; Fang, p. 152.

Story: She is the daughter of Hsi Yü 席豫 [680–748], a vice-president in the Board of Civil Office. Critically ill during T'ien-pao, she gives all her clothes in alms. The last, most treasured garment is finally used to pay for the casting of two Buddha images. When she then dies and is being led off to the underworld the images pursue and rescue her.

197 The daughter of Chief Administrator Liu 劉長史女

Text: *TPKC* 386.3081–2; *Fen-men ku-chin lei-shih* 16.9b–10a; Fang, pp. 152–4, 250–1.

Story: Liu's eldest daughter dies, aged twelve (*var.* seventeen), at his post in Chi-chou 吉州. Her coffin goes with him when he leaves the post in company with his colleague Kao Kuang 高廣 and his son. On the way, encouraged by a maid, the son has a sexual affair with her spirit, who then asks him to help her resurrection. Her father refuses to open the coffin, until the girl herself requests it in a dream. She is then revived and marries her lover.

Note: The story claims to explain the name of a local village, Li-hui ts'un 禮會村.

198 [Li] Fan, prince of Ch'i 岐王範

Text: TPKC 387.3087; *Lei shuo* 8.18a–b; Fang, pp. 154, 247.

Story: With the help of the Taoist master Yeh Ching-neng 葉淨能 the prince [d. 726] petitions heaven for a son. After an initial mistake a monk of the Ching-ai Monastery 敬愛寺 is chosen to die and be reborn as the prince's son. The boy is much drawn to the monastery, but later gives up piety and uses a catapult to shoot down all its pigeons.

Note: Li Fan had one son, Chin 瑾, president of the Imperial Stud. Much given to wine and women, he died suddenly during T'ien-pao: *CTS* 95.3017; *HTS* 81.3602.

199 The T'ai-hua Princess 太華公主

Text: TPKC 387.3087; Fang, pp. 154–5.

Story: Though daughter of Hsüan-tsung's consort Lady Wu 武妃, she is said to be a reincarnation of Kao-tsung's Empress Wang [d. 655] and dislikes her mother. As a child she asks for her rosary and guides the way to it among the late Empress Wang's effects.

Note: Empress Wang was murdered by Wu Tse-t'ien, Lady Wu was related to Wu Tse-t'ien: see *Cambridge history of China,* vol. 3, pp. 243–51, 258, 380–2.

200 A slave of Sun Mien's family 孫緬家奴

Text: TPKC 388.3094–5; *Chin-hsiu wan-hua ku, ch'ien-chi* 19.4a; Fang, pp. 155, 248.

Story: At age six the slave still cannot speak. But suddenly he talks to Sun's mother of scenes and incidents in her youth. He was then her pet wild cat, killed by hunters. King Yama had him reborn as a beggar's son, then finally as slave to a noble family.

201 T'ang Yao-ch'en 唐堯臣

Text: TPKC 389.3110; Fang, p. 155.

Story: When T'ang dies during K'ai-yüan his family engage the geomancer Chang Shih-lan 張師覽 to site the tomb. He sends his disciple Wang Ching-ch'ao 王景超 to do this. But after the burial the T'ang family livestock break into speech to denounce the choice of site on the dead man's behalf. They fall silent only when it is changed.

202 The officer's burial mound 奴官冢

Text: TPKC 390.3112; Fang, p. 156.

Story: Certain crops grown in Mao County are eaten by geese emerging from the nearby tomb of a Later Han officer. The villagers break in to rob the tomb. Bronze geese attack them. Guards in purple robes also fight with the robbers before running to denounce their theft in the county office. The men are arrested, and thirty-odd stolen items are presented to the throne, *ca.* 741.

Note: For Ts'o 鄮 read Mao 鄮, the county which was also the seat of Ming-chou prefecture: *Yüan-ho chün-hsien t'u-chih* 26.629.

203 Li Ssu-kung 李思恭

Text: *TPKC* 390.3118–19; *Lu-i chi* 錄異記 8.6b–7a (*Tao tsang*, fasc. 327, HY 591); Fang p. 241. Ming MS cites *Lu-i chi*, from which this item, with its internal date 896, is demonstrably drawn: see Tu Te-ch'iao, '*Kuang-i chi* ch'u-t'an', p. 404.

204 A battle with thunder 雷鬪

Text: *TPKC* 393.3139 and 464.3818 (**309**); Fang, p. 156.

Story: In late K'ai-yüan dwellers on the Lei-chou 雷州 coast witness a seven-day battle on the surface of the sea between a whale and dozens of thunder gods, leaving the sea red.

Translation: Schafer, *The vermilion bird*, p. 106.

205 Chang Hsü-mi 張須瀰

Text: *TPKC* 393.3140; Fang, pp. 156–7.

Story: In 760–761 (?) Chang delivers livestock for his county employers in Ch'u-chou 滁州. Stopping at a charitable hostel, he sends his man Wang out to stable the donkeys. Wang sees a group of village girls carrying a heavy cart. His own dead daughter is among them, and she asks about family news. Then they leave, bearing the cart into the clouds. Thunder follows: it was a thunder cart.

206 Ts'ai Hsi-min 蔡希閔

Text: *TPKC* 393.3140–1; Fang, p. 157.

Story: Ts'ai, who lives in Lo-yang, hears something fall into his courtyard during a thunderstorm one summer night. It is a woman who speaks no Chinese. After five or six years she speaks enough to explain that she came from a place with different eating habits. There she was gathered up one night by thunder and deposited in Ts'ai's yard.

207 Hsü Ching-hsien 除景先

Text: *TPKC* 393.3141; Fang, pp. 157–8.

Story: Hsü has an unruly younger brother who is indulged by their mother. When Hsü shouts back at his mother he is swept up by thunder into the clouds and required to explain his behaviour. But his words are not understood, so he is ordered to reply in writing, then dropped into a pond outside the family home. He pins a written statement to the wall, and it is duly swept aloft by the wind.

208 Ou-yang the Thunder Defier 歐陽忽雷

Text: *TPKC* 393.3141–2; Fang, p. 158.

Story: Ou-yang Shao 紹 of Kuei-yang 桂陽 is a strong, tough fighter. His official residence in Lei-chou 雷州 is near a miasmal pool which claims many lives locally. He drains it, then does battle with the thunder and lightning unleashed on him. A snake-like creature eventually succumbs, which Ou-yang reduces to powder and consumes. Men of the south call him the Thunder Defier.

209 Ch'eng Pi 成弼

Text: *TPKC* 400.3214–15; Fang, pp. 159–60.

Story: In late Sui times Ch'eng Pi serves a Taoist alchemist on Mount T'ai-po 太白山 and is given tablets to transform copper into gold. Later he returns for more and takes them by force, cutting off his master's hands, feet and head. The master promises him the same fate himself. He makes gold for T'ai-tsung, but cannot give him the recipe. So he suffers the promised penalty. Later his gold is seen as uniquely precious.

Note: Cited by Ch'en Kuo-fu, *Tao tsang yüan-liu k'ao,* Peking 1963, p. 393.

210 The green mud pearl 青泥珠

Text: *TPKC* 402.3237; Fang, p. 160.

Story: The pearl is among relics offered from the far west to Empress Wu. Displayed in the Hsi-ming Monastery 西明寺, it attracts the attention of a Central Asian visitor attending a sermon there. He buys it for 100,000 strings of cash and sets off home. The empress has him seized and recovers the pearl. He explains that it can turn to water a pool of green mud in the far west which encloses rich treasures.

211 The inch-wide pearl 徑寸珠

Text: *TPKC* 402.3237–8; Fang, p. 161.

Story: A Persian traveller sees a square stone outside an inn in Fu-feng 扶風 and buys it for 2,000 cash. Extracting from it a pearl which he hides in his armpit, he sails for home. But the ship threatens to capsize, and the crew look for the treasure which the sea-god wants. The Persian has to produce his pearl and put it in the sea-god's large, hairy hand.

Translation: Schafer, *The golden peaches of Samarkand,* Berkeley and Los Angeles 1963, p. 243.

212 A precious pearl 寶珠

Text: *TPKC* 402.3238; Fang, pp. 161–2.

Story: A man in the time of Empress Wu takes a pearl from the crown of King Wu of Chou and sells it to some Central Asians for a high price. They all go off to sea with it. One of the Central Asians fries the pearl in ghee. Dragons in human form come offering treasure for it, but he refuses. Two dragon maidens appear and fuse with the pearl to form paste. The Central Asian smears this on his feet and walks off across the sea.

213 The 'Purple Goat' 紫羖羯

Text: *TPKC* 403.3251–2; Fang, pp. 162–3.

Story: In 758–759, when forced loans of twenty per cent are levied on the Yangtze valley cities to restore public funds after the rebellion, a monk offers a bottle worth 1 million cash. A Persian puts up the money to buy it and is later questioned in Yang-chou by Teng Ching-shan 鄧景山 [d. 762]. He says the contents, called 'Purple Goat', secure spirit protection and shield from fire and water. The bottle contains twelve pearls.

Note: On the forced loans, see *CTS* 48.2087, *HTS* 51.1347; Denis Twitchett, *Financial administration under the T'ang dynasty,* second edn., Cambridge 1970, p. 35.

214 The myrobalan 訶黎勒

Text: *TPKC* 414.3369–70; Fang, p. 163.

Story: During his campaign against the Arabs Kao Hsien-chih 高仙芝 receives a myrobalan fruit which he puts in his stomacher. Stomach pains and diarrhoea follow. But an Arab elder assures him that now that impurities have been purged the fruit will protect him from sickness. Kao treasures it until his execution in 756, when it disappears.

Note: On myrobalans, see Henry Yule, *Hobson-Jobson,* second edn., London 1985, *s.v.*; Berthold Laufer, *Sino-Iranica,* Chicago 1919, p. 378; Schafer, *The golden peaches of Samarkand,* pp. 145–6.

215 The generals at Lin-huai 臨淮將

Text: *TPKC* 415.3381; Fang, pp. 163–4.

Story: In 760–761 some generals are feasting at night when a giant hand reaches in through the window and a voice asks for meat. They succeed in snaring the hand with rope. It cannot struggle free and the next morning snaps off. It turns out to be a branch of willow, and the matching tree is found by the river, still oozing blood.

216 Ch'i Huan 齊澣

Text: *TPKC* 420.3423 and 467.3846 (**311**); Fang, pp. 164–5.

Story: As civil governor of Ho-nan and prefect of Pien-chou, Ch'i Huan [675–746] has a canal cut. In Chen-yüan 真源 county the excavators open up a dragon hall, exposing dragons, turtles and carp. Ch'i orders the creatures to be transferred to the Huai and Pien Rivers. Various interesting phenomena attend these operations.

Note: The canal cutting is reported in *HTS* 128.4469, with details as given here.

217 Su T'ing 蘇頲

Text: *TPKC* 425.3462; Fang, pp. 165–6.

Story: When serving as commandant in Wu-ch'eng 烏程 county Su T'ing [670–727] goes on a convivial excursion and falls through a bridge into deep water inhabited by monsters. A voice orders him to be borne up to the surface, and he is saved.

218 A fight with a dragon 鬪蛟

Text: *TPKC* 425.3462; Fang, p. 166.

Story: A *chiao* 蛟 dragon in She-chou 歙州 takes many lives. In late T'ien-pao an ox is dragged into the water, but fights back. Days later it emerges victorious. The dragon is believed to be dead.

219 The young oxherd 牧牛兒

Text: *TPKC* 426.3468; Fang, p. 241. A variant of the story is found in *Tu-i chih,* repr. Peking 1983, A.4.

Note: Either wrongly ascribed to *Kuang-i chi,* or transcribed into it from another source.

Story: In the Chin period a boy of Fu-yang 復陽 county takes an ox to pasture. It licks him, leaving white traces on his flesh. The boy dies, and the ox is served as meat to the funeral guests. All who eat the meat turn into tigers.

Translation: de Groot, vol. 4, p. 174.

220 The men of Pa 巴人

Text: TPKC 426.3472; Fang, p. 166.

Story: A party of loggers set about felling pines outside the Temple of T'ai-po 太白 [planet Venus] in Szechuan. An old man describing himself as the god begs them to leave the trees standing. He threatens them with death, then calls in tigers which kill all but five or six, whom he lets off. The felled trees are still there in late T'ien-pao, when the emperor permits them to be used for restoring the temple's inner hall.

Translation: Charles E. Hammond, 'An excursion in tiger lore', *Asia Major*, Third Series, 4, 1991, 94–5.

221 Fei Chung 費忠

Text: TPKC 427.3474–5; Fang, p. 167.

Story: The Fei, a tribe inhabiting Fei-chou 費州, live on upper floors to escape tigers. Fei Chung, whose mother-in-law works as wet-nurse for the prefect Ti Kuang-ssu 狄光嗣, is caught in the open one night during K'ai-yüan and meets some tigers. One proves to be a transformed tribesman appointed to eat him. They agree to substitute another Fei Chung. The man re-enters his tiger skin and leaves. The substitute is later eaten.

Note: On Ti Kuang-ssu (son of Ti Jen-chieh), see Yü Hsien-hao, *T'ang tz'u-shih k'ao*, p. 2246.

222 A tiger's woman 虎婦

Text: TPKC 427.3475; Fang, p. 168.

Story: During K'ai-yüan a woman is married to a tiger without realizing what he is. She finds out when she spies on her husband asleep with a drunken company of tiger guests. Later she asks to be taken on a visit home, and as they cross water pretends to catch sight of his tiger's tail. In shame he flees and never returns.

223 Chi Hu 稽胡

Text: TPKC 427.3475–6; Fang, pp. 168–9.

Story: Chi is a hunter in Tz'u-chou 慈州. One day he encounters the king of tigers, appointed by heaven to control their food, and learns that he is registered as food for this king. They agree to substitute a straw man dressed in Chi's clothes and filled with pig's blood. Chi watches from a tree while the king takes on tiger form, devours the substitute, then reverts to the likeness of a Taoist priest. Chi's name is cancelled from the register.

224 The blue stone 碧石

Text: TPKC 427.3476; Fang, p. 169.

Story: In late K'ai-yüan traps are set in Yü-chou 渝州 to catch tigers. One night a man watches how a trap is sprung by the soul of a tiger-victim (倀鬼) looking like a naked child. When reset the trap catches a tiger. The child then weeping enters the tiger's mouth. Next day a blue stone the size of an egg is found there.

Translation: de Groot, vol. 5, p. 563, with discussion, pp. 554–63. Cf. **228**.

225 'Striped ones' 斑子

Text: *TPKC* 428.3480–1; *Lei-shuo* 8.18a; *Neng-kai chai man-lu* 7.172; *Kan-chu chi* 7.22b; Fang, pp. 169–70, 247, 249, 254.

Story: Mountain sprites (山魈) with specialized hands and feet inhabit Ling-nan 嶺南. They nest in trees. Travellers take cosmetics to give the females and money to give the males. During T'ien-pao a traveller from the north meets a female in a tree, gives her cosmetics and receives shelter and protection from threatening tigers. The mountain sprites work land made available by men and share the produce evenly. Plagues fall on those who cheat.

Translation: Schafer, *The vermilion bird*, p. 113.

226 Liu Chien 劉薦

Text: *TPKC* 428.3481; Fang, pp. 170–1.

Story: Liu, when serving in Ling-nan, meets a mountain sprite and provokes its wrath with an ill-judged remark. The sprite summons a tiger ('striped one'), which seizes Liu. The sprite then taunts him, but eventually calls off the tiger and lets him go. Liu takes days to recover from his fright. He himself is the informant.

Translation: Schafer, *The vermilion bird*, pp. 112–13.

227 Ch'in Tzu-li 勤自勵

Text: *TPKC* 428.3481–2; Fang, pp. 171–2.

Story: In late T'ien-pao Ch'in serves with the army in the Annam and Tibetan campaigns. His wife is induced to remarry in his absence, but on the eve of the wedding hangs herself and is carried off by a tiger. By chance Ch'in has returned and finds her in the tiger's lair. He kills off the whole family of tigers before carrying his wife to safety.

Note: Used by Feng Meng-lung 馮夢龍 in *Ch'ing shih lei-lüeh* 12.334, and *Hsing-shih heng-yen* 5: see Jacques Dars in Lévy, ed., *Inventaire analytique et critique du conte chinois en langue vulgaire*, part 1, vol. 2, Paris 1979, p. 595.

228 The boy of Hsüan-chou 宣州兒

Text: *TPKC* 428.3482; Fang, p. 172.

Story: The boy is approached several times by a spectre leading a tiger. He warns his parents that he is likely to be eaten and then to become the soul of a tiger's victim (倀). He undertakes to lead the tiger into a trap which he will ask his parents to prepare. All this happens, prompted by a dream appearance of the dead boy.

Translation: de Groot, vol. 5, pp. 556–7. Cf. **224**.

229 The flautist 笛師

Text: *TPKC* 428.3482–3; Fang, pp. 172–3.

Story: When An Lu-shan takes T'ung-kuan 潼關 the people of Ch'ang-an take flight. A flautist from Hsüan-tsung's palace theatre finds refuge in a hermitage in the Chung-nan Mountains. His playing charms to sleep a creature with human body and tiger head. The performer then climbs up a tree. The tiger and its companions regret losing the chance of eating him, and after fruitless attempts to reach him they leave. He escapes.

230 Chang Yü-chou 張魚舟

Text: *TPKC* 429.3486; Fang, pp. 173–4.

Story: In Pei-hai 北海 county, Ch'ing-chou 青州, the fisherman Chang Yü-chou lives near Ch'in Shih-huang's Ocean-viewing Terrace. He is visited, *ca.* 780, by a tiger who needs a thorn removed from its paw. Chang does this, and thereafter the grateful tiger regularly brings him gifts of game. Suspected of sorcery, Chang is examined by the county authorities, who verify his story. Eventually the tiger prompts Chang to move away.

231 Wang T'ai 王太

Text: *TPKC* 431.3499; Fang, p. 174.

Story: In Hai-ling 海陵, a place infested with tigers, Wang T'ai and his followers meet one in the wilds. Facing it alone, Wang stuns it with his club. He then takes refuge in the roof of a temple, where he witnesses the return of the tiger spirit he struck. The spirit, now in human form, tells him how to escape death by using a pig smeared with his own blood as a substitute. The tiger eats this, while Wang watches in safety from a tall tree.

232 The man of Ching-chou 荊州人

Text: *TPKC* 431.3499–500; Fang, p. 175.

Story: In the mountains the man meets the soul of a tiger's victim, which covers his body with a tiger skin. He becomes a tiger, eating humans and animals. One day he seeks sanctuary in a Buddhist monastery. A Ch'an master able to tame wild beasts takes him in hand, and he later returns to human form. Going outside one day he is again attacked and transformed, but again recovers and spends the rest of his days in the monastery.

Translation: de Groot, vol. 5, pp. 559–60.

233 Old Liu 劉老

Text: *TPKC* 431.3500; Fang, pp. 175–6.

Story: Liu lives in religious retreat in the mountains of Hsin-chou 信州. He protects the lives of some dedicated geese, but they fall prey to a tiger. Traps are set, but the tiger avoids them. An aged visitor explains that the soul of its last victim is warning the tiger, and can only be neutralized with sour fruit. This is done, and the tiger is caught.

Translation: de Groot, vol. 5, pp. 558–9.

234 A tiger's woman 虎婦

Text: *TPKC* 431.3500–1; Fang, p. 176.

Story: A woman of Li-chou 利州 is seized by a tiger. She becomes its mate and lives for years with the tiger's family, confined and fed in a mountain cave. One night she escapes and is brought home by woodcutters. Her first husband is dead, but his family, who are rice-sellers, take care of her. Her intelligence is dimmed by the experience.

Note: First-hand informant named as Liu Ch'üan-po 劉全白: see also story **287**. A man of this name was prefect of Hu-chou in 794: Yü Hsien-hao, *T'ang tz'u-shih k'ao,* p. 1712.

235 A man of Sung-yang 松陽人

Text: *TPKC* 432.3504; Fang, p. 177.

Story: While cutting firewood, the man is chased up a tree by two tigers. They fail to reach him and bring in a third tiger, referred to as 'Office Manager Chu'. The man fights it off with his cleaver, severing a paw. The tigers leave. But local villagers know where to find Office Manager Chu, who proves to have a recently wounded hand. The magistrate orders his house surrounded and burned. Chu turns into a tiger and flees.

Translation: de Groot, vol. 5, p. 548.

236 Tiger cares for man 虎恤人

Text: *TPKC* 432.3506; Fang, pp. 177–8.

Story: A General Li of Feng-hsiang prefecture 鳳翔府 is seized by a tiger, but pleads with it for his life. The tiger takes him to a pit, where he lives with the cubs, sharing their meat. As the cubs grow up and leave, Li asks to be brought out too. The tiger takes him home and visits him there every three days, until Li asks him politely to desist for the sake of frightened neighbours in the village. After one more visit the tiger complies.

237 Fan Tuan 范端

Text: *TPKC* 432.3506–7; Fang, pp. 178–9.

Story: Fan, a village headman in Fu-ling 涪陵 county, serves the local administrations. But he often turns into a tiger, and neighbours denounce him to the magistrate. Under questioning he admits to craving raw meat and to hunting for it with other tigers. After more of this his mother drives him out. He is sighted later, with a boot still on his one human foot. Mother and son share their grief. He departs and is only rarely seen thereafter.

Translation: Hammond, 'An excursion in tiger lore', pp. 92–3. Hammond notes (p. 94) a mention of this episode, dated 689, in *HTS* 36.954.

238 Shih Ching-yai 石井崖

Text: *TPKC* 432.3507; Fang, p. 179.

Story: First a village headman, Shih later takes up scholarship. Near a stream he overhears a Taoist priest in red preparing to eat him and instructing his servant boys to disarm him first. Shih hides in an inn. When a soldier comes to collect his weapons he secretly keeps his spearhead. Later, forced to travel on, he finds a tiger waiting to attack him, but kills it with the spearhead. The young servants are overjoyed.

239 An ox belonging to Liang-chou folk 洛州人牛

Text: *TPKC* 434.3520; Fang, pp. 179–80.

Story: A domestic ox in Liang-chou grows abnormally large and goes wild, leading an uncontrollable herd of wild oxen. The local military commander pays some Central Asians to lend the hunting beast they are delivering as tribute to the throne. The beast does battle with the ox, which ends with its neck broken and bowels cut out. When these are fed to the beast it resumes the normal size it had before the battle.

240 The oxen of the River Lo 洛水牛

Text: *TPKC* 434.3521; *Chü-t'an lu* A.31ab; Fang, p. 242.

Note: Only T'an K'ai ascribes to *Kuang-i chi.* The Shen MS cites *Wen-ch'i lu* 聞奇錄, the Ch'en collation *Hsü-tu lu* 需讀錄 – presumed to be a corruption of *Chü-t'an lu*, the likely source of this piece. An internal date of 863 is too late for Tai Fu's collection.

241 Wei Yu-jou 韋有柔

Text: *TPKC* 436.3542; Fang, p. 180.

Story: When Wei is magistrate of Chien-an 建安 county, one of his slaves dies owing him forty-five strings of cash. Appearing in a dream to a follower of Wei's skilled in spells, the slave announces that he must repay the debt by being reborn as a horse with distinctive markings. The horse is duly born, and eventually sold to P'ei K'uan 裴寬 [681–755] for thirty strings. P'ei later pays an additional fifteen strings, which clears the original debt.

242 Yao Chia 姚甲

Text: *TPKC* 437.3555–6; Fang, p. 181.

Story: Yao, from Wu-hsing, is sent to a remote spot in the deep south. With him go two favourite dogs. A family slave plots with his own son to kill Yao and return north. When Yao learns this he begs a day's grace and offers his last meal to the dogs, sharing his feelings with them. The dogs refuse the food, then kill the slave, his son and his wife.

243 Liu Chü-lin 劉巨麟

Text: *TPKC* 437.3556; Fang, pp. 181–2.

Note: *TPKC* ascribes this item to *Chih-i chi* 摭異記, but the six-chapter MS versions of *Kuang-i chi* include it. Fang argues for corruption in surviving *TPKC* texts.

Story: Liu, a military commander in Kuang-chou 廣州, has a strong but submissive dog. One night the dog seems to warn him against going on an assignment. Liu does set out, but the dog attacks and kills one of his servants, who proves to have a hidden weapon. He was planning revenge for a beating received from Liu, and the dog knew this.

244 Ts'ui Hui-t'ung 崔惠童

Text: *TPKC* 438.3565–6; Fang, p. 182.

Story: During K'ai-yüan Ts'ui, of Kao-tu 高都, has a violent slave called Invincible 萬敵 and a dog called Yellow Girl 黃女. The dog disappears for a few days, then reappears to attack Invincible, who confesses he has killed and cooked the dog. He produces her buried head in proof, which confirms that he was attacked by her vengeful spirit.

245 Yang 楊氏

Text: *TPKC* 439.3574; Fang, pp. 182–3.

Story: At Yang's residence in Ch'ang-an a woman in black keeps appearing to pester the women, walk about naked, dally with men in public and reveal private affairs. A shaman is unable to keep her away. A family guest tricks the woman by pretending to sleep with her, then steals her shoes. She turns out to be a sheep kept alive at a nearby monastery, with two defective hooves. The animal is killed, and the visitations stop.

246 Ch'en Cheng-kuan 陳正觀

Text: *TPKC* 439.3575; Fang, p. 183.

Story: During T'ien-pao Ch'en, of Ying-ch'uan 穎川, is skilled at cutting off sheep's heads. But one day he cuts into the brain and has to wash his hands clean. The sheep's head bleats. Ch'en, stricken with fear, dies within days.

247 Ts'ui Jih-yung 崔日用

Text: *TPKC* 439.3581; Fang, pp. 183–4.

Story: During K'ai-yüan the prefect's residence at Ju-chou 汝州 is haunted and disused. But Ts'ui [*ca.* 673–*ca.* 722], when appointed, moves in. Ten figures in black enter. They are 'long-life pigs', kept in Buddhist monasteries, but beg for release from a foul existence. He has them butchered, sells the meat to pay for *sūtras* and images, and buries the bones. They return to thank him, give him jewelled swords and foretell his future career.

Note: Ts'ui held the post from 718 to 722: Yü Hsien-hao, *T'ang tz'u-shih k'ao,* p. 618.

248 Li Ts'e 李測

Text: *TPKC* 440.3589–90; Fang, pp. 184–5.

Story: During K'ai-yüan Li Ts'e, a magistrate, finds a featherless, red-fleshed bird coming into his hall. It is immune to cleavers and boiling oil, so he plunges it in a cask into the river. His next post, in early T'ien-pao, is again haunted, by crowds of tiny men. When one is killed the others mourn and bury him. The creatures prove to be rats. Li and his family survive unharmed.

249 Palace guards in T'ien-pao 天寶彍騎

Text: *TPKC* 440.3590; Fang, p. 185.

Story: In early T'ien-pao villages in Han-tan 邯鄲 county are regularly plagued by demons. When three palace guards come by they are warned to beware. That night they catch a rat and force it to identify itself. It is 1000 years old and will become a wild cat if it can bewitch 3,000 humans. It promises to go far away if released, and this happens.

Note: Details of informant: kinsman of Censor-in-chief Ts'ui I 崔懿.

250 Pi Hang 畢杭

Text: *TPKC* 440.3590–1; Fang, pp. 185–6.

Story: In 755 Pi is prefect of Wei-chou 魏州, which falls into the hands of An Lu-shan's rebels. One day his courtroom fills with hundreds of tiny men frisking about. His servants kill one. The remainder mourn and bury the dead with full ceremonial. Then they enter a hole in the wall. They turn out to be rats and are killed with hot water. Days later Pi and his family are all put to death.

Note: A man with the similar name Pi K'ang 畢抗 met his end as prefect of rebel-occupied Kuang-p'ing 廣平 [Ming-chou 洺州] in 755: *HTS* 128.4461; cf. Yü Hsien-hao, *T'ang tz'u-shih k'ao,* p. 1282.

Translation: de Groot, vol. 5, pp. 605–6.

251 Ts'ui Huai-ni 崔懷嶷

Text: *TPKC* 440.3591; Fang, p. 186.

Note: There are two distinct entries, the second without title.

Stories: (*a*) Hundreds of rats run crying around Ts'ui's courtyard on hind legs, watched by the whole family. The building collapses with a crash. Reported to the author by Ts'ui's named grandson.

(*b*) A teenaged girl goes missing and is later found underground at home, with a baby sired by a large rat. To her grief the family kill both rat and child. The girl then dies too.

Translation: de Groot, vol. 5, p. 605: (*b*) only.

252 A Mo-yao of Lang-chou 閬州莫徭

Text: *TPKC* 441.3600–1; Fang, pp. 187–8.

Story: A woodcutter of the Mo-yao tribe is borne by an elephant into marshlands, where an aged elephant needs him to remove a bamboo splinter from its foot and treat the wound. They give him a large tusk and take him home. He sells the tusk in Hung-chou 洪州 to an Iranian merchant, but the authorities submit it to Empress Wu. It contains twin dragon-figures, and she gives the first owner an annual pension for life.

Note: The Mo-yao tribe inhabited the Hunan-Kwangsi region (*Sui shu* 31.898; Schafer, *The vermilion bird*, pp. 51–2): the place-name here should perhaps be written 朗州, which would be closer to Hung-chou than Lang 閬-chou in eastern Szechuan.

253 A hunter of Annam 安南獵者

Text: *TPKC* 441.3601–2; Fang, pp. 188–9.

Story: During K'ai-yüan an Annamite hunter is picked up by an elephant in mountain country and taken to a remote valley. He is directed to climb a tall tree, from which he later sees a huge beast receive homage from a herd of elephants, then eat two of them. He kills the beast with arrows, and the grateful elephants lead him to a store of ivory. The protector-general has it collected, together with bones from the great beast.

254 The prefect's son in Chi-chou 冀州刺史子

Text: *TPKC* 442.3608–9; Fang, p. 189.

Story: (The name was forgotten by the informant.) The prefect sends his son on an errand to the capital, but the son first meets the travelling party of an official's widow. He offers marriage, they form a free union, and the prefect's family proves happy with the match. Before long the woman bolts herself in with the son, who fails to answer calls. She proves to be a wolf, which has all but devoured the man. Her followers all vanish.

Translations: de Groot, vol. 5, p. 570; Wieger, pp. 129–30.

255 A villager of Cheng-p'ing county 正平縣村人

Text: *TPKC* 442.3609–10; Fang, p. 190.

Story: In 765 an aged villager sickens, then vanishes. Later another villager is attacked by a wolf, which he wounds on the brow. Tracks lead back to the old man's house: he indeed has a similar wound. To protect the public his sons take his life, and he turns into a wolf. They submit their case to the magistrate, who pardons their action.

Translations: de Groot, vol. 5, p. 564; Wieger, pp. 126–7.

256 Idem 又

Text: *TPKC* 442.3610; Fang, p. 190.

Story: The same year a young peasant labourer in the same prefecture turns into a wolf after an illness and preys upon children. The father of one victim tries to employ him, but the young man disdains to eat there a second time. He then confesses to his in-born taste for human flesh. Seeing the signs in his mouth, the father beats him to death, as he finally takes on wolf form.

Translations: de Groot, vol. 5, p. 565; Wieger, pp. 127–8.

257 A son of the Chengs 鄭氏子

Text: *TPKC* 442.3616; Fang, pp. 190–1.

Story: While staying in the Ch'ung-hsüan Monastery 重玄寺 near Soochow he meets a pretty girl and enjoys a liaison with her. But the girl's visits to his quarters are controlled by his wife, who employs a holy nun to recite sacred texts: these keep the woman away, and she finally takes leave, explaining that she is a wild cat from the monastery tower.

258 Wei Yüan-chung 魏元忠

Text: *TPKC* 444.3633; *Lei-shuo* 8.14a–b and 14b–15a; *Chin-hsiu wan-hua ku, hou-chi*, 39.7a–b (story *a*); Fang, pp. 191–2.

Note: Two items are kept together in *TPKC*, kept apart in *Lei shuo*.

Stories: (*a*) In his early years of poverty Wei Yüan-chung [*ca.* 637–707] receives freak visitations from animals – an ape, a dog, some rats, some night-birds. He deals with them calmly and philosophically, and the visitations stop. The story ends with a summary of Wei's public career under Empress Wu and Chung-tsung.

(*b*) While yet unknown, he visits Chang Ching-ts'ang 張景藏 and reacts indignantly to his casual reception. Chang predicts an exalted future for him.

259 The son of Wei Hsü-hsin 韋虛心子

Text: *TPKC* 444.3634; Fang, pp. 192–3.

Note: I emend the name from the original Wei Hsü-chi 己, as the man can be identified.

Story: The son of Wei Hsü-hsin [672–741], president of the Board of Revenue, sees an ox-headed man, as shown in pictures of Hell, watching and approaching him. The figure chases him around the courtyard and into a well. It turns into an ape and finally vanishes. The boy is brought out in shock, unable to speak for days. Weeks later he dies.

260 Chang Ch'an 張鋋

Text: *TPKC* 445.3635; *Chin-hsiu wan-hua ku, hou-chi* 40.6b–7a; *Ch'ün-shu lei-pien ku-shih* 24.8ab. Fang, pp. 193–5, 248, 256–7, discusses parallel attribution to *Hsüan-shih chih.*

Story: Returning to Ch'eng-tu after a tour of duty, Chang is invited and entertained in aristocratic splendour by the marquis of Western Pa 巴西侯. Other guests with military titles join the party. One jokingly threatens to eat Chang. A visitor warns of danger from a member of the party: for this he is killed. Chang later awakes to find sleeping animals and stolen treasures all around him. Local folk kill them and recover the treasures.

261 Chang-sun Wu-chi 長孫無忌

Text: *TPKC* 447.3657; Fang, pp. 195–6.

Story: A woman given by T'ai-tsung to Chang-sun Wu-chi [*ca.* 600–659] is bedevilled by a fox. T'ai-tsung accepts advice to summon Ts'ui, an administrator in Hsiang-chou 相州, to exorcize it. He arrives, ritually summons the household gods and orders them to seize the fox. They fail, for it comes from heaven. Ts'ui calls in the Five Peaks, who agree to make the arrest. He then gives sentence and administers the flogging himself. The fox flies off, the woman recovers.

262 The monk Fu-li 僧服禮

Text: *TPKC* 447.3658–9; Fang, p. 196.

Story: In the period 650–655 a man of T'ai-yüan 太原 proclaims himself Maitreya Buddha. Worshippers see his body reach the sky, then grow small again. He relates this to the Buddhist *trikāya* doctrine. The learned monk Fu-li finds this premature appearance of Maitreya anomalous. His devout greeting causes the creature to take its true form as a fox; its accoutrements are paper cash from a grave. The fox flees.

Translation: de Groot, vol. 5, pp. 590–1.

263 Shang-kuan I 上官翼

Text: *TPKC* 447.3659; Fang, p. 197.

Story: In 664–5, while Shang-kuan I is assistant in Chiang-chou 絳州, his son embarks on an affair with a young girl who walks by. A maid-servant observes he is bewitched and tells the father, who exploits the demon's practice of swallowing all his son's meals to feed her poison. This exposes a dying fox, which they burn up. For weeks after this mourners continually appear in their home. Then slowly the manifestations stop.

264 The monk Ta-an 大安和尚

Text: *TPKC* 447.3660; Fang, p. 198.

Story: In the time of Empress Wu a woman calling herself a holy bodhisattva claims insight into people's thoughts. The empress and her court are impressed. The monk Ta-an challenges her. Although she three times identifies the subject of his thoughts, she fails when he meditates on arhatship. With this failure she turns into a fox and flees.

Translation: de Groot, vol. 5, pp. 591–2.

265 Yang Po-ch'eng 楊伯成

Text: *TPKC* 448.3664–5; Fang, pp. 198–9.

Story: While Yang is vice-governor of the metropolitan prefecture in early K'ai-yüan, an outspoken visitor called Wu Nan-ho 吳南鶴 takes possession of his daughter. Yang recognizes a fox at work, but no ritual experts can control it. He returns to his estate and accommodates Wu. A Taoist immortal sent by the monarch in heaven writes charms to summon and expose the fox. It returns to heaven; the daughter awakes as if from a sleep.

Note: Yang Po-ch'eng 陽伯成 was vice-governor of Ho-nan fu in 741: *Chin-shih ts'ui-pien* 81.29b–30a; cf. *T'ang shang-shu sheng lang-kuan shih-chu t'i-ming k'ao* 1.35b.

266 Liu Chia 劉甲

Text: *TPKC* 448.3666; Fang, p. 200.

Story: On the way to a post in Ho-pei, Liu is warned that his pretty wife might be taken by a spirit. That night he covers her with flour and mounts guard, but she is still taken. He follows a trail of flour to a lair deep under a tree growing on a grave-mound: there, attended by a dozen stolen women, is a fox with hundreds of cubs. These are all killed.

267 Administrator Li 李參軍

Text: *TPKC* 448.3666–8; Fang, pp. 200–2.

Story: On the way to a post in Yen-chou 兗州 Li is warned against marriage with the daughter of the prefect T'ao Chen-i 陶貞益. Instead he accepts a match with the daughter of a local gentleman called Hsiao. The splendid wedding is attended by the magistrate. Later, when Li is away on business, his wife's maids seduce passers-by, but they are found out and killed by hunting hounds. Hsiao too is killed by more specialized hounds.

268 The magistrate of Ch'ien-yang 汧陽令

Text: *TPKC* 449.3670–1; Fang, pp. 202–3.

Story: The magistrate decides to take up Buddhist austerities and receives encouragement from a vision of a bodhisattva. The Taoist Lo Kung-yüan 羅公遠, passing through, detects the influence of a fox from heaven and protects him with written charms. Later Lo comes again to deal with a second visitation, by one Liu Ch'eng 劉成 involving the magistrate's daughter. He wins a ritual battle and with Hsüan-tsung's consent banishes the fox to Silla, where the locals devote a cult to him.

Translation: Karl S. Y. Kao, ed., *Classical Chinese tales of the supernatural and the fantastic*, pp. 244–7.

Note: Discussed in Franciscus Verellen, 'Luo Gongyuan, légende et culte d'un saint taoïste', *Journal Asiatique* 275, 1987, 289–91.

269 Li Yüan-kung 李元恭

Text: *TPKC* 449.3671–2; Fang, pp. 203–4.

Story: Li, vice-president of the Board of Civil Office, has a pretty granddaughter who is bewitched by a fox. Li's son converses on scholarship with the fox in human form (Master Hu 胡郎). The girl also receives an elaborate education. Hu is then tricked into revealing his home – a burrow in a bamboo grove, where he is soon dug out and killed.

Note: For other references to Li's stated appointment (in K'ai-yüan), see *T'ang shang-shu sheng lang-kuan shih-chu t'i-ming k'ao* 7.4b.

270 The Venerable Chiao 焦練師

Text: *TPKC* 449.3672–3; Fang, pp. 204–5.

Story: Among the many followers of Venerable Chiao during K'ai-yüan is a woman called Ah-hu 阿胡, who insists on leaving once she has mastered the Taoist techniques, and reveals that she is a fox. Chiao is unable to stop her, so invokes Lord Lao 老君 and begs him to save the Tao from harm by controlling this fox. Lord Lao calls in a divine figure to cut the fox in two.

Note: On Chiao, a female Taoist divine of Mount Sung, see *Li T'ai-po ch'üan-chi* 9.508.

271 Li 李氏

Text: *TPKC* 449.3673–4; Fang, pp. 205–6.

Story: During K'ai-yüan a girl of twelve named Li is the object of a fox's attentions. Then a second fox comes, claiming to be a younger cousin of the first and bearing a grudge against him. He shows her ways to exorcize his cousin, and these take effect. For permanent protection he prescribes certain names written with twigs of peach and placed with charms on the gates. In due course the girl, still unmarried, goes missing.

272 Magistrate Wei 韋明府

Text: *TPKC* 449.3674–5; Fang, pp. 206–7.

Story: During K'ai-yüan Wei is confronted by a fox using the name Ts'ui, who lays claim to his daughter. She becomes delirious. Wei requests a post in Shu 蜀, to seek the services of a Taoist master on Mount O-mei. The fox humiliates the Taoist, so the wedding goes ahead, with suitable gifts. But when Wei's son also falls ill through the foxes the mother learns a way to exorcize Ts'ui, who ends up chastized and banished by heavenly authority.

273 Hsieh Hun-chih 謝混之

Text: *TPKC* 449.3675–6; Fang, pp. 207–8.

Story: During K'ai-yüan Hsieh is the harsh and cruel magistrate of Tung-kuang 東光. After a spring hunt in which many foxes and wolves are killed a murder allegation is lodged against him with the Censorate. Chang Chiu-ling 張九齡 [673–740] sends Chang Hsiao 張曉 to investigate. It emerges that the plaintiffs are really foxes. Despite the force of their claim, hunting hounds are brought in to drive them off.

274 Wang Pao 王苞

Text: *TPKC* 450.3677; Fang, p. 208.

Story: Wang, from Wu-chün 吳君, who once served the Taoist master Yeh Ching-neng 葉靜能, is now a student in the State Academy. He has an affair with a woman, but Yeh perceives that he is consorting with a fox. Yeh then provides a written charm, which has the effect of exposing the fox and summoning her before him. He dismisses her.

275 Administrator T'ang 唐參軍

Text: *TPKC* 450.3677–8; Fang, pp. 208–9.

Story: At his Lo-yang residence T'ang, an austere man, receives an unwanted visit from two men seeking food. He attacks them with a sword, but merely wounds one. The other, revealing that they are foxes, warns him of revenge. When he leaves T'ang takes ritual precautions. These fail, and he employs

Buddhist monks to exorcize the fox. It comes posing as a Buddha, tricks them all into eating meat, then mockingly departs.

276 Yen Chien 嚴諫

Text: *TPKC* 450.3680–1; Fang, p. 210.

Story: Yen, a director of administration in Lo-yang, goes to an uncle's funeral. Some days later the family members remove their mourning garments, reporting that the deceased has so directed. Yen suspects a fox is at work, and when the soul of the deceased refuses contact with him he brings in hunting birds, hounds and armed men to surround the fox. It appears on the roof, avoids all missiles, jumps clear and flees.

277 Administrator Wei 韋參軍

Text: *TPKC* 450.3681–2; Fang, pp. 210–11.

Story: In youth Wei's brothers scorn him as simple, but he proves to have hidden powers. He shows them treasure in the K'un-ming Pool 昆明池 and predicts his own appointment in Jun-chou 潤州. On the way there he passes through K'ai-feng 開封 county, where a fox has bewitched the magistrate's mother. Wei exorcizes it. Later, in Jun-chou, he correctly predicts his own death, his wife's remarriage, and the birth of three sons.

278 Yang's daughters 楊氏女

Text: *TPKC* 450.3682; Fang, p. 211.

Story: Yang's two daughters are both married into the Hu 胡 family, but their mother favours the younger son-in-law. The elder denounces him as a fox and tells them how to expose him, by hanging up a magpie's head at the door and repeating the words: 'He prays for cooked meat.' That is done: the fox duly leaves. It is now a general practice.

Translation: de Groot, vol. 6, pp. 1063–4, linking foxes and the surname Hu (cf. **269**).

279 Hsüeh Chiung 薜迥

Text: *TPKC* 450.3682; Fang, pp. 211–12.

Story: Hsüeh spends several nights wenching in Lo-yang with his followers, then pays the girls ten strings each. But the next night one insists on leaving, despite Hsüeh's refusal. She escapes through a water-channel, turning into a fox and leaving her money behind.

280 Hsin T'i-fou 辛替否

Text: *TPKC* 450.3682; Fang, p. 212.

Story: When Hsin's mother dies her voice continues to be heard from the soul-shrine, and the family reverently obey her. But a cousin skilled in magic comes to watch, performs rituals behind the house and exposes a hairless female fox, which he kills. The voice falls silent.

281 Commoners of Tai-chou 代州民

Text: *TPKC* 450.3683; Fang, p. 212.

Story: A girl and her mother, living alone, receive a bodhisattva who floats in on clouds and decides to join them. The devout villagers are bound to silence. Meanwhile the newcomer sleeps with the girl and makes her pregnant.

When her brother returns from military service the bodhisattva refuses to let him in. So the brother engages a Taoist priest, whose rituals expose a fox. He kills it with a sword.

Translation: de Groot, vol. 5, pp. 592–3.

282 Feng Chieh 馮玠

Text: TPKC 451.3684; Fang, pp. 212–13.

Story: Feng is bewitched by a fox, and his father seeks a cure through a ritual specialist. The fox laments her thwarted hopes to live with him until death. Her parting gift is a set of clothes, which she asks him to keep as a souvenir. He wraps it in his books for secrecy. Later, when he has recovered and passed the metropolitan examination, he gets it out, to find it is paper.

283 Ho-lan Chin-ming 賀蘭進明

Text: TPKC 451.3684; *Sui-shih kuang-chi* 23.9ab; Fang, pp. 213–14.

Story: When Ho-lan Chin-ming is a censor in the capital [756], his brother is bewitched by a fox in Sui-yang 睢陽. She is dutiful in ritual greetings to the family. All receive her 'life-prolonging' gifts on the fifth of the fifth month, though at first they burn them as unlucky. Later one of them asks her to obtain a valuable mirror. She goes as a fox to steal it from another house, but is caught and killed. The bewitching ceases.

Note: On Ho-lan Chin-ming's career, see Fu Hsüan-ts'ung, ed., *T'ang ts'ai-tzu chuan chiao-chien,* vol. 1, pp. 270–5. For the gifts on the fifth of the fifth month, cf. **68**, **290**.

284 Ts'ui Ch'ang 崔昌

Text: TPKC 451.3685; Fang, p. 214.

Story: Ts'ui is studying at his Lo-yang manor house when a young boy comes up and joins him in scholarly discussion. Later the boy brings in an old man, who in his drunkenness vomits up human hair and nails. Ts'ui beheads the man, to the fury of the boy, who says this was the head of his family. The boy then leaves, cursing, and never returns.

285 Chang-sun Chia 長孫甲

Text: TPKC 451.3685–6; Fang, pp. 214–15.

Story: Chang-sun is magistrate of Chung-pu 中部 county in Fang-chou 坊州. His devoutly Buddhist family one day sees a bodhisattva float down on clouds to their house. While they worship him, Chang-sun's son calls in a Taoist master who kills the masquerading fox. A second experience leaves the Taoist worsted. The fox now identifies itself as Hu Kang-tzu 狐剛子, apologizes for the trouble and orders the Taoist to return his fee.

286 Old Wang 王老

Text: TPKC 451.3686; Fang, p. 215.

Story: An old fox lives by the Sung kings' tombs in Sui-yang 睢陽, where the local dogs pay him reverence. The men of Sung hire special hounds from Old Wang of Lo-yang, able to control demons, to deal with this fox. But the hounds pay reverence too. This story has given rise to a traditional joke: 'dogs to catch the wild fox of Sui-yang'.

Note: The text begins 'T'ang . . .', but the story is presented as traditional, from Sung times.

287 Liu Chung-ai 劉眾愛

Text: *TPKC* 451.3686–7; Fang, pp. 215–16.

Story: According to informant Liu Ch'üan-po [cf. **234**], whose estate is near Ch'i 岐, his nurse's son Chung-ai once trapped in his net a predatory creature in the form of a red-skirted woman. He killed her and sank her in a pond. When the creature reappeared, alive, he struck again. She took the form of a fox. Following a Buddhist monk's advice Chung-ai induced the fox to spit out its jewel, which confers power to attract affection.

Translation: de Groot, vol. 5, pp. 593–4.

288 Wang An 王黯

Text: *TPKC* 451.3687; Fang, pp. 216–17.

Story: During T'ien-pao Wang An, son-in-law of Ts'ui Shih-t'ung 崔士同, prefect of Mien-chou 沔州, is bewitched by a fox and hysterically refuses to cross the Yangtze. Ts'ui employs a magician, who mortally wounds the fox: the animal is traced and burned to ash, which Wang consumes, then recovers. Later, as a county deputy, he is approached by a fox-slave offering another sister in marriage. Wang fearfully burns silks for them. But the foxes decide not to proceed.

Translation: de Groot, vol. 6, pp. 1066–7 (first part only).

289 Sun Tseng-sheng 孫甑生

Text: *TPKC* 451.3688; Fang, p. 217.

Story: The Taoist master Sun Tseng-sheng begins life as a falconer. This leads him to a cave full of foxes studying under an old fox-professor. Sun seizes one of their books. Next day a group of men come wanting to buy it back and undertake to teach him its contents if he gives them a copy. Thus he becomes a magician, but sworn to secrecy. He refuses even Hsüan-tsung's demand (*ca.* 755) to divulge the secret arts.

290 Wang Hsüan 王璿

Text: *TPKC* 451.3689; *Sui-shih kuang-chi* 23.9b–10a; Fang, p. 218.

Story: Wang Hsüan, now prefect of Sung-chou 宋州, was good-looking in youth and was bewitched by a fox. Her demeanour earned respect and favour. At the due seasons she regularly presented lavish 'life-prolonging' gifts to family members. She stopped coming when Wang rose to high office.

291 Li Nun 李麐

Text: *TPKC* 451.3689–90; Fang, pp. 218–20.

Story: Li Nun, posted to Tung-p'ing 東平 county, buys the attractive wife of a Central Asian cake-seller. After some happy years together and the birth of a son, he travels with her on official business and discovers she is a fox. Dead, she lies there with her human clothes. The son is fostered with relatives in Lo-yang. Li's new wife mocks the old, until one night the old wife's ghost comes to rebuke her. In 755 the son, aged above ten, is alive and well.

292 Sung P'u 宋溥

Text: *TPKC* 451.3690–1; Fang, p. 220.

Story: During Ta-li Sung P'u, who has a post in Ch'ang-ch'eng 長城 county, tells how in youth he tried to trap a fox by night, but saw it guided away from danger by a demon riding on its back. T'an Chung 談眾 also tells a story about trapping foxes in youth: while he watched from a tree an old man came and called up to him. His brother gave chase, and the old man turned into a fox and fled.

293 Li Ch'ang 李萇

Text: *TPKC* 452.3697–8; Fang, p. 221.

Story: During T'ien-pao Li Ch'ang serves as revenue manager in Chiang-chou 絳州 – a notoriously dangerous job. Attacks soon begin: an attempt to abduct his son, tiles flying through the air. A cousin detects a fox and advises the use of hunting dogs. These kill various foxes. But a disembodied voice complains of his mother's death, then joins Li in social drinking. The invisible fox provides a ritual means to exorcize the haunting.

294 The prefect of Hsin-chou 忻州刺史

Text: *TPKC* 456.3731–2; Fang, p. 222.

Story: The post is associated with natural disasters, and many holders have died. In Kao-tsung's time an imperial guards officer goes there and confronts a black monster. It is a snake spirit, but takes on human form to meet him. It needs help because its huge size has imprisoned it underground. The prefect follows its instructions, opens a stone chamber, sees a black dragon fly out and destroys the snake. The hauntings cease.

295 The magistrate of Yü-kan county 餘干縣令

Text: *TPKC* 456.3732; Fang, pp. 222–3.

Story: Holders of this post rapidly die. It is abandoned, the residence left derelict. But in 712, driven by poverty, a new magistrate comes and insists on confronting the haunting presence there. A series of poltergeist phenomena follow, performed by an object like a white bag. He traces this to an underground chamber, into which he pours huge amounts of boiling water. A snake and its vast brood are found. The hauntings cease.

296 Cavalryman Chang 張騎士

Text: *TPKC* 457.3737–8; Fang, pp. 223–4.

Story: Chang is the informant: when young he sailed with Li Chi 李勣 [594–669] on a sea campaign. Two monster snakes drove their ship on to an island of wrecks, but were distracted by other snakes. The crew sailed off to safety. The ship put in to an island where a giant covered in white hair ate two of the crew. The others fled to sea. They finally reached an island in Ch'ing-yüan 清遠 county, under Nan-hai 南海.

Note: Li Chi led a land campaign against Korea in 645, a land and sea campaign in 668. But Nan-hai was in the far south. And the span of dates strains credulity.

297 A worthy of Chih-hsiang monastery 至相寺賢者

Text: *TPKC* 457.3738–9; Fang, p. 224.

Story: The man has pursued devotions in the *ch'an* hall of this Ch'ang-an monastery since the age of ten. A snake has lived there throughout the same period of forty years, growing huge. One night during K'ai-yüan the man finds a luminous pearl in the snake's hole. Taking it to market, he finds a Central Asian merchant willing to buy, but only at a reduced price, since this is a snake pearl.

298 Li Ch'i-wu 李齊物

Text: *TPKC* 457.3740–1; Fang, pp. 224–5.

Story: Li is demoted from governor of Ho-nan 河南 prefecture to prefect of Ching-ling 竟陵 [746]. White smoke appears on the southern tower – a sign to the locals that the prefect must leave or die. Li refuses to submit. He investigates the smoke, suspects a snake, has its lair dug open and kills it with boiling oil. Its death throes shake the town. Li survives.

299 Yen T'ing-chih 嚴挺之

Text: *TPKC* 457.3741; Fang, p. 225.

Story: When Yen T'ing-chih [673–742] takes up duties as prefect of Wei-chou 魏州, a small snake enters the courtroom and rests on the bench. Yen crushes its head with his ivory tablet. The snake turns into a written charm. Suspecting the work of a magician, Yen investigates, but finds nothing.

Translation: de Groot, vol. 6, pp. 1027–8.

300 A woodcutter in T'ien-pao 天寶樵人

Text: *TPKC* 457.3741; Fang, p. 225.

Story: During T'ien-pao a woodcutter collapses drunk in the mountains. He awakes to find he has been swallowed by a snake and has to cut his way out. He is slow to recover his senses, and thereafter half his body sheds its skin, giving the appearance of vitiligo.

301 Chang Hao 張鎬

Text: *TPKC* 457.3742; Fang, pp. 225–6.

Note: Attribution to *Kuang-i chi* given in Ming MS.

Story: The fortifications of Hung-chou 洪州 remain untouched since their building by Ma Yüan 馬瑗 [14 BC–AD 49]: traditionally, death threatens anyone who alters them. But in 765 Commander in chief Chang Hao repairs them. A pit opens up, with two huge snakes and a brood of young. Chang has them removed to a life-sparing pool, driving out other water creatures there. He dies within days, followed by two junior officers.

Note: Chang's appointment in Hung-chou ran from 762 until his death in 764: *CTS* 11.276; Yü Hsien-hao, *T'ang tz'u-shih k'ao,* p. 1984.

302 A hunter of Hai-chou 海州獵人

Text: *TPKC* 457.3743; Fang, pp. 226–7.

Story: While hunting the man is seized by a large snake from the sea. It takes him and his weapons to an island in the sea and leaves him on a cliff. There he watches the snake fight with an even larger one. Realizing that his help is desired, he kills the larger snake with poisoned arrows. The first snake rewards him with jewels and takes him home.

303 'Carried One' 擔生

Text: *TPKC* 458.3744–5; Fang, p. 227. For the reading 擔 see below.

Story: A student carries around his pet snake ('Carried One') on his shoulders. When it grows too big he releases it in the Fan county 范縣 marsh. It preys on humans for forty years, but spares its old master. His unlikely survival puts him in prison under sentence of death. The snake saves him by flooding the county, sparing only the prison. When Tu-ku Hsien's 獨狐遅 uncle is magistrate there, *ca.* 755, his boat capsizes on the lake.

Note: Compare version in *Shui-ching chu shu* 10.990, discussed by Ch'ien Chung-shu, *Kuan-chui pien*, pp. 824–5.

304 A man of P'u-chou 蒲州人

Text: *TPKC* 459.3754; Fang, pp. 227–8.

Story: Digging a well, the man hits a square stone. He removes it and falls into a deep pit full of hibernating snakes. He lives down there for months, subsisting on air like the snakes. When thunder stirs them to life he clings to one and is brought to the surface. There he learns from a man at a beacon that he is in P'ing-chou 平州.

305 The wife of a clerk in the Board of Revenue 戶部令史妻

Text: *TPKC* 460.3765–6; Fang, pp. 228–9.

Story: During K'ai-yüan the clerk's wife is bewitched and his well-fed horse is unaccountably lean. A Central Asian neighbour skilled in magic explains that she goes riding at night. The clerk watches her set off attended by a maid on a broomstick. The next night the maid rides on the jar in which he lies hidden. When they fly home after a mountain orgy the clerk is left behind. He has to walk back hundreds of miles from Lang-chou 閬州. With the neighbour's help he uses fire to exorcize the demon, a grey crane.

306 Lu Jung 盧融

Text: *TPKC* 463.3811; Fang, p. 229.

Story: In early K'ai-yüan Lu is lying sick when a giant bird flies in. It steps up to his couch and lunges at him with spears held in hands on its wings. But a man walks in to warn off the bird, which then flies off. The man leaves too. Lu is permanently cured.

307 Wang Hsü 王緒

Text: *TPKC* 463.3811–12; Fang, pp. 229–30.

Story: In late T'ien-pao Wang Hsü, an administrative supervisor in T'ai-chou 台州, is on his deathbed. A bird flies into his room, walks to his bed and chirps at him: *ts'iu ts'iu* 取取 ('take, take'). Wang then dies.

308 A great fish of the southern ocean 南海大魚

Text: *TPKC* 464.3818; Fang, p. 230.

Story: Ho Lü-kuang 何履光, military governor of Ling-nan [756–757], comes from a seaside home in Chu-yai 朱崖. He describes three wonders of the sea: 1. A monster fish stuck between two rocky islands, bellowing thunder and spouting muddy rain. 2. An island with toad-like creatures exhaling luminous vapour. 3. A giant snake many miles long, coiled round an island and drinking the sea dry, until swallowed up by another creature.

Note: Discussed by Schafer, *The vermilion bird,* p. 218.

309 A whale 鯨魚

Text: *TPKC* 464.3818; Fang, pp. 230–1.

Note: The same as **204**.

310 A carp 鯉魚

Text: *TPKC* 464.3819; Fang, p. 231.

Story: During K'ai-yüan a snake fights with a carp in Lin-hai 臨海, T'ai-chou 台州. Each is colossal in size. After three days of titanic struggle the carp has battered the snake to death.

311 A great crab of the Southern Ocean 南海大蟹

Text: *TPKC* 464.3819–20; *Lei-shuo* 8.17a; *Kan-chu chi* 7.22a; Fang, pp. 231–2, 246, 253.

Story: A Persian seafarer to India puts in to an island far out to sea, with a single Central Asian inhabitant. This man was washed up from a wreck; he lives on berries and plants, dresses in leaves and grass. Helped by him the crew now load their ship with precious stones that abound in the island. But, as he has warned, the mountain god pursues them in the form of a snake. The claws of a huge crab rise out of the sea to crush its head.

312 Ch'i Huan 齊澣

Text: *TPKC* 467.3846.

Note: The same as **216**.

313 Hsieh Erh 謝二

Text: *TPKC* 470.3870–1; Fang, p. 232.

Story: During K'ai-yüan an impoverished Lo-yang scholar in Yang-chou receives from Hsieh Erh a letter to exchange for money at his home near a pool back in Lo-yang. Knocking on a tree to gain admittance, he is given counterfeit coin. He reports it, and the authorities send divers to bring out a brood of turtles and kill them. Later, when the man receives a post in the south, Hsieh Erh rebukes him. The man and his family die.

Note: On the coinage: Chap. 3, n. 13. On the pool: *T'ang liang-ching ch'eng-fang k'ao* 5.18b and 38b.

314 A fisherman of Ching-chou 荊州漁人

Text: *TPKC* 470.3871; Fang, p. 233.

Story: A fisherman catches an unknown kind of blue fish and decides to cook and eat it himself. The taste disappoints him. Days later a train of riders and carriages arrives, accusing him of killing a king's son and a general. Retribution is promised. The man contracts leprosy and months later dies.

315 Liu Yen-hui 劉彥回

Text: *TPKC* 472.3887–8; *Lei shuo* 8.15a–b; *Shuo-fu* 4.10b; Fang, pp. 233, 244–5, 255–6.

Story: When Liu Yen-hui's father is prefect of Hu-chou 湖州 a turtle is found in a silver mine-pit and presented to him with congratulations. But the father takes back the turtle and releases it. Years later, when Liu Yen-hui himself is on the way to his own post in Fang-chou 房州, the grateful turtle appears to assist his family trapped in a flood.

316 A fisherman of Wu-hsing 吳興漁者

Text: TPKC 472.3888; Fang, p. 234.

Story: A fisherman catches a large turtle standing on four other turtles. He submits it to P'ei 裴, an official in the prefecture. A specialist warns that this is a turtle for kings and if used for trivial divination will bring death. But P'ei uses it on a nest of magpies, which is then destroyed by wind, and to learn the sex of a servant's unborn child, a boy who dies at birth. P'ei finally submits the turtle to the throne.

317 [No title]

Text: TPYL 921.4ab. Fang, pp. 242–3, argues for a wrong attribution to *Kuang-i chi.*

Story: The daughter of the Red Monarch of the South attains immortality and dwells on a mulberry tree, building a nest in the first month. She takes different forms – a white magpie, a woman. Her father, failing to draw her back, burns her out with fire, and she rises to heaven. Certain customs of the first month are explained by this myth.

318 A garden of fungus 芝圃

Text: Lei shuo 8.15b; Fang, p. 245.

Story: On [Mount] Hsien-tu 仙都 there is a garden planted with fungus growths in many different shapes and colours.

Note: Mount Chin-yün 縉雲 in Kua-chou 瓜州 received the title Hsien-tu by imperial decree in 748. Taoists counted it as the Twenty-ninth Grotto Heaven: *Hsien-tu chih* A.1ab (*Tao tsang,* HY 602).

319 A game of dice in a mountain grotto 山洞樗蒲

Text: Lei shuo 8.15b–16a and 60.20a (latter citing *I-yüan*); *Kan-chu chi* 7.20b; Fang, pp. 245, 251, suggesting wrong attribution to *Kuang-i chi.*

Story: A traveller riding through mountains sees two old men playing dice. As he watches them his whip and saddle rot away.

320 Gold sheep and jade horse 金羊玉馬

Text: Lei shuo 8.16a; *Kan-chu chi* 7.20b; Fang, pp. 245, 251.

Story: A snowdrift fails to melt away. When it is dug open a gold sheep and a jade horse appear, each 2 feet high.

321 The pine touched at the tip 摩頂松

Text: Lei shuo 8.16a–b; *Kan-chu chi* 7.21a; *TPKC* 92.606, citing *Tu-i chih* 獨異志 (q.v. A.17) and *T'ang hsin-yü* 唐新語. Fang, pp. 245 and 252, rejects attribution to *Kuang-i chi.*

Story: When Hsüan-tsang 玄奘 set out for the west he touched a pine and instructed it to point west while he was away and point back east when he returned. The pine did this, giving his disciples notice of his expected return.

322 An old man plays the flute 老人吹笛

Text: *Lei shuo* 8.17a–b; *San-tung ch'ün-hsien lu* 18.3a–b; *Kan-chu chi* 7.22a; *TPKC* 204.1555–6, citing *Po-i chih.* Fang, pp. 246 and 253, rejects attribution to *Kuang-i chi.*

Story: While Lü Chün-ch'ing 吕君卿 relaxes with his flute one evening on a river journey, an old man appears and shows him three flutes, in size huge, ordinary and small. The man blows a few notes on the smallest, and the effect is to blow up a storm on the river, endangering the boat. He stops playing and recites four lines of verse.

323 The Lord of Tao trims a tongue 道君剪舌

Text: *Lei shuo* 8.18a; *San-tung ch'ün-hsien lu* 10.10b; *Kan-chu chi* 7.22b; *Lu-i chi* 2.6b–7a; *TPKC* 162.1172, citing *Lu-i chi.* Fang, pp. 246–7 and 254, rejects attribution to *Kuang-i chi.*

Story: Wang Fa-lang 王法朗, a Taoist of K'uei-chou 夔州, has a long tongue which impedes his speech. He daily recites the *Tao-te ching.* One night he dreams that Lord Lao trims his tongue. He awakes to find his speech is normal.

324 A goose shot at Sha-yüan 沙苑射雁

Text: *Chin-hsiu wan-hua ku, ch'ien-chi* 4.9b–10a; *Kan-chu chi* 7.20b; *Chi-i chi* 1.1a–2a (in *Ku-shih wen-fang hsiao-shuo*). Fang, pp. 247 and 251, rejects attribution to *Kuang-i chi.*

Story: Hsüan-tsung, when hunting at Sha-yüan, shoots an arrow which hits a wild goose. The goose flies off. A Taoist at a temple in I-chou 易州 has the arrow brought to him, with the prediction that the owner will arrive in ten years. Hsüan-tsung later flees to Szechuan, visits this temple and sees the arrow there.

325 *'Yü-lun-p'ao'* 鬱輪袍

Text: *Chin-hsiu wan-hua ku, ch'ien-chi* 22.6a; *Kan-chu chi* 7.21b; *Chi-i chi* 2.1b–3a. Fang, pp. 248 and 252–3, rejects attribution to *Kuang-i chi.*

Story: Wang Wei 王維 is acquainted with the prince of Ch'i 岐王 and asks for his support in the metropolitan examination. The prince tells him to compose a work for the lute and arranges for him to perform this before royalty. He makes a good impression and passes top in the examination that year.

326 A parrot calls flowers into bloom 鸚鵡喚花開

Text: *Kan-chu chi* 7.21ab; *Po-i chih* 4–6. Fang, p. 252, rejects attribution to *Kuang-i chi.*

Story: Hsü Han-yang 許漢陽 sails in a boat up a creek with flowers in bud on either side. A parrot calls, and the flowers open in bloom, each with a pretty girl inside. When the flowers fall in the evening, the girls too fall into the water.

327 Shih Ah-ts'o 石阿措

Text: *Kan-chu chi* 7.22b; *Po-i chih* 8–9. Fang, p. 254, rejects attribution to *Kuang-i chi.*

Story: Ts'ui Hsüan-wei 崔玄微 once meets two beautiful girls whose names suggest their true identities – a spirit of the wind (Feng) and a pomegranate (Shih).

328 Ching Yüan-ying 敬元穎

Text: *Kan-chu chi* 7.22b; *Po-i chih* 2–4. Fang, p. 254, rejects attribution to *Kuang-i chi.*

Story: This is the name of a mirror.

Note: In *Po-i chih* there is an extended story in which a girl with this name calls upon Ch'en Chung-kung 陳仲躬. She turns out to be a mirror in the depths of a well.

List of works cited

The works listed here, subdivided into Abbreviations, Primary Sources and Secondary Sources, include the most frequently cited works in Western languages and the great majority of those in Chinese and Japanese. Bibliographical details of all works not included are provided in relevant footnotes throughout the book.

Abbreviations

CTS	*Chiu T'ang shu* 舊唐書. Ed. Chung-hua shu-chü. Peking 1975.
HTS	*Hsin T'ang shu* 新唐書. Ed. Chung-hua shu-chü. Peking 1975.
HY	*Tao tsang tzu-mu yin-te* 道藏子目引得. Harvard-Yenching Institute Sinological Index Series, no. 25. Peking 1935. (Scriptures of the Ming Taoist Canon numbered as listed on pp. 1–37.)
T	*Taishō shinshū daizōkyō* 大正新修大藏經. Tokyo 1924–1935. 100 vols.
TCTC	*Tzu-chih t'ung-chien* 資治通鑑. By Ssu-ma Kuang 司馬光 (1019–1086). Ed. Chung-hua shu-chü. Peking 1956 and 1976. 20 vols.
TPKC	*T'ai-p'ing kuang-chi* 太平廣記. Comp. Li Fang 李昉 et al., 977–978. Ed. Wang Shao-ying 汪紹楹. Repr. Peking 1961. 10 vols.
TPYL	*T'ai-p'ing yü-lan* 太平御覽. Comp. Li Fang et al., 977–984. Sung edn. Repr. Chung-hua shu-chü. Peking 1960. 4 vols.
WYYH	*Wen-yüan ying-hua* 文苑英華. Foochow edn. of 1567. Substantial parts repr. in Chung-hua shu-chü edn., Peking 1966. 6 vols.

Primary sources

An-yang hsien-chih 安陽縣志. By Ch'en Hsi-lu 陳錫輅. Ed. Chu Huang 朱煌. Edn. of 1738.

An-yang hsien chin-shih lu 安陽縣金石錄. By Wu I 武億 (1745–1799) and Chao Hsi-huang 趙希璜. Edn. of 1799.

Chang Chi shih chi 張籍詩集. By Chang Chi 張籍 (766?–830?). Peking 1959.

Ch'ang-an chih 長安志. By Sung Min-ch'iu 宋敏求. Preface dated 1076. In *Ching-hsün t'ang ts'ung-shu* 經訓堂叢書.

Ch'ao-yeh ch'ien-tsai 朝野僉載. By Chang Cho 張鷟. Ed. Chao Shou-yen 趙守儼. Repr. with *Sui T'ang chia-hua* (q.v.). Peking 1979.

Chen-sung t'ang chi-ku i-wen 貞松堂集古遺文. By Lo Chen-yü 羅振玉. Edn. of 1931. Repr. in *Lo Hsüeh-t'ang hsien-sheng ch'üan-chi*, First Series. Taipei 1968.

Ch'eng-wei lu 稱謂錄. By Liang Chang-chü 梁章鉅 (1775–1849). Edn. of Liang Kung-ch'en 梁恭辰, 1884. Repr. in *Min Shin zokugo jisho shūsei* 明清俗語辭書集成, vol. 2, Tokyo 1974, repr. 1978.

Chi-i chi 集異記. In *Ku-shih wen-fang hsiao-shuo* 顧氏文房小說.

Chi Shen-chou san-pao kan-t'ung lu 集神州三寶感通錄. By Tao-hsüan 道宣 (596–667). *T* vol. 52, no. 2106.

Chia-t'ai Kuei-chi chih 嘉泰會稽志. By Shih Su 施宿 et al., 1201. In *Ying-yin Wen-yüan ko ssu-k'u ch'üan-shu*, vol. 486.

Ch'ien chu Tu shih 錢注杜詩. By Tu Fu 杜甫 (712–770). Ed. Ch'ien Ch'ien-i 錢謙益. Peking 1958. 2 vols.

Ch'ien-fu lun chien 潛夫論箋. By Wang Fu 王符. Ed. Wang Chi-p'ei 汪繼培. Peking 1979.

Ch'ien-yen t'ang chin-shih-wen pa-wei 潛研堂金石文跋尾. By Ch'ien Ta-hsin 錢大昕 (1728–1804). In *Ch'ien-yen t'ang ch'üan-shu* 潛研堂全書.

Chih-chai shu-lu chieh-t'i 直齋書錄解題. By Ch'en Chen-sun 陳振孫 (*ca.* 1190–1249+). Ed. Hsü Hsiao-man 徐小蠻 and Ku Mei-hua 顧美華. Shanghai 1987.

Chin-hsiu wan-hua ku (ch'ien-chi, hou-chi, hsü-chi, pieh-chi) 錦繡萬花谷前集後集續集別集. Anon. Preface dated 1188. Edn. of 1536.

Chin-shih hsü-ch'ao 金石續鈔. By Chao Shao-tsu 趙紹祖. Repr. 1860.

Chin-shih hsü-lu 金石續錄. By Liu Ch'ing-li 劉青藜. Pref. 1710. In *Hsüeh-ku chai chin-shih ts'ung-shu* 學古齋金石叢書.

Chin-shih lu chiao-cheng 金石錄校證. By Chao Ming-ch'eng 趙明誠 (1081–1129). Ed. Chin Wen-ming 金文明. Shanghai 1985.

Chin-shih ts'ui-pien 金石萃編. By Wang Ch'ang 王昶 (1725–1806). Edn. of 1805.

Chin-shih wen-tzu chi 金石文字記. By Ku Yen-wu 顧炎武 (1613–1682). In *T'ing-lin i-shu* 亭林遺書.

Chin shu 晉書. Ed. Chung-hua shu-chü. Peking 1974.

Ch'ing shih kao 清史稿. Ed. Chung-hua shu-chü. Peking 1976–1977. 48 vols.

Ch'ing shih lei-lüeh 情史類略. By Feng Meng-lung 馮夢龍 (1574–1646). Ed. Tsou Hsüeh-ming 鄒學明 et al. Changsha 1983.

Chiu T'ang shu chiao-k'an chi 舊唐書校勘記. Comp. Lo Shih-lin 羅士琳 et al. 1872 edn. Repr. Taipei 1971. 2 vols.

Chiu Wu-tai shih 舊五代史. Ed. Chung-hua shu-chü. Peking 1976.

Chou I chu-shu 周易注疏. In *Shih-san ching chu-shu.*

Chou li chu-shu 周禮注疏. In *Shih-san ching chu-shu.*

Chou shu 周書. Ed. Chung-hua shu-chü. Peking 1971.

Ch'u-hsüeh chi 初學記. By Hsü Chien 徐堅 et al. Ed. Chung-hua shu-chü. Peking 1962, repr. 1981.

Chuang-tzu chi-shih 莊子集釋. Ed. Kuo Ch'ing-fan 郭慶藩. Peking 1961.

Ch'un-ch'iu Tso chuan chu-shu 春秋左傳注疏. In *Shih-san ching chu-shu.*

Chung-chou chin-shih chi 中州金石記. By Pi Yüan 畢沅 (1730–1797). In *Ching-hsün t'ang ts'ung-shu* 經訓堂叢書.

Chung-kuo min-shih hsi-kuan ta-ch'üan 中國民事習慣大全. Comp. Fa-cheng hsüeh-she 法政學社. Shanghai 1923. Repr. Taipei 1962.

Ch'ung-wen tsung-mu 崇文總目. In *Ying-yin Wen-yüan ko ssu-k'u ch'üan-shu,* vol. 674.

Chü t'an lu 劇談錄. By K'ang P'ien 康駢 (*chin-shih* 877). Preface dated 895. In *Ying-yin Wen-yüan ko ssu-k'u ch'üan-shu,* vol. 1042.

Ch'üan T'ang shih 全唐詩. Ed. Chung-hua shu-chü. Peking 1960.

Ch'üan T'ang wen [欽定]全唐文. Imperial edn. Preface dated 1814. Repr. Taipei 1965.

Ch'üan Tsai-chih wen-chi 權載之文集. By Ch'üan Te-yü 權德輿 (759–818). In *Ssu-pu ts'ung-k'an* 四部叢刊, First Series.

Ch'üeh shih [御覽]闕史. By Kao Yen-hsiu 高彥休. Preface dated 884. In *Chih-pu-tsu chai ts'ung-shu* 知不足齋叢書, First Series.

Ch'ün-shu lei-pien ku-shih 群書類編故事. By Wang Ying 王罃. Yüan edn. Repr. Yangchow 1990.

Erh-ya chu-shu 爾雅注疏. In *Shih-san ching chu-shu.*

Fa-yüan chu-lin 法苑珠林. By Tao-shih 道世 (d. 683). In *T* vol. 53, no. 2122.

Fen-men ku-chin lei-shih [新編]分門古今類事. In *Ying-yin Wen-yüan ko ssu-k'u ch'üan-shu,* vol. 1047.

Feng-shih wen-chien chi chiao-cheng 封氏聞見記校證. By Feng Yen 封演 (*fl. ca.* 795). Ed. Chao Chen-hsin 趙貞信. Harvard-Yenching Institute Sinological Index Series, Supplement no. 7. Repr. Taipei 1966.

Feng-su t'ung-i chiao-chu 風俗通義校注. Ed. Wang Li-ch'i 王利器. Peking 1981.

Feng-su t'ung-i chiao-shih 風俗通義校釋. By Ying Shao 應劭 (*fl.* AD 173–195). Ed. Wu Shu-p'ing 吳樹平. Tientsin 1980.

Fo-tsu li-tai t'ung-tsai 佛祖歷代通載. By Nien-ch'ang 念常 (d. 1341). In *T* vol. 49, no. 2036.

Han shu 漢書. By Pan Ku 班固 (AD 32–92). Ed. Chung-hua shu-chü. Peking 1962.

Han Yen-hsi Hsi-yüeh Hua-shan pei k'ao 漢延熹西嶽華山碑考. By Juan Yüan 阮元 (1764–1849). In *Wen-hsüan lou ts'ung-shu* 文選樓叢書 (1842).

Ho-shuo fang-ku chi 河朔訪古記. By Nai Hsien 迺賢. In *Ying-yin Wen-yüan ko ssu-k'u ch'üan-shu,* vol. 593.

Hou Han shu 後漢書. Ed. Chung-hua shu-chü. Peking 1965.

Hsi-ch'ing san-chi 西青散記. By Shih Chen-lin 史震林. Preface dated 1738. Repr. Shanghai 1935 in *Chung-kuo wen-hsüeh chen-pen ts'ung-shu* 中國文學珍本叢書.

Hsi-yüeh Hua-shan chih 西嶽華山誌. By Wang Ch'u-i 王處一. Preface dated 1184. In *Tao-tsang*: HY 307.

Hsien-chuan shih-i 仙傳拾遺. In Yen I-p'ing, *Tao-chiao yen-chiu tzu-liao,* vol. 1, Pan-ch'iao 1974.

Hsien-ch'un Lin-an chih 咸淳臨安志. By Ch'ien Yüeh-yu 潛說友. Edn. of 1177. Repr. 1830.

Hsien-tu chih 仙都志. By Ch'en Hsing-ting 陳性定. In *Tao tsang*: HY 602.

Hsü kao-seng chuan 續高僧傳. Comp. Tao-hsüan 道宣 (596–667). *T* vol. 50, no. 2060.

Hsü tzu-chih t'ung-chien ch'ang-pien 續資治通鑑長編. By Li Tao 李燾 (1115–1184). Ed. Chung-hua shu-chü. Peking 1979–.

Hsüan p'in lu 玄品錄. By Chang Yü 張雨 (1277–1350). Preface dated 1335. In *Tao tsang*: HY 780.

Hsüeh chih i-shuo 學治臆說. By Wang Hui-tsu 汪煇祖. Preface dated 1793. In *Ju-mu hsü-chih wu-chung* 入幕須知五種, ed. 1892.

Hua-yang kuo chih 華陽國志. In *Ssu-pu ts'ung-k'an*, First Series.

Huai-nan tzu 淮南子. In *Ssu-pu ts'ung-k'an*, First Series.

I-ch'ieh ching yin-i 一切經音義. By Hui-lin 慧琳 (737–820). In *T* vol. 54, no. 2128.

I-chien chih 夷堅志. By Hung Mai 洪邁 (1123–1202). Ed. Ho Cho 何卓. Peking 1981. 4 vols.

I-wen lei-chü 藝文類聚. By Ou-yang Hsün 歐陽詢 (557–641). Ed. Wang Shao-ying 汪紹楹. Peking 1965. 2 vols.

Jih-chih lu chi-shih 日知錄集釋. By Ku Yen-wu 顧炎武 (1613–1682). Ed. Huang Ju-ch'eng 黃汝成. In *Ssu-pu pei-yao* 四部備要.

Jung-chai sui-pi 容齋隨筆. By Hung Mai 洪邁 (1123–1202). Shanghai 1978.

Kai-yü ts'ung-k'ao 陔餘叢考. By Chao I 趙翼 (1727–1814). Shanghai 1957.

K'ai T'ien ch'uan-hsin chi 開天傳信記. By Cheng Ch'i 鄭棨 (d. 899). In *Pai-ch'uan hsüeh-hai* 百川學海.

Kan-chu chi [景印明刊罕傳本]紺珠集. Preface dated 1137. Ming edn. Repr. Taipei 1970.

Ku-chih shih-hua 古誌石華. By Huang Pen-chi 黃本驥. In *San-ch'ang-wu chai ts'ung-shu* 三長物齋叢書.

Ku Ch'ing-liang chuan 古清涼傳. By Hui-hsiang 慧祥 (*fl.* 667). In *T* vol. 51, no. 2098.

Ku-mo chai chin-shih pa 古墨齋金石跋. By Chao Shao-tsu 趙紹祖. In *Chü-hsüeh hsüan ts'ung-shu* 聚學軒業書.

Ku-wen yüan 古文苑. In *Ssu-pu ts'ung-k'an*, First Series.

Kuang-ch'uan shu-pa 廣川書跋. By Tung Yu 董逌 (*ca.* 1125). In *Hsing-su ts'ao-t'ang chin-shih ts'ung-shu* 行素草堂金石業書.

Kuang-i chi 廣異記. By Tai Fu 戴孚. Ed. Fang Shih-ming 方詩銘. Published with *Ming-pao chi.* Peking 1992.

Kuei-chi to-ying tsung-chi 會稽掇英總集. Comp. K'ung Yen-chih 孔延之. Preface dated 1072. In *Ying-yin Wen-yüan ko ssu-k'u ch'üan-shu,* vol. 1345.

Kuo yü 國語. Ed. Ancient Texts Editorial Team, Shanghai Normal University. Shanghai 1978.

Lei shuo 類說. Comp. Tseng Tsao 曾慥. Edn. of 1626. Repr. Peking 1955. 5 vols.

Li chi chu-shu 禮記注疏. In *Shih-san ching chu-shu.*

Li-shih chen-hsien t'i-tao t'ung-chien 歷世真仙體道通鑑. By Chao Tao-i 趙道一. In *Tao tsang*: HY 296.

Li T'ai-po ch'üan-chi 李太白全集. By Li Po 李白 (701–762). Ed. Chung-hua shu-chü. Peking 1977. 3 vols.

Liang shu 梁書. Ed. Chung-hua shu-chü. Peking 1973.

Lieh-tzu chi-shih 列子集釋. Ed. Yang Po-chün 楊伯峻. Peking 1979.

Lu-i chi 錄異記. By Tu Kuang-t'ing 杜光庭 (850–933). In *Tao tsang*: HY 591.

Lun heng chiao-shih 論衡校釋. By Wang Ch'ung 王充 (AD 27–97). Ed. Huang Hui 黃暉. Peking 1990. 4 vols.

Lun-yü 論語. In *A concordance to the Analects of Confucius*. Harvard-Yenching Institute Sinological Index Series, Supplement no. 16. Peking 1940.

Mao-shan chih 茅山誌. In *Tao tsang*: HY 304.

Meng-ch'i pi-t'an chiao-cheng 夢溪筆談校證. By Shen Kua 沈括 (1031–1095). Ed. Hu Tao-ching 胡道靜. Shanghai 1956. 2 vols.

Min shang shih hsi-kuan tiao-ch'a pao-kao lu 民商事習慣調查報告錄. Comp. Ministry of Legal Administration 司法行政部. [Nanking] 1930. Repr. Taipei 1969.

Ming-pao chi 冥報記. By T'ang Lin 唐臨. Ed. Fang Shih-ming 方詩銘. Peking 1992.

Ming shih 明史. Ed. Chung-hua shu-chü. Peking 1974.

Nan Ch'i shu 南齊書. Ed. Chung-hua shu-chü. Peking 1972.

Nan pu hsin-shu 南部新書. By Ch'ien I 潛易. Ed. Chung-hua shu-chü. Peking 1960.

Nan shih 南史. Ed. Chung-hua shu-chü. Peking 1975.

Nan-yüeh tsung-sheng chi 南嶽總勝集. By Ch'en T'ien-fu 陳田夫 (*fl.* 1163). In *T* vol. 51, no. 2097.

Neng-kai chai man-lu 能改齋漫錄. By Wu Tseng 吳曾 (d. 1170+). Repr. Peking 1960.

Pa-ch'iung shih chin-shih pu-cheng 八瓊室金石補正. By Lu Tseng-hsiang 陸增祥 (1833–1889). Edn. of 1925.

Pao-k'o ts'ung-pien 寶刻叢編. By Ch'en Ssu 陳思 (*ca.* 1200–1259+). In *Shih-wan-chüan lou ts'ung-shu* 十萬卷樓叢書.

Pao-p'u tzu nei-p'ien chiao-shih 抱朴子內篇校釋. By Ko Hung 葛洪 (283–343). Ed. Wang Ming 王明. Rev. edn. Peking 1985.

Pei Ch'i shu 北齊書. Ed. Chung-hua shu-chü. Peking 1972.

Pei-ching t'u-shu-kuan ts'ang Chung-kuo li-tai shih-k'o t'a-pen hui-pien 北京圖書館藏中國歷代石刻拓本匯編. Cheng-chou 1989–1991.

Pei shih 北史. Ed. Chung-hua shu-chü. Peking 1974.

P'ei Hsing Ch'uan-ch'i 裴鉶傳奇. Ed. Chou Leng-ch'ieh 周楞伽. Shanghai 1980.

Pi-shu sheng hsü-pien tao ssu-k'u ch'üeh shu mu 祕書省續編到四庫闕書目. Ed. Yeh Te-hui 葉德輝. In *Kuan-ku t'ang shu-mu ts'ung-k'an* 觀古堂書目叢刊, 1903.

P'ing-chin tu-pei chi 平津讀碑記. By Hung I-hsüan 洪頤煊 (1765–1837). In *Mu-hsi hsüan ts'ung-shu* 木犀軒叢書.

Po Chü-i chi 白居易集. By Po Chü-i 白居易 (772–846). Ed. Ku Hsüeh-hsieh 顧學頡. Peking 1979. 4 vols.

Po-i chih 博異志. By Ku Shen tzu 谷神子 [? = Cheng Huan-ku 鄭還古]. Peking 1980.

Po-wu chih chiao-cheng 博物志校證. By Chang Hua 張華 (232–300). Ed. Fan Ning 范寧. Peking 1980.

San-chia p'ing-chu Li Ch'ang-chi ko-shih 三家評注李長吉哥詩. By Li Ho 李賀 (791–817). Peking 1959.

San-fu huang-t'u 三輔黃圖. In *Ching-hsün-t'ang ts'ung-shu* 經訓堂叢書.

San-kuo chih 三國志. By Ch'en Shou 陳壽 (d. AD 297). Ed. Chung-hua shu-chü. Peking 1959.

San-tung ch'ün-hsien lu 三洞群仙錄. By Ch'en Pao-kuang 陳葆光. Preface dated 1154. In *Tao tsang*: HY 1238.

Shan-hai ching chiao-chu 山海經校注. Ed. Yüan K'o 袁柯. Shanghai 1980.

Shang shu chu-shu 商書注疏. In *Shih-san ching chu-shu.*

Shao-shih-shan fang pi-ts'ung 少室山房筆叢. By Hu Ying-lin 胡應麟 (1551–1602). Peking 1958. 2 vols.

Shih chi 史記. By Ssu-ma Ch'ien 司馬遷 (145–86 BC). Ed. Chung-hua shu-chü. Peking 1959.

Shih ching 詩經. In *A concordance to Shih Ching.* Harvard-Yenching Institute Sinological Index Series. Supplement no. 9. Peking 1934.

Shih-i chi 拾遺記. Attrib. Wang Chia 王嘉. Comp. Hsiao Ch'i 蕭綺. Ed. Ch'i Chih-p'ing 齊治平. Peking 1981.

Shih-san ching chu-shu 十三經注疏. Sung edn. reprinted by Juan Yüan 阮元, 1816. Repr. Kyoto 1971. 7 vols.

Shih t'ung chien-chi 史通箋記. By Liu Chih-chi 劉知幾 (661–721). Ed. Ch'eng Ch'ien-fan 程千帆. Peking 1980.

Shih t'ung t'ung-shih 史通通釋. Ed. P'u Ch'i-lung 浦起龍 (1679–?). Shanghai 1978. 2 vols.

Shu tuan 書斷. By Chang Huai-kuan 張懷瓘 (*fl.* 713–741). In *Ying-yin Wen-yüan ko ssu-k'u ch'üan-shu,* vol. 812.

Shui-ching chu shu 水經注疏. By Li Tao-yüan 酈道元. Commentaries by Yang Shou-ching 楊守敬 and Hsiung Hui-chen 熊會貞. Ed. Tuan Hsi-chung 段熙仲 and Ch'en Ch'iao-i 陳橋驛. [Soochow] 1989.

Shuo-fu 說郛. Comp. T'ao Tsung-i 陶宗儀 (1320?–1402?). 100-*chüan* version. Repr. Shanghai 1927.

Shuo-wen chieh-tzu 說文解字. By Hsü Shen 許慎 (30–124). Edn. of Ch'en Ch'ang-chih 陳昌治, 1871. Repr. Peking 1963.

Sou-shen chi 搜神記. By Kan Pao 干寶 (*fl.* 320). Peking 1979.

Sou-shen hou-chi 搜神後記. Attrib. T'ao Ch'ien 陶潛 (365–427). Ed. Wang Shao-ying 汪紹楹. Peking 1981.

Ssu-k'u ch'üan-shu tsung-mu t'i-yao 四庫全書總目提要. Edn. of 1795.

Sui-shih kuang-chi 歲時廣記. By Ch'en Yüan-ching 陳元靚 (*ca.* 1200–1266). Forty-*chüan* version in *Shih-wan-chüan lou ts'ung-shu* 十萬卷樓叢書. Repr. in *Sui-shih hsi-su yen-chiu tzu-liao hui-pien* 歲時習俗研究資料匯編, Taipei 1970, vols. 4–7.

Sui shu 隋書. Ed. Chung-hua shu-chü. Peking 1973.

Sui T'ang chia-hua 隋唐嘉話. By Liu Su 劉餗. Ed. Ch'eng I-chung 程毅中. Repr. with *Ch'ao-yeh ch'ien-tsai* (q.v.). Peking 1979.

Sung kao-seng chuan 宋高僧傳. Comp. Tsan-ning 贊寧 (919–1001). In *T* vol. 50, no. 2061.

Sung shu 宋書. Ed. Chung-hua shu-chü. Peking 1974.

Ta T'ang chiao-ssu lu 大唐郊祀錄. In *Shih-yüan ts'ung-shu* 適園叢書.

Ta T'ang K'ai-yüan li 大唐開元禮. In *Ying-yin Wen-yüan ko ssu-k'u ch'üan-shu,* vol. 646.

Ta T'ang liu-tien 大唐六典. Edn. of Konoe Iehiro 近衛家熙, 1724. Repr. Taipei 1962.

T'ai-ch'ing chin-ch'üeh yü-hua hsien-shu pa-chi shen-chang san-huang nei-pi wen 太清金闕玉華仙書八極神章三皇內祕文. In *Tao tsang*: HY 854.

T'ai-p'ing huan-yü chi 太平寰宇記. By Yüeh Shih 樂史 (930–1007). Edn. of 1803.

T'ang chih-yen 唐摭言. By Wang Ting-pao 王定保. Peking 1959 and Shanghai 1978.

T'ang fang-chen nien-piao 唐方鎮年表. By Wu T'ing-hsieh 吳廷燮. Ed. Chung-hua shu-chü. Peking 1980. 3 vols.

T'ang hui-yao 唐會要. By Wang P'u 王溥 (922–982). Ed. *Kuo-hsüeh chi-pen ts'ung-shu.* Shanghai 1935.

T'ang kuo-shih pu 唐國史補. By Li Chao 李肇. Ed. Shanghai ku-chi ch'u-pan-she. Shanghai 1957 and 1979.

T'ang liang-ching ch'eng-fang k'ao 唐兩京城坊考. By Hsü Sung 徐松 (1781–1848). In *Lien-yün-i ts'ung-shu* 連筠簃叢書. Repr. in Hiraoka Takeo, *Chōan to Rakuyō: shiryō*, Kyoto 1956, pp. 1–74.

T'ang-lü shu-i 唐律疏議. By Chang-sun Wu-chi 長孫無忌 (*ca.* 600–659) et al. Ed. Liu Chün-wen 劉俊文. Peking 1983.

T'ang shang-shu sheng lang-kuan shih-chu t'i-ming k'ao 唐尚書省郎官石柱題名考. By Lao Ko 勞格 and Chao Yüeh 趙鉞. In *Yüeh-ho ching-she ts'ung-ch'ao* 月河精舍叢鈔, 1886.

T'ang shih chi-shih 唐詩紀事. By Chi Yu-kung 計有功 (d. 1161+). Shanghai 1965, repr. Hong Kong 1972. 2 vols.

T'ang ta chao-ling chi 唐大詔令集. Comp. Sung Min-ch'iu 宋敏求 (1019–1079). Peking 1959.

T'ang wen ts'ui 唐文粹. By Yao Hsüan 姚鉉 (968–1020). In *Ssu-pu ts'ung-k'an,* First Series.

Tao-hsüan Lü-shih kan-t'ung lu 道宣律師感通錄. By Tao-hsüan 道宣 (596–667). In *T* vol. 52, no. 2107.

Tao tsang 道藏. See above, under HY.

Teng k'o chi k'ao 登科記考. By Hsü Sung 徐松. Ed. Chao Shou-yen 趙守儼. Peking 1984. 3 vols.

Ts'e-fu yüan-kuei 冊府元龜. By Wang Ch'in-jo 王欽若 (962–1025) et al. Edn. with preface of Li Ssu-ching 李嗣敬, 1642.

Tu-i chih 獨異志. By Li Jung 李冗. Ed. Chang Yung-ch'in 張永欽 and Hou Chih-ming 侯志明. Peking 1983.

Tun-huang pien-wen chi hsin-shu 敦煌變文集新書. Ed. P'an Chung-kuei 潘重規. [Taipei] 1984.

T'ung tien 通典. By Tu Yu 杜佑 (735–812). In *Kuo-hsüeh chi-pen ts'ung-shu* 國學基本叢書.

Tzu-t'ung ti-chün hua-shu 梓潼帝君化書. In *Tao tsang*: HY 170.

Wang Chien shih chi 王建詩集. By Wang Chien 王建 (b. 766?). Ed. Chung-hua shu-chü. Peking 1959.

Wang Fan-chih shih chiao-chi 王梵志詩校輯. Ed. Chang Hsi-hou 張錫厚. Peking 1983.

Wang Fan-chih shih chiao-chu 王梵志詩校注. Ed. Hsiang Ch'u 項楚. Shanghai 1991.

Wei shu 魏書. Ed. Chung-hua shu-chü. Peking 1974.

Wen-hsüan 文選 Comp. Hsiao T'ung 蕭統 (501–531). 1869 reprint of Sung edn. Repr. Taipei 1971.

Wen-yüan ying-hua pien-cheng 文苑英華辨證. By P'eng Shu-hsia 彭叔夏. Preface dated 1204. Kuangtung repr. of *Wu-ying tien chü-chen-pan shu* edn. Repr. in *WYYH*, vol. 6.

Wu-sheng ch'u-t'u chung-yao wen-wu chan-lan t'u-lu 五省出土重要文物展覽圖錄. Peking 1958.

Yang Ying-ch'uan chi 楊盈川集. By Yang Chiung 楊炯 (650–after 693). In *Ssu-pu ts'ung-k'an*, First Series.

Yen Lu-kung chi 顏魯公集. By Yen Chen-ch'ing 顏真卿 (709–785). In *Ying-yin Wen-yüan ko ssu-k'u ch'üan-shu*, vol. 1071.

Yen Lu-kung wen-chi 顏魯公文集. By Yen Chen-ch'ing. Ed. Huang Pen-chi 黃本驥. In *San-ch'ang-wu chai ts'ung-shu* 三長物齋業書, 1845.

Yen-shih chia-hsün chi-chieh 顏氏家訓集解. By Yen Chih-t'ui 顏之推 (531–591+). Ed. Wang Li-ch'i 王利器. Shanghai 1980.

Ying-yin Wen-yüan ko ssu-k'u ch'üan-shu 景印文淵閣四庫全書. Taipei 1983–1986.

Yu-yang tsa-tsu 酉陽雜俎. By Tuan Ch'eng-shih 段成式 (803?–863). Ed. Fang Nan-sheng 方南生. Peking 1981.

Yung-chou chin-shih chi 雍州金石記. By Chu Feng 朱楓. In *Hsi-yin hsüan ts'ung-shu* 惜陰軒業書.

Yüan Chen chi 元稹集. By Yüan Chen (779–831). Ed. Chi Ch'in 冀勤. Peking 1982. 2 vols.

Yüan-ho chün-hsien t'u-chih 元和郡縣圖志. By Li Chi-fu 李吉甫 (758–814). Ed. Ho Tz'u-chün 賀次君. Peking 1983.

Yüan-ho hsing tsuan 元和姓纂. By Lin Pao 林寶. In *Ying-yin Wen-yüan ko ssu-k'u ch'üan-shu*, vol. 890.

Yüeh-fu tsa-lu 樂府雜錄. By Tuan An-chieh 段安節 (*fl.* 894–907). In *Chung-kuo ku-tien hsi-ch'ü lun-chu chi-ch'eng* 中國古典戲曲論著集成, vol. 1. Peking 1959.

Yün-ch'i yu-i 雲谿友議. By Fan Shu 范攄 (*fl.* 860–873). Peking 1959.

Secondary sources

AHERN, Emily M. *The cult of the dead in a Chinese village*. Stanford 1973.

BIRNBAUM, Raoul. 'Secret halls of the mountain lords: the caves of Wu-t'ai shan'. *Cahiers d'Extrême-Asie* 5, 1989–1990, 115–40.

BOODBERG, Peter A. 'Marginalia to the histories of the northern dynasties'. *Harvard Journal of Asiatic Studies* 4, 1939, 230–83.

CATZ, Rebecca D., ed. and trans. *The travels of Mendes Pinto*. Chicago 1989.

CHAVANNES, Edouard. *Le T'ai chan, essai de monographie d'un culte chinois*. Paris 1910.

CH'EN Ch'iao-i 陳橋驛. *Shao-hsing ti-fang wen-hsien k'ao-lu* 紹興地方文獻考錄. Hangchow 1983.

CH'EN Kuo-fu 陳國符. *Tao tsang yüan-liu k'ao* 道藏源流考. Peking 1963.

CH'EN P'eng 陳鵬. *Chung-kuo hun-yin shih kao* 中國婚姻史稿. Peking 1990.

CH'ENG I-chung 程毅中. 'T'ang-tai hsiao-shuo so chi' 唐代小說瑣記. *Wen-hsüeh i-ch'an* 文學遺產. 1980.2, 52–60.

CH'ENG I-chung. 'Lun T'ang-tai hsiao-shuo ti yen-chin chih chi' 論唐代小說的演進之跡. *Wen-hsüeh i-ch'an* 1987.5, 44–52.

CHIANG Shao-yüan 江紹源. *Chung-kuo ku-tai lü-hsing chih yen-chiu* 中國古代旅行之研究. Vol. 1. Shanghai 1935, repr. 1937. [Trans. by Fan Jen as Kiang Chao-yuan, *Le voyage dans la Chine ancienne, considéré principalement sous son aspect magique et religieux*, Shanghai 1937.]

CH'IEN Chung-shu 錢鍾書. *Kuan-chui pien* 管錐編. Peking 1979. 4 vols.

CH'IEN Pao-ts'ung 錢寶琮. 'T'ai-i k'ao' 太一考. *Yen-ching hsüeh-pao* 燕京學報 12, 1932, 2449–78.

CHU Ying-p'ing 朱迎平. '*Ling-kuai chi* pu shih Liu-ch'ao chih-kuai' 靈怪集不是六朝志怪. *Wen-hsüeh i-ch'an* 文學遺產 1987.1, 18.

COLLIS, Maurice. *The grand peregrination, being the life and adventures of Fernão Mendes Pinto.* London 1949.

DAVIS, A. R. *T'ao Yüan-ming (AD 365–427): his works and their meaning.* Cambridge 1983. 2 vols.

DE GROOT, J. J. M. *The religious system of China, its ancient forms, evolution, history and present aspect, manners, customs and social institutions connected therewith.* Leiden 1892–1910. 6 vols.

DES ROTOURS, Robert. *Traité des fonctionnaires et Traité de l'armée, traduits de la Nouvelle histoire des T'ang.* Leiden 1948. 2 vols. Rev. and corrected edn. San Francisco 1974.

DEWOSKIN, Kenneth J. 'The Six Dynasties *chih-kuai* and the birth of fiction'. In Andrew H. Plaks, ed., *Chinese narrative: critical and theoretical essays*, Princeton 1977, pp. 21–52.

DOOLITTLE, Justus. *Social life of the Chinese: with some account of their religious, governmental, educational, and business customs and opinions.* New York 1865. 2 vols.

DUDBRIDGE, Glen. *The Hsi-yu chi: a study of antecedents to the sixteenth-century Chinese novel.* Cambridge 1970.

DUDBRIDGE, Glen. *The tale of Li Wa: study and critical edition of a Chinese story from the ninth century.* London 1983.

DUDBRIDGE, Glen. 'Tang tales and Tang cults: some cases from the eighth century'. *Proceedings of the Second International Conference on Sinology*, Section on Literature, Academia Sinica, Nankang 1990, 335–52.

DUDBRIDGE, Glen. 'The goddess Hua-yüeh San-niang and the Cantonese ballad *Ch'en-hsiang T'ai-tzu*'. *Chinese Studies* (*Han-hsüeh yen-chiu*) 8.1, 1990, 627–46.

DUDBRIDGE, Glen. 'The tale of Liu Yi and its analogues'. In Eva Hung, ed., *Paradoxes of traditional Chinese literature*, Hong Kong 1994, pp. 61–88.

EBERHARD, Wolfram. *The local cultures of south and east China.* Trans. A. Eberhard, Leiden 1968.

EBREY, Patricia Buckley, and GREGORY, Peter N., eds. *Religion and society in T'ang and Sung China.* Honolulu 1993.

ELLIOTT, A. J. A. *Chinese spirit-medium cults in Singapore.* London 1955.

FAURE, Bernard. 'Relics and flesh bodies: the creation of Ch'an pilgrimage sites'. In Susan Naquin and Chün-fang Yü, eds., *Pilgrims and sacred sites in China,* Berkeley and Los Angeles 1992, pp. 150–89.

FU Hsüan-ts'ung 傅璇琮. *T'ang-tai shih-jen ts'ung-k'ao* 唐代詩人叢考. Peking 1980.

FU Hsüan-ts'ung, ed. *T'ang ts'ai-tzu chuan chiao-chien* 唐才子傳校箋. Peking 1987–1990. 4 vols.

FUKUI Kōjun 福井康順, ed. *Shinsenden* 神仙傳. Tokyo 1983.

FUKUNAGA Mitsuji 福永光司. 'Kōten jōtei to Tennō taitei to Genshi tenson: Jukyō no saikō shin to Dōkyō no saikō shin' 昊天上帝と天王上帝と元始天尊—儒教の最高神と道教の最高神. *Chūtetsu bungakkai hō* 中哲文學會報 2, 1976, 1–34.

GAULD, Alan, and CORNELL, A. D. *Poltergeists.* London 1979.

GOTŌ Shukudō 後藤肅唐, 'Jofuku tōrai no densetsu ni toite' 徐福東來の傳説に説て. *Tōyō bunka* 東洋文化 (1926) 25, 60–70; 26, 49–61; 27, 63–72; 28, 55–63; 29, 44–51.

HANABUSA Hideki 花房英樹 and MAEGAWA Yukio 前川幸雄. *Gen Shin kenkyū* 元稹研究. Kyoto 1977.

HIRAOKA Takeo 平岡武夫. *Chōan to Rakuyō: shiryō* 長安と洛陽: 資料. Kyoto 1956.

HOU Ching-lang 侯錦郎. *Monnaies d'offrande et la notion de trésorerie dans la religion chinoise.* Mémoires de l'Institut des Hautes Études Chinoises, vol. 1. Paris 1975.

HSIA Chen-ying 夏振英. 'Hsi-yüeh Hua-shan ku-miao tiao-ch'a' 西嶽華山古廟調査. *K'ao-ku-hsüeh chi-k'an* 考古學集刊 5, Peking 1987, 194–205.

HSIAO Teng-fu 蕭登福. *Tao-chiao hsing-tou fu-yin yü Fo-chiao mi-tsung* 道教星斗符印與佛教密宗. Taipei 1993.

HSIAO Teng-fu. *Tao-chiao yü mi-tsung* 道教與密宗. Taipei 1993.

HU Fu-ch'en 胡孚琛. *Wei Chin shen-hsien Tao-chiao: Pao-p'u tzu nei-p'ien yen-chiu* 魏晉神仙道教: 抱朴子內篇研究. Peking 1989.

JOHNSON, David. 'The City-God cults of T'ang and Sung China'. *Harvard Journal of Asiatic Studies* 45, 1985, 363–457.

JORDAN, David K. 'Two forms of spirit marriage in rural Taiwan'. *Bijdragen tot de Taal-, Land- en Volkenkunde* 127, 1971, 181–9.

JORDAN, David K. *Gods, ghosts, and ancestors: the folk religion of a Taiwanese village.* Berkeley and Los Angeles 1972.

JUAN Ch'ang-jui 阮昌鋭. 'T'ai-wan ti ming-hun yü kuo-fang chih yüan-shih i-i chi ch'i she-hui kung-neng' 臺灣的冥婚與過房之原始意義及其社會功能. *Chung-yang yen-chiu yüan min-tsu-hsüeh yen-chiu-so chi-k'an* 中央研究院民族學研究所集刊 33, 1972, 15–38.

KAO, Karl S. Y., ed. *Classical Chinese tales of the supernatural and the fantastic: selections from the third to the tenth century.* Bloomington 1985.

KARLGREN, Bernhard. 'Legends and cults in ancient China'. *Bulletin of the Museum of Far Eastern Antiquities* 18, 1946, 199–365.

KATSUMURA Tetsuya 勝村哲也. '*Kanshi kakun Kishinhen* to *Enkon shi* o megutte' 顏氏家訓歸心篇と冤魂志をめぐって. *Tōyōshi kenkyū* 東洋史研究 26, 1967, 350–62.

KLEEMAN, Terry. *A god's own tale: the Book of Transformations of Wenchang, the Divine Lord of Zitong.* Albany 1994.

KU Chieh-kang 顧頡剛. 'Ssu-yüeh yü wu-yüeh' 四嶽與五嶽. In *Shih-lin tsa-chih ch'u-pien* 史林雜識初編, Peking 1963, pp. 34–45.

KU Chieh-kang. '*Chuang-tzu* ho *Ch'u-tz'u* chung K'un-lun ho P'eng-lai liang-ko shen-hua hsi-t'ung ti jung-ho' 莊子和楚辭中昆崙和蓬萊兩個神話系統的融合. *Chung-hua wen-shih lun-ts'ung* 中華文史論叢 10 [1979.2], 31–57.

LÉVI, Jean. 'Les fonctionnaires et le divin: luttes de pouvoirs entre divinités et administrateurs dans les contes des Six Dynasties et des Tang'. *Cahiers d'Extrême-Asie* 2, 1986, 81–110.

LEWIS, I. M. *Ecstatic religion, an anthropological study of spirit possession and shamanism.* Harmondsworth 1971.

LI Chien-kuo 李劍國. *T'ang ch'ien chih-kuai hsiao-shuo shih* 唐前志怪小說史. Tientsin 1984.

LI Feng-mao 李豐楙. *Liu-ch'ao Sui T'ang hsien-tao lei hsiao-shuo yen-chiu* 六朝隋唐仙道類小說研究. Taipei 1986.

LI Tsu-huan 李祖桓. 'Huang-ho ku-ch'iao shu-lüeh' 黃河古橋述略. *Wen-shih* 文史 20, Peking 1983, 63–74.

LI Tzu-ch'un 李子春. '*Hsi-yüeh Hua-shan pei* mi-te ts'an-shih i p'ien' 西嶽華山碑覓得殘石一片. *Wen-wu ts'an-k'ao tzu-liao* 文物參考資料 1957.5, 80–1.

LIU Tun-chen 劉敦楨. 'Su-chou Yün-yen ssu t'a' 蘇州雲巖寺塔. *Wen-wu ts'an-k'ao tzu-liao* 文物參考資料 1954.7, 27–38.

LU Hsün 魯迅 [pseud. of CHOU Shu-jen 周樹人]. *Lu Hsün ch'üan-chi* 魯迅全集. 20-vol. edn. Shanghai 1973.

LU Hsün. *Chung-kuo hsiao-shuo shih-lüeh* 中國小說史略. In *Lü Hsün ch'üan-chi,* vol. 9.

MATSUZAKI Kenzō 松崎憲三, ed. *Tō Ajia no shiryō kekkon* 東アジアの死靈結婚. Tokyo 1993.

MCMULLEN, David. *State and scholars in T'ang China.* Cambridge 1988.

MCMULLEN, David. 'The real Judge Dee: Ti Jen-chieh and the T'ang restoration of 705'. *Asia Major,* Third Series, 6, 1993, 1–81.

MIYAKAWA Hisayuki 宮川尚志. *Rikuchō shi kenkyū: seiji shakai hen* 六朝史研究: 政治社會篇. Tokyo 1956.

MIYAKAWA Hisayuki. *Rikuchō shi kenkyū: shūkyō hen* 六朝史研究: 宗教篇. Kyoto 1964.

NAKAMURA Jihee 中村治兵衛. *Chūgoku no shāmanizumu no kenkyū* 中國のシヤーマニズムの研究. Tokyo 1992.

NEEDHAM, Joseph. *Science and civilisation in China.* Vol. 2: Cambridge 1956; vol. 3: 1959; vol. 5, part 1: 1985; vol. 5, part 2: 1974; vol. 5, part 5: 1983.

ODA Yoshihisa 小田義久. 'Godō daijin kō' 五道大神考. *Tōhō shūkyō* 東方宗教 48, 1976, 14–29.

OESTERREICH, T. K. *Possession, demoniacal and other, among primitive races, in antiquity, the Middle Ages, and modern times.* Trans. D. Ibberson, London 1930.

OKAMOTO Saburō 岡本三郎. 'Meikon setsuwa kō' 冥婚說話考. *Tōyōshikai kiyō* 東洋史會紀要 4, 1945, 135–63.

ONO Katsutoshi 小野勝年. *Nittō guhō junrei gyōki no kenkyū* 入唐求法巡禮行記の研究. Tokyo 1964–1969. 4 vols.

POTTER, Jack M. 'Cantonese shamanism'. In Arthur P. Wolf, ed., *Religion and ritual in Chinese society*, Stanford 1974, pp. 207–31.

REISCHAUER, Edwin O. *Ennin's diary: the record of a pilgrimage to China in search of the law.* New York 1955.

SARGANT, William. *The mind possessed: a physiology of possession, mysticism and faith healing.* London 1973.

SAWADA Mizuho 澤田瑞穗. *Jigokuhen – Chūgoku no meikaisetsu* 地獄變 – 中國の冥界說. Kyoto 1968.

SAWADA Mizuho. *Shinsenden* 神仙傳. In *Chūgoku koten bungaku taikei* 中國古典文學大系, vol. 8. Tokyo 1969.

SAWADA Mizuho. 'Sōdai no shinju shinkō – *Ikenshi* no setsuwa o chūshin to shite – ' 宋代の神咒信仰 – 夷堅志の說話を中心として. Repr. in *Shūtei Chūgoku no juhō* 修訂中國の咒法, Tokyo 1992, pp. 457–96.

SCHAFER, Edward H. *The golden peaches of Samarkand: a study of T'ang exotics.* Berkeley and Los Angeles 1963.

SCHAFER, Edward H. *The vermilion bird: T'ang images of the South.* Berkeley and Los Angeles 1967.

SCHIPPER, K. M. *L'empereur Wou des Han dans la légende taoïste.* Paris 1965.

SCHIPPER, K. M. '*Gogaku shinkyō zu* no shinkō' 五嶽真形圖の信仰. *Dōkyō kenkyū* 道教研究 2, Tokyo 1967, 114–62.

SCHURHAMMER, Georg. 'Fernão Mendez Pinto und seine "Peregrinaçam"'. *Asia Major* 3, 1926, 71–103 and 194–267.

SEIDEL, Anna. 'Imperial treasures and Taoist sacraments – Taoist roots in the apocrypha – '. In Michel Strickmann, ed., *Tantric and Taoist studies in honour of R. A. Stein*, vol. 2 (Mélanges chinois et bouddhiques, vol. 21), Brussels 1983, pp. 291–371.

SHIGEHARA Hiroshi 繁原央. 'Chūgoku meikon setsuwa no futatsu no kata' 中國冥婚說話の二の型. In Matsuzaki Kenzō, ed., *Tō Ajia no shiryō kekkon*, Tokyo 1993, pp. 471–84.

SHIH Che-ts'un 施蟄存. *Shui-ching chu pei lu* 水經注碑錄. Tientsin 1987.

STEELE, John. *The I-li or Book of etiquette and ceremonial.* London 1917. 2 vols. Repr. Taipei 1966.

STEIN, Rolf A. 'Les fêtes de cuisine du taoïsme religieux'. *Annuaire du Collège de France*, 71e année, 1971–1972, 431–40.

STEIN, Rolf A. 'Spéculations mystiques et thèmes relatifs aux ≪cuisines≫ du taoïsme'. *Annuaire du Collège de France*, 72e année, 1972–1973, 489–99.

STEIN, Rolf A. 'Conceptions relatives à la nourriture (Chine)'. *Annuaire du Collège de France*, 73e année, 1973–1974, 457–63.

STEIN, Rolf A. 'Religious Taoism and popular religion from the second to seventh centuries'. In Welch and Seidel, eds., *Facets of Taoism*, pp. 53–81.

STRICKMANN, Michel. 'The Mao shan revelations: Taoism and the aristocracy'. *T'oung Pao* 63, 1977, 1–64.

STRICKMANN, Michel. 'On the alchemy of T'ao Hung-ching'. In Welch and Seidel, eds., *Facets of Taoism*, pp. 123–92.

STRICKMANN, Michel. *Le taoïsme du Mao chan: chronique d'une révélation.* Paris 1981.

STRICKMANN, Michel. *Mantras et mandarins: le bouddhisme tantrique en Chine.* Unpublished MS.

SUN Ch'ien 孫潛. See under YEN I-p'ing.

TAKEDA Akira 竹田旦. *Soryō saishi to shiryō kekkon – Nikkan hikaku minzokugaku no kokoromi* 祖靈祭祀と死靈結婚 – 日韓比較民俗學の研究. Kyoto 1990.

T'ANG Ch'ang-ju 唐長儒. 'Tu "*T'ao-hua yüan chi* p'ang-cheng" chih-i' 讀桃花源記旁證質疑. In *Wei Chin Nan-pei ch'ao shih lun-ts'ung hsü-pien* 魏晉南北朝史論叢續編, Peking 1959, pp. 163–74.

T'ANG Chiu-ch'ung 唐久寵 'Fan Ning *Po-wu chih chiao-cheng* p'ing-lun' 范寧博物志校證評論. In *Chung-kuo ku-tien hsiao-shuo yen-chiu chuan-chi* 中國古典小說研究專集 6, Taipei 1983, pp. 315–31.

THOMAS, Keith. *Religion and the decline of magic: studies in popular beliefs in sixteenth and seventeenth century England.* London 1971.

THOMPSON, Paul. *The voice of the past: oral history.* Second edn. Oxford 1988.

TS'AO Hsün 曹汛. 'Tou-lu Jung yü Tou-lu Ts'e' 豆盧榮與豆盧策. *Wen shih* 文史 35, 1992, 212.

TS'EN Chung-mien 岑仲勉. *Yüan-ho hsing-tsuan ssu-chiao chi* 元和姓纂四校記. Shanghai 1947.

TSUKAMOTO Zenryū 塚本善隆. 'Koitsu Rikuchō *Kanzeon ōkenki* no shutsugen – Shin Sha Fu Sō Fu Ryō no *Kōzeon ōkenki*' 古逸六朝觀世音應驗記の出現 – 晉謝敷宋傅亮の光世音應驗記 *Silver Jubilee volume of the Zinbun kagaku kenkyusyō Kyōto University* 創立二十五周年記念論文集, Kyoto 1954, 234–50.

TSUNG Li 宗力 and LIU Ch'ün 劉群. *Chung-kuo min-chien chu-shen* 中國民間諸神. Shih-chia-chuang 1987.

TU Cheng-sheng 杜正勝. 'Shen-mo shih hsin she-hui shih?' 什麼是新社會史? *Hsin shih-hsüeh* 新史學 3.4, 1992, 95–116.

TU Te-ch'iao 杜德橋 [G. DUDBRIDGE]. '*Kuang-i chi* ch'u-t'an' 廣異記初探. *Hsin Ya hsüeh-pao* 新亞學報 15, 1986, 395–414.

T'U Yüan-chi 涂元濟. 'Kun hua huang-lung k'ao-shih' 鯀化黃龍考釋. *Min-chien wen-i chi-k'an* 民間文藝集刊 3, 1982, 35–49.

TWITCHETT, Denis. *Financial administration under the T'ang dynasty.* Second edn. Cambridge 1970.

TWITCHETT, Denis. 'The composition of the T'ang ruling class: new evidence from Tunhuang', in Arthur Wright and Denis Twitchett, eds., *Perspectives on the T'ang,* New Haven and London 1973, pp. 47–85.

TWITCHETT, Denis C., and WRIGHT, Arthur F., eds. *The Cambridge history of China.* Vol. 3, *Sui and T'ang China, 589–906.* Cambridge 1979.

UCHIDA Michio 內田道夫. *Kōhon Meihōki* 校本冥報記. Sendai 1955.

UCHIDA Michio. 'Kō U shin monogatari' 項羽神物語. Repr. in his *Chūgoku shōsetsu kenkyū* 中國小說研究, Tokyo 1977, pp. 241–59.

UCHIDA Tomoo 內田智雄. 'Meikon kō' 冥婚攷. *Shinagaku* 支那學 11.3, 1944, 311–73.

UCHIYAMA Chinari 內山知也. *Zui Tō shōsetsu kenkyū* 隋唐小說研究. Tokyo 1977.

UCHIYAMA Chinari. 'Chū Tō shoki no shōsetsu – *Kōiki* o chūshin to shite' 中唐初期の小說 – 廣異記を中心として. In *Kaga hakushi taikan kinen Chūgoku bunshi tetsugaku ronshū* 加賀博士退官記念中國文史哲學論集, Tokyo 1979, pp. 527–41.

WAN Man 萬曼. *T'ang chi hsü-lu* 唐集敍錄. Peking 1980.

WANG Chung-min 王重民. *Tun-huang ku-chi hsü-lu* 敦煌古籍敍錄. Peking 1979.

Wang Kuo-liang 王國良. '*Yu-ming lu* yen-chiu' 幽冥錄研究. In *Chung-kuo ku-tien hsiao-shuo yen-chiu chuan-chi* 中國古典小說研究專集 2, Taipei 1980, pp. 47–60.

WATSON, James L. 'Of flesh and bones: the management of death pollution in Cantonese society'. In Maurice Bloch and Jonathan Parry, eds., *Death and the regeneration of life*, Cambridge 1982, pp. 155–86.

WATSON, James L., and RAWSKI, Evelyn S., eds. *Death ritual in late imperial and modern China.* Berkeley, etc., 1988.

WEINSTEIN, Stanley. *Buddhism under the T'ang.* Cambridge 1987.

WELCH, Holmes, and SEIDEL, Anna. *Facets of Taoism: essays in Chinese religion.* New Haven and London 1979.

WIEGER, Léon. *Folk-lore chinois moderne.* Ho-chien fu 1909. Repr. Farnborough 1969.

WOLF, Arthur. 'Gods, ghosts, and ancestors'. In Wolf, ed., *Religion and ritual in Chinese society*, Stanford 1974, pp. 131–82.

WU Jung-tseng 吳榮曾. 'Chen-mu-wen chung so chien-tao ti Tung-Han Tao-wu kuan-hsi' 鎮墓文中所見到的東漢道巫關係. *Wen wu* 文物 1981.3, 56–63.

WU Yü-ts'ang 吳雨蒼. 'Su-chou Hu-ch'iu shan Yün-yen ssu t'a' 蘇州虎丘山雲巖寺塔. *Wen-wu ts'an-k'ao tzu-liao* 文物參考資料 1954.3, 69–74.

YANG Liu-ch'iao 楊柳橋. '"T'ao-wu" cheng-i' 檮杌正義. *Wen shih* 文史 21, 1983, 100.

YEN I-p'ing 嚴一萍. *T'ai-p'ing kuang-chi chiao-k'an chi* 太平廣記校勘記. Pan-ch'iao 1970. (Transcribes variants recorded by Sun Ch'ien in 1668.)

YEN I-p'ing. *Tao-chiao yen-chiu tzu-liao* 道教研究資料. Pan-ch'iao 1974. 2 vols.

YEN Keng-wang 嚴耕望. *T'ang-tai chiao-t'ung t'u-k'ao* 唐代交通圖考. Taipei 1985–1986. 5 vols.

YU, Anthony C. '"Rest, rest, perturbed spirit!": ghosts in traditional Chinese prose fiction', *Harvard Journal of Asiatic Studies* 47, 1987, 397–434.

YÜ Chia-hsi 余嘉錫. *Ssu-k'u t'i-yao pien-cheng* 四庫提要辨證. Repr. Peking 1980.

YÜ Hsien-hao 郁賢皓. *T'ang tz'u-shih k'ao* 唐刺史考. Hong Kong and Nanking 1987. 5 vols.

Index

This index incorporates two kinds of reference. References to numbered stories as listed in the Appendix appear in **bold** type, and page references to the main text appear in roman type.